The Circle of the
Baal Shem Tov

Abraham J. Heschel

The Circle of the
Baal Shem Tov

Studies in Hasidism

Edited by Samuel H. Dresner

The University of Chicago Press
Chicago and London

ABRAHAM J. HESCHEL (1909–72), born in Poland to a long line of Hasidic rabbis, was one of the most prominent and beloved scholars of Judaism in the twentieth century. SAMUEL H. DRESNER, a rabbi and scholar of Jewish thought, earned his doctorate in Hasidism under Abraham Heschel.

The University of Chicago Press, Chicago 60637
The University of Chicago Press, Ltd., London
© 1985 by The University of Chicago
All rights reserved. Published 1985
Printed in the United States of America
92 91 90 89 88 87 86 85   5 4 3 2 1

BM
750
· H47
1985
Cy.2

Library of Congress Cataloging in Publication Data

Heschel, Abraham Joshua, 1907–1972.
  The circile of the Baal Shem Tov.

  Bibliography: p.
  Includes index.
  1. Hasidism—Biography.   2. Hasidism—History.
I. Dresner, Samuel H. II. Title.
BM750.H48   1985   296.8′33′0922 [B]   84-16340
ISBN 0-226-32960-7

Contents

Introduction

Heschel as a Hasidic Scholar

T HE LOSS OCCASIONED BY THE DEATH OF RABBI ABRAHAM JOSHUA
Heschel in 1972 has been felt with increasing poignancy. Time has
not served its customary conciliatory function. The passing years have
only emphasized the immensity of the void and the unique stature of the
man.

For the Christian world, what Reinhold Niebuhr once described as a
"commanding and authoritative voice . . . in the religious life of America" has been silenced. Both Catholics and Protestants sought out
Heschel's opinions on theological and social issues, because they believed
these opinions represented an authentic Jewish perception expressed by
one whose wisdom, piety, and integrity they esteemed. This fraternity
with the Christian community manifested itself, for example, in Heschel's
persuasive presence at the Second Vatican Council and in his close bonds
with leading figures of the Protestant church. It had its basis in the
prophetic call for a just society and in what Heschel described as "Depth
Theology"—those underpinnings of religion, such as humility, compassion, faith, and awe, which characterize the community of all true men of
spirit.

For the Jewish world, the death of Abraham Heschel has, of course,
been an incomparably greater blow. Jewry has lost a scholar, a thinker, a
poet, and a social reformer of the first rank. One of Heschel's unusual
qualities was the universality of his concern. His interests were not
limited to any single epoch or subject but embraced the totality of Jewish
experience. Vertically, there was hardly a major topic in the history of
Jewish thought which he did not plumb. In a time of growing specializa-
tion, most scholars prefer to restrict themselves to a single aspect of
Judaism. Not so Heschel. He contributed major works in a number of
fields: Bible (*The Prophets*), Rabbinics (*Torah min Hashamayim*),
Hasidism (*Kotzk*), Theology (*Man Is Not Alone, God in Search of Man,*
and *Who Is Man?*), and Ethics (*The Insecurity of Freedom*), among
others. It was this mastery of virtually the entire Jewish creative experience which contributed to the richness of Heschel's own thinking. If his
scholarship moved readily across the vertical dimension from the Bible to

contemporary thought, his Jewish concern was just as remarkably horizontal. By this I mean his understanding of, sympathy for, and acceptance by almost the entire spectrum of Jewish life—from the Zionists and the Hebraists to the Yiddishists, and from the Reform and Conservative to the Orthodox and the Hasidim. Though himself eschewing labels, identifying wholly with none of these schools, and all the while holding his own views, Heschel established good relations with each of the factions, since he believed each represented, in greater or lesser measure, an affirmation of Jewish life. Heschel's breadth expressed the quality of his ʾahavat yisraʾel (love of Israel).[1]

Heschel was intimately familiar with the Jewries with whom he resided. The liquidation of East European Jewry had left him as one of the few authentic interpreters of that great period of Jewish life and thought. He knew not only the Jews of Germany and America as well, but also was thoroughly conversant with the contemporary general culture of those countries. I recall the observation of Eugen Taeubler, Mommsen's successor as professor of classics at Heidelberg, that Heschel had a better grasp of German culture than the German-born faculty of the American academic institution in which Taeubler found himself in the forties. The same could have been said for Heschel's understanding of the pragmatic, open, and socially oriented American society which he came to appreciate soon after his arrival here in 1940, and for which, in time, he served as a leading spokesman.

Gifted with a moving literary style in four languages (Yiddish, Hebrew, German, and English), Heschel has left us a precious written legacy. Much of his work was produced at a prodigious rate in the language he mastered last, English, and comprises one of the most impressive bodies of writing by a single modern Jewish thinker. No one has yet picked up the pen he has set down, nor plumbed the depths of the Jewish mind so tellingly, nor so moved the heart. If it is true that the Jewish community's recognition of Heschel was belated, following rather than preceding that accorded him by Christians, then there is all the more reason for pain that

1. "My father" [he wrote] "used to tell me a story about our grandfather." [Abraham Joshua Heschel, rabbi in Opatów (Apt) and later in Miedzybórz (Mezbizh), after whom Heschel was named, was popularly known as the Lover of Israel (ʾOhev Yisraʾel), the inscription on his grave and the title of his book.] He was asked by many other rebbes, "How come your prayers are always accepted and our prayers are not?" He gave the following answer: "You see, whenever some Jew comes to me and pours out his heart and tells me of his misery and suffering, I have such compassion that a little hole is created in my heart. Since I have heard and listened to a great many Jews with their problems and anguish, there are a great many holes in my heart. I'm an old Jew, and when I start to pray I take my heart and place it before God. He sees this broken heart, so many holes, so many splits, that He has compassion for my heart, and that's why He listens to me. He listens to my prayers." ("Hasidism," Jewish Heritage 14, no. 3 [1972]:21)

we can no longer expect from Heschel yet another startling book, another bold act of prophetic leadership, or another moving reaction to a challenging issue.

The publication of this volume is evidence of the implication of Heschel's death for Hasidic scholarship. In no other field of study is his loss felt more keenly, for only now have a growing number of students begun to take seriously Martin Buber's long-denied claim, that Hasidism was the most significant phenomenon in the history of religion during the past two centuries. The new academic and popular interest in Hasidism is apparent from the surprising quantity of original works and reprints on the subject being published in Hebrew (see any recent issue of *Kiryat Sefer*), the growing number of English publications, and the spate of courses being introduced in colleges. While the "decline" of the Hasidic movement has received generous attention from scholars, the evidence of its communal and intellectual vitality is only now beginning to receive a hearing. If not on the same exalted level as in its first three generations, the movement has nevertheless continued with unabated vigor, regularly producing a formidable series of leaders and a constantly growing, if uneven, literature. Despite early separatist tendencies, Hasidism returned to (and was admitted by) the official Jewish community, while in the second half of this century—even after the Holocaust—it has shown itself capable of taking root in the democratic societies of the West. Consider, for example, the fact that a disproportionate number of Jews who have made signal contributions to contemporary culture—Agnon in literature, Chagall in art, and Buber and Heschel in philosophy— emerged from a Hasidic milieu. All this, if touched on by publicists, has by and large been ignored by scholars. Heschel, whose studies on Maimonides and Abrabanel demonstrated his understanding of the Spanish epoch, argued that the "golden period" of Jewish history was not in Spain but in Eastern Europe. For him the acme of Eastern European Jewry had been Hasidism, the high point of post-talmudic Jewish history.

While Heschel's specifically Hasidic studies are confined to the essays in this volume on the circle of the Besht (Baal Shem Tov = the master of the good name), the founder of Hasidism, and to the monumental work on Rabbi Menahem Mendel of Kotzk, his other writings often reflect Hasidic sources and insights. Indeed, the more familiar one becomes with Hasidic literature, the more one understands how Heschel drew upon these sources. The influence of Hasidism is reflected in Heschel's contributions to the understanding of the phenomenology of prophecy and of *ruah hakodesh* (the holy spirit). There are, for example, clear echoes of Hasidic concepts and concerns in Heschel's excursions upon the Sabbath as a bride, upon "divine pathos," the "ineffable," "radical amazement," the illusion of God's absence, the "holy dimension" of all reality, the

"primacy of inwardness," the criticism of "panhalachism," the centrality
of prayer, the "dignity of words," and the "endless yearning." Some of
the section headings in *Man Is Not Alone* might, in fact, be transposed to
a book on Hasidic philosophy. In the final chapter of Heschel's work on
Maimonides, where he described the great philosopher's last years when
he abandoned his scholarly undertakings for a life of *imitatio Dei*, one
catches a reflection of the tzaddik for whom "living" Torah is more
important than "writing" Torah.[2]

The State of Hasidic Research

To understand Heschel better as a scholar of Hasidism, it would
be helpful to review the general state of Hasidic research. One might
describe it as both promising and problematic.

It is promising because of the growing number of scholars, both in
Israel and the Diaspora, who have directed their efforts to the subject of
Hasidism. There are several reasons which might be suggested for this
increased interest. One reason is spiritual. It has to do with what Daniel
Bell has called the "exhaustion of modernity," that is, the failure first of
technology and then of "culture" (literature—art—music) as substitutes
for religion. After several centuries in which "natural" man has explored
the secular kingdom in search of redemption, there has again emerged a
receptivity to the sacred dimension of reality. This accounts, in good
measure, for the attentiveness to the Hasidic movement, the last great
flowering of the Jewish spirit. A second reason for the growing interest in
Hasidism is historical. The catastrophic end of a thousand years of
Eastern European Jewish communal life has stimulated considerable
effort to document and understand what was previously taken for granted
and, consequently, in good measure, overlooked. Studies on Hasidism,
formerly so scant, are today considered of sufficient interest to warrant
their publication in major scholarly journals. Formerly, no courses in
Hasidism had been offered at institutions of higher learning, even Jewish
institutions; today, the number rises each year, as does the number of

2. More explicit cases of how Hasidic sources are used in Heschel's writings are abundant. For example, the startling title Heschel chose for his youthful volume of Yiddish
poems, *Der Shemhameforash Mentsh*, "Man, the Ineffable Name of God," can be traced to
Hasidic-kabbalistic origins. According to a form of gematria introduced by the kabbalists
that permitted "filling," *milui ʾalafim*, where each letter of a Hebrew word receives the
numerical value not of the letter itself but of the name of the letter "filled" with alefs, the
value of the ineffable Name, YHVH (*Yod Heʾ Vaʾv Heʾ*), becomes 45 (= 20 + 6 + 13 + 6),
which is equivalent to the simple gematria of the Hebrew for "man," *ʾadm* = 1 + 4 + 40 =
45! Thus, through the process of gematria, "man is the ineffable Name of God" (*Keter Shem
Tov* [Brooklyn: Kehot, 1972], p. 74, § 292).
   One further study in Hasidism was Heschel's "Unknown Documents in the History of
Hasidism" (Yiddish), *YIVO Bleter* 36 (1952):113–35.

doctoral dissertations on or related to Hasidism. One product of the new research is the publication of the first critical edition of a classic Hasidic book with full commentary, which provides a key that will unlock many difficulties for the student and sets an example which others will no doubt follow.[3]

Hasidic research, however, is also problematic. So little has been done in the past that is of lasting value and upon which one can build. Anti-Hasidic prejudice in the West kept many students from contributing to this field and rendered the work of others ineffective. With the absence, until very recently, of university-level courses in Hasidism and professorships, fellowships, or research grants, few were encouraged to enter a field with so bleak a future. Of the studies which have appeared, most are characterized either by overenthusiasm or lack of sensitivity. Hasidism has been either romanticized or maligned. Indeed, the absence of a balanced approach to the subject has been a major obstacle. New movements are bound to engender advocates and critics. Hasidism, because of its nature and its claims, aroused a storm of controversy that has persisted down to our very day. Fervor characterized both its proponents and its enemies. Attack was followed by counterattack, forgery by counterforgery; the burning of books, excommunications, and courting the interference of government authorities were the order of the day. In time, matters quieted down, partly because the Hasidic movement had grown so powerful that it had to be received back into the community. Much of the more modern literature, however, has remained impassioned, extreme, and bitter. As a result, the contemporary scholar has at his disposal few evenhanded and well-informed studies congruent with Hasidism's depth and breadth. The sad fact is that we possess hardly a handful of significant works. Heschel himself observed in 1952 that "in the field of Jewish scholarship there are few subjects about which so much has been written in so dilettantish a manner as the history of Hasidism. Few researchers have followed the fine example set by Eliezer Tzvi Hakohen Zweifel with his work, *Shalom ʿal Yisraʾel* (Zhitomir, 1868—69) . . . Samuel Abba Horodezky's important monographs did not concern themselves sufficiently with details. Dubnow, in his noteworthy *History of Hasidism*, paid more attention to the opponents of Hasidism, the Mitnagdim, than to Hasidism itself . . ."[4]

The lack of surviving documents is a second obstacle to a proper understanding of the movement. Referring to the post-Holocaust situation, Heschel noted in the same article that " . . . we remain unsure of thousands of simple facts: biographical dates, bibliographic details, iden-

3. Dov Ber, Maggid of Miedzyrzecz (Mezeritch), *Maggid Devarav Leyaʿakov*, ed. and commentary by R. Schatz-Uffenheimer (Jerusalem: Hebrew Univ. Press, 1976).
4. See Heschel, "Unknown Documents in the History of Hasidism."

tification of names, etc. This sorry state of affairs is due in part to the fact that research on Hasidism suffers from a dearth of documents."[5] While Heschel was writing about the post-Holocaust condition, such a vacuum had, in fact, long prevailed in the great Jewish libraries of Western Europe and America, upon which most historical research on Judaism was dependent. The author of a work on Shabbetai Tzvi observed that it is easier to write a study on that subject than on some noted Hasidic figure, for while manuscripts about Sabbateanism were being avidly collected by the Jewish librarians of the West, Hasidic documents, even the most valuable, though readily accessible, were virtually ignored. The librarians followed the example of their doyen, Steinschneider, the master bibliographer who insatiably ransacked every nook and cranny in search of a Hebrew manuscript, but freely admitted that he knew next to nothing about Hasidic literature. Sabbateanism, though heretical, was after all a curiosity, while Hasidism was a contemporary calamity, a "malady of Judaism."[6]

A case in point is Elkan Adler, the noted English barrister, book collector, and son of the former chief rabbi. While his anti-Hasidism seems a somewhat gentler British version, it no doubt played a role in what he felt was of value to collect. The description he gives in his travel book of "Hasidic" joy on Simhat Torah around the turn of the century in Jerusalem includes seeing himself as "Gulliver among the Brobdingnagians, when the monkeys patronized him . . . If the tune of the Chassidim is funny, . . . a Chassidish howl, . . . [and] the harmonization rather like a Chassid's nightmare after a heavy supper of Beethoven! . . . the manner in which they make the Hakafoth, or circuits of the Synagogue, during the Rejoicing of the law, is funnier still. It was comical and shocking to see venerable gray beards pirouetting on their toes like some European fairy of the pantomime, but it was highly appreciated, and I had to simulate satisfaction for fear of being rebuked, as Michal was when she objected to King David's 'dancing with all his might.' "[7] An unusual combination of Jewish knowledge and aristocratic wealth, Adler literally scoured the earth in search of rare Hebrew books. He managed to collect manuscripts at the rate of about one hundred a year and to visit each of the continents, except Australia, half a dozen times or so in search of them.[8] Yet the catalog of his manuscripts reveals hardly a single Hasidic work.

5. Ibid.
6. See S. Baron, "Steinschneider's Contribution to Historiography," *Alexander Marx Jubilee Volume* (New York: Jewish Theological Seminary, 1950), English section, p. 95.
7. Adler, *Jews in Many Lands* (Philadelphia: Jewish Publication Society, 1905), pp. 50–55.
8. Ibid., pp. 12–13.

Another problem in Hasidic research is the separation, by predeliction or circumstance, between some Hasidic scholarship and familiarity with Hasidic life. In other disciplines, such disjuncture may not have serious consequences. The essence of Hasidism, however, was the living reality of which the written word, impressive and vast as it is, is only a reflection. Hasidism was more than the philosophy which could be distilled from its classics. It was a certain style of life. With the demise of Eastern European Jewry, the living tradition was severely attenuated. Heschel writes:

> [It] is a tragedy that this great movement is essentially an oral movement, one that cannot be preserved in written form. It is ultimately a living movement. It is not contained fully in any of its books . . . [In] other words, Hasidism has a very personal dimension . . . To be a Hasid is to be in love with God and with what God has created. Once you are in love you are a different human being . . . That is the history of Hasidism. Indeed, he who has never been in love will not understand and may consider it a madness. That is why there is so much opposition to Hasidism, more than we are willing to admit.[9]

Some modern scholars, not familiar or sympathetic with Hasidic life, may be limited almost exclusively to its literature and by necessity approach their subject like astronomers, biologists, . . . or tourists.

Hasidic literature itself, finally, is intrinsically difficult to penetrate. It is enigmatic, terse, usually the work of a disciple transcribing the words of his master, often written in a poor Hebrew which is nothing more than a translation of the original spoken Yiddish,[10] characterized by allusions to kabbalistic formulae, and presupposing a knowledge of the rabbinic texts. The writings of Hasidism, though filled with brilliant insights and profound exposition, present a formidable obstacle to the student. One need only observe that although Hasidic literature numbers about 3,000 items, we lack a bibliography, an adequate study of its nature and extent, a comprehensive anthology, and a critical edition of and commentary to even a handful of its classic texts.[11]

9. "Hasidism," *Jewish Heritage* 14, no. 3 (1972):14–16.
10. A reference to this problem is found in the introduction to *Teshuᶜot Hen* by R. Gedaliah of Linitz, one of the earliest followers of the Besht. The editor of the book, a disciple of R. Gedaliah and a son of the author of *Shivhey Habesht*, explains that difficulties in comprehending the text may be due to the profundity of the ideas, the errors of the printer, and the limits of his own understanding in transcribing the text. "Or perhaps the meaning of the author was altered in [my] translating from one language [Yiddish] to another [Hebrew], and it was as a 'tongue of stammerers' to me. For it is known that the task of translating from one tongue to another is considerable, in that care must be taken neither to add nor detract from the intent of the author . . . " (*Teshuᶜot Hen* [Berdichev, 1816; rpt. Jerusalem: S. Reifen, 1964], p. 15).
11. A century ago Solomon Schecter believed that Hasidic literature consisted of some "200 volumes." See his *The Chassidim* (London: Jewish Chronicle, 1887), p. 22. The Mosad

In a little-known article,[12] Heschel once suggested that the attitude toward Hasidism of the scholars of the West was yet another example of their wholesale rejection of the Ashkenazic tradition in favor of the supposedly more liberal, "cultured," and decorous Sephardic mode. To demonstrate his point, he included one of his rare references to contemporary writers:

> In the modern period, its [the Sephardic] influence permeated other Jewish groups, especially in Germany. It was the admiration of the 19th-century German Jewish scholars for the Sephardic Middle Ages that determined the mood of the modern "Science of Judaism" (*Wissenschaft des Jüdentums*).
>
> The scholars of emancipated German Jewry saw in the Spanish period the "Golden Age" of Jewish history, and celebrated it as a happy blend of progress and traditionalism upon which they desired to model their own course. In their research they went to the point of applying the cultural standards of the "Golden Age" to the literature of later centuries. For some Jewish scholars, any Jewish literature dating after 1492, the year in which Jewish life in Spain ceased, was not considered worthy of scholarly investigation. Their example was followed in forming the curricula of the higher schools of Jewish learning, which gave no place to works written after 1492 and before the beginning of modern Hebrew literature.
>
> This desire for inner identification with the Spanish Jewish period reflected itself in the synagogue architecture of the 19th century. Liberal Jewish synagogues in Central Europe were built in the Moorish style, as if the stucco arabesque, horseshoe arches, and dados of glazed and painted tiles were the most apt possible expressions of the liberal Jew's religious mood.
>
> Hand-in-hand with the romantic admiration of the Sephardim that became one of the motifs of Reform Judaism in Germany went social aspirations, too. The social standing of the few Sephardim in Germany was superior to that of the Ashkenazim, and the leaders of the new Reform movement, anxious to develop a new and more advanced way of Jewish life that would abandon the traditional forms still adhered to by the Jewish masses, often blatantly imitated the manners of the Sephardim. In the Portuguese synagogues they found that solemnity and decorum which they missed in the old *shul*. It was hardly for scientific reasons that the Sephardic pronunciation of Hebrew was introduced in the early "temples."

Harav Kook of Jerusalem, under the general editorship of Dr. Yitzhak Raphael and the authorship of Shalom H. Parush, is publishing a bibliography of Hasidic literature. See also the fine translation of R. Nahum of Chernobyl's *Light of the Eyes* by A. Green, published by Paulist Press in 1982.

12. "The Two Great Traditions," *Commentary* 5 (1948):420–21.

. . . [T]he modern Ashkenazic Jew, particularly in Central Europe, often came to lose his appreciation of the value of his own original way of life. He developed an embarrassed aversion for the dramatic, for the moving and vivid style, whether in the synagogue or in human relations. For him dignity grew to mean something to be achieved by strict adherence to an established, well-balanced, mannerly form, undisturbed by an eruption of the sudden and spontaneous . . . Thus Hermann Cohen wrote in 1916 that the elimination of the dramatic manner from the worship of East European Jews would turn the synagogues into "seats of true culture."

This lack of understanding for and alienation from the values of the Ashkenazic traditions became complete. Describing the way in which the Hasidim prayed, a prominent Jewish historian, in a work first published in 1913 and reprinted in 1931, could write:

"The [Hasidic] movement did not signify a gain for religious life; the asset that lay in its striving for inwardness was more than cancelled out by the preposterousness of its superstitious notions and of its unruly behavior . . . According to its principles, Hasidism meant a total revolt against the divine service [*sic!*]; nothing could have made the untenability of the latter more striking than the fact that great numbers of people should turn away from it, not out of skepticism or doubt, but out of a most intense yearning for piety . . . Hasidism contributed to the deterioration rather than to the improvement of the divine service . . . its noise and wild, restless movements brought new factors of disturbance . . . It is no wonder that at such a time complaints were made about the lack of devoutness and attention, about the disorder and interruptions. The divine service stood in need of a thorough renovation and restoration if it was to survive. The modern age [read: the Reform movement—AJH.] supplied both."

The book referred to by Heschel is *Der jüdische Gottesdienst*, the standard work on Jewish liturgy, by Ismar Elbogen, one of the leading figures in *Die Wissenschaft des Judentums* (the movement for the scientific study of Judaism).[13] Other expressions of this point of view have not been uncommon. For example, according to the system of organization of the standard library catalog for Judaica, "Hasidism" is listed under the rubric, "sects," along with the Essenes, the Karaites, and the Samaritans.[14] As early as 1887, perhaps the most distinguished figure associated with the development of American Jewish scholarship, Solo-

---

13. Ismar Elbogen, *Der jüdische Gottesdienst in seiner geschichtlichen Entwicklung* (Leipzig: Fock, 1913), p. 392.

14. Freimann, A., *Katalog der Judaica* (Frankfurt: Lehrberger, 1922), p. ix. Also listed under this rubric are the Saducees and the Pharisees.

mon Schecter, had published a sympathetic article on Hasidism in English ("The Chassidim," first read before the Jews College Literary Society, 13 November 1887, later printed in the *Jewish Chronicle*, and reprinted in his *Studies in Judaism*). Virtually none on this continent were to emulate him. Among the more than seventy volumes of the *Jewish Quarterly Review*, the more than forty volumes of the *Proceedings of the American Academy for Jewish Research*, and the more than fifty volumes of the *Hebrew Union College Annual*, only a handful of articles relating to Hasidism have appeared—and these, more often, to anti-Hasidism![15] It would be fair to conclude that the approach to Hasidism of *Die Wissenschaft des Judentums* was perpetuated, until most recently, by its American advocates.

Among the few scholars of the West who repudiated the outlook of *jüdische Wissenschaft* and contributed to a reawakening of interest in Hasidism have been Martin Buber and Gershom Scholem. Their motives were only partly the same.

Buber opposed *jüdische Wissenschaft*'s stress on rationalism, philology, and positivism; its pursuit of a historiography "which sees the past as a meaningless 'promiscuous agglomeration of happenings,'" thus fragmenting "Jewish history into many tiny problems."[16] Scholem understood *jüdische Wissenschaft* as the "academic mortician" of Judaism. Referring to the polemical purposes of the Western scholars, who, in the throw of emancipation, were embarrassed by and sought to dismiss the unpleasant evidence of mysticism in Judaism, he writes:

> Factors that have been emphasized and were considered positive from the world-view of assimilation and self-justification now require an entirely new analysis in order to determine what their actual role was in the development of the nation. Factors which were denigrated will appear in a different, more positive light from this point of view . . . It is possible that what was termed degeneracy will be thought of as a revelation and light and what seemed to [the nineteenth-century historians] will be revealed as a great living myth . . . not the washing and mummification of the dead, but the discovery of hidden life by removal of the obfuscating masks.[17]

15. E.g., M. Wilensky, "Some Notes on Rabbi Israel Loebel's Polemic Against Hasidism," *Proceedings of the American Academy for Jewish Research* 30 (1962):141–51; Y. Eliach, "The Russian Dissenting Sects and Their Influence on Israel Baal Shem Tov, Founder of Hasidism," *PAAJR* 36 (1968):57–81; E. Etkes, "The System of R. Hayim of Volozhin as a Response of the Community of the Mitnagdim to Hasidism" (Hebrew), *PAAJR* 39 (1972):1–46 (Hebrew section); J. Weiss, "The Great Maggid's Theory of Contemplative Magic," *Hebrew Union College Annual* 31 (1960),137–48.

16. David Biale, *Gershom Scholem* (Cambridge, Mass.: Harvard Univ. Press, 1979), p. 46. See M. Buber, "Jüdische Wissenschaft," *Die Welt* 11–12 (October 1901); *Jüdische Bewegung* (Berlin: Jüdische Verlag, 1920), 1:48–58.

17. Biale, *Gershom Scholem*, p. 11. Translation emended by editor—SHD.

Although both Buber and Scholem were agreed in their rejection of the apologetic-rationalist-philological approach of *Die Wissenschaft des Jüdentums*, the two were subsequently to follow different directions in their work. A reading of their controversy on the proper post-*Wissenschaft* approach to Hasidism is of considerable interest; for our purposes, moreover, the two approaches help to provide a context within which to view the contributions of Abraham Joshua Heschel.[18]

Toward the beginning of the century, Buber, through his lyric German rendition of the Hasidic tale, brought the startling message of Hasidism to the Western Jew, and to the Gentile. He was only the best-known figure of the neo-Hasidic revival which included such writers as Berdichevsky, Peretz, Horodezky, and Y. Steinberg, most of whom were nationalists or members of the intelligentsia, rebelling against the traditional pattern of Jewish study.

Gershom Scholem and his school repudiated not only *jüdische Wissenschaft* but neo-Hasidism as well, particularly Martin Buber's understanding of Hasidism. They pointed to Buber's preference for Hasidic legend over the discursive writings, as well as to his penchant for exposition which emphasized mysticism or existential "decision" at the expense of the real meaning of the text and the centrality of tradition. Though Scholem would not have gone as far as Hurwitz who attacked neo-Hasidism for "searching for pearls in piles of garbage," he did adopt almost all of Hurwitz's "critique of Hasidism as a quietistic movement" and of Sabbateanism as a model of historical vitality.[19] He acknowledged Buber's contribution as a groundbreaking effort, but argued that it glossed over the less attractive aspects of Hasidism, was self-serving, and was overly selective in its emphasis. As Buber's general thinking moved from mysticism to existentialism, so did his understanding of Hasidism. Thus during the first phase, before World War I, he dealt with the "ecstatic quality" of Hasidism. Later, he emphasized Hasidism's "hallowing of the everyday" and its concern for the "concrete here and now."

The approach of the dominant Scholem school is no less problematic. Scholem credited the period of Shabbetai Tzvi as the watershed of modern Jewish history. He viewed the false messiah as a liberator who broke the millennial rabbinic hegemony and thereby facilitated, in

18. See G. Scholem, "M. Buber's Interpretation of Hasidism," in *The Messianic Idea in Judaism* (New York: Schocken, 1971), pp. 227–51; idem, "M. Buber's Conception of Judaism," in *On Jews and Judaism in Crisis* (New York: Schocken, 1976), pp. 126–72; R. Schatz-Uffenheimer, "Man's Relation to God and World in Buber's Rendering of the Hasidic Teaching," in *The Philosophy of Martin Buber*, ed. Paul Schilpp and Maurice Friedman (La Salle, Ill.: Open Court, 1967), pp. 403–35; Martin Buber, "Replies to My Critics: On Hasidism," idem, pp. 731–41; Biale, pp. 165–69; M. Buber, "Interpreting Hasidism," *Commentary* 36, no. 3 (1963):218–25.

19. Biale, *Gershom Scholem*, p. 48. Cf. Stanley Nash, "The Psychology of Dynamic Self-Negation in a Modern Hebrew Writer, Shai Hurwitz (1861–1922)," *PAAJR* 44 (1977):81–93. See now S. Nash, *In Search of Hebraism: Shai Hurwitz and His Polemics in the Hebrew Press* (Leiden: Brill, 1980).

greater or lesser measure, the emergence of such movements as Haskalah, Zionism, Reform, and Hasidism. For Scholem, "pluralism" replaced
"normative" as the key word in the new Jewish historiography, providing, alongside of halakhah and philosophy, a place for mysticism, and
even such undercurrents as antinomianism.[20]

While contributing significantly to the understanding of the Hasidic
text, both as to its historical authenticity and its relation to the older
Kabbalah, the Scholem school betrays at times its own selective weakness
for the gnostic, the quietistic, and the supposedly Sabbatean elements in
the literature of Hasidism. Critics have made their points. R.J.Z. Werblowsky sees Scholem's attempt to raise Sabbateanism to the level of
rabbinic Judaism as a dangerous misreading of Jewish history; Kurzweil
questions Scholem's historical objectivity in view of the latter's anarchical
emphasis on the irrational in contrast to the halakhic and rational elements in Judaism; Jacob Katz is doubtful whether historical sources
support a causal relationship between Sabbateanism and modern Jewish
movements;[21] while M. Piekarz argues that numerous Hasidic state-
ments, which Scholem traces to Sabbatean texts, merely share a common
source in classical Musar works such as *Sheney Luḥot Habrit* and *Re'shit
Ḥokhmah*.[22]

Die Wissenschaft des Judentums, because of its stress on polemics and
rationalism, either ignored or demeaned Hasidism. Buber, the foremost
representative of the neo-Hasidic revival, while cultivating the tale and
showing the contemporary relevance of several of the central Hasidic
themes, can be faulted for often interpreting Hasidism in terms of his
personal philosophy, whether mystical or existential. Scholem, who
opened modern Jewish historiography to the dimension of the mystical
and the mythical, tended to overlook the moral and the enduring religious message of Hasidism, by virtue of his concentration on the kabbalistic and the Sabbatean, as well as his distance from Hasidic life itself.

---

20. For an example of the attractiveness of Sabbateanism to a contemporary novelist,
see Isaac Bashevis Singer, *A Young Man in Search of Love* (New York: Doubleday, 1978),
p. 7. Cf. Samuel Dresner, "Is Bashevis Singer a Jewish Writer?" *Midstream* 27, no. 3
(1980):42–47.

21. Cf. Biale, *Gershom Scholem*, pp. 155, 172–74, 192–93, and the bibliography cited
there. For Buber's response to Scholem's strictures, see Martin Buber, "Replies to My
Critics," pp. 731–41, and above, n. 18.

22. *Bimey Tzemiḥat Hahasidut* (Jerusalem: Mosad Bialik, 1978). A more polemical
approach is adopted by H. Lieberman, "How Jewish 'Researchers' Explore Hasidism"
(Hebrew), *'Ohel Raḥel* (Brooklyn: Empire Press, 1980), 1:1–49. Cf. Scholem, *Devarim
Bago* (Tel Aviv: Am Oved, 1975), p. 300, n. 20.

Several significant studies have appeared since Scholem's death: Schweid, "Mysticism
and Judaism according to Gershom Scholem" (Hebrew), *Jerusalem Studies in Jewish
Thought*, Supplement 2 (1983); R. Shatz, "Gershom Scholem's Interpretation of Hasidism
as an Expression of His Philosophy of Idealism" (Hebrew), in *Gershom Scholem: The Man
and His Work* (Hebrew) (Jerusalem: Israel National Academy for Science, Magnes Press-
Mosad Bialik), pp. 48–63.

Both Buber and Scholem rejected Jewish tradition as a pattern for their personal lives, and both pursued theories which support their own positions. Buber's central emphasis on Hasidism was upon the existential decision. (A favorite tale of his is about the Master who asked his disciples, "What is the most important thing in the world?" One answers, "the Sabbath"; another "prayer"; a third, "Yom Kippur." "No," the master explains, "the most important thing is whatever you are doing at the moment!")

> Buber as a religious anarchist rejected the notion of an authoritative revelation and historical tradition. Out of hostility toward both orthodox halakhic Judaism and rational Jewish philosophy, Buber rejected the burden of tradition and created his counterhistory by a subjective, mythopoeic "act of decision."[23] Scholem also labels himself a religious anarchist, but . . . he means something quite different from Buber. Scholem . . . argued that Judaism actually consists of an anarchistic plurality of sources . . . When Scholem calls himself a religious anarchist, he means that the historical tradition, which is the only source of knowledge we have of revelation, contains no one authoritative voice. All that can be learned from the study of history is the *struggle* for absolute values among conflicting voices of authority. Scholem is an anarchist because he believes "the binding character of the Revelation for a collective has disappeared. The word of God no longer serves as a source for the definition of possible contents of a religious tradition and thus of a possible theology."[24]

Buber's stress upon mysticism and/or existential decision in Hasidism and Scholem's search for Sabbatean influences both reflect antinomian sympathies.

23. "Buber is dissatisfied with Hasidism because it does not expand the realm of revelation," argues Rivkah Schatz-Uffenheimer, "and in this he sees its failure . . . [But], if Hasidism had been more universal and had dared to broaden the 'horizon of revelation,' instead of confining itself from the start to the revelation in the Torah, it would have achieved this greatness at the price of antinomianism, . . . and is it not thus that we must understand Buber's position?" ("Man's Relation to God and World," p. 419).
    In a letter to Franz Rosenzweig, Martin Buber writes that he discontinued religious observances after he became bar mitzvah, at the age of thirteen, and Gershom Scholem testified that "the early Buber developed a deep aversion to the Law, to *halakhah* in all its forms." . . . Buber was a "man who with complete radicalism stood aloof from the institutions of Judaism as a cult, and whom nobody ever saw in a synagogue during the almost thirty years he lived in Israel." (M. Buber, *Briefwechsel aus sieben Jahrzehnten*, ed. Grete Schaeder [Heidelberg: 1975], 3:141; Gershom Scholem, "Martin Buber's Conception of Judaism," in *Jews and Judaism in Crisis* [New York: Schocken, 1976], p. 129; see also pp. 133–34. Cf. Franz Rosenzweig, "The Builders: Concerning the Law," in *On Jewish Learning*, ed. N. N. Glatzer [New York: Schocken, 1955], pp. 72–92; Ernst A. Simon, "Martin Buber and the Faith of Israel" [Hebrew], *Divrey Iyyun* [Jerusalem: 1958], pp. 13–56; Arthur Cohen, "Martin Buber and Judaism," in *Leo Baeck Yearbook* 25 [London: Secker and Warburg, 1980], pp. 287–300; Nahum N. Glatzer, "Reflection on Buber's Impact on German Jewry," in *Leo Baeck Yearbook* 25, pp. 301–9).
    24. Biale, *Gershom Scholem*, pp. 80, 98.

For Heschel, Hasidism was neither romanticism, rebellion, nor an affirmation of orthodoxy. He could not be labeled a neo-Hasid, though he forsook the Hasidic enclave for the broader Western society; nor did he find Hasidism shot through with Sabbatean elements, though he was well aware of the origins and history of the movement. Indeed, in his understanding of Hasidism, Heschel had no peer. His grasp of the entire range of Jewish literature—biblical, rabbinic, philosophic, and mystical—enabled him to discern in what sense Hasidic writings were a continuation of or a departure from the past, where they were original, what elements of earlier Jewish thought they accepted or rejected, and what problems they attempted to address. Philosophically, he was able to place Hasidism within a wider intellectual context; historically, he sought to gather those bits of evidence which, properly evaluated and pieced together, might reveal a hitherto unknown aspect of a personality or an event. Heschel's mastery of Hasidic texts themselves was such that when works were cited during discussions, he usually had no need to see the printed volume to quote from it extensively. Heschel's control of the material was joined by highly disciplined study habits. During his relatively short life, characterized by some wandering and dislocation, Heschel was the author of more than a dozen major works in several different languages.

Despite the fact that Hasidic literature is characterized by considerable shortcomings, which we have already alluded to, the effect of the publication and dissemination of the early Hasidic writings was as a series of thunderbolts that shattered as well as enlightened. Of those who read these treatises, few remained unmoved, some becoming angry critics of the new movement, others fervent followers. So avidly did the devotees pore over these books in the years that followed that they virtually devoured them, and soon a first edition in good condition could hardly be found. Hasidic literature was, and was meant to be, evocative as well as cognitive, addressing the soul and the mind at once. The "word," so central to the entire Hasidic enterprise, was, in its written form, says Heschel, "a voice, not a mere idea." To him, whose approach to Hasidism was never that of pure research, the task of the present student of this literature becomes, therefore, "how to hear the voice through the words." Heschel's trenchant observations are contained in his preface to a study of R. Jacob Joseph of Polonnoye, author of the first and, in some ways, still the most significant Hasidic book:

> The Holy of Holies in the Temple at Jerusalem was a place which only the High Priest was allowed to enter once a year, on the Day of Atonement. Now even the Holy of Holies was occasionally in need of repair. To provide for such an occasion, there

were openings in the Upper Chamber leading [down] through the ceiling of the Holy of Holies and close to its walls. Through these openings they used to lower the workmen in boxes (*Tevot*), which were open only to the walls, "so that they should not feast their eyes on the Holy of Holies.". . . It is said that the Upper Chamber of the Holy of Holies was even less accessible than the Holy of Holies, for the High Priest entered the Holy of Holies once a year, whereas the Upper Chamber was entered only once in fifty years to see whether any repairs were required.

The great Hasidim were the repair men of the Holy of Holies. In Hebrew *tevot* means both boxes and *words*. It was through the word that they entered the Holy of Holies. In the Hasidic movement the spirit was alive in the word. It was a voice, not a mere idea. It emanated in words that had the power to repair, to revive, to create.

Judaism today is in need of repair. The spirit is stifled, the word is emaciated; we do not know how to find access to the "Upper Chamber."

Hasidism withers when placed on exhibition. Its substance is not perceptible to the eye. It is not enough to read its written word; one must hear it, one must learn to be perceptive to the voice. Fortunately there are words in many of its records which still ring with the passion and enthusiasm of those who spoke them. The problem is how to hear the voice through the words.

Neither the Baal Shem nor most of his disciples have written down their utterances. One of the very few who did write was Rabbi Yaakov Yosef. The surprise, the joy, the refreshment which the publication of his books brought to the Jewish world are quite understandable to those who are acquainted with the spiritual atmosphere of the eighteenth century. It was like questioning the Ptolemaic theory in the time of Copernicus. These books offered a transvaluation of accepted values, a fresh vision of what is at stake in Jewish faith and existence, and a singular sensitivity for the divine. These are words that originated in Paradise, said one of the contemporaries. In other books one must read many pages until the presence of God is sensed; in the writings of Rabbi Yaakov Yosef, God's presence is felt on each page.[25]

Heschel's Hasidic understanding went beyond books. He was intimately familiar with Hasidism as a living phenomenon, was privy to the legacy of tradition handed down from several Hasidic dynasties because of his early upbringing and continued association, and had remarkable

25. Preface to S. Dresner, *The Zaddik* (New York and London: Abelard-Schuman, 1960; rpt. New York: Schocken, 1974), pp. 7–8.

sensitivity to the core of Hasidic authenticity as it was transmitted from generation to generation. Without acquaintance with the oral tradition of the movement, and with Hasidism as a living phenomenon, Hasidic scholarship, in Heschel's opinion, faces a major obstacle, which the demise of East European Jewry serves to emphasize. His published views on this central issue revolve around the preparation of his last major work, the powerful two-volume Yiddish study on Rabbi Menahem Mendel of Kotzk.

Why, in his waning years, Heschel determined to write his one major Hasidic work on the later master of Kotzk rather than the movement's founder, the Baal Shem Tov, whose life and thought had occupied him for decades, Heschel did not tell us. Perhaps the formidable problems which the paucity of historical sources presented for a comprehensive work on the Baal Shem—the need to collect, collate, and interpret scattered hints and pieces of information to establish dates, names, and places, comparing different versions of manuscripts and/or early prints, as well as contending with numerous other conflicting theories which would have to be presented and refuted—comprised too wearying a project for the final years of his life. A book on Kotzk, on the other hand, might almost write itself. Whether or not this explanation as to the subject of the study satisfies our curiosity, there is a second problem about the language of the study which Heschel himself answers: namely, why he wrote his book on Kotzk in Yiddish. Surely, he knew that to do so was to limit severely the work's future readership and that either English or Hebrew would have been preferable from the point of view of the future use of the book. In explaining that he resolved to use Yiddish as the language of the work in order to preserve the authentic legacy of Kotzk, Heschel's understanding of the relationship between the oral tradition and Hasidic scholarship comes to the fore:

> The words of the Kotzker Rebbe have simmered within me all my life. Even when not in agreement, I felt their powerful thrust. Though my way has not been without hardship, when thinking of the Kotzker Rebbe everything difficult became easier. Rabbi Mendel occupied himself with problems which, though we may not always be aware of them, disturb us to this very day. The answers he proposed may be hard for modern man to accept, but his perception was revolutionary, his impact shattering. Whoever is for but an hour in the presence of the Kotzker will never again give way to smugness.
>
> One of the qualities of the Kotzker Rebbe was a marvelous gift in formulating his thoughts in a tense, sharp and brilliant manner. Reading those of his aphorisms which have been preserved in the distinctive manner in which they were uttered, that is, in Yiddish, reveals an extraordinary style and power. Unfortunately, those

who published Rabbi Mendel's words translated them into Hebrew, for seldom in Jewish history has the talent for conversion
into felicitous Hebrew been so lacking as among those learned
Jewish circles in Poland of the last century. Consequently, a number of his sayings . . . are garbled. That I understand them despite their ambiguous Hebrew formulation is due to the fact that
in my youth I heard many of these aphorisms in their original
Yiddish. It was my good fortune to have known Rabbi Ben Tzion
and Rabbi Moses Judah, who had visited Rabbi Mendel, as well
as a large number of Hasidim who were thoroughly imbued with
the way of the Kotzk. From them I learned many of the aphorisms which I cite in this book.

    . . . Some oral statements have survived which are more cor-
rect than their literary form. While the oral tradition preserved
what was spoken by the rabbis, the literary text conveys them
only as they were translated into Hebrew. One who has been
close to Hasidic life knows with what reverence the words of the
masters were transmitted after they were "heard." One literally
lived with them, was nourished by them: every effort was taken
to transmit such words accurately.

    *Whoever attempts to describe Hasidism on the basis of literary
sources alone without drawing upon the oral tradition, ignores the
authentic living source and is dependent upon material artificial
in character. In the absence of the oral tradition and a proximity
to Hasidic personages, one can scarcely describe Hasidism. Its
essence was rarely expressed in writing, and that which was written
down was translated into Hebrew in a style which seldom captured
the living tongue of the masters. Hasidic literature is a literature of
translation, and not always successful translation. In order to
understand Hasidism one must learn how to listen and how to
stand close to those who lived it* [Emphasis S.H.D.].

    Surrounded by so many great scholars, why did none of them
write down R. Mendel's words, as students of other Tzaddikim
had? The Kotzker himself asked his disciple, R. Yehiel Meir, to
record his teachings, but he did not. In my opinion it was because
of an unwillingness to do so in Yiddish. The words R. Mendel
spoke in Yiddish were not easily rendered into Hebrew. To translate them exactly was not possible, while to record them in Yiddish was not acceptable. Thus Kotzk remained an oral tradition.

    . . . What I have written in this book about the Kotzker,
whether his personality or his way, reflects the tradition of Kotzker Hasidim . . .[26]

It has been suggested that the low estimate in which Hasidism was
formerly held in scholarly circles may have encouraged Heschel in his

___

26. *Kotzk: In Gerangel far Emesdikeit* (Kotzk: The struggle for integrity), 2 vols., (Tel
Aviv: Hamenora, 1973), pp. 7–10.

earlier writings to omit all but the most necessary references to Hasidic material in support of his theories. The tragic end of Eastern European Jewry, however, brought new respect for what it had produced. This, together with the growing acceptance of Heschel's own works, permitted him to make more open use of Hasidic literature. It is of interest that Heschel's first book, *Der Shem Hameforash Mentsh* (1933), a youthful volume of Yiddish poetry, was not listed in the initial bibliography of his works which appeared in 1959, but is present in the updated 1965 version.[27]

Heschel observed privately more than once that "after the Holocaust, Jewish scholarship should be devoted to that which advances Yiddishkeit." He was warning that in the terribly weakened position in which Jews now found themselves, with their very survival at stake, and with the demise of the great centers of Jewish authority and guidance, they dared not expend their limited resources on hairsplitting studies or on the exposure of the unseemly side of Jewish life. Heschel was speaking to a situation in which some Jewish scholars were content to edit texts, collect footnotes, and frown upon ideas, questioning, for instance, whether there was such a thing as Jewish theology, while others explored the Jewish "underworld," dwelling upon forgeries and heresies.[28] Heschel preferred to devote himself, in a series of seminal works, to delineating wide areas of Jewish creativity—biblical, rabbinic, medieval, and Hasidic. Even his popular survey of Eastern European Jewry, which reflects the enduring values of a thousand years of Ashkenazic Jewry, stands in marked contrast to the explorations of the occasionally insipid, bizarre, and ribald. If Heschel may be faulted, it is in his tendency toward Hasidic apologetics and his preference to stay clear of the ignoble and dark features which are inevitable in a world which included millions. To limit Jewish research in any way, however praiseworthy the motive, may result in an incomplete view of the subject. The reader and the student must submit the final verdict as to the relative reliability of those who sought, for whatever reasons, to portray a different and often more negative picture than did Heschel.

Heschel as a Scholar of Hasidism

Perhaps the single most important project which Heschel left unfinished at his untimely death, a project to which he was uniquely suited and the completion of which students and scholars of Judaism had

27. *Between God and Man: From the Writings of Abraham J. Heschel*, (ed. F. A. Rothschild (1959; rev. rpt. New York: Free Press, 1965).
28. An examination of the topics selected for doctoral dissertations in Jewish studies during the past thirty years unfortunately confirms Heschel's concern.

long awaited, was his work on the life and thought of the Baal Shem Tov, the renowned eighteenth-century founder of the Hasidic movement.[29] We do not know when Heschel first made plans to write this comprehensive work, but while in Cincinnati (1940–45) he was already methodically gathering material. Perhaps the destruction of Hasidic life in Eastern Europe made him turn from those areas of Jewish thought in which he had been engaged, primarily Bible and medieval philosophy, to a study of the movement he considered to be, in some ways, the final flowering of post-biblical Jewish history. Heschel's agony over the Holocaust during the years in Cincinnati, while failing to influence public policy directly, led to his memorable portrait of Ashkenazic Jewry, *The Earth Is the Lord's*, in which he sketched its lasting qualities.[30]

Whatever the reasons, Heschel's book on the Besht was never written. Other works and projects, coming in quick succession, always postponed the book that must have been dearest to his heart. The closest he came was his investigation of R. Menahem Mendel of Kotzk,[31] which was finished at the very end of his life, as if at least one major statement on Hasidism had to be made before death snatched him away. In that book, a part of which he adapted into English as *A Passion for Truth*,[32] he dealt,

29. Heschel's plan is indicated in the introductory note to his first published essay on the history of Hasidism, the Yiddish study, "Reb Pinkhes Koretzer" (*Yivo Bleter* 33 [1949]:9), which he described as "a chapter from the author's work on *the Besht and his circle*" (emphasis SHD). By July 1947 Heschel had completed his essays on R. Pinhas of Korzec and R. Gershon of Kutov (ibid., p. 48).

30. In an interview with Heschel in 1963, the Yiddish journalist, Gershon Jacobson, recorded Heschel's recollections as a newcomer to America.

"I was an immigrant, a refugee. No one listened to me. Let me mention three examples: In 1941 I met with a prominent Jewish communal leader, a devoted Zionist. I told him that the Jews of the Warsaw ghetto endure in the belief that American Jewry is working ceaselessly on their behalf. Were they to know of our indifference, the Jews in Warsaw would perish from shock. My words fell on deaf ears. In 1942 or 1941, I was at a convention of Reform rabbis. A representative of the Quakers appeared, demanding that the rabbis adopt a resolution to have food parcels sent to the Jews in the ghettoes and concentration camps. The appeal was turned down. The rabbis explained that they could not do it officially, because it might aid the Germans by sending food into their territory. In 1943 I attended the "American Jewish Conference" of all Jewish organizations, to appeal that they act to extinguish the flames which had engulfed Eastern European Jewry. The "Conference" had a long agenda—Eretz-Yisrael, fascism, finances, etc.—the last item of which was Jews under the Germans. By the time they reached this issue, almost all the representatives had left. I went away brokenhearted."

"What then, in fact, did you do?"

"I went to Rabbi Eliezer Silver's synagogue in Cincinnati [where Heschel resided. R. Silver was actively involved in saving Jews during the Holocaust.], recited Psalms, fasted, and cried myself out. I was a stranger in this country. My word had no power. When I did speak, they shouted me down. They called me a mystic, unrealistic. I had no influence on leaders of American Jewry." (*Day-Morning Journal*, 13 June 1963)

I thank Dr. Zanvel Klein for calling this interview to my attention.

31. *Kotzk.*

32. *A Passion for Truth* (New York: Farrar, Straus and Giroux, 1973; repr. ed., New York: Noonday, 1974).

as well, with the Besht. True, his purpose was to contrast the way of the Besht with that of Kotzk, the main subject of the work, but in his remarks on the Besht he condensed a number of valuable insights into the founder of Hasidism, as well as allowing himself a personal statement:

> I was born in Warsaw, Poland, but my cradle stood in Mezbizh (a small town in the province of Podolia, Ukraine), where the Baal Shem Tov, founder of the Hasidic movement, lived during the last twenty years of his life. That is where my father came from, and he continued to regard it as his home . . . The earliest fascination I can recall is associated with the Baal Shem, whose parables disclosed some of the first insights I gained as a child. He remained a model too sublime to follow yet too overwhelming to ignore . . .
>
> Years later I realized that, in being guided by both the Baal Shem Tov and the Kotzker, I had allowed two forces to carry on a struggle within me. One was occasionally mightier than the other. But who was to prevail, which was to be my guide? Both spoke convincingly, and each proved right on one level yet questionable on another.
>
> In a very strange way, I found my soul at home with the Baal Shem Tov and the Kotzker. Was it good to live with one's heart torn between the joy of Mezbizh and the anxiety of Kotzk? . . . I had no choice: my heart was in Mezbizh, my mind in Kotzk.
>
> I was taught about inexhaustible mines of meaning by the Baal Shem; from the Kotzker I learned to detect immense mountains of absurdity standing in the way. The one taught me song, the other—silence. The one reminded me that there could be a Heaven on earth, the other shocked me into discovering Hell in the alleged Heavenly places in our world.
>
> The Baal shem made dark hours luminous; the Kotzker eased wretchedness and desolation by forewarnings, by premonitions. The Kotzker restricted me, debunked cherished attitudes. From the Baal Shem I received the gifts of elasticity in adapting to contradictory conditions.
>
> The Baal Shem dwelled in my life like a lamp, while the Kotzker struck like lightning. To be sure, lightning is more authentic. Yet one can trust a lamp, put confidence in it; one can live in peace with a lamp.
>
> The Baal Shem gave me wings; the Kotzker encircled me with chains and entered into joys with my shortcomings in mind. I owe intoxication to the Baal Shem, to the Kotzker the blessings of humiliation.
>
> The Kotzker's presence recalls the nightmare of mendacity. The presence of the Baal Shem is an assurance that falsehood dissolves into compassion through the power of love. The Baal Shem suspends sadness, the Kotzker enhances it. The Baal Shem

helped me to refine my sense of mystery; the Kotzker warned me
of the constant peril of forfeiting authenticity.
. . . My origin was in Mezbizh [the town of the Besht]. It gave
me nourishment. Following the advice of the old Chortkover
Rebbe, R. David Moses, the uncle and second husband of my
father's mother, my father settled in Warsaw. There I spent my
younger years among Kotzker Hasidim. I am the last of the generation, perhaps the last Jew from Warsaw, whose soul lived in
Mezbizh but whose mind was in Kotzk.[33]

From Heschel's childhood on, there were Hasidic leaders who looked
to him as one with unique promise for renewing Hasidic life. That was
not to be, at least not in the way that they had hoped. Descended
from Hasidic nobility on both his father's and his mother's side, young
Heschel's talents were early recognized, and though he was only a child of
ten at the time of his father's death, the Hasidim began to bring him
kevitlekh (petitions) and wished him to become their rebbe. "We
thought," said the rebbe of Kopyczynce (Kopitchinitz), a cousin and
brother-in-law, "that he would be the Levi Yitzhak of our generation." A
byword after his departure was that "had Heschel become a rebbe, all the
other rebbes would have lost their Hasidim."[34] While his education had
always been directed with special care in the selection of his teachers,
even more attention was now paid in view of his promise, and it was
during this period of his life that the influence of the remarkable Kotzker
Hasid, Reb Bezalel, his teacher from the age of nine to twelve and a half
(described by Heschel's childhood friend, the writer, Yehiel Hofer), was
most keenly felt. But awareness of the worlds "outside" was stirring, and
the young Heschel did not accede to the wishes of the Hasidim. Heschel's
curiosity was too consuming to ignore what lay beyond the narrow
borders of the Jewish society of piety and learning of his ancestors in
which he had been raised. Hofer related how, at the age of seven or eight,
Heschel once surprised him by compiling a detailed catalog of the bolts of
cloth which were piled in high columns in Hofer's father's millinery store,
giving such information as color, material, quantity, price, etc., as an
example of how Heschel insisted on mastering whatever new phenomenon drew his attention. Heschel's interest in secular studies began
at about age fifteen or sixteen. His decision to leave Warsaw for Vilna and
later Berlin to gain a secular education was received with concern. His
mother, an unusual woman, clever and strong, who maintained their
shtibl (the Hasidic house of prayer) after her husband's death and
appreciated her son's gifts, noticed that she no longer heard him chanting

33. Ibid., pp. xiii–xv; *Kotzk*, p. 10.
34. Quotations for which no sources are given come from this writer's conversations with
Heschel, or from family members.

the Talmud from his room, for he was now engaged in learning Polish, and she inquired why. He told her of his plan and she communicated her concerns to the family in Vienna and Warsaw. A meeting of the family in Vienna was called by the Tchortkover Rebbe[35] which Heschel may have attended. His mother's brother, the Novominsker Rebbe of Warsaw, at whose table Heschel grew up and one of the most powerful influences upon his life, tried to dissuade him, and agreed only when he saw that it was to no avail. "You can go," he told Heschel, "but *only* you." It was on a Saturday night after the close of the Sabbath that Heschel left Warsaw, changing his Shabbos hat for an ordinary weekday cap, and accompanied by his cousin, a son of the Novominsker Rabbi.

Just before the young Heschel was to depart his ancestral home in Poland for the secular society of the West, an old Hasid came to bid him farewell. Following the admonition that one should take leave with a word of Torah, the Hasid quoted the Mishnah (Avot 5:8) which cites, as "one of the ten miracles of the Temple in Jerusalem," that, no matter what the provocation, "the holy flesh [of the sacrifice] did not ever become polluted." Then he told how R. Barukh of Miedzybórz (Mez-bizh) explained the passage: "One of the most wondrous miracles was, indeed, *lo' hisriaḥ besar kodesh mey‘olam*, which is to say, 'the holy flesh'—that is, the people Israel—'did not become polluted, *mey‘-olam, from the world.'"

"Avraham," the old Hasid concluded, taking him by the shoulders, "remember the word of R. Barukh. *Lo' hisriaḥ besar kodesh mey‘olam.* You, Avraham, you holy flesh, do not become polluted from the world!"

The Novominsker Rebbe, mentioned above, is important for another reason. One of Heschel's major contributions as a religious thinker was his analysis of Jewish piety. He was a phenomenologist. He held that discursive reason, while essential, was, alone, inadequate in penetrating the inner recesses of religion. This could better be achieved through a description of the religious phenomena itself, which, much as the artist's

35. I.e., R. Israel. He was the son of R. David Moses, the first Tchortkover Rebbe, who was married later in life to his niece, Heschel's father's mother, Rachel Leah, both having been widowed from their first spouses. R. David Moses was a son of the famed R. Israel of Ruzhin, while Rachel Leah was both his daughter-in-law and his granddaughter. Indeed, the Ruzhiner died in her arms. After the death of her first husband, R. Abraham Joshua Heschel of Miedzybórz, Heschel's grandfather, she brought her son, Heschel's father, to the court of Czortków (Tchortkov) where he was raised. Since R. Israel of Ruzhin knew intimately those who knew the maggid of Miedzyrzecz, whose great-grandson he was, and since the oral record was handed down with such care, this is an instance, which Heschel once cited in conversation, of how reliable traditions going back to the earliest generations of Hasidism were available to him. (Cf. A. Twerski, *The Genealogy of Tchernobil and Ruzhyn* [Lublin, 1938], p. 120 [Hebrew].)

In addition to being descended on his father's side from R. Israel of Ruzhin, R. Abraham Joshua Heschel of Opatów, and R. Dov Ber of Miedzyrzecz, Heschel counted on his mother's side R. Levi Yitzhak of Berdichev and R. Pinhas of Korzec.

canvas, would have the power to evoke another level of comprehension. In composing his now classic picture of Jewish piety, Heschel drew from the lives and writings of holy men of the past, as well as from his own personal experience, but equally important were the living models he had known in his youth. One whom he identified was the rabbi of Minsk Mazowiesk (Novominsk).

Rabbi Alter (a name added for long life) Israel Simon (after his grandfather) Perlow (1874–1933) was Heschel's mother's twin. The Novominsker's grandfather was a son-in-law of Rabbi Solomon Hayim of Kedainai (Kaidenov) in White Russia, situated between Minsk and Vilna. It is there that the family lived. The father of the Novominsker, Jacob (1847–1902), was advised to "bring his type of Hasidism to Poland," and settled in Minsk Mazowiesk (Novominsk), just outside of Warsaw, established a yeshivah and a large synagogue with an impressive *hof* (court). The privations of World War I drove the Novominsker himself, who succeeded his father in 1902 (though he had been at the head of the yeshivah since its founding in 1896), to remove to Warsaw, where he remained. His principal published work was *Tif'eret 'Ish*. The Novominsker was an unusual tzaddik. Famed for his talmudic learning and as a kabbalist, his piety, Torah, and love of Israel were well-known. He presided at the third Sabbath meal, the *Shalosh Seudos*, in a mood of ecstasy: his songs and words of Torah were wonderful, while his gestures and his face were marvelous to behold. He helped to bring Heschel's father to Warsaw, found a suitable place for him, and after the latter's early death, acted as mentor to the family. His uncle liked to have the young Avraham sit at his right hand when he spoke before the Hasidim at the Sabbath table.[36]

> His life [Heschel observed], was consistent with his thought . . .
> He was a complete person. Not one minute of the day was
> allowed to pass without attempting to serve God with all of his
> strength. He gave himself over to a tremendous task: the service
> of the Almighty at every moment with every act. An ordinary
> *Minhah* prayer was like Yom Kippur elsewhere, and on the Sab-
> bath, as he put each morsel of food into his mouth, he would say,
> *Lekoved Shabbos Kodesh* "for the honor of the holy Sabbath."
> This latter custom was not practiced even by my father, while the
> Gerer Hasidim who were the majority in Poland and followed
> the austere teachings of Kotzk, opposed it as excessive expression
> of one's feelings.[37]

36. Cf. H. Rabinowicz, *The World of Hasidism* (London: Valentine, 1970), pp. 164–66; A. Bromberg, *Hasidic Leaders* (Jerusalem: Hamakhon Lehasidut, 1963), 20:124–68 (Hebrew).

37. Heschel's appreciation of his uncle is confirmed by other sources. So admiring was he of him that the Gerer Rebbe, the ranking Hasidic leader in Poland, used to send his Hasidim

Heschel left Warsaw for Vilna to study and graduate from the secular, Yiddish real-gymnasium there, joining, during his stay, the newly formed group of Yiddish poets, Yung Vilno, which later included writers such as Abraham Sutzkever and Hayim Grade, who recalled in what high regard the youthful Heschel had been held. Shlomo Beillis, a fellow poet, a Communist who still resides in Warsaw, described his impressions of Heschel. ". . . with the deep eyes of a *talmid ḥakham*, he came from a world far different from mine." When they took walks through the forest, Heschel "would surprise me by bringing along his dark hat and, upon entering the woods, would put it on. When I inquired for the reason, he replied in his soft voice: 'I don't know if you will understand. To me a forest is a holy place, and a Jew does not enter a holy place without covering his head!' "[38]

Heschel moved west, to the University of Berlin and the *Hochschule für die Wissenschaft des Judentums*, to the Frankfurt *Lehrhaus*, to England, and, finally, to America. He claimed he was no longer a Hasid. He had indeed abandoned the Hasidic style of dress and of restricted social contacts for the larger world, both Jewish and German. Heschel wrote:

> In my childhood and in my youth I was the recipient of many blessings. I lived in the presence of quite a number of extraordinary persons I could revere. And just as I lived as a child in their presence, their presence continues to live in me as an adult. And yet I am not just a dwelling place for other people, an echo of the past . . . I disagree with those who think of the present in the past tense . . . [T]he greatest danger is to become obsolete. I try not to be stale. I try to remain young. I have one talent and that is the capacity to be tremendously surprised, surprised at life, at ideas. This is to me the supreme Hasidic imperative.[39]

To the end Heschel remained an anomaly. Most of those who had left the narrow Hasidic milieu of Eastern Europe for the modern, open

---

to visit the Novominsker and would himself call upon him whenever the Gerer was in Warsaw. This writer has seen a *kevitl* from the Gerer Rebbe to the Novominsker. When the Gerer Rebbe sought someone to head the powerful Agudas Yisroel organization, he remarked that there was only one person in all of Poland whom he could recommend without qualification: the Novominsker Rebbe; and when his followers asked whom they should consult upon his departure for a visit to the Holy Land, the Gerer again responded: the Novominsker. Hillel Zeitlin observed: "Whenever I felt depressed and needed to repent, I visited the rabbi of Novominsk" (Rabinowicz, *The World of Hassidism*). The chief rabbi of Tel Aviv, Rabbi Yedidiah Frankel, said, "The picture I have in my mind of a perfect tzaddik is the rabbi of Novominsk. His profound wisdom, his constant learning, the depth of his Kabbalistic mastery, his majestic face, the smile which never left his face, his love of all Israel, his refusal to utter a critical word about another, were unforgettable."

38. Shlomo Beillis, "The Beginnings of Yung Vilno," in *Die Goldene Keit*, pp. 18–19; cf. E. Schulman, *Yung Vilno* (New York, 1946).
39. Heschel, "In Search of Exaltation," *Jewish Heritage* 13, no. 3 (1971):29.

society of the West—especially if they pursued studies in the human-
ities—exchanged the one world for the other, often repudiating their
Hasidic origins. This was true even of those engaged in Jewish research.
The art, philosophy, and literature of the West, as well as its power and
apparent freedom, were more than attractive: they were overwhelming.
The enthusiastic reviews of Heschel's early works, *Die Prophetie* and
Maimonides, confirmed how highly he was considered according to the
West's own scientific and literary standards. Nonetheless, while master-
ing European *Kultur* and *Wissenschaft* and recognizing their values,
Heschel retained his own religious position and even his Hasidic bias.

In an address before the annual convention of American Reform
rabbis in 1952, he gave a memorable description of the conflict he
experienced between Berlin and Warsaw, between the intellectual claim
of the university and the way of Torah:

> I came with great hunger to the University of Berlin to study phi-
> losophy. I looked for a system of thought, for the depth of the
> spirit, for the meaning of existence. Erudite and profound schol-
> ars gave courses in logic, epistemology, esthetics, ethics and
> metaphysics. They opened the gates of the history of philosophy.
> I was exposed to the austere discipline of unremitting inquiry and
> self criticism . . .
>
> Yet, in spite of the intellectual power and honesty which I was
> privileged to witness, I became increasingly aware of the gulf that
> separated my views from those held at the university. I had come
> with a sense of anxiety: how can I rationally find a way where
> ultimate meaning lies, a way of significance? Why am I here at
> all, and what is my purpose? I did not even know how to phrase
> my concern. But to my teachers that was a question unworthy of
> philosophical analysis.
>
> I realized my teachers were prisoners of a Greek-German way
> of thinking. They were fettered in categories which presupposed
> certain metaphysical assumptions which could never be proved.
> The questions I was moved by could not even be adequately
> phrased in categories of their thinking.
>
> My assumption was: man's dignity consists in his having been
> created in the likeness of God. My question was: how must man,
> a being who is in essence the image of God, think, feel and act?
> To them, religion was a feeling. To me, religion included the in-
> sights of the Torah which is a vision of man from the point of
> view of God. They spoke of God from the point of view of man.
> To them God was an idea, a postulate of reason. They granted
> Him the status of being a logical possibility. But to assume that
> He had existence would have been a crime against epistemology.
>
> The problem to my professors was how to be good. In my ears
> the question rang: how to be holy. At the time I realized: There

is much that philosophy could learn from Jewish life. To the phi-
losophers: the idea of the good was the most exalted idea, the
ultimate idea. To Judaism the idea of the good is penultimate. I
cannot exist without the holy. The good is the base, the holy is
the summit. Man cannot be good unless he strives to be holy . . .

I did not come to the university because I did not know the
idea of the good, but to learn why the idea of the good is valid,
why and whether values had meaning. Yet I discovered that
values sweet to taste proved sour in analysis; the prototypes were
firm, the models flabby. Must speculation and existence remain
like two infinite parallel lines that never meet? . . .

In those months in Berlin I went through moments of profound
bitterness. I felt very much alone with my own problems and anx-
ieties. I walked alone in the evenings through the magnificent
streets of Berlin. I admired the solidity of its architecture, the
overwhelming drive and power of a dynamic civilization. There
were concerts, theaters, and lectures by famous scholars about
the latest theories and inventions, and I was pondering whether
to go to the new Max Reinhardt play or to a lecture about the
theory of relativity.

Suddenly I noticed the sun had gone down, evening had arrived. *From what time may one recite the Shema in the evening?*[40]
I had forgotten God—I had forgotten Sinai—I had forgotten that
sunset is my business—that my task is "to restore the world to
the kingship of the Lord."

So I began to utter the words of the evening prayer.

> *Blessed art thou, Lord our God,*
> *King of the universe,*
> *who by His word brings on the evening twilight . . .*

On that evening in the streets of Berlin, I was not in a mood to
pray. My heart was heavy, my soul was sad. It was difficult for
the lofty words of prayer to break through the dark clouds of my
inner life.

But how would I dare not to *davn*? How would I dare to miss
evening prayer? "Out of *emah*, out of fear of God do we read
the Shema."[41]

Contact with Western culture, particularly with German Jewry, its
synagogues and academies of higher Jewish learning, made Heschel all
the more certain that Hasidic thinking and living contained a treasure

40. The first words of the Mishnah dealing with the evening prayer.
41. A play on *Me'eymatai* (From what time), the first word of the Mishnah dealing with
evening prayer, which is taken to mean "out of *'eymah*." It comes from the Hasidic master,
Rabbi Levi Yitzhak of Berditchev. See Heschel's *Man's Quest for God* (New York:
Scribner's, 1954), pp. 94–98, and "Toward an Understanding of Halakha," *Yearbook of the
Central Conference of American Rabbis* 63 (1953):386–91.

which should be made available to the emancipated Jew. His early studies on prophecy and Maimonides had stressed themes such as the divine pathos, the striving for prophecy, and *imitatio Dei*—concepts to which he had been sensitized by Hasidism. But what of Hasidism itself? What of that immense repository of surprising beauty and startling wisdom of which the West was not only ignorant but contemptuously ignorant? Where should one begin? Hasidism constituted a panorama of hundreds of remarkable spiritual figures, each with his own special way, and a literature whose books were precious, because, according to R. Pinhas of Korzec, unlike other works, one did not have to turn countless pages in them to find God. Before understanding the contributions of its notable leaders and the meaning of its most important books, one had to address the phenomenon of the Hasidic movement's creator, the Baal Shem Tov. This was the task to which Heschel began to direct himself.

Some idea of how Heschel intended to proceed in his work on the Baal Shem comes from an early outline of the book (or part of the book) which I found in his files:

1. The Love of God
2. Love for Israel—Love for Evil-Doers
3. Descending into Hell [to Redeem the Sinner]; Self-Sacrifice
4. [Faith?] in the Tzaddik
5. Humility
6. Evil
7. The Value of the Common Deed
8. The Relation to [?]
9. Messiah
10. Sadness
11. Strictness in Observing the Law
12. Truth
13. The Hasid
14. To Study Musar
15. The Besht on Himself
16. The Talmudic Sages
17. Bodily Movement [in Prayer]
18. "Serve Him in All Your Ways"
19. Limits of the Way of the Besht
20. Yearning
21. The Study of Torah
22. The Tzaddik

This outline is, of course, neither complete nor final. The topics, for example, seem not to be arranged in any particular order. No provision is made, moreover, for the historical studies of the circle of the Besht which, in revised form, were presumably to comprise the first part of the work. But what is significant about the outline is that it enables one to contrast Heschel's view of what should comprise the main subjects of Hasidism with that of other scholars.

Heschel did not, as we have noted, complete the work on the Besht which he had planned. One would have wished to possess a comprehensive statement from him, even a single essay, on the meaning of Hasidism. Unfortunately, almost all of his published Hasidic research is of a technical nature. He rarely even lectured on the subject, nor, I believe, did he ever offer a formal course on Hasidism at the Jewish Theological Seminary, where he taught for over twenty years, or elsewhere. His scanty lecture notes, however, do provide brilliant, if all too brief, insights. At one point he even hints at the reasons for his reticence. "Young boys are shy," his notes read. "Too shy to lecture on Hasidism. It is too personal. Too intimate. I remained a boy even after becoming a man!"

While it is to be regretted that the detailed monographs dealing with the circle of the Baal Shem failed to lead to a full-length evaluation of the doctrine of Hasidism and its significance—especially since Heschel's textual and historical studies were generally done not for their own sake but in order to distill the meaning of the material he researched—there are a number of scattered remarks in his notes, in his more popular writings, and in *A Passion for Truth*, which point to what he wished eventually to say. Obviously, they must not be taken as his measured and scholarly view either of the movement or of the man who was its founder:

Hasidism [he writes] was neither a sect nor a doctrine. It was a dynamic approach to reality. That was its essence. It succeeded in liquifying a frozen system of values and ideas. Everything was neatly labelled—good and evil, clean and unclean, safe and dangerous, rich and poor, *rashaʿ* and *tzaddik*, *mitzvah* and *ʿaverah*, beautiful and ugly, truth and falsehood. But, such a division is artificial. Life cannot be enclosed in boxes. Values are often ambiguous. What, for example, is beauty? Something in itself, or an experience born when a person who loves the beautiful discovers it? In attaching oneself to the source of all unity, the Hasid learned to bend every action to the ultimate goal. Hasidism opposed the externalization of the maggid's preaching and the idolatry of the talmudist's learning. It attacked the inclemency of intellectuality, the rigidity of legalism, a system of life which had become chilly. The Hasid studied the Talmud also to experience its soul, to envision worlds. Hasidism brought warmth, light, enthusiasm; it set life aflame. It was one of the great conquests of Jewish history. The admonition not to fool others was given a new turn: don't fool yourself. Truthfulness, wholeheartedness was central. The aphorism became a mode for Hasidic thinking. The parable took on new power. Doctrines affected life and were transformed into attitudes and facts. Hasidism learned how to fight with the enemies' weapons—the evil urge (*yetzer hara*ᶜ) and joy (*simḥah*). It taught that holiness was something concrete and positive. To redeem the sparks was earthly serving. There are two ways of instilling discipline: knowledge of the law and understanding its meaning: Halakhah and Kabbalah. At a time when the spectacular phenonenon of *lamdanut* (talmudic learning) was praised, Hasidism stressed ᶜ*anavah* (humility), the imponderable, the inaudible. It taught reverence, enthusiasm. It taught that scholarship for its own sake could be an idol, that God is greater than sin.[42]

It was a time when the Jewish imagination was nearly exhausted. The mind had reached an impasse, thinking about impossible possibilities in Talmudic law. The heart was troubled by oppressive social and economic conditions, as well as the teachings of ascetic preachers. Then a miracle occurred. It was as if Providence had proclaimed, "Let there be light!" And there was light—in the form of an individual: Reb Israel, son of Eliezer, Baal Shem Tov, "master of the Good Name" (ca. 1690–1760) . . .

He was born in a small town in the province of Podolia, Okop, to poor and elderly parents. Orphaned as a child, he later eked out a living as an assistant teacher of little children (*belfer*). Tradition has it that at the age of twenty he went into seclusion in the Carpathian Mountains for spiritual training and preparation for his calling. There he lived for several years as a digger of clay, which his wife sold in the town where she kept house. When he was thirty-six, he revealed himself as a spiritual master. Later he settled in Mezbizh [i.e., Miedzybórz] . . . where he died in 1760.

The Baal Shem was the founder of the Hasidic movement, and Mezbizh was the cradle in which a new understanding of Judaism was nurtured. When millions of our people were still alive in Eastern Europe and their memory and faith vibrated with thought, image, and emotion, the mere mention of Reb Israel Baal Shem Tov cast a spell upon them. The moment one uttered his name, one felt as if his lips were blessed and his soul grew wings. . . . During his lifetime, Reb Israel inspired a large number of disciples to follow him. After his death his influence became even more widespread. Within a generation, the insights he had formulated at Mezbizh had captivated the Jewish masses with new spiritual ideas and values. And Mezbizh became the symbol of Hasidism. Rarely in Jewish history has one man succeeded in

42. This paragraph is drawn from Heschel's lecture notes.

uplifting so many individuals to a level of greatness . . . No one in the long chain of charismatic figures that followed him was equal to the Baal Shem.

Hasidism represents an enigma. It is first of all the enigma of the impact of one great man, the Besht . . . who in a very short time was able to capture the majority of the Jewish people and to keep them under his spell for generations. What was there about him that was not to be found in other great Jewish personalities like Maimonides or even Isaac Luria or Akiba? . . . The answers given are partly sociological, partly historical; I believe there is also a Hasidic answer to this Hasidic riddle . . . [in] the following story:

In Poland in the eighteenth century, a king was nominated, not as a matter of heritage but of election. Noblemen would get together from all over the country and . . . elect a king. The king could also be a citizen of a foreign country, so whenever a king died and there was a possibility of election, many princes and aristocrats from all over Europe would vie for that honor. And this is what happened. The king passed away and immediately various princes, eager to become king of Poland would send their representatives to Poland . . . each . . . sing[ing] the praises of his candidate. "He is the wisest of all men," one . . . said. "He is the wealthiest," said another. "The kindest," said a third. This went on for days, and no decision was reached. Finally one representative decided he would take his candidate, the prince himself, bring him to the people and say: "Here he is, look at him, see how grand he is!"

And that man was elected.

Many Jews talked about God, but it was the Besht who brought God to the people. This is perhaps the best answer to the question of how to explain the unbelievable impact in such a short time of this great man.

Reb Israel Baal Shem Tov revealed the Divine as present even in our shabby world, in every little thing, and especially in man. He made us realize that there was nothing in man—neither limb nor movement—that did not serve as vessel or vehicle for the Divine force. No place was devoid of the Divine. He taught that the Tzaddikim who grasped the bond between Creator and creature were blessed with so great a power that they were able to perform marvelous acts of mystical unification in the sphere of the Divine. Furthermore, every man in this world could work deeds that might affect the worlds above. Most important, attachment to God was possible, even while carrying out mundane tasks or making small talk. Thus, unlike the sages of the past, who delivered discourses about God, the Baal Shem, like the wise man in the parable, brought God to every man.

. . . The Baal Shem brought about a radical shift in the religious outlook of Jewry. In ancient times the sanctuary in Jerusalem had been the holy center from which expiation and blessing
radiated out to the world. But the sanctuary was in ruins, the
soul of Israel in mourning. Then the Baal Shem established a new
center: the Tzaddik, the Rebbe—he was to be the sanctuary. For
the Baal Shem believed that a man could be the true dwelling
place of the Divine. He brought about the renewal of man in
Judaism. The Jewish people is not the same since the days of the
Besht. It is a new people. Other pesonalities contributed great
works; they left behind impressive achievements; the Besht left
behind a new people. To many Jews the mere fulfillment of reg-
ulations was the essence of Jewish living . . . The Besht taught
that Jewish life is an occasion for exaltation. Observance of the
Law is the basis, but exaltation through observance is the goal.
. . . Other great teachers bore the message of God, sang His
praises, lectured about His attributes and wondrous deeds. The
Baal Shem brought not only the message; he brought God Himself to the people. His contribution, therefore, consisted of more
than illumination, insights, and ideas; he helped mold into being
new types of personality: the Hasid and the Tzaddik. . . . [T]he
greatness of the Besht was that he was the beginning of a long
series of . . . moments of inspiration. And he holds us in his spell
to this very day. He who really wants to be uplifted by commun-
ing with a great person whom he can love without reservation,
who can enrich his thought and imagination without end, that
person can meditate about the life . . . of the Besht. There has
been no one like him during the last thousand years.[43]

Descendant of a Hasidic dynasty and heir of the living tradition at its
most vital source, master of the philosophical and historical-critical
method of the West as well as possessing unusual creative gifts, Heschel
was perhaps the one scholar who might have given us the definitive work
on Hasidism.

Historical Studies

The essays before us constitute historical studies which Heschel
published as preliminary to a proper understanding of the Besht and the
foundations of Hasidism. If the intended work was planned in two
volumes—one to deal with the history and the second, the teachings of
the Besht—these four essays would have supplied much of the material
for the first volume.

43. A composite from "Hasidism," *Jewish Heritage* 14, no. 3 (1972):14–16, and *A
Passion for Truth* (New York: Farrar, Straus and Giroux, 1973), pp. 3–7.

Besieged by controversy, Hasidism had emerged in the eighteenth century as a reform movement which engendered bitter opposition. Its early writings, such as the *Toldot Ya'akov Yosef* (Korzec, 1780), were largely polemical, attacking not only the decline of Judaism into legalism and asceticism, but also the corruption of Jewish life itself. To correct the malaise, Hasidism boldly proposed a new type of leader, the tzaddik, a new kind of service to God which was not limited to Torah study and worship but embraced "all one's ways," and a new mood of joy and exaltation. Along with this program came the advocacy for the establishment of separate synagogues. A furious clash of forces followed, producing a polemical literature from the Mitnagdim, as the opponents of the Hasidim were called.

Though the Hasidim, at first separatists themselves and later excluded by the ruling group, finally rejoined the general community, the remnants of the early opposition never disappeared. The bitterness which provoked the excommunications of the first generations was still felt in the twentieth century. Its tone could be heard in the anti-Hasidic satire in the East and the aggressively critical reports by historians in the West. If Hasidim were drunkards, and tzaddikim little deities dabbling in witchcraft,[44] then it should come as no surprise that the Besht himself was the object of stinging jibes. "Ignoramus" and "sorcerer" were the two terms most commonly applied to him. In an atmosphere where Western scholars, such as Graetz, were so critical of Hasidism, it was natural that disturbing questions would continue to be raised: Did the Baal Shem, in fact, ever live? Do we possess any evidence about him from contemporary sources, apart from the hagiography which accumulated after his death? What do we know of his early followers? What was their relationship to the Frankists and the Sabbatean heresy?

Adored by some and reviled by others, the subject of miracle legends and scurrilous gossip, the inspiration for subsequent communities of the faithful as well as decrees of excommunication, the Baal Shem himself seemed shrouded in mystery. How to get behind the legend to the man? If a historian of Polish Jewry of the distinction of Mayer Balaban despaired in the 1920s and 1930s of finding any verifiable historical evidence about the founder of Hasidism,[45] consider the difficulties that confronted schol-

44. Graetz, *History of the Jews* (Philadelphia: Jewish Publication Society, 1898), 5:375–81.

45. "According to Balaban, all that is left to us concerning the life of the founder of the Hasidic movement is pure legend. To him, therefore, no responsible historian should attempt to write an historical treatise on this topic. 'A legend is a piece of folk poetry and it should not be dissected. We must take the legend as it is, or not use it at all.' There are no historical facts whatsoever against which to test these legends about the Baal Shem Tov . . . Balaban is dubious as to whether any genuine evidence relating to the founder of the Hasidic movement will ever be found. 'Israel Baal Shem Tov was a simple man. He did not

ars, after the Holocaust had destroyed most of the primary sources, as well as the movement's living tradition.

Heschel felt it vital that the historical basis for the rise of Hasidism be established to whatever extent it was still possible. To do so meant examining the entire eighteenth-century rabbinic literature for occasional references to and hints of the early Hasidic figures. The libraries of Hebrew Union College and, especially, of the Jewish Theological Seminary provided him with a unique opportunity for a systematic and thorough review. His work was severely hampered by the disastrous fire at the latter institution in 1966 which destroyed or made unavailable many of the rare volumes he needed. With the help of the book dealer, Jaker Biegeleisen, Heschel also began to rebuild his own Hasidic library, though he could not replace the valuable material, including rare manuscripts, he had lost in Europe. In 1949, aware of the presence in America of some of the central figures of the Hasidic remnant who had survived, he founded the YIVO Hasidic Archives, which functioned under his guidance and was directed by Moses Shulvass, to search out what could still be salvaged. Heschel believed that there was a reliable oral tradition going back to the early Hasidic period, if only one knew where to look

---

participate in the public life of the Jewish community, and did not come into contact with the leading personalities of his age. He did not compose books himself and did not write introductions to the books of others.' Neither did he engage in business activity nor have any communication with the Polish noblemen. There is therefore nowhere to look for traces of his activities. All we have is a multitude of legends—which often contradict each other." (I. Biderman, *Mayer Balaban: Historian of Polish Judaism* [New York: Biderman Book Committee, 1976], pp. 204–5; cf. M. Balaban, *"Hasidut," Hatekufah* 18 (1923):488.) Balaban's strict delimitation of the role of legend was made, in part, in reviewing the exaggerated claims of S. Setzer's biography of the Besht (in the periodical *Bicher Velt* 1, nos. 4–5 [1922]:406–7).

Balaban's general view of Hasidism was one of disapproval. He claimed that Hasidism had a negative influence upon family life and was one of the major causes of the decline of Polish Jewish culture. Summarizing Balaban's view, Biderman writes that "Polish Jewish culture . . . came to fruition during the Seventeenth Century, later to deteriorate under the twofold impact of the misfortunes which beset Polish Jewry from outside and the decay brought about by the mystical and hasidic movements from within the community" (p. 174). At least three factors must be considered in assessing Balaban's disapprobation: (1) The highly critical views of Heinrich Graetz; (2) the fact that Balaban's knowledge of Hebrew, according to one Jewish historian who was his student, did not allow him to master the sources sufficiently to gain a proper understanding of Hasidism; and (3) Balaban's descent from a family of Mitnagdim. One ancestor was a cosigner, with the rabbi of Lwów, of the 1792 excommunication of the Hasidim, while Balaban's grandfather "was known for his opposition to the Hasidim and was a principal supporter of Rabbi Ornstein, rabbi of Lemberg (i.e., Lwów) from 1804 to 1839," a leading opponent of the Hasidic movement. "Opposition to Hasidism was characteristic of the Balaban family," concludes Biderman, "and the young Mayer Balaban remained faithful to the family tradition."

One of the major objectives of Heschel's studies was to refute the point of view represented by Balaban, arguing, that, indeed, "there are . . . historical facts . . . against which to test these legends about the Baal Shem Tov," to the point of affirming that the Besht did, in fact, "come into contact with leading personalities of his age."

and how to listen. The YIVO Archives were, therefore, used as well for fieldwork and oral histories.[46]

In Heschel's relentless search, no document which might illuminate the origins of Hasidism was overlooked. Even rare and early Polish periodicals were scrutinized. Scholars who brought him their discoveries in this field almost always found that Heschel had been there before them. By exhaustively exploring the literature of the early eighteenth century for new information and by reexamining known material and allusive oral traditions, Heschel sought to move toward a historical understanding of the Besht. The major results of Heschel's early work are the essays in this book, originally published in Hebrew and Yiddish, in which he attempted, for the first time, to chart the lives and describe the teachings of the personalities of the intimate circle which the Besht had gathered about him as disciples, colleagues, or both. These monographs constitute an indispensible corpus of research preliminary to a proper understanding of the Besht, the founder of Hasidism.

Four (or five, if we include R. Moses of Kuty) of the leading figures in the group associated early with the Besht are discussed in the following essays. A number of almost equal importance are not. Heschel did not give us portraits of others from the Besht's circle, such as R. Nahman of Horodenka (grandfather of R. Nahman of Bratslav), whose early ascent to Palestine helped set a pattern among Hasidism for the love of the Land;[47] or R. Jacob Joseph of Polonnoye, the chief literary disciple of the Besht, whose books are the main record of the Baal Shem's teachings; or of R. Dov Ber, the Maggid of Miedzyrzecz who succeeded to the leadership of the movement after the death of the Besht; or of R. Judah Leib Pistener.[48] No doubt, Heschel intended eventually to deal with these and other figures. I have located some significant unpublished material in his files which has yet to be examined.

Strictly speaking, none of the figures whom Heschel has described in these essays can simply be called a "disciple" of the Besht. R. Nahman and R. Pinhas, critics at first, became disciples who were also colleagues, while R. Isaac of Drohobycz seemed to have remained somewhat distant until the end. (His son R. Yehiel Mikhel of Zloczew, on the other hand, became one of the most fervent fighters for the way of the Besht. It was before his house in Brod that the first Hasidic book, *Toldot Ya'akov Yosef*, by R. Jacob Joseph of Polonnoye, was publicly burned.) In any case, those who comprised the circle of the Besht did not submerge their

---

46. See the introductory remarks to A. Heschel, "Unknown Documents in the History of Hasidism."

47. See ibid., pp. 115–19.

48. R. Jacob Joseph of Polonnoye held him in such esteem that he published his eulogy of him (*Toldot Ya'akov Yosef* [Korzec: Katz, 1780], p. 92d).

individuality to the Besht: at times they were partners, at times opponents, at times followers. What each of them shared in common was the
possession of immense personal talents and their role as the conscious
object of the Besht's missionary efforts.

Previous to Heschel's studies, these figures had been vague and unclear. Some, like R. Gershon of Kuty, R. Nahman of Kosów, and R.
Isaac of Drohobycz (Drobitch), were occasionally quoted or told about;
only R. Pinhas of Korzec had left a body of teachings. In Heschel's adept
hands, these men are revealed as formidable scholars and striking personalities who, no doubt, would have played a role in any period of Jewish
history. In reading these essays, one beholds the image of historical
figures and not simply legendary ghosts.

Heschel's thorough examination of eighteenth-century rabbinic literature enabled him to add important facts to what was already known. The
close relationship between the earliest members of the "circle" of the
Besht and such significant personalities of the time as R. Hayim Hakohen
Rapoport of Lwów, R. Meir Margoliot of Lwów, R. Eleazer Rokeah of
Amsterdam, and R. Ezekiel Landau of Prague is confirmed and explored
in Heschel's studies. The brother-in-law of the Baal Shem, R. Gershon of
Kuty, emerges as one of the central figures of his time, suggesting a
reevaluation of our understanding of his role in eighteenth-century Jewish history, as well as the role of certain other Hasidic figures. R. Gershon
was a halakhic authority respected by R. Ezekiel Landau of Prague, and
by R. Jonathan Eybeschütz, as well as a communal figure who was
accepted as a leading representative of Palestinian Jewry. Heschel presents a fascinating picture of R. Gershon in the notable Constantinople
Jewish community where Ashkenazim and Sephardim esteemed and
worked with one another. The position of R. Gershon can be better
appreciated by our new knowledge that a person of such eminence as the
wealthy printer and regular visitor to the sultan's court, Moses Soncino,
who "administered the funds raised by R. Ezekiel Landau in Poland for
the Ashkenazim in Jerusalem," was a close friend of R. Gershon's and, in
fact, acted as intermediary in the correspondence between the Besht and
R. Gershon. R. Gershon traveled to the Land of Israel from Constantinople accompanied by R. Abraham Rosanes and R. Isaac Rosanes,
among the most noted rabbis of the community. Soon after his arrival, R.
Gershon was offered the post of rabbi of the Ashkenazic community of
Jerusalem. Heschel's long article, marked by new insights and suggestions, has encouraged considerable further research into R. Gershon
Kutover's role in eighteenth-century Palestine. Persuasive evidence is
now available that the early Hasidic leaders occupied a more important
position than was formerly believed among the pilgrims of the period.

It is in the essay on R. Gershon that Heschel published an important discovery: a reference to the Besht made during his lifetime by R. Meir Teomim, the head of the Yeshivah in Lubartów (Levertof) and father of the noted talmudist and author of *Peri Megadim*, who writes: "I have seen in a letter from the Holy Land what the Hasid, our master and teacher, R. Gershon, may his light continue to shine, wrote to his well-known [*mefursam*] brother-in-law, the Baal Shem Tov, may his light continue to shine." The source of this statement, a talmudist and father of a halakhic authority, the term used, "*mefursam*," and the fact that it is one of the very few contemporary references to the Besht, "refutes the claims of scholars that the Besht led a secluded existence and was unknown during his lifetime except to a small circle."[49]

Apart from Heschel's contribution to the history of Hasidism in these essays is his analysis of Hasidic thought. In his essay on R. Pinhas of Korzec, for example, he delineated the ideological conflict which occurred early in the history of the movement, in which each side claimed that it possessed the true meaning of the Besht's legacy. The maggid of Miedzyrzecz (Mezeritch) had stressed the centrality of Kabbalah and established *devekut* as the highest goal. For him, the awareness that all is God would lead man to understand that this world is but so many veils which must be cast aside to enter into the divine embrace. His language is strongly Lurianic, with spiritual ascent beyond time and place the all-consuming goal. For R. Pinhas, on the other hand, the stress is elsewhere. This world is no illusion. It is the place, and now is the time, where man must labor diligently and unremittingly to perfect himself. To escape the world is to violate the Psalmist's admonition that one must first "turn from evil" and only then "do good." R. Pinhas, who had favored R. Jacob Joseph of Polonnoye and not the maggid as successor to the Besht, emphasized moral virtue and simple faith.

The present essays are not all of a single type. The articles on R. Gershon of Kuty, R. Pinhas of Korzec, and R. Nahman of Kosów are finished works. The essay on R. Isaac of Drohobycz, not published in a scholarly journal, is much less elaborate. Published in Hebrew and Yiddish and in various stages of completeness, the essays which constitute the present volume should be understood as preliminary studies which would undoubtedly have been edited or recast to make up part of the work on the Besht which Heschel had planned.

Among the challenges to the editor and translators were the technical nature of some of the material, the frequent play upon Hebrew words, and the kabbalistic concepts which could be rendered only with difficulty into concise English. Our hope was to remain faithful to the author's words; our dilemma was to make these writings understandable to

49. See below, pp. 71–76, 98–99.

the reader of English beyond the narrow circle of Hasidic scholarship. Toward this end, a series of supplementary footnotes and explanations within the text itself has been provided, always in brackets [ ]. While nothing is omitted, highly technical material has at times been placed in footnotes or in an appendix, and on a few occasions, the material has been rearranged for ease of reading. For the benefit of those pursuing Hasidic scholarship, subsequent published research on the subjects dealt with by Heschel has been summarized in the notes, and the relationship of these studies to Heschel's positions has been pointed out. The important work of two Israeli scholars, Piekarz and Barnai, has been especially noted. The relevant research has thus, to a considerable extent, been brought up to date.

Though not uniform, the transliteration has been executed with an attempt at some consistency. For the ease of the reader, diacritical marks have been minimized, while established English spellings of Hebrew words have been maintained. The transcription follows the generally accepted norm in works of scholarship, with the following exceptions: we have used *sh* (instead of *ŝ*) to transliterate the Hebrew letter *shin*, *tz* (instead of *ṣ*) to transliterate the Hebrew letter *tzadi*, and *ey* (instead of *ê*) to designate the hard *e*.

The titles of scholarly works have usually been translated, while the titles of rabbinic works have almost always been transliterated. Generally, the titles of rabbinic works bear no relationship to their contents and sometimes sound odd in translation.

For the most part, we have either eliminated or shortened the honorific titles that characterize references in rabbinic works to both the living and the dead.

Place names are given according to the spellings in Berl Kagan's *Hebrew Subscription Lists* (New York: Library of the Jewish Theological Seminary of America and Ktav Publishing House, 1975). When an alternate spelling is given, that spelling reflects the Yiddish name of the town or city—e.g., Kozienice (Kozhnitz). For a list of the Eastern European towns and villages mentioned in this book, the reader may refer to the Gazetteer.

Dates, almost always given by the author according to the *anno mundi*, are presented as follows: In dates of publication, the year is simply given according to the common-era date in which most of the Jewish year fell—e.g., the publication date for the *Luḥot ʿEdut* is given as 1755, even though three or four months of A.M. 5515 actually fell in 1754. In other contexts, the Jewish year often is spread out over the two years of the common era in which it fell—e.g., 1743/4 (C.E.) for A.M. 5504. In cases in which a month is given, only the correct year is cited, e.g., 10 Tishri 1748 where the original has 10 Tishri 5509.

Some comments on the individual articles: For the chapter on R. Pinhas of Korzec, the translators have had the advantage of consulting both the Hebrew and Yiddish versions of this essay. The two differ slightly. Our translation is an amalgam. In several places, material from the chapter on R. Nahman of Kosów which would prove too specialized for the English reader has been placed in footnotes; another small section was made into an appendix. The Drohobycz piece, the most unfinished of the chapters, required some rearrangement of the text.

The essays in this volume originally appeared as follows:

"Rabbi Pinhas of Korzec" (Hebrew), *Alei ʿAyin: The Salman Schocken Jubilee Volume* (Jerusalem: Schocken, 1948–52), pp. 213–44; "Reb Pinkhes Koritzer" (Yiddish) *Yivo Bleter* 33 (1949); 9–48.

"Rabbi Gershon Kutover: His Life and Immigration to the Land of Israel" (Hebrew), *Hebrew Union College Annual*, 23 (1950–51): part 2, pp. 17–71.

"Rabbi Nahman of Kosów, Companion of the Baal Shem" (Hebrew), *The Harry A. Wolfson Jubilee Volume*, ed. Saul Lieberman et al. (New York: American Academy for Jewish Research, 1965), Hebrew section, pp. 113–41.

"Rabbi Isaac of Drobitch" (Hebrew), *Hadoʾar Jubilee Volume* (New York: Hadoar, 1957), pp. 86–94.

Parts of this Introduction appeared earlier in a slightly different form in two articles published in *Judaism*: "The Contribution of Abraham Joshua Heschel" (vol. 32, no. 1, pp. 57–69) and "Hasidism through the Eyes of Three Masters" (vol. 32, no. 2, pp. 160–69).

The present work, begun more than ten years ago, was undertaken to honor the memory of Rabbi Abraham Joshua Heschel and to enrich our knowledge of the Hasidic movement. Because of the problems already delineated in making available such a book to the English reader and to the nonspecialist, as well as the desire to produce a work of reliable scholarship, a number of experts, both here and abroad, were consulted in various capacities at different stages of the work. While their contributions have added to the quality of the work, I do not absolve myself from responsibility for any mistakes. I wish to acknowledge my indebtedness to the following: Dr. Zanvel Klein of the University of Chicago, who carefully reviewed most of the manuscript as the work proceeded, correcting numerous errors, making valuable suggestions, and contributing significantly to its final version; Dr. Ada Rappaport-Albert of the University of London, the principal translator of the chapter on R. Gershon of Kuty; Dr. Martin Samuel Cohen of the Jewish Theological Seminary Library, the principal translator of the notes to that chapter, who compiled the Gazeteer and the Bibliography; Rabbi Gedalia Rabinowitz of the Hebrew Theological College (the son of the Monastritche Rebbe from whom Heschel obtained two important manuscripts for the chapter, "R. Pinhas of Korzec"), who was constantly available to the editor; Dr. Moses Shulvas of Spertus College of Judaica, a companion of Heschel's during his student years in Berlin and the first director of the YIVO Hasidic Archives which Heschel had established, who generously provided information from his understanding of East European Jewish history; the late Rabbi Arye Kaplan and Dr. Mordecai Goldman of Spertus College of Judaica, who interpreted several kabbalistic and rabbinic passages; Rabbi Elliot Gertel and Dr. Karen Sager, who reviewed the manuscript for style and consistency; and Mrs. Norma Gavin who typed it.

SAMUEL H. DRESNER

The University of Chicago Press gratefully acknowledges Sylvia Heschel's granting permission for the work of the late Abraham J. Heschel to be published in this volume.

The Circle of the
Baal Shem Tov

One

Rabbi Pinhas of Korzec

The Grandfather

MANY WERE THE SORROWS THAT THE JEWS SUFFERED FROM THE TIME they were exiled from their land, but none more terrible than the persecutions of 1648–49 (*gezeyrot taḥ vetat*). The dead exceeded those killed during both the Crusades and the Black Death in Western Europe. Some 700 communities were destroyed,[1] while those that remained were left penniless and terrified. Their wounds still unhealed, these Jewish communities faced yet further agony. Taking advantage of their desperate situation, the Catholic church was urging them to embrace the cross, but to little avail. Despite the terrors of persecution and the tragic consequences of the Sabbatean movement, most of the Jews preferred death to conversion. Yet there were, here and there, those for whom the persistent efforts of the Church bore fruit and who, under terrible pressures, forsook the faith of Israel. Some, it must be added, even did so willingly. It was a time in the history of Israel when they were compelled to gather together every ounce of strength to survive the attacks upon their lives and to defend themselves from the treacherous blood libels, as well as from other decrees that were regularly promulgated against them. In such critical times, with their very lives in jeopardy, who could be concerned with renegades and apostates?

Some Jews of that period indeed did respond. They were moved to take leave of the security of their homes, the affection of their families, and the honor of their communities, and wander through the land, sometimes disguised as strangers or beggars, on a personal mission to their fellows. Among such men as these were the *maggidim* and the *mokhiḥim*, itinerant preachers, who spoke to the community "without having been appointed by the rabbinical courts, but with permission of the Holy One, blessed be He."[2] In the region of Reisan at this time lived a humble Jew by the name of R. Pinhas [the grandfather of R. Pinhas of Korzec (Koretz)], neither a rabbi nor a communal leader, neither the

1. Dubnow, *Divrey Yemey ʾAm ʿOlam* (Tel Aviv: Dvir, 1933–40), 7:22.
2. [Binyamin Wolf ben Matityahu], *Toharot Hakodesh* (Bialozórka: Mordecai b. Samuel, 1806), Introduction. [1st edition: Amsterdam, 1733.]

1

author of books nor the head of a yeshivah, who would "travel from town to town to admonish the children of Israel." Yet he differed from other itinerant preachers in one basic way. Whenever he received payment, he would keep for himself only enough for his minimal needs, contributing the rest toward maintenance of the synagogue.[3]

Reviving dead bones was the task R. Pinhas took upon himself. He would travel from place to place, urging the apostates to repent, offering them money, or promising them a share in the world to come, even his own share, if only they would swear to recite each day, "*Shema* *Yisra'el*—Hear O Israel, the Lord our God, the Lord is One . . . " "Do whatever wickedness you wish," he would tell them, "but say *Shema* *Yisra'el.*"[4] R. Pinhas knew that one spark from the smoldering embers of the spirit might consume all the thorns and thistles, and that even to save one soul, it was worth forsaking his portion in the future world. Because of his efforts many Jews returned to the faith of Israel.

Among those who prepared the way for the emergence of the Hasidic movement was R. Pinhas, the elder.

The *mokhiah* of Polonnoye, a disciple of the Baal Shem Tov, used to say, "The Messiah will stand fast for every Jew, even for the wicked, maintaining that they are right (*az zey zenen gerekht*). And because he defends them, searching for some bit of worthiness in their lives by which he might exonerate them, they will be led to repent. Here is the path to redemption. For it is through repentance that we shall be redeemed." He also used to say: "A lesser tzaddik loves the lesser wicked, while a greater tzaddik loves and finds merit even in the totally wicked. For whoever discovers some virtue in God's creatures has in him something of the Messiah. Therefore it must be that before Messiah appears, Elijah the Prophet will come to establish peace in our world, in order that Messiah

---

3. MS. Uman, fol. 45b. I have been fortunate to find four collections of manuscripts in the United States containing an abundance of rich material regarding the history of R. Pinhas of Korzec (Koretz) and his doctrine: MS. Cincinnati (Hebrew Union College #62); MS. Shapiro [R. Solomon Shapiro]; MS Kitvey Kodesh; and MS. Uman (the last two are in the possession of my relative, the Admor of Monestrisht, Rabbi Isaac Joel Rabinowitz).

4. *Midrash Pinhas* (Bilgorey, 1929), p. 81. Regarding the matter of converts during this period, cf. Azriel Nathan Frank, *Meshumadim in Poilen* (Warsaw, 1923), pp. 4–15; N. M. Gelber, "Der Taufbewegung unter den polnischen Juden im XVIII Jahrhundert," *MGWJ* 67 (1924): 225–40. John Serafinovich (see Dubnow, *History of the Jews in Russia and Poland* [Philadelphia: Jewish Publication Society, 1916–20], 1:173), who converted to Christianity in 1710, was notorious "for his allegations against the Jews which were spread throughout almost the entire world" (Israel Halpern, ed., *Pinkas Va'ad 'Arba' Ha'aratzot* [Jerusalem: Mosad Bialik, 1945], p. 265). MS. Uman, fol. 45b: "There is the tale of a woman who had amassed great wealth from the many villages that she controlled. She was an evil person and would not allow herself to speak to a Jew. After numerous ingenious efforts, he [R. Pinhas] succeeded in talking with her privately and convinced her to recite the *Shema'*, so that in the end she rejected her heresy." Ibid.: "I have heard from the very lips of our master and teacher, may the memory of a righteous man live forever, that this was the father of the rav [R. Pinhas of Korzec]." Most sources, however, relate these stories to R. Pinhas the Elder [the grandfather of R. Pinhas of Korzec].

should be able to find a portion of virtue in every man. For, without peace, it would be impossible for both plaintiff and defendant to be worthy. If one is right, then the other is wrong."[5]

R. Pinhas, who befriended the wicked, took pity upon animals, for they, too, were God's creatures. "Once, upon seeing a peasant driving an oxen-drawn wagon laden with lumber along a muddy road, he spent all of his money to buy the wood, only to throw it off the cart into the mud in order to spare the oxen pain. For the peasant had been beating them, as Gentiles do when the roads are muddy."[6]

The Father

According to a tradition, R. Pinhas the elder, the guide to apostates, was descended from R. Nathan Shapiro (d. 1633), kabbalist, rabbi of Cracow, and author of the *Megaleh 'Amukot*. R. Pinhas died before the year 1726. His son, Abraham Abba, was the rabbi of a small Lithuanian town.[7] When a son was born to Abraham Abba in 1724/5 or 1725/6, he called him Pinhas, after his grandfather.[8] Later the tzaddikim of Karlin (Lithuania) said of the child, that a soul such as his "comes to repair our world only once in 500 years."[9]

The child was born in Shklov (in the province of Mogilev) whose Jewish community was noted for its Torah scholars. The city of Shklov, then under Polish rule, suffered because it was located near the Russian and Swedish borders. Finally, in 1708, the Swedes destroyed it. In addition to military threats from without, the Jews were persecuted as much from inner threats of anti-Semitic decrees. An example of the mood of the time is reflected in the words of one contemporary Polish author: "As there is no freedom for a noble without *liberum veto*, so there is no Jewish *matzah* without Christian blood." Though in former centuries and in other lands the blood libel had at times reached the proportions of a plague, nowhere and at no other time do we find the plethora of decrees dealing with the blood libel as in Poland in the short period between 1730 and 1750.[10] Because R. Abraham Abba was accused of the blood libel, perhaps as a result of his father's (the elder R. Pinhas's) efforts among the converts to Christianity, an activity the priests surely frowned upon, he

5. MS. Uman, fol. 145b.
6. Ibid.
7. *Maseket 'Avot 'im Be'ur Torat 'Avot* [of Joshua Heschel Rabinowitz (New York: Rechtman, 1926)], p. 18.
8. Ibid. MS. Cincinnati, fol. 99b, indicates that R. Pinhas was thirty-five years old when the Besht died, which was, according to *Midrash Pinhas*, p. 89, on the 7th of Sivan, 1760. Consequently, R. Pinhas was born in 1726. In the yahrzeit lists in MS. Kitvey Kodesh, the name of his mother is given as Sarah Rachel Sheindel.
9. Yerahmiel Moses of Kozienice (Koznitz), *Shema' Shlomo* [Pietrokov, 1928], 2:12.
10. Dubnow, *Divrey Yemey 'Am 'Olam*, 1:84.

and his family were forced to flee from Shklov and settle in the little village of Miropol in Volhynia.[11] Miropol and Kaminka were twin towns between which flowed the river Tloshts.

Far from the land of his birthplace, R. Abraham Abba was compelled to forsake the rabbinate and earn his living as a preacher. He could not even find a communal position as maggid, but had to travel from town to town, preaching in synagogues and earning his livelihood as best he could.[12] R. Tzvi Merabbenu,[13] known by the name R. Hirsh Kaminker, then served as local preacher (*maggid mesharim*) in Kaminka, one of the communities R. Abraham Abba frequented.

R. Pinhas the Kabbalist

R. Pinhas, the son of Rabbi Abraham Abba, had mastered not only the Talmud and its commentaries,[14] but also several of the secular branches of knowledge.[15] "An expert in the disciplines of grammar, geometry, mathematics, and other subjects," he was among the few of his time who urged that "one must acquire such learning in one's youth."[16] He devoted himself to the study of the philosophical works of the Middle Ages, but found little solace in them. He later observed that philosophy was no longer worthy of his consideration.[17] He sought a more spiritual way of thinking and discovered it in the wisdom of the Kabbalah, particularly in the *Zohar*, whose mysteries he continued to explore throughout his life. Never has a Jew expressed more love for the *Zohar* than did R.

11. According to the descendants of R. Pinhas. Biber, *Mazkeret Lagedoley ʾOstroha* [Berditchev: Mefitzey Haskalah, 1907], p. 211. From *Shivḥey Habesht* (Kopys: Israel b. Isaac Jaffe, 1815), p. 20c; ed. and trans. Dan Ben-Amos and Jerome R. Mintz (Bloomington: Indiana University Press, 1970), #124, pp. 146–49, it appears that R. Abraham Abba did not live in Miropol when he met the Besht, because when he was in Miropol at that time, he had to lodge as a guest with the layman elected to serve as head of the community (*parnas*) for the month.

[Heschel's references to *Shivḥey Habesht* are to the first edition (Kopys, 1815) and to the Horodezky edition (Berlin, 1922). Since the Horodezky edition is now available only in a later printing (Tel Aviv, 1947) which has different pagination, we are referring to the first, 1815, edition and to the English translation: *In Praise of the Baal Shem Tov*, ed. Dan Ben-Amos and Jerome R. Mintz (Bloomington: Indiana University Press, 1970); hereafter cited as Ben-Amos.)

12. MS. Shapiro.

13. R. Samuel Miropol, *Tifʾeret Shemuʾel* (New York: Orios Press, 1926), p. 7.

14. His manuscript on *Yoreh Deʿah* and *ʾEven Haʿezer* was extant in Shepetovka. Horodezky, *Haḥasidut Vehaḥasidim* (Berlin: Dvir, 1922), 1:142.

15. *Midrash Pinḥas*, p. 21.

16. MS. Cincinnati, fol. 99b.

17. "*Atzund tzu nidrik far mir*" (now beneath me), *Midrash Pinḥas*, p. 17.

The Guide to the Perplexed by Maimonides had been so dear to R. Pinhas that he "studied it from cover to cover a thousand times" (MS. Sipurim Yekarim). Hasidim related that he refused to lend his copy of *The Guide to the Perplexed*, "because having the writings of Maimonides in one's home is a prescription for piety" [*a segulah tzu yiras shomayim*].

Pinhas.[18] He gave thanks to God that he had not been born before the *Zohar* was written. "The *Zohar* sustained my soul."[19] "The *Zohar* helped me to be a Jew."[20] "In matters of both the spirit and the flesh the *Zohar* is a guide."[21] "The bitter taste of the exile is ever with me. . . . Only when I immerse myself in the study of the *Zohar* do I find peace."[22] "I achieve inner tranquillity only in prayer or in the study of the *Zohar*. Everywhere else one finds both angels and demons . . . and this brings great distress to man. The *Zohar* alone is of the tree of life."[23] And when his student, R. Raphael, sought guidance on how to free himself from pride and pressed the matter, R. Pinhas advised: "Study the *Zohar*." "But, I do study the *Zohar*," he replied. "Then study it even more."[24] When once he was asked for a nostrum for earning a livelihood, he advised, "Learn the *Zohar*."[25] Take care, he would warn his students, "lest three days pass without the *Zohar*."[26]

R. Pinhas sought to "hide himself" in God, and observed that "while

18. [Betzalel Joshua of Galina,] *Tosefta Lemidrash Pinḥas* [Lwów: Mates Spiegel, 1896], p. 75, and MS. Kitvey Kodesh, chap. 7, fol. 19b: "He praised the *Zohar* because of its wide dissemination, as it is written, 'and it will be propagated far and wide in every generation.' With it, every tzaddik will be able to revive all souls. This is not true of a book written by an individual tzaddik, which is only effective in reviving individuals on the same level as he. [Of the books related to the *Zohar*] the *Reʿaya Mehemna* (Faithful Shepherd) is the clearest. It does not contain the difficulties (?) found in the *Zohar* proper, or in [such examples of zoharic literature as] the *ʾIdra*, the *Saba*, and others. This is for the above-mentioned reason, that it 'will be propagated far and wide in every generation' [and hence, every soul has access to it]."

"The same is true of the [biblical] books of the Prophets. Since their influence is propagated to even the lowest level, every individual can assume to understand them. These books therefore revive [the spirit] of all mankind. It is because of this propagation [to lowly worldly levels] that [the mysteries of these books] are clothed in stories."

R. Solomon, a disciple of R. Pinhas, said, "Before the time of the Baal Shem Tov, the [destiny of the] world rested on the small volumes of the *Zohar*, which stood in the uppermost cabinets, even though no one studied them" (MS. Cincinnati, fol. 105b).

"The soul said to the rav (i.e., the maggid of Miedzyrzecz) that he deserved to have heavenly matters revealed to him, not because of his great learning in the Talmud and Codes but because of his prayer. He would constantly pray with great *kavanah*, and because of that, he reached the highest rung." *ʾImrey Tzaddikim* [ed. D. Frankel (Husiatyn: Philip Kabalha, 1899)], p. 207.

19. *Geʾulat Yisraʾel*, with commentary *Nofet Tzufim Veḥayot Hakodesh*, pt. 2 (Ostróg: Aaron & Son, 1821), #72: "*Hot mikh derhalten bei mein leben.*" [It kept me alive.]

20. MS. Uman fol. 130b; MS. Kitvey Kodesh, pt. 7, fol. 15b; *Tosefta Lamidrash Pinḥas*, p. 21.

21. *Geʾulat Yisraʾel*, #29.

22. "*Ikh ken mikh nisht kilin, ela be-es she-ani lomed Zohar ha-kadosh, shpor ikh mikh op.*" (I cannot cool myself down. When I study the holy *Zohar*, however, then I am able to compose myself.) *Geʾulat Yisraʾel*, #105.

23. MS. Kitvey Kodesh, pt. 5, fol. 22a.

24. *Midrash Pinḥas*, p. 77.

25. "Also he would counsel all those in his circle to study the *Zohar* in its entirety each year" (*Geʾulat Yisraʾel*, #29).

26. Guttman, *Torat R. Pinḥas Mikoretz*, [3d ed. (Tel Aviv: Mosad Harav Kook, 1953)], p. 217.

with other books one must search laboriously to find God, with the *Zohar* (and, to a lesser degree, in the book *᾿Or Haḥayim* [a commentary to the Torah by R. Hayim ibn Attar (1696–1748)]) one can find Him with ease."[27] R. Pinhas longed to reach the "inner Torah" through which one comes "to know God."[28] Consequently, he held the study of the *Zohar* above the study of the Talmud. For when a man studies the Talmud, he is on the level of *katnut* [constricted consciousness], as the Talmud teaches, "the legal debates of the Abaya and Rava are a *davar katan*, a small thing" (*BT* Sukkah 28a), but when he studies the *Zohar* he is "on the level of *gadlut* [expanded consciousness]."[29] One must understand this statement of R. Pinhas not as a denigration of the sages of the Talmud, but rather as a criticism leveled against the then-accepted method of talmudic study. For

> the central purpose of study of the Tanaim and the Amoraim (the Talmudic sages) was to penetrate the mysteries of the Torah. They knew the secret of its innermost essence and searched for it even in the plain meaning of the text (*peshat*). However, in our days the inner meaning of the Torah is forgotten and only the plain meaning remains. The inner meaning of Torah reflects *moḥin degadlut* [expanded consciousness]; the plain meaning reflects *moḥin dekatnut* [constricted consciousness]. And in *moḥin dekatnut* there is distortion. That is why when one studies the simple meaning of the Torah with his fellows, he may grow proud, which is not the case when he studies the *Zohar*.[30]

Further: "While the Kabbalah was written in the Land of Israel, the Talmud was written outside of the Land of Israel. The Babylonian Talmud is characterized by externality."[31] "The Talmud represents the World of *Beri᾿ah* [Creation, the universe of the Throne and the Chariot, where good and evil are intermingled], while the *Zohar* represents the World of *᾿Atzilut*" [Emanation, the universe of the *sefirot*, where only good exists].[32] "One who studies the Talmud alone, constantly building dialectical towers, is destined to remain barren."[33]

In R. Pinhas's writings a statement unparalleled in the literature of Hasidism appears: "This generation does not learn as much Torah as in

27. *Tosefta Lamidrash Pinḥas*, p. 70.
28. Ibid., p. 77.
29. *Ge᾿ulat Yisra᾿el*, #82. "Each day new meanings emerge" from the *Zohar* (MS. Kitvey Kodesh, chap. 7, fol. 10a).
30. Addenda to *Midrash Pinḥas*, p. 71. [In Kabbalah, the terms *moḥin degadlut*: "expanded consciousness," and *moḥin dekatnut*: "constricted consciousness," respectively, refer to the mature and immature states of the Supernal Mentality, which are reflected in human mental states.]
31. Ibid., p. 95.
32. *Ge᾿ulat Yisra᾿el*, #17.
33. MS. Cincinnati, fol. 24b.

former years, for there is more *yirat shamayim* [fear of heaven; piety] now than there was in those times. And it is because of this [that there was not enough piety then] that they had to busy themselves with Torah. Indeed, there are places in which they study Torah today (Lithuania?), where there is no fear of God at all."[34]

This sharply caustic remark, which was probably not meant to be taken literally, nevertheless distressed many Hasidim.[35]

Besides the *Zohar,* R. Pinhas mastered other kabbalistic works, such as the *Pardes Rimonim* (Orchard of Pomegranates) by Moses Cordovero (1522–70), the writings of the Ari (Isaac Luria, 1534–72), and *Sheney Luhot Haberit* (Two Tablets of the Covenant) by Isaiah Horowitz (1556–1640). So influenced was he by the book, *Maggid Mesharim* (The Righteous Mentor), by Joseph Caro (1488–1575), which contains halakhic and mystical teachings revealed to the author by an angelic mentor (maggid), that he began to follow its prescriptions for fasting and other ascetic practices. Subsequently, he confided to a disciple that the book "affected his health, because he ate so little in accordance with its demands."[36] Held in high esteem by him, this book "rarely left his table," for, he declared, "one must revere words that were spoken from Heaven." When he was told that in the book *Shivhe Ha'ari* [In Praise of the Ari], Luria is quoted as demeaning the *Maggid Mesharim*, he replied that the author of *Shivhe Ha'ari* was "a liar."[37]

Despite the abject poverty which R. Pinhas suffered, he gave himself to the study of Torah and the service of God, supported only by the meager earnings of his father, and refused "all manner of help" from others. Once his father, an itinerant preacher, was delayed on the road, "and conditions reached such a state that not even one penny remained." R. Pinhas took ill and "did not know where to turn for food . . . Some offered him money," but he rejected it, and put his trust in God.[38] Another time it was suggested to him that he become a teacher of small

34. *Ner Yisra'el* [*Likutey Rav Hai Ga'on* (Warsaw, 1798; rpt. Israel: 'Otzar Haposkim, 1968)], *likutim mêharav r. pinhas mikoretz*, #23.

35. R. Isaac Judah Yehiel Safrin of Komarno, *Netiv Mitzvotekhah* (Jerusalem, 1947), Torah, pt. 1, #12, comments on this statement: "They have printed a lie in his [R. Pinhas's] name, for his holy mouth never uttered such words. We possess many collections of his sayings, and this statement is not found among them. Some scoffers must have printed these foolish words. Woe to the ears of those who have heard such things. I swear . . . that words like this never came from the holy mouth of R. Pinhas whose behavior, well-known to us from the reports of the disciples who served him, was ever that of a guardian of the Torah who warned that one must study it for its own sake (stressing that) the study of Torah is the very essence of the life of a Jew." The disputed passage, however, is found in other collections and was omitted by the printers (!) in *Likutey Shoshanim* (Munkács, 1889).

36. MS. Cincinnati, fol. 109a.

37. Ibid., fol. 52a. Cf. *Pe'er Layesharim* (Jerusalem: Isaac David Halevi Rosenstein, 1921), p. 14a.

38. MS. Kitvey Kodesh, chap. 9, fol. 3a; MS. Shapira.

children, "but, knowing that this might hinder his service of God,[39] he disapproved the proposal and trusted in the Lord." According to a tradition, Providence arranged that people should come to his house to exchange currency, and, as a result, he was able to earn a livelihood as a money-changer in his home.[40] In the end, however, he was compelled to accept a position as a *melamed* and found work in a village near Polonnoye.[41]

Korzec

R. Pinhas was shy and withdrawn.[42] Far from according him honor, people crudely called him, "the black *melamed*." R. Judah Leib was then serving as the preacher (maggid) in Polná and was known simply as *Hamokhiah*, "the Reprover." He recognized the great holiness of R. Pinhas and loved him dearly. The *mokhiah* had a private *mikveh* in the bathhouse and permitted R. Pinhas to use it whenever he wished. So dear to R. Pinhas was immersion in the *mikveh* that he once endangered his life because of it.[43] [R. Pinhas would similarly disregard danger when performing other *mitzvot*, as we see from the following account.]

Once the day before Passover, when he had to cross the river in order to bake *mitzvah matzot*,[44]

> the peasants were repairing the bridge which had been damaged through flooding. It was mortally dangerous to cross, because the peasants at that time were murderous. But R. Pinhas trusted that the Lord would help him. Firm in his faith, he proceeded, and the Lord did send him aid in the form of a Jewish tailor who suddenly appeared carrying clothing from the duke. Apparently, the tailor gave R. Pinhas some of the clothing to carry, so that the peasants would think he, too, was one of his workers, and they did not harm him. The tailor warned the peasants not to harass

39. *Se vet ihm shattin la-avodas ha-Shem*. [It will harm him when it comes to serving God.] R. Nahman of Brazlaw also did not want "anyone of our circle to be a *melamed*." Nathan b. Naftali Herz, *'Alim Laterufah* (Warsaw: Bratzlav Publishing, 1930), p. 130. [Cf. *Sihot Haran*, #240.]

40. MS. Kitve Kodesh, chap. 9, fol. 3a.

41. R. Abraham Isaac (head of the rabbinic court of Zinkevitz), *Sipurey Tzaddikim* (Vienna, 1922), no. 44.

42. When later he became famous, he said, "*Ikh hob nit koneh shlemus gevehn, nor veil ikh hob gelernt unteren oiven. Akhshav, veil ikh zetz mikh oiben ohn lernern, veis ikh nit vos se shteit.*" [I only earned perfection when I studied behind the oven (*oiven*). Now, however, because I sit up front (*oiben*) and study, I do not understand what is plainly written." Note the pun on "oven" (*oiven*) and "up front" (*oiben*).] MS. Kitvey Kodesh, chap. 7, fol. 6a. "The private, unknown acts of man alone are important, for blessing is found only in that which is hidden from the eye" *Nofet Tzufim* (Lwów: Abraham Joshua Heschel, 1865), pt. 2, § 1, #106. [See *Taanit* 8b.]

43. *Sipurey Tzaddikim*, no. 44.

44. [Matzot made the day before Passover are called "*mitzvah matzot*."]

R. Pinhas should they see him later unaccompanied. Nevertheless, when he passed them again on the way home, one of them struck him on his foot with a club.[45]

From Polná, R. Pinhas traveled to Korzec which was situated on the river Korczyk. A Jewish community had existed in Korzec since the sixteenth century, and by 1765, the Jewish population had reached 937. About that time Count Chartoriski built a weaving factory in Korzec in which some 120 Jews worked, at first forcibly and afterward voluntarily.[46] Korzec was at that time an important center of Torah. R. Yitzhak-Isaac Hakohen, author of *Berit Kehunat ʿOlam*, was appointed head of the Jewish court of Korzec at the age of thirteen in 1766. R. Yitzhak-Isaac, of whom R. Pinhas said "that his good character was evident already at birth,"[47] was a master of both the halakhic and mystical writings who would instruct his students "each day in Talmud and codes." Among his students was the later-renowned R. Efrayim Zalman Margoliot. R. Yitzhak-Isaac Hakohen's piety was reflected in his habit of "wrapping himself in shrouds day and night." On the door of his house were inscribed the words:

"To speak with the rav about worldly matters is only permissible if they are pressing, but one is free to speak to him about spiritual matters at any time, for the road is long and the provisions scanty."[48]

Though we do not know precisely when R. Pinhas settled in Korzec, it would seem that he lived there for many years, so that even after his departure he was known as "R. Pinhas Koretzer." As his fame spread so did the name of the city. When he resided in Korzec, they say, he suffered such poverty that he and his family often went hungry. R. Pinhas, however, "was unperturbed" and would sit in the house of study and "serve God with devotion." Others "saw nothing special in him" because he hid his true qualities, until an incident occurred which caused them to understand "that he possessed eyes which could see, and he saw." Then they began to show him honor.[49]

A description of this incident is found in the manuscript Sipurim Yekarim:

> After the Baal Shem Tov had taken ill, R. David Ostrer asked him to whom he should "travel" when [the Besht] was no longer with them [i.e., whom he was to select as master].

45. MS. Kitvey Kodesh, chap. 9, fol. 3a.
46. *Encyclopedia Judaica* (Berlin: Eschkol, 1934), vol. 10, col. 325.
47. MS. Cincinnati, fol. 72a.
48. Yitzhak-Isaac b. Joel Hakohen, *Sheʾelot Uteshuvot Zikhron Kehunah* [Lwów: Kugel, Lewin & Co., 1863], Introduction; Isaac b. Joel Hakohen, *Berit Kehunat ʿOlam* [Lwów: Judith b. Tzvi Hirsch, 1796], Introduction; Biber, *Mazkeret Lagedoley ʾOstraha*, pp. 217–21. See *BT* Ketubot 67b. He was thirty-five years of age when he died in 1788.
49. *Bet Pinḥas* [Bilgorey, 1926], p. 12.

The Besht replied: to the maggid of Miedzyrzecz (Mezritch) and to R. Pinhas of Korzec (Koretz).

So it was that following the Besht's death, R. David began to travel to the maggid. For R. Pinhas did not "preside" [over a group of disciples] in the first years after the death of the Baal Shem.

It had been customary for R. David Ostrer to send a beautiful *etrog* to the Besht each year as a gift [for Sukkot]. Under the new conditions, he would send an etrog [both] to the maggid and to R. Pinhas.

It once happened that the Gentile messenger bearing the etrog was delayed, so that he still had not arrived in Korzec the day before Sukkot. Heavy rains and flooded roads, which had contributed to a general shortage of etrogs, now left the community of Korzec without a single one!

The congregation was already in the midst of their prayers on the morning of the first day of Sukkot, when R. David's messenger at last arrived. R. Pinhas made the blessing over the etrog [after he had put it together with the palm branch, myrtles, and willow, comprising the four kinds of plants used on the Feast of Tabernacles]. Subsequently the rest of the congregation also fulfilled the commandment of the "four kinds." R. Pinhas then went to the prayer-reader's stand, recited the *Hallel* psalms, and made the required *ni anu im* [while reciting the *Hallel* psalms, the "four kinds" are "shaken" in sequence toward all directions of the compass, as well as upward and downward, reflecting the omnipresence of the Divine]. When the prayers were finished, the worshipers all approached and wished him [R. Pinhas] a happy holiday [for evidently he had "seen" that the etrog would arrive in time].

R. Pinhas remarked that until then he had not wished to take upon himself the onus of being a leader (*manhig*), but during the holidays, he had recognized that a pact had been made in Heaven for him to accept the yoke. From that point on he began to "preside."

R. Pinhas and the Baal Shem Tov

While R. Pinhas dwelt in seclusion so as to perfect his soul, the Besht, whose fame had by now begun to spread, was busy renewing the hearts of the masses and stirring a whirlwind within the spirits of the select. Among the latter was R. Judah Leib of Polna who had become a *mokhia* on the advice of the Besht and was among the first who sought to spread the teachings of the Baal Shem. One may surmise that it was from him that R. Pinhas heard of the greatness of the founder of Hasidism.

Years had passed, however, since the time the Besht had revealed himself, and still R. Pinhas remained at a distance. Often he wanted to visit the Besht, but his father, R. Abraham Abba, "both a Lithuanian and opinionated" and in whose eyes the Besht counted for nothing, restrained him, constantly remonstrating his son: "Where do you think you are traveling to?" R. Pinhas's desire to meet the Besht at last overcame all obstacles. Once, it is told, R. Pinhas traveled about with the rabbi of Rowne (Rovno) to collect ransom money to redeem captives, for one of those imprisoned was a relative of theirs. R. Pinhas said to the rabbi, "I have heard that the Besht will spend the Sabbath in the holy community of Kaminka.⁵⁰ Let us go to him. Perhaps he will help us, and it will then no longer be necessary for us to weary ourselves with travel [to collect money]." R. Abraham Abba, R. Pinhas's father, happened to be in Kaminka at that time as well, and, consequently, both father and son became followers of the Besht.⁵¹

This meeting apparently took place not long before 1760, the year in which the Besht died, since according to a tradition, R. Pinhas visited the Besht only three times;⁵² and, furthermore, though the Besht was R. Pinhas's elder by many years—for the latter would have been in his thirties when he met him—R. Pinhas's relation to the Besht was not that of a disciple bowing before his master, but rather that of half comrade, half student.

R. Pinhas joined himself to the Besht and accepted his basic teachings. "From the day that I was with the Besht," R. Pinhas said of himself, "God helped me toward the truth. And I walk in the path of King David, may he rest in peace."⁵³

In the Besht, R. Pinhas saw one who blazed a new path in serving God. He used to emphasize the fact that he followed "the way of the Baal Shem Tov," with whom a new era in Judaism had begun. "Since the time when people began to follow the way of the Baal Shem Tov, many customs instituted by R. Judah the Hasid have been abrogated."⁵⁴

50. According to a tradition of the descendants of R. Samuel Kaminker, the Besht used to visit the city of Kaminka each year, because R. Tzvi Kaminker, the elder zaddik of his generation, had testified to the holiness of the Besht, and gained him acceptance among many tzaddikim. Miropol, *Tifʾeret Shmuʾel*, p. 6. The visits of the Besht to Kaminka are also mentioned in *Shivḥey Habesht*.

51. This exceptionally long note appears in the Endnotes; see p. 183.

52. MS. Kitvey Kodesh, chap. 10, fol. 5a.

53. MS. Cincinnati, fol. 108a.

54. *Peʾer Layesharim*, #178. [R. Judah the Hasid of Regensburg (d. 1217), a noted figure of the *Hasidey Ashkenaz* movement in medieval Germany and the author of its most important literary work, *Sefer Ḥasidim* (ed. princ.: Bologna: Abraham b. Moses Hakohen, 1538). He introduced a number of ascetic practices into Ashkenazic Jewry. Cf. Scholem, *Major Trends in Jewish Mysticism*, 3d ed. (New York: Schocken, 1946), chap. 3.] See *Sheʾ elot Uteshuvot Divrey Ḥayim* [by R. Hayim Halbertstam, the Tzanzer Rav, a subsequent Hasidic master] (Warsaw: Abraham Cahana, 1930), pt. 1, *ʾeven haʿezer*, #8: "The later

A loyal disciple of the way of R. Pinhas once noticed a man who, because he used to study before saying his prayers, did not pray at daybreak. He warned him to say the Shema in its proper time. "Even though some Hasidim pay little attention to praying early in the morning," he added, "nevertheless the essence of Hasidism began with the Besht and his disciples, and since they were careful about this, with what authority do you alter it?"[55]

The Besht taught "that it is better to serve the Lord in joy, without self-mortification, which brings one to despair"[56] and forbade his disciple, R. Jacob Joseph, to fast "more than the Law requires or than is necessary."[57] Apparently under the influence of the Besht, R. Pinhas abandoned the way of self-mortification which he had followed from his youth and taught that "one can worship Heaven through eating."[58] In contrast to the words of the heavenly maggid who instructed R. Joseph Karo that one must "eat only sparingly," R. Pinhas now declared: "Here below they know more than on high, for one should eat and, through eating, serve the Lord."[59] It was from the Besht that he learned "how to eat before the Lord."[60] In earlier times, Hasidim would "keep themselves away from seventy permissible gates, lest they enter one forbidden gate."[61] The Besht came and taught, "Be not fanatical in whatever [mitzvah] you perform. For this is none other than the work of the Yetzer Hara' [Evil Urge], which seeks so to terrify you over not fulfilling your obligations that you are brought to despondency."[62] Likewise, taught R. Pinhas: "One need not be fanatical [in doing the mitzvot] or quail [that he has not kept them properly], lest, Heaven forbid, he bring down upon himself divine punishment."[63] R. Pinhas "was careful not to be severely

---

sages (aharonim) should not ignore the words of the earlier masters (kadmonim) . . . for in comparison to their wisdom, Torah knowledge, and piety, we are as nought. We must therefore accept their words wholeheartedly, even when they appear to conflict with the Talmud . . . In our community, however [of all the admonishments in R. Judah the Hasid's ethical will], we are only particular that a woman should not have the same name as her mother-in-law." [R. Judah's ethical will (#23) warns that a man should not marry a woman who has the same name as his mother. In many communities this admonition was ignored, chiefly because it had no basis in the Talmud. See Pithey Teshuvah, yoreh de'ah 116:6, and 'even ha'ezer 2:7]. See also Shalom Rokeach of Belz, Dover Shalom (Przemyśl: Amkrant and Freund, 1910), p. 53.

55. Pe'er Layesharim, p. 19a. The expression "the essence of Hasidism" ['ikar hahasidut] suggests the existence of Hasidim before the time the Baal Shem Tov revealed himself. On this question see Dinaburg, "The Beginning of Hasidism and Its Social and Messianic Element," Zion 9 (1944):186–97.

56. Tzava'at Harivash (Warsaw, 1853), p. 10 [rpt. New York: Kehot, 1975), #56].

57. See his letter to R. Jacob Joseph, Shivhey Habesht, p. 8d [Ben-Amos, #49].

58. MS. Cincinnati, fol. 109a.

59. MS. Kitvey Kodesh, chap. 5, fol. 6b.

60. Ibid., chap. 10, fol. 3a.

61. Hovot Halevavot, shaar hateshuvah, chap. 5.

62. Tzava'at Harivash, #46.

63. MS. Cincinnati, fol. 22b.

meticulous of the law, for through this we extend the exile, Heaven forbid."[64]

R. Pinhas not only accepted the doctrine and a number of the customs of the Baal Shem Tov, but also received helpful personal guidance from him. It is told that

> R. Pinhas once became obsessed with the idea that there is a natural law governing all things. The Besht came to the city, and R. Pinhas visited him. The Baal Shem said to him, "Why is the wickedness of Amalek greater than that of all other nations? It is because Amalek sinned in explaining all miracles according to natural law." R. Pinhas understood that these words were directed at him. After the *Minhah* service, he returned to the Baal Shem Tov, who then said, "And what is the solution? It is the fact that prayer is answered. People pray and are answered!" R. Pinhas then prayed that this obsession might leave him, and it did.[65]

As we have already remarked, R. Pinhas did not simply accept all the Besht taught, as a disciple would his master, and was not averse to debating him on matters of faith and the service of God. According to a tradition, he received three teachings from the Besht,[66] and the Besht received three teachings from him.[67] He once remarked: "I know the *kavanah* for eating just as well as the Besht."[68] Nor was he hesitant even to declare: "Wisdom flows only from me. It would never even have crossed over from the Baal Shem Tov's doorway" [and, hence, would not have been accessible to others].[69] In some matters, he disputed the Besht. R. Pinhas instructed people to put on *tefillin* during the intermediary days of the Passover and Sukkot festivals, and remarked that in this regard he had argued with the Besht who taught that tefillin not be used, in accordance with the proscription of the *Zohar*. R. Pinhas responded that in order to avoid violating the opinion of the *Zohar*, one could put on

64. Ibid., fol. 103a.

65. Ibid., fol. 57a.

66. "[1] How to induce a blessing for those who are childless, together with charms for conception; [2] the mystery of the nose, explaining why nostrils are on the bottom; and [3] the mystery of why one must close the wine bottle used for Kiddush after the cup is filled." *Torat ʾAvot* [i.e., *Masekhet ʾAvot ʾIm Beʾur Torat ʾAvot* (New York: Rechtman, 1925)], p. 18. Another version is found in MS. Kitvey Kodesh, chap. 19, fol. 3a.

67. "[1] Closing the windows after lighting the Sabbath candles, lest the light of the candle be seen by the Evil Forces (*Hitzonim*), who would then derive nourishment from the holiness of the Sabbath light; [2] the mystery of [curing] the ague; and [3] the mystery of the two branches of myrtle [which one smells before reciting the Kiddush on Friday night]" (*Torat ʾAvot*, p. 18).

68. *Peʾer Layesharim*, p. 12a.

69. "*Hokhmos kummen nor fon mir aroes, avol min ha-Baal Shem Tov, vohlt es nit iber gegangen (afilu) iber der tir*" (MS. Cincinnati, fol. 81b).

tefillin only if it was done without the blessing and simply as a strap, but not sanctimoniously to fulfill the mitzvah.[70]

The students of R. Pinhas knew that some of the customs of their master were different from those of the Besht and were careful not to change them. It was the Baal Shem's habit to recite the entire Book of Psalms on the day before Rosh Hodesh. When R. Pinhas's disciple, R. Raphael, heard from one of his associates that he did the same, he was annoyed and instructed him to say Psalms "deliberately on another day, in order that it might be known that this was not the custom of R. Pinhas, but rather that of the Besht. For we must follow the tradition of the former."[71]

The Besht extended special honor to R. Pinhas. Once the Besht said to him: "In the years of my youth I used to feel that when I lifted my hands worlds would tremble. But now I feel nothing." R. Pinhas replied: "And I feel that when I raise my hands worlds do tremble."[72]

R. Pinhas and the Besht's Disciples

Shortly before his death, R. Jacob of Anipol asked the Besht to describe each of his disciples. And he did so. When he inquired about R. Pinhas, the Besht said: "About so great and holy a one as he, there is no need to ask."[73]

How highly R. Pinhas was esteemed in the circle of the Besht is apparent from the following story.

R. Pinhas had once spent Passover with the Besht. Because he was feeling ill, R. Pinhas went to the *mikveh* only in the morning before the seventh day of Passover, but did not go toward the evening. During the evening service, R. Pinhas suddenly felt that his prayer might have saved the Besht from death had he gone to the mikveh that evening. Now he realized that his prayer would be to no avail, and relied on the Besht [to save himself with his own prayer]. When the prayers were over the Besht asked R. Pinhas: Did you immerse yourself in the mikveh this evening? R. Pinhas smiled faintly. The Besht, realizing that R. Pinhas had not, said: "Alas! Had you gone to the mikveh this evening I would have been able to go on living. But now I must die. For the one depends on the other."[74]

70. Ibid., fol. 93b.
71. *Pe'er Layesharim*, p. 10b.
72. MS. Kitvey Kodesh, chap. 10, fol. 3a.
73. MS. Cincinnati, fol. 81b. R. Jacob is mentioned also in *Shivhey Habesht*, p. 11b [Ben-Amos, #62].
74. MS. Shapiro. "I myself heard R. Raphael state in the name of his master, R. Pinhas, that it is not necessary to immerse oneself in the *mikveh* on Friday in preparation for the

R. Pinhas remained in Miedzybórz with the Besht, who died there on Shavuot in 1760 at the age of seventy.[75]

Though the soul of the Besht ascended to Heaven, R. Pinhas believed "that sixty years after his death he would return to this world," adding, "Who knows in what land he will appear."[76] He said further: "Many years after a tzaddik enters the future World he is transformed into a Divine Name, and he becomes a light for the fear of God." He had heard this from R. Tzvi, the son of the Baal Shem Tov. R. Tzvi told him that he had once spent a night in a terrifying forest. His father appeared to him in a dream and told him, "In the next world a tzaddik is transformed into a Divine Name. You should meditate on the Name [alluded to in the prayer], *Ana Bakoah*, for I am that Name."[77]

R. Pinhas used to tell of wonders performed by the Besht and his disciples.[78] R. Raphael, the loyal disciple of R. Pinhas, once remarked: "It is said that at the close of the Sabbath one should speak about the Besht, or be silent."[79]

The Besht and the Maggid of Miedzyrzecz

Many were the disciples of the Besht, some of whom—like the *mokhiah*, R. Leib of Polonnoye, or R. Jacob Joseph, who later gained

---

Sabbath, when that Friday falls on a Festival, or for that matter, on the intermediary festival days in preparation for the holiday, i.e., going to the *mikveh* on Hoshanah Rabba for the Seventh Day of Sukkot. As he put it, *Bedarf men mehr mikveh vi yom tov?* 'Is *mikveh* more important than Yom Tov itself? [i.e., the Festival—Yom Tov—purifies one more than the *mikveh*]. And the intermediary day is itself a festival.'

"The only time when R. Pinhas would go to *mikveh* [on the intermediary days of a festival] in the afternoon, was on the eve of the seventh Day of Passover, because of the incident [mentioned in the text]."

This same story is found with minor changes in *Shivhey Habesht*, p. 35d [Ben-Amos, #247]. There it is reported: "On the seventh day of Passover, while at prayer, [R. Pinhas] saw that it was decreed that the Besht would soon pass away because of his struggle against (the sect of) Shabbetai Tzvi."

75. The year of the Besht's birth is not mentioned in *Shivhey Habesht*. Dubnow, *Toldot Hahasidut* [Tel Aviv: Dvir, 1930–32], p. 43, fixes it as 1700. R. Abraham Jacob of Sadagura, who certainly was in possession of old traditions, mentioned at the *Hilula* [celebration at the anniversary of the death] of the Maggid of Miedzyrzecz on the 19th of Kislev, 1881, "that both the Besht and the Maggid had reached a full old age. The Besht lived to be seventy (?) and the Maggid about seventy-seven." See the notes of R. Solomon, the son of R. Abraham Jacob of Sadagura, in a manuscript belonging to the Admor of Kopyczyńce (Kopitschinitz) [R. Abraham Joshua Heschel], fol. 200a. The year of the Besht's death is mentioned in *Midrash Pinhas*, p. 89, as well as in MS. Cincinnati, fol. 101.

76. R. Moses of Slavuta reports that he heard this from his father, R. Pinhas. MS. Cincinnati, fol. 101a.

77. MS. Cincinnati, fol. 81b. "And R. Raphael said that he heard from the Rav [R. Pinhas] that he should meditate on the name [alluded to in the words] *kabbel rinat* [in the prayer *Ana Bakoah*]."

78. Ibid., p. 100, and elsewhere. Horodezky (*Hahasidut Vehahasidim*, 1:143), writes that R. Pinhas had doubts about the alleged "miracles" of the Besht.

79. *Pe'er Layesharim*, p. 20b.

renown as the author of *Toldot Ya akov Yosef*—served him for many years. But when the time came to choose a successor, the Hasidim[80] chose none of these, but rather R. Ber, a relatively new face in Miedzybórz who was with the Besht only in his latter years. "He visited the Baal Shem Tov but twice, remaining the second time for a half year. The Baal Shem gave over to him all of his teachings. Each evening R. Ber would come to him. He would teach him at night in order that there should be no jealousy among the other Hasidim."[81] The followers of the Besht, who apparently were unaware that he had chosen R. Ber, refused to accept his authority. Only two or three of the youngest disciples attached themselves to him.[82]

It was natural for his ascension to the throne of the master to stir opposition among the circle of those who had surrounded the founder of Hasidism, for R. Ber differed from the Besht in personality, life-style, and even, to some extent, philosophy. One has reason to believe that R. Jacob Joseph, the "foremost exponent of the Besht's teachings," had hoped to fill the place of the master himself. It is known that the appointment of R. Ber made him feel slighted. It is told "that R. Jacob Joseph once was traveling through Miedzyrzecz, where R. Ber had established the new center for Hasidism, and wished to see him personally. However, the maggid, R. Ber, was already conducting himself in such a grand manner that a servant stood outside of his door when R. Joseph wished to enter. The servant, who did not recognize R. Jacob Joseph, stopped him. R. Jacob Joseph, known for his angry disposition, slapped him, entered the room of R. Ber, removed his hat, and said to him in Polish, 'Are you a *poritz* [Polish landowner], that you must have a watchman standing at your door'? The maggid explained apologetically that because of his poor health someone had to guard his door. The maggid asked him to be seated. R. Jacob Joseph, however, did not remain for long."[83]

In a short while the fame of the maggid spread, and Miedzyrzecz became the single most important Hasidic center. Many students, among them noted Torah scholars and remarkable personalities, came to warm themselves by his flame. Hasidism, which in the time of the Besht, had been limited principally to Podolia, Volhynia, and Galicia, pressed on-ward beyond the border of these lands during the reign of the maggid and

---

80. [Yiddish text: "the Besht."]

81. According to R. Abraham Jacob of Sadagura. See above note 75. Compare *Shivhey Habesht*, p. 11c [Ben-Amos, #62]: "When the maggid, may his memory be for a blessing, departed from the Besht, the Besht blessed him. And afterward the Besht bent his head that he might receive a blessing from him, but the maggid hesitated. Thereupon the Besht took the maggid's hand and placed it upon his own head, so that he blessed him."

82. Such as R. Nahum of Chernobyl and R. Mendel of Vitebsk. R. Mikhal of Zloczew visited the Maggid, but not as a disciple. See the notes by R. Solomon of Sadagura, MS. Admor of Kopyczyńce, fol. 169.

83. Ibid., fol. 118b.

won a considerable following in Lithuania and Belorussia. Among the disciples of the Besht, the maggid alone achieved renown during his lifetime. The period of his activity was less than thirteen years, but during this time Hasidism became a formidable movement, led by men whom he had appointed to spread the teachings of their master in many lands. Later, even R. Jacob Joseph was forced to admit the importance of the new center. It is reported that he said: "What can we do? Since the day that the Baal Shem died, the Shekhinah has packed her bags and moved from Mezbizh (Miedzybórz) to Mezeritch (Miedzyrzecz), and we are obliged to bow our heads."[84] Even though this acknowledgment refers to the new center rather than the new leader, R. Jacob Joseph, in a sermon given on *Shabbat Hagadol* in 1765, does mention the Torah that he heard in the maggid's name and refers to him as "the Hasid, our teacher, Dov Ber Tortziner."[85] R. Ber, on the other hand, did not consider R. Jacob Joseph qualified to become a leader.[86]

R. Pinhas did not accept the succession of R. Ber with enthusiasm. Indeed, he pointed out that it was R. Jacob Joseph whom the Baal Shem considered his most able and cherished disciple. He would quote the Besht as saying, "God will thank me for having provided Him with such a Yosele [Jacob Joseph] as this."[87] "He held the rabbi of Polonnoye in very high esteem and said that even in the days of the sages who composed the Mishnah there was never such a mind as his."[88] He testified that R. Jacob Joseph once "received a letter from Heaven,"[89] and extolled his books when they were published: "Never have there been books like these, for they are Torah from paradise."[90] "None of the new books which have been written during the past seventy years possesses the quality of truth,

---

84. Ibid.; *Horodezky*, 1:109.

85. *Ben Porat Yosef, derush leshabbat hagadol*, 1765 (Korzec: [Abraham Samson Katz of Raszkow and Abraham Dov of Khmelnik,] 1781), p. 87c. R. Ber lived in Torczyn at the time he became a follower of the Besht, *Shivhey Habesht*, p. 11a [Ben-Amos, #62]. Dubnow, *Toldot Hahasidut*, p. 101, errs in asserting that R. Jacob Joseph "does not specifically mention the name of the maggid anywhere in his books."

86. "I heard from R. Dov Katz, a member of our community, that once the rav, R. Joseph, *maggid mesharim* of Polonnoye, was with the maggid of Miedzyrzecz. The latter requested R. Joseph to do him a favor when he returned home, and was assured it would be done. Long afterward, the maggid saw R. Joseph again and asked him if he had done what he had requested from him. R. Joseph replied that upon reaching home, the matter had slipped his mind. Exclaimed the maggid: "*Hei! Hei! vie ken eyer vort teyer zein etzel ha-Shem Yisborakh?*" (Oh! Oh! How, then, can your word be valued by God [if you do not even keep a promise to a friend]"? (MS. Cincinnati, fol. 49a)

87. *Midrash Pinhas*, p. 65. And R. Pinhas added: "*ve'ani 'omer Ha-Shem-Yisborakh vet mir danken vos ikh hob im tzu geshtelt azoi ein Rafael*" (and I say, God will thank me for having provided him with such a Raphael). R. Raphael succeeded R. Pinhas as leader of his disciples.

88. *Pe'er Layesharim*, p. 14a.

89. Ibid., p. 11b. [Cf. Dresner, *The Zaddik*, chap. 3.]

90. Ibid., p. 31a.

except for the books of the rabbi of Polonnoye, for there are no books like his in all the world, apart from 'Or Haḥayim [by R. Hayim ben Attar]."[91]

So highly did R. Pinhas honor R. Jacob Joseph that he would travel all the way to Polonnoye to spend the Sabbath with him.[92] Once he took along R. Barukh [of Miedzybórz]. the grandson of the Besht, whom R. Pinhas had raised in Ostróg. R. Barukh later told the following story: After the Sabbath a messenger arrived for R. Pinhas informing him that he must return home at once, because of pressing affairs which awaited him. Now it so happened that at that hour the holy rabbi of Polonnoye was meditating [hitboded] in his private room. R. Pinhas was troubled and did not know what to do. To delay returning home until after the seclusion of the rabbi of Polonnoye was not possible, since such periods of meditation usually lasted twenty-four hours or more. To depart without leave-taking was likewise unthinkable. Thus the holy R. Pinhas asked me to go to the rav, to the room of his seclusion, and request him to give R. Pinhas permission to return home on urgent business. When R. Pinhas asked this of me, I found myself in a dilemma: if I went to the room of the rabbi, I was afraid I might disturb him; if I did not go, I would disobey R. Pinhas . . . Therefore I suggested to him that both of us go to his room together.

"And so it was," R. Barukh related, "that the two of us approached R. Jacob Joseph's door. It was warped and in disrepair. As my hand touched the knob, it fell to the floor, and the door opened by itself. As soon as we entered the room, we saw to our amazement that a heavenly maggid [mentor] was studying with him! So frightened was R. Pinhas that he would not stay there. But I remained standing in the room. And it is because of this that I know what an angel is!"

"I had known," R. Barukh added, "that the rabbi of Polonnoye had a [heavenly] maggid with whom he studied. But my grandfather, the Besht, saw that this maggid was not one of the true maggidim, and so he took that maggid away from him and gave him another one of the true maggidim."[93]

One may conjecture that R. Pinhas—who was so close to R. Jacob Joseph that he used to say, "I and the rav of Polonnoye"[94]—considered the latter as the one most qualified to sit upon the Besht's chair. It is said that R. Pinhas met R. Jacob Joseph and made the following critical allusion to R. Ber, upon whose head the Hasidim had just set the crown of leadership:

91. Ibid., p. 20b.
92. *Shivḥey Habesht*, p. 21d [Ben-Amos, #131]; *Pe'er Layesharim*, p. 14b.
93. *Butzina Denehora Hashalem* [New York: Yeshivah Ohr Mordecai, n.d.], p. 9.
94. MS. Cincinnati, fol. 52b.

I am astonished that when the king himself is not wearing his crown, it is hung upon a peg! Is the crown not sufficiently important when not in royal use for it to be set upon a human head for safekeeping? Why, then, is it not worn temporarily by one of the king's courtiers, that there might not be such desecration of honor? But the answer is thus: The man upon whose head the crown would be put when the king himself is not wearing it might grow arrogant and say to himself: "Now I am like the king." But the peg is without feelings and incapable of arrogance![95]

R. Pinhas did not recognize the maggid of Miedzyrzecz as the leader of the generation. He questioned his interpretation of Hasidism and his way of conduct. The Besht's door had been open to all callers; he had moved freely among the people, going out to his flock, even traveling to where they lived. In ill-health,[96] the maggid kept to his room and received his Hasidim only once a week. R. Pinhas did not favor that style of leadership. "Of what benefit to them is the maggid of Mezeritch," he observed, "since he has secluded himself for so many years?" In connection with this statement a disciple of R. Pinhas once remarked about another Hasidic *tzaddik*, "that he is not able to help the people, because he finds it difficult to eat a meal or mix socially with them."[97] In a period of crisis, when R. Pinhas needed divine aid to revoke a decree that threatened Poland, he expressed regret that R. Nahman of Horodenka had departed the country, leaving no one else of comparable greatness in that generation to whom he could turn. This took place during the lifetime of the maggid.[98]

The Way of R. Pinhas and the Way of the Maggid

R. Pinhas felt that his was not the way of the maggid. The latter introduced the method of the Ari (R. Isaac Luria) into the teaching of the Besht and taught his students mysteries of the Kabbalah, expositions on the writings of the Ari, *kavanot*, and *yihudim*.[99] "The maggid taught that

95. M. E. Guttman, *R. Pinhas Mikoretz*, p. 1; indications of the disagreement between R. Jacob Joseph and other zaddikim over the correct interpretation of the doctrine of the Besht are preserved in M. Bodek, *Seder Hadorot Hehadash* [n.p., n.d.], pt. 1, p. 34.
96. The maggid was ill when he first visited the Besht. *Shivhey Habesht*, p. 11a [Ben-Amos, #62].
97. MS. Cincinnati, fol. 80a.
98. See n. 198.
99. "In his [the maggid's] holy words, there are allusions which clarify many passages from the '*Etz Hayim* ['The Tree of Life' by R. Hayim Vital, the primary classic of Lurianic Kabbalah] and the *kavanot* of the Ari" (*Maggid Devarav Leya'akov* [Korzec: Solomon of Luck, 1784], Introduction). [See now the Jerusalem 1976 edition, the Magnes Press, edited by R. Schatz-Uffenheimer, with introduction and commentary.] Cf. *Vikuha Raba* (Munkács, 1894), p. 25a. "Once the rav [the maggid] rebuked a man for publicly expounding the Kabbalah. He responded: Why then, sir, do *you* expound the Kabbalah in public? The rav

the essence of serving the Creator, blessed-be-He, was *devekut*, 'cleaving to God,' and *hitlahavut*, 'burning enthusiasm,'"[100] "to be bound up with the Lord in ecstasy."[101] The way of *devekut*, he said, is through wisdom and meditation. "The process of attaching oneself to God is true wisdom, and this is derived from the [higher states of] consciousness (*mohin*)."[102] "If one wishes to join himself to the Creator, blessed be He, he should bind himself to the attribute of wisdom,"[103] "for wisdom gives life to all things, and no change can occur in the world without wisdom."[104]

This course of thought was further developed by the maggid's disciple, R. Shneur Zalman, who taught that the essence of all things was intellectual contemplation (*hitbonenut*) on the greatness of God. For "the fear of God cannot be attained without such contemplation."[105]

Contrariwise, R. Pinhas criticized those who wanted to learn "secrets of the Torah" and were not "fearful of hearing more than was proper" for them.[106] "One must not overly trouble oneself to achieve lofty rungs of insight, but rather should serve God with unquestioning simplicity; and if one is deserving of ascending to such a spiritual height, this will come of itself. It once happened that a man prayed that he might acquire the Holy Spirit (*ruah hakodesh*), but his prayer was only half successful. He indeed received a spirit, but it was something other than the holy (*ruah belo kedusha*)!"[107] R. Pinhas opposed relying on one's intellect alone, which he believed separates man from God. When worldly "widsom" became widespread, he observed, the holy spirit withdrew.[108] R. Pinhas did not expound on the secrets of the Torah.[109] He preferred to teach his students honesty and humility rather than *yihudim* and *kavanot*, believing that the way to the service of God is through the purification of one's character. From his students he sought that they first "turn away from evil" and only then "do good."

His disciple, R. Raphael, explained the differences in their ap-

---

replied: I teach [the Kabbalah publicly] in a way that leads people to understand that all the teachings found in the book *'Etz Hayim* are also to be found in this world and in man himself. But you, sir, do nothing more than expound the teachings as they are written in the *'Etz Hayim*. Since the mouth cannot speak about purely spiritual matters, you are thus transforming that which is spiritual into that which is physical." (*'Imrey Tzaddikim*, p. 86)

100. *'Or Torah* (Lublin, 1910), p. 50.
101. *'Or Ha'emet* (Zhitomir, 1901; rpt. Jerusalem: Yahadut, 1967), p. 3a.
102. Ibid., p. 35.
103. *Maggid Devarav Leya'akov*, p. 4a.
104. Ibid., p. 11b.
105. See R. Shneur Zalman's letter to R. Abraham of Kalisk. Mordecai Teitelbaum, *Harav Miladi Umifleget Habad* (Warsaw: Toshiah, 1910–13), pt. 1, p. 234; cf. *Likutey Torah*, Num. 1.
106. *Ner Yisra'el, Likutim Meharav R. Pinhas Mikoretz*, #12.
107. Guttman, *R. Pinhas Mikoretz*, p. 22.
108. *Midrash Pinhas*, p. 82.
109. *Likutim Yekarim* (Lwów: Judah Solomon Rappaport, 1792), p. 35; *Midrash Pinhas*, p. 25.

proaches. There are two ways to serve God. The first way is to seize hold of one's evil qualities and crush them, "for one who slays the beast reaches prayer and *devekut.*" This was the way of R. Pinhas, and it is called, "Let Haman be cursed." The second way, which was that of R. Shneur Zalman and similar to that of the maggid, was ever to contemplate the greatness of the Creator and to labor toward *devekut*, in which process evil would be nullified of itself. This way is called, "Let Mordecai be blessed."[110]

Just as R. Pinhas rejected the way of the maggid, the way of R. Pinhas was repudiated in Miedzyrzecz. According to a Hasidic tradition, on R. Shneur Zalman's second trip there, he stopped in Korzec. R. Pinhas welcomed him warmly and urged him to remain with him so that he might instruct him in the language of the birds and other lofty matters. R. Shneur Zalman apparently remained in Korzec for a period, but would not forsake the way of the maggid.[111] Later when he arrived in Miedzyrzecz, the maggid said: "R. Pinhas wanted to teach you the language of the birds and the rest, but I will teach you the higher *yihud* and the lower *yihud.*"[112]

It is told that once when R. Abraham the Angel, son of R. Ber of Miedzyrzecz, saw R. Schneur Zalman off on a journey, he advised the latter, "Ride, ride, pay no attention to the horses." (*"Fohr, fohr, kuk nit oif die ferd."*) He was alluding to R. Pinhas, who

> was a man of exceptional humility and truthfulness. For many years of his life he struggled to achieve truth, by seeking first to banish all darkness and only afterward permitting light to enter. Consequently his Hasidim were few, for not many could expel the darkness completely. R. Abraham's parting message, however, was hinting at another way. He said that we should ignore the horses [which represent the animal traits in man, and not spend all of our efforts attempting to banish them]. Instead, one should "ride" by speaking words of wisdom. For a little light will drive away much darkness.[113]

A grandson of the R. Shneur Zalman said, "The reason they call us [the followers of his grandfather] by the name *Habad* is because of our

---

110. MS. Cincinnati, fol. 87a.

111. The story goes that he was instructed in many things by R. Pinhas and that he said, "I have received the qualities of truth and humility from R. Pinhas of Korzec." Teitelbaum, *Harav Miladi*, pt. 1, p. 9. From (overhearing) a conversation R. Pinhas had with his wife, R. Shneur Zalman learned the substance of his sermon on "How lovely are thy steps in sandals" (Song of Songs 7:2), which is printed in his *Likutey Torah*. See *Bet Rabi* (Berdichev: H. Y. Sheftel, 1902), pt. 1, p. 62a.

According to another tradition, R. Pinhas gave him the explanation of a Midrash which was helpful to him later. *Bet Pinhas*, p. 3.

112. *Bet Rabi*, pt. 1, fol, 3b.

113. Ibid., pt. 1, p. 44b.

preoccupation with instilling a higher state of consciousness (*mohin*) in our followers, rather than emphasizing traits of character."[114]

Despite their differences, the maggid accorded great honor to R. Pinhas and was fully in agreement, for example, with his opposition to the Jews fleeing Ukrainia at the time of the persecutions under [Ivan] Gonta [the Cossack leader of the Haidamacks] in 1768.[115] It is related that once when the maggid was ill and his bed was in the house of study, he delayed reciting the prayer for the santification of the new moon. To his disciples he explained:

"Be not surprised at the delay. R. Pinhas is in Korzec, and his prayer is even now piercing the heavens."[116]

They say that once, when a new king of Poland was to be elected, R. Pinhas traveled to the maggid, that they might take counsel with one another and decide which nobleman should sit upon the throne.[117] At their meeting, R. Pinhas reviewed the candidates one by one, pointing out their shortcomings. At the name of Count Poniatowski, however, R. Pinhas expressed the opinion that this was the proper man. The maggid agreed that the count was acceptable. Subsequently, the Polish noblemen in fact elected [Poniatowski], without a single dissent, to be king of Poland.[118]

According to another legend R. Pinhas once visited the maggid and even participated at his *tish*, the communal meal at the rabbi's "table," "since [R. Pinhas] was too humble to conduct *tish* himself."[119] Another tale relates that when the wife and children of the maggid fell ill, the latter sent for R. Pinhas. He came to Miedzyrzecz, entered the house of the

114. Ibid., pt. 1, p. 44a. See above, p. 6. [Habad is an acronym for *Hokhmah Binah Da 'at*, "Wisdom, Understanding and Knowledge."]

115. See below, n. 191.

116. MS. Kitvey Kodesh, chap. 10, fol. 1b. For another version see Guttman, *R. Pinhas Mikoretz*, p. 14.

117. R. Ber held the position of maggid in Miedzyrzecz and in Korzec during the period of R. Pinhas's residence there. He signed a letter, dated 1767, "*Maggid Mesharim* of the holy community of greater Miedzyrzecz and of the holy community of Korzec." Kahana, *Sefer Hahasidut* [Warsaw: n.p., 1922], p. 163. In the eighteenth century Miedzyrzecz was considered part of the district of Korzec; cf. Dubnow, *Toldot Hahasidut*, p. 80. See also the maggid's approbation to the book, *Halakhah Pesukah* by R. Todros of Rovney, printed in 1765 in Turka: "The lowly Dov, son of our master and teacher, R. Abraham, may the memory of the righteous endure in the world to come, *maggid mesharim* of the Holy community of greater Miedzyrzecz and of the holy community of Korzec." At this time R. Pinhas lived in Korzec.

It is not certain, however, that the maggid and R. Pinhas actually lived in Korzec at the same time. The incident mentioned above regarding the maggid waiting for R. Pinhas to finish his prayers, might imply that at that time they did. See n. 116 above.

118. MS. Sipurim Yekarim. King August II died in 1763. On 7 September 1764, Stanislav August Poniatowski [Stanislaus Augustus Poniatowski] was elected king.

119. R. Shneur Zalman was then in Miedzyrzecz. *Bet Rabi*, pt. 1, p. 3a. See there, as well, the story about the Ari revealing himself to the maggid.

maggid, and said: Many [powers of] Judgment (*dinim*) reside here." He instructed them to gather all the sick in one room, where R. Pinhas began to pray. They forgot, however, to bring the maggid's wife who was in another room. All were restored to health, except the wife of the maggid, who passed away.[120] The year of her death was, it appears, considerably before 1773, the year of the maggid's death.[121]

Even at that time, Hasidim were inclined to praise their rebbe to the heavens, often even at the expense of other tzaddikim. When the maggid's disciples proceeded to do likewise, R. Pinhas seems to have taken it as a personal affront. He once heard that people said that the maggid "elevated prayer."[122] R. Pinhas observed, "It is *I* who have elevated prayer."[123] Since his close disciples were aware of the friction between their master and R. Ber, they did not repeat the teachings of the latter in the presence of R. Pinhas. But in Korzec there was a simpleminded fellow who told R. Pinhas the following in the name of the maggid: [It is written,] "Who wishes to express (*yemallel*) the strength of God? He [must] declare all of His praise (*tehillato*)" (Psalms 106:2). [This implies that] if a person wishes to annul heavenly judgments, he must recite the entire book of Psalms (*Tehillim*). R. Pinhas replied: "It is I who have said [that]."[124] Under the maggid's influence, the Hasidic movement ex-

---

120. MS. Kitvey Kodesh, chap. 9, fol. 6b.

121. It may have taken place during the early period of the maggid's leadership, since the maggid lived "separated from women [i.e., without a wife] for many years" (cf. *Maggid Devarav Leyaʿakov*, Introduction), and died in 1773 (Horodezky, *Torat Hammagid Mimezeritch Vesihotav* [Berlin: Eynot, 1923], p. 15).

122. According to *Peʾer Layesharim*, p. 12a, the Maggid himself said this.

123. "*Ikh hob oifgehoiben davenen*" (MS. Cincinnati, fol. 45a).

124. Ibid. In *Teshuʾot Hen* by R. Gedaliah of Linitz, *parshat vayigash*, we read: "From the late, renowned Hasid, our master and teacher, R. Meshulam Zusman, may his memory be a blessing and endure in the world to come, I heard a commentary . . . on the verse, "Who wishes to express (*yemallel*) the strength of God? He [must] declare all of His praise' (Psalms 106:2). He said that the word *yemallel* comes from the same root as [the word *mollel* in] the expression, 'one who rubs (*mollel*) ears of parched corn' (*Mishnah* Maʿasrot 4:5), which has the connotation of 'crumbling' and 'sweetening.' The verse, 'Who wishes *yemallel* the strength of God?' thus, means, 'Who can ameliorate the powers of [the Sefirah of] Strength (*Gevurah*) [which is the source of Judgment]?' The answer is 'He [must] declare all of His praise (*tehillah*).' [The word *tehillah* refers to *Tehillim*, the Psalms, and therefore, the verse refers to] one who recites the entire book of Psalms at one sitting."

In *Rishpey 'Esh Hashalem*, #125, by R. Mordecai of Neskhiz [Brody: Moses Lieb Harmelin, 1874], this item is quoted in the name of "my master, may the memory of this holy zaddik be for a blessing" (the maggid of Zloczew?). R. Tzvi Elimelekh of Dynów, *Igra de-Pirka* [Lwów: Moses Schumfeld, 1858], #348, mentions it, without giving the source, only as a teaching "I have received." In *Midrash Pinhas*, p. 27, however, we find: "For many troubles and concerns, such as making a living, etc., he (R. Pinhas) instructed that one recite the book of Psalms from beginning to end without any interruption, even omitting the *yehi ratzon* prayer, which is usually said after each section of the book, until one has completed them all." This same nostrum is likewise quoted in the name of R. Moses Savraner as "a tradition from zaddikim."

[The latter is further cited as saying that while the phrase "without any interruption" is

panded, and the Hasidic way began to be practiced openly by a growing number of people. This did not sit well with R. Pinhas who all his life had demanded humility and did not consider Hasidism to be a mass movement. He said: "How dare we consider ourselves Hasidim?" Although the disciples of the maggid did not put on their tefillin on the intermediate days of the festivals,[125] R. Pinhas commanded his followers to do so and likewise differed with them in not having *hakafot* on the eve of *Shemini ʿAtzeret*, "except on rare occasions with select individuals."[126]

The strained relationship between R. Pinhas and the active and influential circle of the maggid continued to increase until at last bitter controversy broke out. As a result of this, R. Pinhas was compelled to leave the city of Korzec shortly before the year 1770.[127]

In Korzec, where R. Ber served for some time as the maggid, there were apparently many Hasidim who were devoted to him. The rabbi of Korzec, R. Yitzhak Isaac, was the son-in-law of the rabbi of Miedzyrecz, R. Tzvi Hirsh, and was considered a disciple of the maggid. Under their influence many kabbalistic books, which had previously been restricted, were published, so that for a time Koretz became the most important center for their dissemination. More than ninety percent of the books printed there were kabbalistic.[128] Among those who wrote approbations in support of the publication of these kabbalistic works were friends of R. Pinhas. However, he himself did not lend his hand to this, perhaps because he opposed their distribution.

R. Pinhas, who used to say, "How dare we consider ourselves Hasidim!,"[129] turned a number of the maggid's followers from his house because he could not bear their affectation of mannerisms similar to those of the maggid. These people stirred up strife by complaining that he was at odds with the maggid. When R. Pinhas heard about this he exclaimed, "Do these people of the maggid really believe that I am at odds with him? Were I to go along the maggid's path, or he mine, there would be fire."[130]

taken to mean, between the beginning and the end of the Book of Psalms, that is, not to utter a single other word during one's recitation, "I explain it thus: without any interruption between the heart and the mouth, that is, that they should be in complete harmony during one's recital of the whole book of Psalms" ([Isaiah Borokovitz], *ʾAsefat ʾAmarim* to Psalms [Warsaw, 1883], Introduction. See also *Mayim Rabbim* [Warsaw: A. Schriftgiessen, 1899; rpt. Jerusalem, 1964], pp. 13, 20).]

125. Shalom Rokeach, *Sefer Dover Shalom* (Przemyśl: Amkroit and Freund, 1910), p. 12.

126. *Torat R. Pinhas Mikoretz*, p. 223. [The *hakafot* are ritual circumambulations of the synagogue.]

127. R. Pinhas died in 1790 or 1791 after having lived in Ostróg "more than twenty years" (Biber, *Mazkeret Lagedoley ʾOstraha*, p. 211).

128. Hebrew printing began in Korzec in 1776 or earlier, and many of those engaging in publishing there founded printing houses of their own in other cities. See Aryeh Tauber, *Mehkarim Bibliografiim* (Jerusalem: The University Press, 1932), pp. 15 ff.

129. *Torat R. Pinhas Mikoretz*, # 223.

130. MS. Cincinnati, fol. 45a. The meaning of the last words "*hayinu mesarfim*," which

At the head of the maggid's followers who took issue with R. Pinhas was R. Solomon of Luck,[131] later preacher in Sokal, who was called "R. Solomon Lutzker-Koretzer."[132] A relative of the maggid,[133] he published the latter's teachings in *Likutey'Amarim, Maggid Devarav Leya'akov* (Korzec, 1781), the most important source of the maggid's thought. He also published editions of major kabbalistic works,[134] drawing upon the important body of kabbalistic manuscripts which were kept in the *bet midrash* in Miedzyrecz.[135] Due to the efforts of R. Solomon, the first two

---

we translated as, "there would be fire," is not clear. From MS. Kitvey Kodesh, chap. 3, fol. 8a, where the reading is, "Had I invaded . . . (*gevehn arein treten*)" [in the past-perfect tense], one gets the impression that the incident took place after the maggid's death in 1773. According to the version in MS. Cincinnati and the tradition of Ostróg (see above n. 127), however, the incident occurred during the maggid's lifetime. The writer of the two manuscripts heard the story from "an old man from Korzec, R. Isaac the son of R. Solomon, who in his city was called 'R. Isaac Glazier.'" He knew R. Pinhas well, lived in Korzec at that time, and was a guest of R. Raphael of Bershad during the summer of 1827. Another reason for R. Pinhas's departure from Korzec was the "bitter dispute with regard to ritual slaughterers (*shoḥetim*). This was because of envy, since R. Moses, son of R. Pinhas, together with his partners, had a business interest in the only abbatoir in the city" (Kitvey Kodesh). It is clear, however, that the matter of the *shoḥetim* was only secondary since, R. Moses, the cause of the envy, remained in Korzec even after his father departed (according to MS. Cincinnati). The version in *'Even Shetiyah*, by Hayim Cohana (Munkacs: Menahem Mendel Hager, 1930), p. 19, stating that R. Pinhas left Korzec because of a plague, is refuted by the testimony of an eyewitness, as well as by the family tradition (see n. 131).

131. According to the tradition of R. Pinhas's descendants (*Mazkeret Legedoley 'Ostroha*, p. 211), R. Solomon's son-in-law and his partner in the publishing house in Poryck (Poritzk) was R. Abraham, the son of R. Yitzhak Isaac of Korzec. R. Yitzhak Isaac, the head of the Jewish court of Korzec, wrote of R. Solomon: "my dearly beloved friend and scholar, noted for his learning and piety, the perfect sage, devout Hasid . . . " (*Hakaneh 'al Hamitzvot* [Poryck, 1786]).

132. R. Jacob Isaac of Lublin in his approbation to the book, *Divrat Shlomo* (Zolkiew, 1848; rpt. Jerusalem: Ma'ayan Hokhmah, 1955).

133. *Maggid Devarav Leya'akov*, Introduction; *Divrat Shlomo, parshat balak*. It is told that to R. Solomon was given the privilege of arranging the twelve loaves of bread at the maggid's table. R. Solomon's disciple, R. Shalom of Belz, used to say: "I am the third after the Besht, for my master, R. Solomon, was the disciple of the maggid" [who was the disciple of the Besht]. R. Solomon died in 1813 in Sokal. See *Dover Shalom*, p. 12.

134. In the introduction to *Maggid Devarav Leya'akov*, R. Solomon writes that, together with his partner, R. Simon, he published the *Zohar* (1775), *Tikkune Zohar* (1780), *Sefer Yetzirah* (1779), and the *Shoshan Sodot* (1784). In this introduction he signs his name, "Solomon of Luck, now residing here in the holy community of Korzec." In 1786 he established a printing press in Poryck with his son-in-law and another partner which continued until 1788. There he published five books. See Yaari, "Bibliographical Miscellany," *Kiryat Sefer*, 20 (1943):102. [Cf. regarding the publishing of *Maggid Devarav Leya-'akov*, Rivka Schatz's introduction to her edition of this work (Jerusalem: Magnes Press [The Hebrew University], 1976).]

135. "With the holy manuscripts of the Ari, may his memory endure into the future world, which are in our local *bet hamidrash*, a whole variety of writings had been gathered by zealous scholars who had formerly dwelt here, as those who know our community can affirm, may God be praised. In acquiring this particular holy book (of the Ari's writings), our elders have told of the enormous efforts made by the late tzaddik, the distinguished rabbi, the Hasid, our master, Mordecai, may his memory live on in the future world, who was the *maggid mesharim* of our community, may its Creator and Possessor guard it" (*Maḥberet Hakodesh* [Korzec: Johann Anton Krüger, 1783]). Previously one had refrained

Hasidic books—*Toldot Ya'akov Yosef* (Korzec, 1780) and *Ben Porat Yosef* (Korzec, 1781)—were printed.[136] R. Solomon was renowned for his devotion to the teachings of his master.[137] The maggid had taught him "all the principles of faith and the ways to serve God, from which he departed neither to the right nor to the left, as is well-known."[138] R. Pinhas was not the only one with whom he came into conflict. Toward the end of his life, he also engaged in an argument with the students of the maggid of Złoczew (Zlotchov), making it necessary for R. Moses Lieb of Sasów to compose a letter which would quiet the controversy.[139]

The polemic against the way of the maggid of Miedzyrzecz did not end with the conflict between R. Solomon and R. Pinhas. The battle between these two forms of Hasidim—the one, scholarly, speculative, and aristocratic; the other, that of the Ukrainian tzaddikim, poetic, moralistic, and popular—continued for generations. Among the examples of this controversy is the well-known antagonism of the Besht's grandson, R. Barukh of Miedzybórz, an admirer of both R. Pinhas and R. Jacob Joseph,[140] toward R. Shneur Zalman of Lady[141] and R. Levi Isaac of Berdichev;[142] the polemic between R. Abraham of Kalisk and R. Shneur Zalman;[143] and also the complaints of R. Asher of Stolin, the disciple of R. Solomon of Karlin, against the Habad Hasidim.[144]

---

from disseminating kabbalistic works. Their appearance during these years was due to the influence of the maggid and his disciples.

136. In the introduction to *Maggid Devarav Leya'akov*, he mentions that he had already published *Ben Porat Yosef*. However, in the edition which I am using [Lwów, 1865], his name is not mentioned as the publisher [nor is it in the first edition, Korzec, 1781].

137. When R. Solomon was appointed as maggid of Sokal, the rabbi there was a *mitnaged*, praying according to the Ashkenazic rite and putting on *tefillin* during the intermediary days of the festival [contrary to the custom of the Baal Shem and his followers]. "On the first intermediary day after his arrival, R. Solomon's friends very much feared the outbreak of dissension between them." *Dover Shalom*, p. 12.

138. *Seder Hadorot Hehadash*, pt. 1, p. 78.

139. See the end of *Likutey Ramal* [by R. Moses Judah Leib of Sasów (Cernăuţi [Tchernovitz], 1866)].

140. R. Barukh was raised in the home of R. Pinhas in Ostróg (*Butzina Denehora Hashalem*, p. 9). He used to say, "May I be counted among the *tzaddikim* (*Zohar, vayakhel*). Master of the world, when I say '*tzaddikim*' I do not mean *them* (*Ikh mein nit zay*) [the famous tzaddikim of his time]. I mean (*Ikh mein*) the rav, R. Pinhas of Ostróg [and Korzec] and the rav of Polonnoye" (p. 12).

141. R. Lipa of Khmelnik testified that the conflict between R. Barukh and R. Shneur Zalman was reminiscent of the "disagreement between Rabban Gamaliel and R. Eliezer ben Azariah, in which Rabban Gamaliel proclaimed that only those students would be admitted to the house of study whose inner thoughts and feelings paralleled their outward actions [i.e., who were absolutely honest; consequently few entered], while R. Eliezer removed the guard at the door to the house of study and gave permission for all students to be admitted" (*Butzina Denehora Hashalem*, p. 22).

142. Ibid., p. 25.

143. R. Abraham of Kalisk admonished R. Shneur Zalman, because he was accustomed "to clothe the words of the holy Besht with the words of the holy Ari, may his memory be for a blessing." About R. Shneur Zalman's book, the *Tanya*, R. Abraham wrote: "I do not find

On the other hand, R. Solomon was not the only one who took issue with the way of R. Pinhas. "There were many who left the rav [R. Pinhas] with questions."[145]

"Certain tzaddikim opposed R. Pinhas." They accused him of not possessing the proper "preparation for prayer." This is the testimony of R. Zusya of Anipol, who stood in close relationship to R. Pinhas.[146] Who these tzaddikim were is not recorded, but, from the various allusions to them that have been preserved, we can surmise that they were from the school of the maggid, among whom was R. Levi Isaac of Berdichev, who objected when the names of the maggid and R. Pinhas were once mentioned to him in the same breath.[147]

The maggid of Miedzyrzecz taught that genuine prayer requires *hitlahavut*. If one "prays with *hitlahavut*," the *Shekhinah* rests upon him, but if one does not pray with *hitlahavut*, the *Shekhinah* does not rest upon him."[148] For from the mitzvah which a man performs "below, abundant joy is aroused above. The principle is that one should be moved to great *hitlahavut* from one's joy on earth, in order that a divine joy should be aroused in Heaven."[149]

From this it follows that in prayer "one must put all his strength in the words he utters, moving from letter to letter, until he is no longer aware of what surrounds him."[150] Many of the disciples of the maggid adopted the way of *hitlahavut*, particularly R. Levi Isaac of Berdichev, who, when he was about to pour forth his prayer before the Lord, "would tremble violently and could not remain in one spot because of the awe he felt. If he was praying in one corner of the room, he might very well be in another a moment later, because of his violent and wonderful movements. Those who were with him felt the hair on their head stand on end, their hearts melt, and the crookedness within them made straight by the sound of his

it of much benefit in saving souls . . . In their approach to almost all their Hasidim, our teachers took great care with their words, speaking only *musar* (ethical teachings) and striving to bring them to faith in the sages." R. Abraham's principal concern was with the enhancement of character. Disseminating secrets of the Kabbalah to the public, he felt, might lead to dangerous consequences. "Too much oil may, Heaven forbid, cause the light to be extinguished . . . Why should the fool with money but no understanding purchase wisdom?" *Kiryat Sefer* 1 (1924):144 ff. [Also see *Likutey 'Amarim* (= *Tanya*), *'Igrot Hakodesh*, #27 (Brooklyn, N.Y.: Kehot, 1973), pp. 563–65; David Tzvi Hillman, *'Igrot Ba'al Hatanya Uveney Doro* (Jerusalem: Hamesorah, 1953), #58, p. 105.]

144. Dubnow, *Toldot Hahasidut*, p. 481.
145. MS. Cincinnati, fol. 46a.
146. R. Zusya was with R. Pinhas more than once. MS. Cincinnati; Elimelekh b. Hayim Shapiro, *Divrey 'Elimelekh* [Warsaw: Halter and Shuldberg, 1890–91], *rimzey isru hag* (as cited in the *Menorat Zahav* [Warsaw, 1902], p. 62.
147. This exceptionally long note appears in the Endnotes; see p. 000.
148. *Maggid Devarav Leya'akov* (Korzec, 1784), p. 9b.
149. Ibid., p. 20a.
150. Ibid., p. 11a.

voice."¹⁵¹ To reach the level of *hitlahavut*, Hasidim would devote themselves to various kinds of preparation for it. It was believed that without
such preparation, it was not possible to receive the holy heavenly be-
neficence [*shefa*], for "the stirring from below must precede the stirring
from above." Because of the need to make themselves ready, they would
often even delay the time of prayer.

R. Pinhas, however, did not hold with

> those who always prayed with excessive energy and in a loud
> voice. For, he said, it is stated in the *Zohar* that he who slays the
> dragon is given in marriage the king's daughter, which is, prayer.
> Consequently, a man must wait to see whether or not prayer has
> been given to him [and he must not press the matter]. He related
> how once a man came to him complaining that he was afflicted
> with idolatrous thoughts. He replied on the above lines. For if
> prayer is not given to man from Heaven and he wishes to take
> the hand of the king's daughter without permission, as above, it
> is sheer effrontery in the face of Heaven, and (even) where the
> honor of a mere mortal teacher is involved, there is a ban. Idola-
> try is called a "banned thing" (*herem*), as it is said: "for it is a
> banned thing" (Deut. 7:26); hence [that man] is afflicted with
> these idolatrous thoughts and [R. Pinhas] instructed him to agree
> to be placed under the ban (as a penance). The *Zohar*, he ex-
> plained, suggests that one should recite his prayers only after
> adequate preparation and with due deliberation . . . He explained
> that "slaying the dragon" means a man should think of himself as
> nothing at all; then the king's daughter will be given to him. The
> sign that prayer has been given to him is when tears flow from his
> eyes. For twice the numerical value of dim'ah ("tear") is *Rahel*
> (Rachel), *the daughter of Malkhut* (Sovereignty), as is well
> known. He related, too, how once a distinguished visitor com-
> plained that his associates never seemed to pray along with him:
> one would study, the other would sleep. He [R. Pinhas] said to
> him: "You will observe that when I lead the service everyone
> prays together with me." And so it was indeed. "You pray," he
> said to the man, "before your prayer has really been given to
> you. But when prayer has been given from Heaven and is called
> 'the king's daughter,' representing *yihud* ('union') on high, then
> there is *yihud* here on earth." Understand this.¹⁵²

151. M. Bodek, *Seder Hadorot Hehadash*, p. 25. See *Sheney Hame'orot* (Kishenev,
1896), p. 96. [Cf. S. Dresner, *Levi Yitzhak of Berditchev* (New York: Hartmore House,
1975), pp. 92–99.]

152. *Midrash Pinhas*, p. 19. [Louis Jacobs, in *Hasidic Thought* (New York: Behrman,
1976), pp. 25–27, has commented on this passage. " . . . R. Pinhas does not believe in trying
to storm Heaven. Rather his approach is that of the passive way in which the worshiper
prepares himself to receive an influx of the divine grace. The motif of the hero who slays the
dreaded dragon and receives the hand of the princess is applied by the *Zohar* to prayer. R.

R. Pinhas opposed *"sharf davenen,"*[153] namely, the exceptional vigor and exertion expressed by some so as to reach *hitlahavut*. Since "worship is divine,"[154] and worship and worshiper are part of one whole, for there can be no prayer without one who prays, it follows that worship is not within the domain of man. Of what avail, then, are all his exertions? R. Tzvi, the son of the Besht, once said to R. Pinhas that "one must prepare oneself in order to receive the holiness of the Sabbath . . . To which R. Pinhas replied: 'When one receives a gift from Heaven about which one knows nothing . . . how can he prepare himself for it?!' "[155]

Pinhas understands it to mean that true prayer is a divine gift, from which it follows that it must not be snatched at will, any more than the hero is allowed to take the princess by force. To do so is sheer effrontery (*hutzpah*), and the penalty for one guilty of *hutzpah* to a scholar, say the rabbis, is for him to be placed under the ban (*herem*), i.e., to be ostracized for a time. If this is the penalty where the honor of a mere human is at stake, how much more so where God's honor is at stake. Now the term *herem* in the verse from Deuteronomy is used for idolatry. Hence the man guilty of taking Heaven by storm is afflicted with idolatrous thoughts. . . . If only he could learn quietly to await the divine grace, not demanding, but patiently making himself ready to receive, he will not be bothered by such thoughts any longer . . .

"R. Pinhas then elaborates on the theme of passivity by introducing the typical Hasidic idea of self-annihilation. This means stilling the ego, or, in stronger terms, killing it. When man has become as 'nothing,' demanding nothing for himself, then the divine grace can freely flow down to him. When that happens his experience is completely authentic and uncontrived, and so his tears of joy or of sorrow flow automatically.

"R. Pinhas now introduces a kabbalistic idea. There are ten *sefirot*, powers or potencies in the godhead. The lowest of these is known as *Malkhut* ('Sovereignty'), because it is through this that God's dominion is exercised. Now this aspect of Deity is also known as the *Shekhinah* ('Divine Presence'), conceived of in feminine terms. There are two further aspects of *Malkhut*, one known as Leah, the other as Rachel, after Jacob's two wives. Thus Rachel is the 'king's daughter,' and authentic prayer comes from this aspect of Deity as a gift. Now the word for 'tear' (*dimʿah*) is formed from the letters *dalet, mem, ʿayin, hêh*, the total numerical value of which is 119 (*dalet* = 4, *mem* = 40, *ʿayin* = 70, hêh = 5). Twice 119 is 238. Rachel also has the numerical value of 238 (*rêsh* = 200, *het* = 8, *lamed* = 30). At least two freely flowing tears are an indication of complete authenticity. One cannot easily contrive to have tears flow. Finally, union with the king's daughter represents unification in the realm above and here on earth. Hence where there is authentic prayer all pray together. But R. Pinhas's visitor, great though he was, was too concerned with his own spiritual progress, enough at least to be bothered about why his associates failed to pray together with him. As a result he was always in a state of isolation in his prayers and was therefore quite unable to influence others."]

153. MS. Cincinnati, fol. 83a.

154. Ibid., fol. 8b.

["People think that they pray *before* the Holy One, blessed be He. But that is not so. Prayer itself is, in fact, divine (*tefilah hiʾ ʿatzmut ʾelohut mamash*), as it is written '*huʾ tehilatekhah huʾ elohekhah*'—'your prayer is your God' (Deut. 10:21)" (*Midrash Pinhas*, p. 18, #52).

In this understanding, prayer is more than man's dialogue with himself, more even than communion with God. It is itself a part of God! Rabbi Jacob Joseph, the primary source of the teachings of the Besht, writes: "I have heard from my master (the Baal Shem Tov) that the *Shekhinah* is called 'prayer,' as it is explained in the (mystical) writings '*Vaʾani tefilah*—and I (the Lord), *am* prayer' (Psalms 109:4)," *Tzafnat Paneyʿah* (Korzec: Abraham Samson Katz of Raszków and Abraham Dov of Khmelnik, 1782), p. 1a.]

155. *Midrash Pinhas*, p. 33.

The Relationship between R. Pinhas
and His Contemporaries

According to one of his disciples, those tzaddikim who differed
with R. Pinhas "did not understand" properly the matter of "preparation" (*hakhanah*) for prayer. They thought it sufficient to

> simply walk back and forth in one's room. But this is not so.
> Each word one speaks, even one's lying down to sleep, every-
> thing that transpires during the night from the time of the eve-
> ning prayer until morning—all are preparation for the morning
> prayer. And, likewise, everything one does from the morning
> prayer until the afternoon prayer is in preparation for the latter
> service. R. Pinhas used to say: "I anticipate a prayer for eight
> days. The same is true of the Sabbath. By Wednesday, I can rec-
> ognize if the coming Sabbath will be an exciting one." Regarding
> R. Pinhas's objection to intensive prayer (*sharf davenen*), he
> meant that one should not begin one's prayer with intensity
> (*sharfkeit*), but should proceed step by step, so that one might
> ascend in devotion to the principal parts of the service,namely,
> the *Shema*ᶜ and the ʿ*Amidah*. Likewise, one should not [attempt
> to pray] with more heart than he has at that time. Rather, in
> accordance to his heart, so should he pray. One of the noted dis-
> ciples of R. Pinhas, R. Solomon, said (in criticism of R. Levi
> Isaac): "I pray with more fervor than does the Berdichever Rav."
> He said further that by the conclusion of the service he, like R.
> Pinhas, would reach so exalted a rung of prayer that it was
> beyond their capacity to utter any words. They left it up to God.
> "You, O Lord, finish our *davenen*!"[156]

R. Yehiel Mikhel, the maggid of Zloczew, too,

> was at odds with R. Pinhas, because the latter had established the
> custom for his disciples to drink a little liquor and a little mead.
> R. Mikhel, who used to say that even a little confuses the mind,
> refused to as much as taste it.[157] When R. Joshua, a tzaddik from

---

156. MS. Cincinnati, fol. 83a: "And he said: 'There is no one left now who knows
anything about prayer. Neither he himself, nor our master and teacher (R. Raphael), may
his memory be for a blessing. Only the great ones such as R. Solomon, may his memory be
for a blessing, knew. But, R. Moses, may his light shine, the son of the rav (R. Pinhas), also
knows, for he said: "Had I the strength, I could pray." I heard this from his son, R.
Joseph.'" [It is not clear who the source of this passage is.]

157. Ibid., fol. 84b. "(R. Pinhas) observed about a certain town: 'How can wisdom dwell
there, since they drink so little wine? For we have learned in the Gemara (*BT* Yoma 76b),
'wine . . . makes one wise'" (R. Leibush Shohet, *Likkutim Yekarim*, p. 96). He also once
remarked, "Drinking strengthens the love between Jews" (p. 172). .

Hasidim used to drink whiskey before retiring, calling it, "the Besht's *Kriat Shema*ᶜ"
('*Irin Kadishin Tinyana* [Bartfeld, 1887], p. 22). "Since it is the body which is the major
obstacle, standing as a barrier between the soul and the Torah, to annul the body is to

the city of Mikolajow, had to travel through Korzec, R. Yehiel—
who was older than he—ordered him not to remain over the Sabbath with the rav [R. Pinhas]. And so it was. Before the onset of
the Sabbath, [R. Yehiel] visited the rav, but when the rav asked
him to spend the Sabbath with him, he refused and departed.
Many years afterward, when he returned to Korzec and went to
see the rav, the latter paid no attention to him and did not speak
to him, for he was apparently still rankled from the previous visit.
R. Joshua complained: "How am I guilty? It was R. Yehiel who
commanded me not to remain." It availed nothing. Later, R.
Yehiel himself came to visit the rav.[158]

Opposition to points of view held by R. Pinhas did not cease with his
death. R. Nahum of Chernobyl, who "praised R. Pinhas highly," on
being reminded of a reason (*ta'am*) which the latter gave regarding a
certain matter, observed that "his soul was sweet (*mata'amim*)." However, R. Nahum added, " . . . after the death of the tzaddik, difficulties arise even over things which did not appear problematic during his
lifetime."[159]

On the other hand, we know there were others of his time who
enthusiastically supported R. Pinhas. R. Isaiah of Dinovitz, a disciple
of the maggid of Miedzyrzecz, to whom R. Pinhas had once written a
marvelous letter on ecstasy and the ascension of the soul,[160] spent the
Sabbath with him in Ostróg and said of him: "What we so-called good
Jews comprehend after six months of mental torment, R. Pinhas grasps in

---

strengthen the soul. Witness the fact that the soul speaks [uncensored] when one is
intoxicated" (*Toldot 'Aharon, drush lepurim* [Berdichev: Israel Beck, 1817], fol. 77b). "It is
customary for most people to drink mead on Erev Shabbat after coming from the bath. The
reason for this is . . . that they will thereby experience a deeper love [of God] during the
minhah and *ma'ariv* prayers, for the prayers on the eve of the Sabbath require greater fervor
and *kavanah* than all the prayers of the week, as is well-known. However, there are those
who drink too much, until they no longer know the difference between ["Blessed be
Mordecai" and "Cursed be Haman" (see *BT* Megilah 7b)]" (*Likutim Yekarim*, [Mezyrów,
1794], p. 33a). The maggid of Miedzyrzecz used to say: "There are two kinds of redness.
One is [associated with the *sefirah* of] Strength (*Gevurah*) [the source of stern judgment (cf.
Pardes Rimonim 10:3)]. The second is [the red color of] wine, which represents joy.
Through the second redness, all [harsh judgments associated with the] first redness are
ameliorated. As a parable, we see that when a king is in a happy mood, even individuals who
are not otherwise worthy are admitted to his presence" (*Maggid Devarav Leya'akov*, p. 11;
'Or Torah, parshat vayehi, p. 23a). On the other hand, R. Shmelke [Horowitz] of Nikolsburg
(*Divrey Shmu'el* [Lwów: Moses Hakohen, 1862], *hanhagot*, p. 12) said: "One may only
drink alcohol if he is free of passion, and then only moderately. He must never become
drunk, Heaven forbid."
    158. MS. Cincinnati, fol. 46a.
    159. MS. Kitvey Kodesh, chap. 6, fol. 4a. R. Nahum said this in the presence of R. Jacob
Simon, the son of R. Pinhas.
    160. The letter is published at the end of *Ḥesed Le'avraham* [(Cernaŭti: Meshulam
Heller, 1851), p. 25b]. According to the MS. *Sipurim Yekarim*, R. Nahum said of him that
· he was a "divine philosopher [*filisof 'eloki mima'al*]."

one leap."[161] R. Nahum of Chernobyl once visited R. Pinhas together
with the son-in-law of his daughter, R. Shalom [Shakhne] Prohovitchner,
who was then a young man, and he counted [R. Pinhas] as a miracle
worker and a great mind.[162] R. Hayim Krasner, a disciple of the Besht,
said about R. Pinhas: "Truly, truly, he is remarkable, unique in his
generation."[163] R. Jacob Joseph of Polonnoye once brought R. Pinhas to
him by sending a carriage, and R. Pinhas spent the Sabbath with him.
Although it was R. Jacob Joseph's unaltered custom to lead the communal prayer, this time he revoked his oath in the presence of three Jews and
honored R. Pinhas to act as *shaliaḥ tzibbur*. "It is reported that he
observed later that since the Besht died he had never heard such
praying."[164] Once a man came to R. Jacob Joseph seeking a cure for

161. "R. Isaiah of Dinovitz once spent the Sabbath with the rav [R. Pinhas]. After the
first Sabbath meal [Friday evening], [R. Isaiah] spoke of the rav, and the old man [R. Isaac
ben Solomon (see above, n. 130)] heard him say, 'Long life to him. We have also gotten to
know God a bit. (*Lang leben oif ihm. Mir hobn zikh oikh a bissel mit Got derkennt.*)' After
the second Sabbath meal [Saturday noon, the old man] saw that [R. Isaiah] was very pleased
with the rav (R. Pinhas), and he heard him [R. Isaiah] say, 'He has no equal. . . .' Once in
R. Isaiah's house, the old man heard him say, 'The little bit of intelligence in serving God for
which we and our brethren—called good Jews—spend half a year struggling for [*vos mir
darfn horiven oif ein shtikel sekhel*], comes to the rav (R. Pinhas) intuitively.' After
Havdalah [Saturday evening], R. Isaiah remarked to some others, 'Who will accompany me
to R. Isaakel (R. Yitzhak Isaac), the rabbi of [the city of] Korzec, for I want to get to know
him (see n. 48)?' To which the above-mentioned elder replied, 'I will.' And he went with
him to R. Isaakel's house. Now, R. Isaakel, who was already in his nightclothes, was
confused at their approach and said: "My master, where are you going?" R. Isaiah
answered: 'To you, for I would become better acquainted with you. Tell me what you said
Friday at the Sabbath table.' Embarrassed, he repeatedly refused, saying, '*Siz kein ma'aseh
nit*' (It was nothing at all). Later, he related numerous *gematriot*. [R. Isaiah] then told him,
'*Dos laygt avek. Es nitzt nit la'avodas Ha-Shem-Yisborakh* (Lay this [interpretation through
gematriot] aside). It is of no help in serving God. I too practiced the method of interpretation
by means of *gematriot* but have abandoned it. But [what is helpful is] that which at first you
said "is nothing at all [*kein ma'aseh nit*]"'" (MS. Cincinnati, fol., 46).
162. MS. Uman, fol. 96a. [R. Shalom Shakhne of Prohovitch was the son of R. Abraham
Hamalakh, and grandson of the maggid. He married the daughter of R. Abraham of
Kristishov, who in turn was married to a daughter of R. Nahum of Chernobyl. R. Shalom
Shakhne had been raised by R. Nahum after his father's early death.]
163. MS. Cincinnati, fol. 95b. Perhaps it was after this that he was referred to at the time
as "R. Pinhas the Great."
164. Ibid., fol. 53a. [R. Jacob Joseph, author of the first Hasidic work, *Toldot Ya'akov
Yosef*, whose books are the main source for the teachings of the Besht, was the latter's
foremost disciple. At first he opposed the way of the Besht, and several versions are given of
his conversion. The single version reported in the name of R. Jacob Joseph reports that he
came to visit the Besht and "while praying, I wept a great weeping, the like of which I had
never wept in all my life. I understood that this weeping was not from myself" (but from the
Besht). It was then that he decided to attach himself to the Baal Shem (*Shivhey Habesht*,
p. 8a [Ben-Amos, #47]). "I heard the following from Rabbi Zusya of Anipol regarding the
time he traveled from his brother, Rabbi Elimelekh, by way of Zolkiew. 'I stood in a certain
place in the *bet hamidrash* to pray. The prayer which I prayed was pure and clear like the
prayer of the Besht, and I did not know the cause. Then they told me that this place was the
place of the author of the book, *Toldot Ya'akov Yosef*'" (ibid., #113). (See Dresner, *The
Zaddik*, chap. 2.) The Besht was told that "heavenly secrets were revealed to him not

someone who was ill. "I cannot help you," he told him, and sent him to R. Pinhas.[165] In the eyes of R. David Halperin, the rabbi of Ostróg and Zasláw, who knew the Besht's opinion "regarding all the noted figures of his generation," R. Pinhas was apparently numbered among the first four.[166]

Among the distinguished figures of the time who honored and visited R. Pinhas were the "Grandfather" of Shpola;[167] R. Leib the son of Sarah;[168] the brothers, R. Shmelke of Nikolsburg and R. Pinhas of Frankfurt, the author of the *Hafla'ah*;[169] R. Jacob Joseph, the maggid of Ostróg and author of *Rav Yevi*,[170] who stood in very close friendship with R. Pinhas.[171]

> R. Elimelekh of Lezajsk said: "To know R. Pinhas of Korzec is a prescription for piety (*segulah tzu yiras shomayim*)." Upon hearing this, R. Elimelekh's son, R. Eleazer, decided to travel to R. Pinhas. While sitting at the latter's "table," R. Eleazer heaved a sigh: "*Tatte!*" ["Oh, Father in Heaven!"]. To which R. Pinhas retorted: "Perhaps He isn't your father at all!" R. Eleazer was silenced. When he returned home and reported to his parent what had happened, R. Elimelekh pursued the matter: "And what did you answer him back?" "I didn't answer him at all," R. Eleazer confessed. "You should have told him: It is written in Scriptures, '*she'al avikha*' (Deut. 32:7)—*Men leit zikh a tatte*. One can at least borrow a father'"![172]

R. Pinhas was likened by those intimate with him to the Besht himself. The Besht's disciples used to say: "If all the wonders performed by the Ari are recorded in the book, *Shivhey Ha'ari* (In Praise of the Ari), then we have seen more from the Besht." R. Solomon, the disciple of R. Pinhas added: "If all [the wonders] performed by the Baal Shem Tov are those which have been reported and there are no others, then I have seen

---

because he had mastered the Talmud and Codes, but because his prayer was always marked by great *kavanah*" (*Tzava'at Harivash*, #41). Typical of the Besht's teachings on prayer is the following: "Before he begins to pray, a man should decide that he is ready to die in that very prayer. There are those so intense in their worship and who give so much of their strength to prayer, that if not for a miracle they would die after uttering only two or three words. It is only through God's great kindness that such people live, that their soul does not leave them as they cleave to God in prayer" (*Tzava'at Harivash*, #57).]

165. MS. Uman, fol. 95b; MS. Kitvey Kodesh, chap. 6, fol. 5a.
166. *Mazkeret Lagedoley 'Ostroha*, p. 338.
167. Guttman, *R. Pinhas Mikoretz*, p. 28.
168. MS. Cincinnati, fol. 45a.
169. *'Eser Orot* [by Israel Berger; Pietrkov, 1910], pp. 2-5.
170. *Mazkeret Lagedoley 'Ostroha*, p. 211.
171. MS. Cincinnati, fol. 83b.
172. R. Yehezkel Shinover, *Divrey Yehezkel, parshat ma'asey* (see Hullin 11b). (*She'al* = both "ask" and "borrow.")

more from the Rav [R. Pinhas] . . ."[173] Another disciple of R. Pinhas [R. Raphael?] observed that had the generation been worthy, R. Pinhas would have been Messiah, and this calculation was consistent with Maimonides' prediction.[174]

R. Pinhas of Korzec and the Haidamak Pogroms

"In this bitter exile of ours each day we inherit new sorrows, and each day we wonder what our fate will be," writes one contemporary, concluding with the prayer: "May the Holy One, blessed be He, send the Righteous Redeemer speedily and in our time!"[175] R. Pinhas was tormented over the suffering of his people and the misery of exile. Though convinced that it was in his power to hasten the Messiah and with him the redemption, he was determined not to "force the end." "I could bring the Messiah as easily as one takes a hair out of milk or as one lifts straw from the ground (*azoi vi di shtroy oif tzu hoiben*), but I can be trusted [not to abuse this power]. . . . This power was given to me, because the Lord knows that I can be trusted with it."[176]

He always hoped to settle in the Land of Israel[177] and urged others to do so, often recounting its virtues. "He [R. Pinhas] once suggested to a visitor who had been there, that, while at prayer, he sketch in his mind the Holy Land, with all its lakes and rivers. . . . 'How great is the power of imagination,' said R. Pinhas. 'I, who have never been in the Holy Land, can, nonetheless, conjure up a picture of the very faces of those who dwell there at this moment.'"[178] Even before the celebrated immigration to Palestine of R. Mendel of Vitebsk and his followers in 1777, R. Pinhas had decided to settle there. He made two separate attempts, but, as with the Besht, neither succeeded. Shortly before the month of Tammuz in 1768, R. Pinhas determined "to go up to the Holy Land."[179] All the

173. MS. Kitvey Kodesh, chap. 6, 5a. " . . . and he told many wonderful stories how R. Pinhas, without any special effort, would cure people suffering from the ague. Sometimes he would say to the person, come and look at my face when I say *borkhu*, and the person would be healed. To some he would say nothing, but just stood near them . . . " (Ibid.)

174. [Matityahu Ezekiel] Guttman, *Torat R. Pinhas Mikoretz* (Bilgorey, 1941), p. 8. See R. David Ibn abi Zimra, *Magen David* (Amsterdam: Asher Anshel b. Eliezer, 1713), p. 39b: "The messianic age will surely not begin later than 500 years" [before the sixth millennium. This implies that the messianic age would have to begin before the Hebrew year 5500 (1740). Accordingly, the Messiah would have to be born before 1740. R. Pinhas was born in 1725 or 1726. See n. 8.]

175. R. Israel of Satanow, ʿ*Ateret Tifʾeret Yisraʾel* [Warsaw: Samuel Orgelbrand, 1871], p. 5d.

176. MS. Kitvey Kodesh, chap. 3, fol. 5a.

177. "He said that it was his firm desire to settle in the Land of Israel." [MS. Cincinnati? See n. 179.]

178. *Tosefta Lamidrash Pinhas*, p. 4b.

179. "When R. Pinhas planned to go up to the Land of Israel, he said that it was his firm desire to settle in a 'city of refuge,' since it could harbor murderers and one might hide there.

necessary preparations had been made, even to the hiring of wagons. Suddenly he fell ill. "He knew that he was dangerously sick and took to bed. R. Simon Ashkenazi, who was standing behind him, heard R. Pinhas say: 'O Lord, if it is your will that I not go up to the Land of Israel, then I shall not go.' Once having uttered those words, he immediately recovered. For what reason God did not wish him to leave remained a puzzle, for he knew he had a good purpose in going. It was only some time later that he understood why Heaven had prevented him—because of the decree [of the Haidamak pogroms]."

The Czarina Catherine, who planned to expand the borders of Russia by annexing parts of the Ukraine which were east of the Dnieper and which belonged to Poland, incited the Ukrainians against the Poles. In 1764, Russian troops marched against Polish Ukraine to destroy the Confederation of Bar. They were accompanied by Cossacks from the slopes of the Dnieper, who fell upon both Poles and Jews with religious fervor. A decree from the czarina was widely circulated which read: "Since it is established that both the Poles and the Jews have joined in mocking our faith [Russia was Orthodox and Poland Roman Catholic], we dispatch this order and command . . . [that you] cross the Polish border and, with Heaven's assistance, kill every Pole and Jew, the defilers of our holy religion . . ." Later, however, when the czarina heard reports of the barbaric atrocities which were being committed, she declared that the order was nothing but a forgery. Nevertheless, the "golden letter," as it became known, brought immeasurable benefit to the Haidamaks in their bloody efforts.[180]

The year 1768, which one contemporary saw as the year when the Messiah would come,[181] brought misfortune and destruction to many

---

Perhaps he had the city of Safed in mind, since it is the holiest of the cities of refuge" (MS. Cincinnati, p. 45a). [The "cities of refuge" were asylums where an accidental killer would be secure from a kinsman's vengeance. See Exod. 21:13 and Num. 35:11 ff.]

180. Dubnow, *Divrey Yemey 'Am 'Olam*, chap. 7, p. 97. [See Dubnow, *History of the Jews in Russia and Poland* (Philadelphia: Jewish Publication Society, 1916), 1:180–87.]

181. "While I lay upon my bed, this thought came to me: The year 5528 [1768] after creation, will be the year of the redemption. Its gematria is *kashahar* ['as the dawn' = 5528]. For I have seen that every redemption occurs on the eighth year of the decade. Thus redemption from Egypt was in 2448 [1313/2 B.C.E.], and the entrance into the Land of Israel occurred in 2488 [1273/2 B.C.E.]. In 2928 [833/2 B.C.E.] the first Temple was built, and in 3408 [353/2 B.C:E.] the second Temple. As I write this, however, *kashahar* 'like the dawn' has become *kaheresh* ['like the deaf,' as in the verse,] 'I am like the deaf (*kaheresh*), I do not hear (Psalms 38:14).' I have seen that catastrophies brought by our many sins [also occur in the eighth year of the decade]: The First Temple was destroyed in 3338 (423/2 B.C.E.), and the Second Temple in 3828 (67/8 C.E.). (I do not have at hand the book *Seder 'Olam* to check my theory about eights.) [This is in accordance to the talmudic tradition which states that the First Temple stood for 410 years, and the second, 420, with a seventy-year hiatus between the two.] . . . In our time, it is well-known that in 5408 (1648) [*Tah*, see n. 1], a massacre occurred in the Polish Ukraine, because of our many sins, at the hand of the savage Chmelnitzki—may his memory be erased. Also in our time, in the year 5518 [1757], our holy Torah was burned. This occurred on the fourth of Marheshvan [17

communities in the Ukraine. The Ukrainian Haidamaks and the Cossacks attacked the Poles—especially the priests and the landed class—
and the Jews. "Tens of thousands of Jews were killed, until it was almost
no longer possible to number them, in all close to one hundred thousand.
Many cities and villages in an area about fifty miles long and twenty wide
were utterly destroyed . . . It is impossible to describe. One can simply not
bring pen to paper."[182]

The rebellion commenced in April, and in various cities in the province
of Kiev masses of Jews were murdered. At the news of the slaughter,
thousands of Jews, together with members of the Polish upper class,
sought refuge in the fortified city of Uman,[183] the wealthiest community in
all the domain of Count Pototzki of Kiev. The Jews and Poles joined in its
defense, firing upon the Haidamaks who were besieging the city. Uman
fell, and on the fifth of Tammuz (18 June) a large number of Jews who had
taken refuge in the synagogue to defend themselves were put to the
sword. With "the Uman massacre," however, Russian and Polish forces,
acting in concert, silenced the unrest, and the Haidamak movement came
to an end.[184]

October] in the city of Kamenetz, in the region of Podolia. The entire Mishnah, the talmudic
tract of *Berakhot*, the *Tikuney Hazohar*, and the large edition of *Shulhan ʿArukh* were
burned in the main street. All this was a result of the heretic, Shabbetai Tzvi, may his
memory be erased. [God's] hand was set against us in the form of a decree [for the burning]
from the bishop. During the conflagration on that day, he was seized by epilepsy which
became increasingly severe, until he died a cruel death on the fifth of Kislev (18 November)
of that year. May God so punish all our enemies who rise up against us to do us evil! And,
now, in the year 5528 [1768] a slaughter took place in the Ukraine in the fourth and fifth
months, Tammuz and Av—May they be turned into a season of Joy and gladness!—where
tens of thousands were murdered." (R. Israel of Satanów, ʿAteret Tifʾeret Yisraʾel, parshat
behukotai) In parshat behar, he writes, "God's Law was burned in the city of Kamenetz. The
Mishnah, the [*Shulhan ʾArukh* containing the commentary of the] *Turey Zahav*, the
Tikuney Hazohar, and the talmudic tract of *Berakhot* were all burned in the main street . . .
A vow was taken to fast on the fourth of Heshvan . . . and he arose from fasting (?) on the
night of the seventh of Heshvan in the year 5529 [1768]." [Cf. A. Yaari, *Kiryat Sefer* 23
(1946–47), p. 158.]

182. Ibid., *parshat behukotai*. According to a letter of another contemporary, the number of the slain was estimated to be fifty to sixty thousand (cf. Gurland, *Lekorot Hagezerot
ʿal Yisraʾel* [Cracow, 1889], pt. 3, p. 30. [See also B. Weinryb, *The Jews of Poland*
(Philadelphia: Jewish Publication Society, 1972), pp. 204 ff.] In Uman alone "the number
of Jews slain was around thirty thousand" (cf. [Simon] Bernfeld, *Sefer Hademaʿot* [Berlin:
Eschkol, 1923–26], pt. 3, p. 302). R. Israel of Satanov's careful specifications of the places
where the pogroms occurred is a sign of similar accuracy in regard to the numbers killed.
The details he affords us regarding the burning of books (see preceding note) are likewise of
importance; it is especially interesting that the *Tikuney Hazohar* was among the books
condemned to the flames. According to another source the bishop wanted to burn only
"rabbinic literature (*torah shebeʿal peh*) . . . leaving (unscathed) the Five Books of Moses
and the *Zohar*" (Balaban, *Latoldot Hatenuʿah Hafrankit* [Tel Aviv: Dvir, 1934], p. 187; cf.
pp. 185–89).

183. For example, the Jews of Shargorod. (*Shivhey Habesht*, p. 79 [Ben-Amos, #50].)
[Six months before his death, R. Nahman moved from Bratzlaw to Uman, primarily
because he wanted to live in this city of martyrs.]

184. Dubnow, *History of the Jews*, 7:97–100; Bernfeld, *Sefer Hademaʾot*, 3:290–302.

Said the rav of Polonnoye (R. Jacob Joseph):

Two years before the flight [in 1766], R. Tzvi, the son of the
Besht, saw his father in a dream. At the time, [R. Tzvi] was in
trouble over a considerable debt which he owed to the landown-
ers and could not repay. He asked his father:
"Do you know of my predicament?"
"I do," he answered.
"Who told you?"
"Those who travel the crossroads told me."
"Who are the travelers?"
"Abraham, Isaac, and Jacob [said the Besht]. They journey the
byways to learn of the sorrows of Israel, which they then relate at
the graves of the tzaddikim. They told me of your trouble. But I
have no time now to speak with you, for I must hasten to annul
the plots of the thieves who are called Haidamaks."
This dream occurred about three weeks before Passover.[185]

How did R. Pinhas react to the persecutions? One of his disciples
reported

that before the decree was promulgated, on the eve of the Sabbath in the month of Tammuz 1768, he went to the *mikveh*,
where he beheld a sword flying in the world—may Heaven deliver us—and grew faint. Afterward he rose and went to the
house of study to lead the services and felt such a pain in his
head and heart that he was forced to leave the lectern. (Others
say that it was when he prayed *minhah* [the afternoon prayer],
that he saw a sword flying in the world—may Heaven deliver us!)
The young man who took his place prayed so quickly that he
completed *ma'ariv* [the evening prayer] before nightfall. Had he
waited to lead *ma'ariv* until it was actually the Sabbath, the
heavenly decree [against the Jews] would have been annulled.
    R. Pinhas said: "I know that had I been able to sleep, I could
have annulled the decree, for sleep 'sweetens the harsh judgments' . . . But I was not able to sleep until after Yom Kippur.
On the Eve of Rosh Hashanah, I had wanted to pour out my soul
in tears before the Lord that it might help annul the decree. But
when I was about to pray the *selihah* (the penitential prayer)
Zakhor Brit, [which is recited on the day before Rosh Hashanah],
I began to feel a pain in my heart and head and was forced to
step down from the lectern and recite the *selihot* like any ordinary Jew. Nor was I able to weep (even though he was very
much given to weeping), and I was in anguish lest the holiday
period pass (Heaven forbid!) without tears. But on Rosh Hashanah, the holiness of the day so overcame me that I wept freely

185. *Shivhey Habesht*, p. 26a [Ben-Amos, #171].

before the Lord. Later, after the close of Yom Kippur, I tasted just a bit of food, lay down, and slept soundly until morning. It was then that I felt certain that the decree was annulled."[186]

So shaken were they by these tragic events that Ukrainian Jewry began in massive numbers to flee to Poland.[187]

One aged and renowned sage, as soon as he heard the annunciation of the decree . . . warned the holy community of Tetiev, and sent messengers as well to many other communities, telling them:
"After the persecutions of Chmelnitzki in 1648 and 1649 (*Taḥ* and *Tat*), a ban (*ḥerem*) was declared throughout Lithuania, Poland, and Turkey that no Jew henceforth be permitted to live in the land of Ukrainia. Apply to yourselves the passage, 'And you shall not take anything from the forbidden thing (*ḥerem*)' (Deut. 13:18). Therefore, all the possessions which you have acquired in this land are forbidden. [That you have survived undisturbed for so long] is only because in the year 1648 a heavenly edict decreed that concerning you there would be fulfilled what is written in Scriptures: 'And the Lord said, My spirit will not rest with man forever since he is flesh, and his days will be 120 years' (Gen. 6:3) . . . which is according to the explanation of Rashi on that passage: 'I shall delay my anger for 120 years, and if by then they will not have repented, I will bring the flood upon them.' Consequently, I say to you that should you flee, forsaking all your possessions and taking nothing from the *ḥerem*, you will be delivered, but if, out of concern for your position, you take with you even a trifle from the *ḥerem*, you will not be saved."
And as he predicted, so it was. The majority of the people hearkened to the words of the rav, fled, and were saved, but those who remained [in the Ukraine] died horribly—strangled and slaughtered, burned and stoned. Even among those who escaped, there were a few who took along a small portion of their possessions, and they too died along the way.[188]

R. Pinhas, however, opposed the "flight" and attempted to influence the Jews to remain where they were. Later he observed that had it not been for his efforts, "there would have not remained, heaven forbid, a Jewish foot (from Poland) to Lwów."[189] But even among his closest associates, there were not many who agreed with him.[190] Only the maggid extended some support. "The maggid of Miedzyrzecz did not order them

186. *Peʾer Layesharim*, p. 15b, and manuscripts.
187. *Shivhey Habesht*, pp. 31,102, 119[Ben-Amos, ##40, 45, 51, 171, 210].
188. Gurland, *Lekarot Hagezerot*, pt. 3, p. 31. See Dubnow, *History of the Jews*, 7:100: "This *ḥerem* against Ukrainia has no basis in fact and only reflects the sentiment of the people."
189. MS. Cincinnati, fol. 56a.
190. "They were too frightened and weak to support me, both in Zaslav and Zwiahel (the cities in which many members of his circle lived)" (ibid.).

to flee," and it appears that he advised the Jews to hide in the forests and wait until the calamity would pass.[191]

R. Pinhas also said: "For the coming year I have managed that the Holy One, blessed be He, will replace the massacre [which is destined for us] with an epidemic—heaven forbid. I did so for two reasons: The first [is found in the verse]: 'I beg You, let us rather fall into the hand of the Lord for His mercies are many [and let us not fall into the hand of man' (Sam. 24:14). I.e., if the Jews must be punished for their sins, it would be better to exchange, in the place of a massacre, which is the work of man, an epidemic, which is the work of God]. The second reason is that there should not be a desecration of God's name, since a massacre is only against the Jews, while epidemics break out principally among the Gentiles. And because of my concern for this matter, I have endangered my very self." For in that year R. Pinhas's wife died.[192]

"During the epidemic [R. Pinhas continued] I did not worry about myself at all, for I knew that I had spoken no lie and whoever does not lie, his days are lengthened." As long as he had fish for the Holy Sabbath, the epidemic touched neither him nor his household. But afterward, when he was not able to find fish, his wife died and also his servant of whom he was very fond. At the time of her death, his wife had still been nursing his son, Elijah, and no other woman wanted to continue the nursing for fear of contracting the plague. So the rav said: "Whichever woman will take my son and nurse him, I promise that the plague will not visit her, nor her husband, nor her household . . ." One woman accepted and nursed the child. When she fell ill, showing signs of the disease, her husband reported this to the rav. He ordered that she come to him and look him square in the face. She did so. At once her face turned different colors, and she was cured on the spot. That is how the husband of the woman told the story.[193]

---

191. "They did not dress in white on the Sabbath; nor lead the congregation in prayer" (ibid.). Evidently R. Pinhas and R. Ber spoke out on communal issues and were able successfully to implement their opinions among the people.

192. This event apparently took place in 1769. R. Pinhas's prayer follows the way of the Besht. In the Besht's letter to his brother-in-law, R. Gershon Kutover, which was printed in Korzec, in 1781 (during the lifetime of R. Pinhas), it is written: "On Rosh Hashanah, 1750, I ascended into heaven—as is known—and I beheld a fearful indictment [against the Jews], until it seemed that Samael [Satan] would be given the power to destroy whole communities and lands. So I staked my life and prayed: "Let us fall now into the hand of the Lord [for His mercies are great], and let us not fall into the hand of man" (see 2 Sam. 24:14). My prayer was granted that in the place of this [i.e., anti-Jewish pogroms incited by man, we would receive God's punishment of] a terrible epidemic, the like of which had never occurred in all the lands of Poland or those nearby. And so it was that an indescribable epidemic spread [in Poland] and the other lands" (*Ben Porat Yosef*, end).

193. MS. Cincinnati, fol. 56a.

After the death of his wife, Treyna—the mother of R. Meir and R. Moses—he took another wife, Yuta, and from her were born R. Jacob Simon and R. Ezekiel.[194] He also had a daughter whose name was Rachel-Sheindel.[195]

R. Pinhas and the Polish Government

Although the situation of Polish Jewry during that period was critical, R. Pinhas argued that

> it was the Jews who dwelt in Germany who suffered the bitterest exile of all. For no Jew is permitted to remain there without a *prava* (special permit), or to keep more than one of his children with him in the country. And all this is so, because the Jews [in Germany] are indistinguishable from the Gentiles in their dress and speech. The exile in the land of Ishmael [Turkey] is not as bitter as in Germany, because Jews there are at least distinguished by language, though not by dress. However in Poland where both their clothing and language are different, the exile is less bitter than anywhere else.[196]

The Polish government was then in a stage of both political and social decline. Russia, Prussia, and Austria were about to divide Poland between them. R. Pinhas championed the Polish cause and had harsh things to say against Russia, then the leader of the anti-Polish coalition. He described the Russians as "rats" who knew nothing at all "of truth,"[197] and with his prayers fought all his days to annul the decree of annihilation which hung over the Polish kingdom.

His disciple, R. Raphael, related:

> Before the Russians entered the land of Poland, R. Pinhas felt the peril and said that he thought "that there was no one in the whole country who had the strength to prevent the danger except for R. Nahman Horodenker.[198] However [R. Pinhas added], R. Nahman was then preparing to depart for the Land of Israel. Now as long as R. Nahman resided in Poland *that* nation [Russia]

194. According to the records of the yahrzeits at the end of MS. Kitvey Kodesh.

195. *Mazkeret Lagedoley 'Ostroha*, p. 212. Apparently she was named after R. Pinhas's mother. See above, n. 8.]

196. MS. Cincinnati, fol. 102.

197. Ibid., fol. 73b.

198. "*Ikh hob nit gefilt azoine pleitzes.*" Lit: "I did not feel shoulders broad enough in anyone." "He held him [R. Nahman Horodenker] in highest esteem, would speak his praises, and said that, according to the Midrash, one who praises the tzaddikim is as if he would study the mysteries of the Chariot (*merkavah*)." (MS. Cincinnati, fol. 99b.) R. Nahman's son, R. Simhah, was the father of R. Nahman of Bratslaw and the son-in-law of Edel (Udel), the Besht's daughter.

did not cross over the Dnieper River. Despite many attempts
their soldiers failed to enter Poland. But on the day that R. Nahman traversed the Dniester on his way to the Land of Israel, the
Russian troops crossed the Dnieper.[199] And [of those able to stop
them] I alone remained in the land. So I decided that I would
pray with a sizable congregation and therefore traveled (in the
year 1764 or 1765)[200] to the holy community of Zasláw for the
Sabbath, for there were many Jews there.[201] I traveled there, even
though it was with some uneasiness.

[Previously, R. Pinhas had always declined an invitation to the
city] from R. David of Ostróg, who was then the head of the
court in the holy community of Zasláw[202] and who had repeatedly
invited R. Pinhas, through R. Solomon, may his memory be for a

199. R. Nahman departed for the Land of Israel in 1764 (R. Simhah of Zalovitz, ʾ*Ahavat
Tziyon*, 6:15). In that same year Russia dispatched its armies into Poland, in connection
with the Confederation of Bar.

200. R. David Halperin (who is mentioned in this story) died in 1765. Consequently, R.
Pinhas's journey must have taken place in 1764, after R. Nahman had departed for
Palestine, or in 1765.

201. In 1764 the Jewish population in Zasláw, at that time the largest community in
Volhynia, was 2,161. (See Mahler, *Yiden in Amolikin Polin* [Warsaw: Farlag Yiddish Buch,
1958], p. 181.)

202. R. David Halperin, rabbi of Zasláw and of Ostróg, the son of R. Israel Harif
Halperin, succeeded his father as rabbi of Ostróg in 1735. He was a "noted Hasid" and a
beloved disciple of the Besht, who resided in his home whenever he came to Zasláw. In 1745
his approbation was given to R. Raphael Emanuel Hai Riki's book, *Mishnat Hasidim* (a
selection of *kavanot* for prayer taken from the writings of the Ari, together with the
Sephardic order of prayers.) At that time, there resided in Ostróg, R. Abraham Meshulam
Zalman (son of the author of the book, *Hakham Tzvi*, and the brother of R. Jacob Emden),
who was the son-in-law of R. Yuzpa, the richest Jew of his day in the land of Volhynia. In
1737, R. Abraham became rabbi of the *kloiz*. His father-in-law spent a large sum to have
him appointed rav of the entire community, but important members of the Halperin family
and those laymen who revered the Besht and his circle chose R. David Halperin as rabbi.
The fire of dissension apparently raged for many years. When R. David complained about
this to the Besht, he advised him to resign the post in Ostróg. R. David became rabbi of
Zasláw in 1746. His brother, R. Joel of Leszniów, was the father-in-law of R. Pinhas
Horovitz, author of the *Haflaʾah*. (See *Mazkeret Lagedoley* ʾ*Ostroha*, pp. 97–101, 106; S.
Kahan, ʿ*Anaf* ʿ*Etz* ʾ*Avot* [Cracow: Kahan, 1903], p. 6.) R. David died and was buried in
Ostróg in 1765. In his will, which was published in *Darkey Tzion* (Polonnoye, 1798; see
Mazkeret Lagedoley ʾ*Ostroha*, p. 338), he made the following provisions: He left 4,000
gulden for charity. Six hundred gulden he designated for the *mokhiah* of Polonnoye, the
maggid of Miedzyrzecz, the maggid of Zloczew, and R. Pinhas of Korcez—each of whom
was to receive 150 gulden. One hundred gulden each were bequeathed to R. Wolf Kutzis of
Miedzyrzecz, to the maggid of Bar, to R. Zalman of Miedzyrzecz, and to his brother, R.
Leib. To the poor of the Land of Israel, R. Mendel of Przemyślany was to distribute 200
gulden. R. Nahman of Horodenka and R. Fridl received 150 gulden each. Both R. David,
the son-in-law of the rabbi of Stepan, and "R. Tzvi, the son of the Rav Baal Shem," were left
100 gulden each . . . The maggid of Ostróg received 30 gulden. Further on he writes: "My fur
coat should be given to the rabbi, the *mokhiah* of Polonnoye, together with my bequest of
money for him . . . and the hat which I recently acquired . . . should be given to the rabbi, our
master and teacher, Pinhas of Korzec together with my bequest of money for him." R.
Mendel of Przemyślany and R. Nahman of Horodenka had already emigrated to the Land
of Israel in 1764 (Cf. ʾ*Ahavat Tzion*).

blessing, to visit him. Wealthy and aged, R. David was a leader
of the Jewish community. Before the Besht died, R. David had
inquired of him regarding all the notables of his generation. And
the Besht answered about each one. Now certain of their stature,
he [R. David] wanted them to be his guests. So he would invite
first one and then another. When he sent R. Solomon after the
rav [R. Pinhas], the latter took counsel with R. Solomon himself:
"What do you think? Who am I [R. Pinhas asked in humility] to
visit him [R. David], since he is aged and I am but a young
man?" For the rav was about thirty-five years of age at the death
of the Besht. And R. Solomon answered: "You should not travel
there." So it was that he did not go. Consequently, it was awk-
ward for him now to come at his own initiative, for the Sabbath.

R. Pinhas continued, "I made a pretense of needing one hundred and fifty gold pieces for the redemption of captives. Having
done so, I traveled through Zevehl. And there people joined
me.[203] When I came to the holy community of Zasláw, I found
there (R. Leib) the mokhiah of Polonnoye[204] and the rav of
Frankfurt-am-Main who was then the head of the court of Lechovice (in Volhynia).[205] They had been brought there in regard to a
legal suit about stores which the prince had built, for which one
ruble had been promised them from each store. [The mokhiah's
presence] caused me much anguish. For the purpose in my coming was to lead the worship service, but I knew it was the custom
of the mokhiah to do so [no matter where he was]. The mokhiah
was old, and when he saw me in the bathhouse, he said at once:
"You shall pray with me." I said to him: "Where will you pray?"
And he answered: "In R. David's synagogue." "Good," I
answered, "then I will pray in the house of study [and not in the
synagogue]."

And so it was. He [R. Pinhas] led the services in the house of
study.

For some twenty-two years, no one knew the reason for his trip
to Zasláw. When he was old and close to death, he told us this
story and said that the worship [of that Shabbat] had been so sub-
lime it had, in truth, driven that nation [the Russians] out of the
land and has kept them out ever since. R. Raphael added: If,
after the prayer [of R. Pinhas], we still suffer so much from that
nation [the Russians], imagine what it would have been like without his prayer!"[206]

203. Friends of R. Pinhas lived in Zeiahel (Zevehl).
204. He died on the 21st of Tevet 1770 (Horodezky, *Hahasidut Vehahasidim*, 1:138).
205. R. Pinhas Horowitz became the rabbi of Frankfurt in 1772. (M. Horovitz, *Frankfur-
ter Rabbinen* [Frankfurt a.M.: Commisionsverlag der Jaeger'schen Buchhandlung, 1885],
pt. 4, p. 96.)
206. MS. Cincinnati, fols. 99–100; MS. Kitvey Kodesh, chap. 5, fol. 4a.

On the Passover before his death R. Pinhas said about Russia: "No one before me had ever stepped into such filth (*Shum adam hat nit areinget-reiten batume zu*). For had anyone trudged in filth such as this, he would have drowned. Would that I might live but two more years." R. Pinhas died in 1790 (1791?). His disciple, R. Raphael, explained: "Had he lived two more years, he would have destroyed that nation [the Russians], as well as the Kaiser and France."[207]

In 1792, the second division of Poland took place.[208]

207. MS. Cincinnati, fol. 73b.
208. In July 1792, Russian troops attacked Ostróg and the inhabitants were saved "by a miracle" (*Mazkeret Lagedoley 'Ostroha*, p. 25).

Two

Rabbi Gershon Kutover: His Life and
Immigration to the Land of Israel

To illuminate the figure of R. Abraham Gershon Kutover, brother-in-law of the Baal Shem Tov, would contribute significantly to the understanding of early Hasidism and to the history of the Besht himself. In the few published studies about R. Gershon biographical material is sparse.[1] Over the past years I have been fortunate to discover several manuscripts which shed new light on the activities of the Besht and his circle and have helped to clarify certain facts and dates connected with the lives of the founders of the Hasidic movement. Some of these documents bear on R. Gershon Kutover. The present study is based primarily on an analysis of the following letters written by R. Gershon: (a) A fragment of his first letter from Jerusalem; (b) his letter of recommendation concerning R. Hayim Yeruham and R. Meir de Segura; (c) a manuscript version of his well-known letter to the Besht of 5507 [1747/8],[2]

1. S. Dubnow, "The First Hasidim in the Land of Israel" (Hebrew), *Pardes* 2 (1984):201–14; S. A. Horodezky, *Oley Tzion* (Tel Aviv: Gazit, 1947), pp. 136–41; Y. Halperin, *The First Immigration of Hasidim to the Land of Israel* (Hebrew) (Jerusalem and Tel Aviv: Schocken, 1947), pp. 11–16. [Since Heschel's study, due in some measure to his pointing to the *Pinkas* Constantinople manuscript (JTS MS. 4008) as a historical source, further research has appeared, particularly by Y. Barnai. See A. Yaari, *Emissaries of the Land of Israel* (Hebrew) (Jerusalem: Mosad Harav Kook, 1951); G. Scholem, "Two Letters from the Land of Israel" (Hebrew), *Tarbiz* 25 (1956): 429–40; A. Yaari, "Notes to G. Scholem's 'Two Letters from the Land of Israel'" (Hebrew), *Tarbiz* 26 (1956):109–12; D. Brilling, "Die Tätigkeit des Jerusalemer Sandboten Petachja b. Jehuda Wahl Katzenellenbogen in Westeuropa (1735–1750)," *Festschrift Dr. I. E. Lichtigfeld* (Frankfurt a.M., 1964); D. Brilling, "On Emissaries from Palestine in Germany" (Hebrew), *Sura* 4 (1964); Y. Barnai, "Pekidei Erez Israel Be-Kushta," *Encyclopedia Judaica*, 1974 Yearbook. pp. 249–50; Y. Barnai, "The Jewish Community in Jerusalem in the Middle of the Eighteenth Century" (Hebrew), *Shalem* 2 (1976):193–240; Y. Barnai, "On the Immigration of R. Abraham Gershon of Kutov to the Land of Israel" (Hebrew), *Zion* 42 (1977):110–19; Ch. Katz-Shteiman, "Concerning Y. Barnai's Notes on the Immigration of Abraham Gershon of Kutov to the Land of Israel" (Hebrew), *Zion* 42 (1977):306–10; A. Rubenstein, "Stories of Self-Disclosure in *Shivhey Habesht*" (Hebrew), *Aley Sefer* 6–7 (1979):157–86; *Hasidic Letters from Eretz-Israel* (Hebrew), ed. Y. Barnai (Jerusalem, 1980); Y. Granatsztajn, *The Disciples of the Baal Shem Tov in the Land of Israel* (Hebrew) (Tel Aviv, 1982), pp. 19–70. This work, while using much material from Heschel's study, fails to cite it.]
2. [Throughout this essay, except here, Heschel dates the Hebron Letter 5508 (1747/8). See e.g., below, n. 132, and Appendix, document 1. This suggests that "5507" is a misprint. (See Barnai, "On the Immigration of R. Gershon to Israel," 42:113, n. 17.]

which I have called the "Hebron Letter"; this manuscript, which was supplied me by the late Rebbe of Kobryn,[3] is far superior to the text of the published version of the letter; (d) a letter to R. Tzvi, the scribe of the Baal Shem Tov; (e) and a letter from Jerusalem dated 5517 (1756). Of these, only letters (c) and (e) had been known previously. In addition to other manuscripts now in the YIVO Hasidic Archives in New York, I have made use of the Jewish Theological Seminary's valuable collection of correspondence relating to Jewish settlement of the Holy Land during the period concerning us. This collection, MS. 4008, I refer to as "the *Pinkas* of Constantinople" (*Pinkas Kushta*).

Kabbalist and Ascetic

R. Abraham Gershon apparently spent many years in the town of Kuty (Kutov); hence the name "R. Gershon Kutover," as he is still known. His brother, R. Aaron,[4] and possibly his father (R. Ephraim?), also lived in Kuty. It is said that he served for a while as judge (*dayan*) in the rabbinical court of the kabbalist, R. Moses, who was both rabbi of Kuty,[5] and, according to family tradition, his brother-in-law.[6]

A member of the "Society of Hasidim" in Kuty headed by R. Moses,[7] R. Gershon was given to extreme piety and asceticism,[8] sometimes not eating from the end of one Sabbath to the start of the next. According to one account, a Jew tried to emulate him, fasted "*hafsakot*" [i.e., with only brief interruptions in a long period of total abstention from food], and, as a result, died. R. Gershon attended his funeral. At the cemetery, he kicked the corpse and shouted before the whole gathering: "*Rasha*ᶜ, *rasha*ᶜ (wicked, wicked fellow)! Why did you kill yourself? Why did you try to imitate me and fast beyond your capacity?"[9]

R. Gershon was an expert kabbalist[10] who used Lurianic *kavanot* [a

3. [R. Barukh Yosef Zak; d. 1949.]
4. *Shivḥey Habesht*, p. 19a [Ben-Amos, #116].
5. An oral tradition; cf. *Letters of the Baal Shem Tov and His Disciples* (Hebrew), ed. R. David Frankel [Lwów: Frankel, 1923], p. 7. [For biographical information on R. Moses, see this volume, pp. 113–117, 148.]
6. *'Ohaley Shem* [of Samuel Noah Gottlieb (Pinsk: M. M. Glauberman, 1912)], p. 149.
7. *Shivḥey Habesht*, p. 19a [Ben-Amos, #54].
8. It is said that at one point he separated from his wife as an act of abstinence; see *Shivḥey Habesht*, p. 9d [Ben-Amos, #54]. Cf. *Devarim ʿArevim* [Munkacs: Ehrman, 1903], pt. 1, p. 5a.
9. R. Abraham of Slonim, *Yesod Haʿavodah* [Warsaw: Meir Y. Halter, 1892], pt. 3, p. 85.
10. R. Jonathan Eibeshütz refers to him as *harav hehasid hamefursam hamuflag batorah umekubal 'eloki* (the famed Hasid and rabbi, brilliant scholar of Torah, and divine kabbalist) in his *Luḥot ʿEdut* (Altona: Aaron Katz, 1755), p. 57a. The Ashkenazic Jews of Palestine described him in 1767, after his death, as *harav hamuvhak hamekubal 'eloki hasida kadisha* (the brilliant rabbi, divine kabbalist, and holy Hasid), see [A. Lunz, "Dovev Siftey

meditative technique] in prayer and followed kabbalistic ritual and custom.[11] On one occasion he said to the Baal Shem Tov: "So long as you are still able to say the words, 'Blessed art Thou,' of your own volition, know that you have yet to arrive at the true intent (*kavanah*) of worship. For one must be so stripped of selfhood that he has neither the awareness nor the power to pray a single word."[12]

The extent of R. Gershon's renown in his own generation as a distinguished kabbalist may be perceived from the fact that R. Jonathan Eybeschütz, in citing the letter of commendation for R. Hayyim Yeruham Vilna, signed by R. Gershon, describes the latter as "the rabbi, famed for piety, expert in Torah, and a divine kabbalist."[13]

R. Gershon himself related how he perceived that harsh heavenly judgments (*dinim*) were settling upon the ship on which he was journeying to the Land of Israel. To revoke them he sought to immerse himself in water. When the ship stopped at an island, all the passengers disembarked and went out for a walk. R. Gershon, however, took off his clothes, left them aboard ship, and dove into the sea. While he was immersing himself in the water, the ship began moving. When R. Gershon came out of the water and saw the ship was sailing off, he thought to himself: "What shall I do now? If I climb ashore I shall not be able to utter any words of holiness, as I am naked; furthermore, I shall surely find nothing to eat or drink." He decided to pursue the ship. (He was confident in his ability to swim well for he had once seen a Jew drowning in the Dniester and had dived in and swum about half a parasang to save him.) So he did it. R. Gershon began swimming and caught up with the ship, but its sides were high and coated with pitch and there was nothing for him to grasp. Though he shouted for help, his voice was not heard over the noise of the ship, which once again pulled away. He swam as hard as he could until he began sinking, bobbing up and

---

Yesheynim," 2 (1887)]. *Yerushalayim*, pt. 2, p. 157; *Birkat Ha'aretz* [ed. Barukh Hakohen (Jerusalem: Frumkin, 1904)], p. 67c.

11. *Shivhey Habesht*, p. 8b [Ben-Amos, #46]. At R. Gershon's request, the Baal Shem Tov wrote down for him "novellae and mysteries"; see *Ben Porat Yosef* [Korzec, 1781], end. It is told in *Shivhey Habesht*, p. 4a [Ben-Amos, #15] that it was his custom to recite *kiddush* "over twelve [Sabbath] loaves of *halah*" [a kabbalistic custom; see A. Wertheim, *Halakhot Vehalikhot Bahasidut* (Jerusalem: Mosad Harav Kook, 1961), pp. 150–51].

12. R. Israel of Kozienice (Koznitz), *'Avodat Yisra'el* [Jozefów, 1842], *parshat metzora'*. See also the *Heykhal Haberakhah* [of Isaac Safrin (Lwów, 1869; rpt. Brooklyn, N.Y.: Joseph Weiss, 196?)] to Deut. 22:6: "As R. Gershon said . . . to his brother-in-law, the Baal Shem Tov, even before the former had accepted the latter's eminence: 'So long as one's worship remains swathed in language, and he is aware of sound and thought, one has still not reached the *kavanah* (the true mystical intention) of prayer.'" Cf. the same work to Deut. 28:38: "As long as one remains aware of oneself, one has not reached the true intention of prayer." "Cf. the *Notzer Hesed* [of Isaac Safrin (Lwów, 1856)], p. 29.

13. *Luhot 'Edut*, p. 57. [Cf. Isaac Safrin, *Notzer Hesed*; see above n. 10, below p. 73, and Appendix to this chapter, document 2.]

down, unable to utter a word—even his final confession. Thought R. Gershon: "Not only am I going to drown but I shall also lose my share in the world to come" (for he was virtually a suicide). Suddenly an Ishmaelite [Turk] appeared on deck. When he saw R. Gershon he lowered a small boat, pulled R. Gershon into it, and brought him back to the ship. R. Gershon lay astern for two hours, vomiting because of all the water he had swallowed. When he got up, he put on his clothes and wanted to reward the Ishmaelite for having saved him. But he was nowhere to be found. R. Gershon then said: Surely he was none other than "that Arab" (i.e., Elijah the Prophet [who often comes disguised as an itinerant Arab merchant]).[14]

It is told that R. Gershon once spent the Sabbath in the town of Hanipol. Upon his return, he said to the Baal Shem Tov: "I experienced a great light there—the light of R. Samson who lived in that city before 1648."[15] R. Pinhas of Korzec considered R. Gershon "a miracle worker" (*ba'al mofet*).[16]

His Relationship with the Besht

For reasons unknown to us, R. Gershon left the town of Kuty and settled in Brody.[17] Around the same time, his father died and his divorced sister, Hannah, became the wife of R. Israel Baal Shem Tov. As is well-known, the Baal Shem Tov had kept his true ways secret at first and had assumed the guise of one who was uneducated. To R. Gershon— the talmudist, kabbalist, and man of spiritual refinement—the Baal Shem appeared to be utterly worthless. The book, *Shivhey Habesht* (In praise

14. [See *BT* Berakhot 6b. Heschel's practice, repeated often in this essay, is to closely paraphrase the original passage, using quotation marks only for exact quotations.] *Shivhey Habesht*, pp. 9c–d [Ben-Amos, #53]. The author of *Shivhey Habesht* heard this story from Gedaliah (of Linitz), who had heard it from "the rabbi and Hasid, our teacher, Tzvi of Kamenets." R. Tzvi had heard it from R. Gershon. The procedure of "sweetening" instances of rigorous judgment by means of ritual immersion in water was taught by the Baal Shem Tov, as is evident from the section of *kavanot* to be recited in a ritual bath found in the *Sefer Keter Shem Tov* [(Brooklyn, N.Y.: Kehot, 1972), pp. 4–5, #2. See *Sefer Ba'al Shem Tov* of Simon Menahem Mendel of Gowarczów (Lodz, 1938), pt. 2, *parshat yitro*, #12], and cf. *Degel Mahane 'Efrayim*. [See also Joshua Mondshein, *Shivhey Ha-Baal Shem Tov* (Jerusalem: Hanahal, 1982), pp. 163–64.]

15. *Shivhey Habesht*, p. 17c [Ben-Amos, #102]. The town should be Ostropol. R. Samson of Ostropol is revered among the tzaddikim. His marvelous and trenchant remarks on the Kabbalah are quoted in many books; he himself wrote the commentary *Dan Yadin* to the *Sefer Karnayim*. "He was killed during the disturbances of 1648 while in his synagogue still wearing his prayer shawl and phylacteries"; see R. Hayim Joseph David Azulai, *Shem Hagedolim*, personalities, letter *shin*, #180.

16. See below, n. 203.

17. R. Gershon's residence in Brody, according to the traditional account, must have preceded his sister's marriage to the Baal Shem Tov; see the *Shivhey Habesht*, p. 2d [Ben-Amos, #8].

of the Baal Shem Tov), records the struggles that ensued, R. Gershon's
doubts and reservations, and how the relationship changed between him
and the Besht. The details need not be discussed here.[18] A measure of R.
Gershon's initial antipathy, at any rate, is reflected in the story of his
attempting to persuade his sister to divorce the Baal Shem Tov, even
though that bit of advice was not given lightly. R. Gershon considered
divorce to be "a very grave matter." He used to say, "The letters of [the
Hebrew word] *get* [writ of divorce, spelled *gimel tet*] never appear next to
each other in that order anywhere in the Torah . . . To divorce one's wife,
therefore, is an attempt to [do what is unnatural]." . . .[19] Heaven frus-
trated R. Gershon's counsel, however.

When his eyes were opened, R. Gershon began to regard his brother-
in-law as "a man in whom there was the spirit of God," whose capacities
to foretell the future knew no spatial bounds. He once told R. Jacob
Joseph of Polonnoye, who was visiting him in Brody, "Something just
happened to me which my brother-in-law, Israel, had predicted last year.
After services, I had been studying Mishnah, and [at the moment] was
concentrating on one particular section of the text. My brother-in-law
said to me then, 'Do you realize what you have just read?' And he
revealed the future by means of the text I had been studying."[20]

R. Gershon became deeply attached to his brother-in-law, receiving
"moral instruction" from him. After R. Gershon settled in the Land of
Israel, the Baal Shem Tov wrote him "new insights and mystical inter-
pretations." "Review the words of moral instruction which I have given,"
he asked him, "letting them come readily to mind always, meditating
over them and considering them carefully. You are bound to find various
kinds of 'sweetness' in each teaching, for what I have told you 'is no vain
matter.'"[21]

R. Gershon's faith in the Baal Shem Tov was firm and unquestioning.
He asked the latter to pray on his behalf and that of his household and to

18. This exceptionally long note appears in the Endnotes; see pp. 185–86.
19. ["To put together something which is intrinsically separate."] MS. Uman, p. 83a.
[Cf. Ben-Amos, #19.]
20. The author of the *Shivhey Habesht* heard this story from R. Jacob Joseph (*Shivhey
Habesht*, p. 24b [Ben-Amos, #151]). Cf. the remarks of R. Menahem Mendel of Lubavitch
in '*Or Hatorah*, pt. 1, p. 170a: "Thus do we learn what was written regarding the Baal Shem
Tov and his brother-in-law, R. Gershon of Kuty, to wit, that in learning this particular
mishnah, he (i.e., the Baal Shem Tov) forecast four events that were still in the future." The
story cited in the *Dover Shalom* [of Tzvi Michelson (Przemyśl, 1910)], p. 141, is only
acceptable if we change the locale from Kuty to Brody.
21. *Letters of the Baal Shem Tov and His Disciples*, p. 4. The Baal Shem Tov admonished
R. Gershon for not keeping his vow of abstinence (see *Shivhey Habesht*, p. 9d [Ben-Amos,
#54]) and also wrote quite severely to him after the latter dared to excommunicate the
Sephardic sage (p. 10a [Ben-Amos, #56]). That R. Gershon was volatile and easily angered
in his youth may be deduced from various references in the *Shivhey Habesht*, e.g. "He
struck the Baal Shem Tov," p. 9d [Ben-Amos, #54]), and "He excommunicated the man
Tiktiner," p. 19a [Ben-Amos, #116]).

send him an "amulet for general purposes." Subsequently, he spread among the scholars of the Land of Israel the account of the Baal Shem Tov's reputation and his wondrous deeds.[22] He described the Baal Shem Tov in the following terms:

> Mouth which utters profundities, contender for the hidden mysteries of the All-Merciful, for the treasured secrets of the saints . . . master of the recondite, of the excellent knowledge of the Most High, "light of Israel, pillar on the right, the strong hammer," pious and unusual man, the divine kabbalist.

In 1756/57 [about ten years later], he wrote even more passionately:

> My beloved friend, closer to me than a brother, remember your brother well and accept my affectionate words as a seal upon your arm, for love is strong as death, more wonderful than the love of women. And do not withhold from your brother who yearns with thirst to hear your pleasant words, . . . my beloved friend, most dear to my heart, the light of my eyes.[23]

R. Gershon's fondness for the Baal Shem was mutual. The latter addressed him in a letter as "My beloved brother-in-law, dear to me as soul and heart, I refer to the eminent rabbinical scholar, the pious one, renowned for his learning and fear of God." The Baal Shem Tov used to send him money from time to time,[24] and even delivered to his own disciples teachings in R. Gershon's name.[25]

---

22. *Birkat Ha'aretz*, #327.

23. Ibid., #327, 328. [Cf. Y. Barnai, *Hasidic Letters from Eretz-Israel* (Hebrew), Jerusalem.]

24. *Letters of the Baal Shem Tov and His Disciples*, p. 1d.

25. *Divrey Moshe* [of Moses of Dolina (Polonnoye, 1801)] to *parshat bo'*: "I heard my holy teacher, the divine Hasid the Baal Shem Tov, himself, warn others regarding the alacrity necessary for men of his type during prayer, if they are to escape from inappropriate thoughts (Heb.: *mahshavot zarot*, i.e., during prayer). And in the name of his brother-in-law, R. Gershon of Kuty, he quoted a fine parable regarding those who do not bother themselves with this matter and, indeed, are unable to determine if such inappropriate thoughts have entered into their minds during prayer or not, which is as follows: There was once a very dangerous road along which were the hiding places of thieves and highwaymen who would lie in wait for travelers—but it was the only path through the forest (and therefore could not be avoided). These criminals would come out of hiding upon seeing a traveler, and rob, pummel, beat, and wound him. Travelers, therefore, made it their business to run at top speed down this path, so as to get away before the robbers could emerge from their hiding places. Once, two fellows were traveling together, one dead drunk and one sober. When they reached the forest, the sober one ran as fast as he could, and escaped without injury. The drunkard, of course, walked slowly at his leisurely pace, as a result of which the murderers beat him severely, but because of his drunken stupor, he remained entirely oblivious. When the two met again, the first was amazed and asked the other how he avoided being killed after having received such terrible wounds, while the latter found the former's amazement even more perplexing—for as far as he was concerned, he had succeeded in traveling safely, until his friend showed him the wounds all over his own body, as well as his blood-stained garments. Nonetheless, his amazement continued unabated, for he could not remember a thing."

R. Gershon was not given to public discourses, neither as a lecturer nor a preacher. Perhaps for this reason he was not one of those who undertook to spread the way of the Baal Shem Tov among the people. He remained a recluse, a kabbalist who shunned fame and everything associated with it. In this respect, his position within the circle of the Baal Shem Tov was similar to that of R. Meir Margoliot, the rabbi of Ostróg and author of *Me'ir Netivim*, who likewise played no active part in the propagation of his master's teachings.

Among the "Scholars of the Kloiz"

When R. Gershon first settled in Brody, it was the most important Jewish community of Galicia in size, as well as in scholarship and wealth.[26] The city was the domain of the powerful Potocky family, whose nobles had granted the local residents a variety of exemptions and privileges. Under the protection of the Potockys, the economic life of the town flourished. It is said that the Potockys made a practice of stationing horsemen along the roads to persuade merchants, en route to sell their wares in Lwów, to journey instead to Brody. Although the story may be apocryphal, it is clear that any Jew trading under the protection of such eminent masters could travel anywhere in the land without fear of being robbed of his merchandise by other noblemen; the Potocky holdings were spread throughout the country, and their subjects could always turn for help to one of their lessees or representatives.[27] The Jews of Brody maintained commercial links with Breslau, Leipzig, and the cities of Romania and Turkey. Brody attracted visitors from distant lands; there is even evidence of some Turkish Jews having settled there.[28]

Brody achieved its position of leadership not only because of its wealthy and politically well-connected residents but also by virtue of its scholars, who were renowned throughout the Jewish world. "In those days, the city was the very perfection of beauty, filled with sages. From Brody hundreds of legal decisions emanated to all Israel. The local houses of study had the greatest scholars of the land, so that 'the earth was filled with knowledge.' It was 'a city in which righteousness lodges.'" According to R. Ezekiel Landau, author of *Noda᷄ Bihudah*, "it is impossible to relate [the full extent of] charitable activity in Brody. In my opinion the merit of the alms it gives to the poor alone would account for

26. In 1765, toward the end of Polish rule, there were 7,197 Jews in Brody, while there were only 6,195 in Lwów. Cf. M. Balaban, *Dzieje Żydów w Galiczji* (Lwów: Nakl. Ksieyarni Polskiej B. Poloniec Kiego, 1916), p. 94.

27. According to Abraham Braver, writing in *Hashiloah* 22 (1910):152.

28. N. M. Gelber, "*Pinkas* of the Brody Burial Society" (Hebrew), *Jahrbuch der Jüdisch Literarischen Gesellschaft* 13 (1920), #20–29, pp. 122–23.

its prosperity."[29] Many elderly rabbis settled in Brody after retiring from their posts elsewhere.

During this period, a house of study (*bet midrash*), which became one of the most important institutions for the learning of Torah in Polish Jewish history, was founded in Brody by one of the town's dignitaries, "the well-known and wealthy" R. Jacob Babad,[30] who was a merchant of silk, wax, and especially skins. In this study house, famed as the *kloiz* of Brody, were gathered "princes, distinguished rabbis, and scholars . . . the holy ones of the holy community of Brody," who had come there from numerous localities to give themselves to the pursuit of Torah day and night. Among them were leading halakhic authorities of the generation, as well as ascetics and kabbalistic scholars. Some were later to become rabbis of communities in many countries. Difficult halakhic questions were addressed to them from all corners of the Diaspora, for they enjoyed widespread fame.

Among the best-known scholars of the *kloiz* were "the excellent and pious rabbi," our master and teacher, R. Mordekhai Hasid (the Pious), whose death "left no one equal to him,"[31] the extraordinary kabbalist, R. Hayim Tzanzer,[32] R. Isaac Horowitz, son-in-law of R. Jacob Babad, the founder of the *kloiz*, who later became rabbi of Hamburg,[33] and the learned R. Ezekiel Landau, later rabbi of Prague, famed for his work, *Noda^c Bihudah*. Around 1713/14, the well-known scholar and pietist, R. Eleazar Rokeah was appointed rabbi of Brody. He remained there until 1735, when he accepted the rabbinate of Amsterdam.[34] He was succeeded in Brody by the learned R. Jacob Yukel Horowitz who had served previously as rabbi of Bolechów.[35] The maggid [preacher] of the town during that period was the famous orator, R. Ephraim.[36]

---

29. Landau, Ezekiel, *Derushey Hatzlah* [Warsaw: 1899], #4, p. 18. In 1731, R. Levi b. Solomon of Brody wrote in his *Bet Levi* (Żolkiew, 1732): "I dwell amid a holy people in a city marked by splendor and refinement, and filled with sages."

30. Regarding him, see below, n. 126.

31. He died 6 Av 1736; see Gelber, "*Pinkas*," #52. I have discussed him elsewhere. [We have no published work dealing with R. Mordecai by Heschel, but his files do reveal material about him as well as others. See now M. Piekarz, *The Beginnings of Hasidism* (Hebrew) (Jerusalem: Mosad Bialik, 1978), pp. 87–88, n. 66.]

32. This exceptionally long note appears in the Endnotes; see pp. 186–88.

33. Two of R. Jacob Babad's other sons-in-law were also "sages of the *kloiz*"—R. Naftali Hirtz and R. Hayim Landau, the chiefs of the rabbinical courts of Kowel and Podkamien, respectively. See this volume, pp. 160–65, for information on R. Isaac Horowitz's relationship with R. Isaac of Drohobycz.

34. [See Mondschein, p. 12. For other references to R. Eleazar of Amsterdam and his relationship to the early circle of the Baal Shem Tov, see pp. 74, 92–93.]

35. *Zikhronot R. Dov Mibolihov*, ed. M. Vishnitzer [Berlin: Klal Verlag, 1922], p. 43.

36. He died 18 Adar 1749; see Gelber, "*Pinkas*," #78. Prior to Brody, he had been maggid in Cracow and Rzeszow (Risha).

Hasidic tradition has it that R. Gershon was one of the "scholars of the *kloiz*." The tradition is plausible. The restored text of the "Hebron Letter" shows that he was close to R. Jacob Babad, founder of the *kloiz*.[37] His friendship with R. Ezekiel Landau, one of its most notable figures, may well have begun during R. Gershon's tenure in the *kloiz*.

At that time there were four rabbinical courts in Brody, each headed by its own presiding judge.[38] According to one source, R. Gershon was a presiding judge.[39] Such a position may not have paid well enough to sustain its occupant. It is related that even the rabbi of the city, R. Jacob Horowitz, earned only "approximately 2 (Rhenish) gulden a week."[40] R. Gershon, gifted with a pleasant voice,[41] also acted as the second cantor [*hazan sheni*] of the *kloiz*.[42] Throughout his time, R. Gershon was teaching and training disciples.[43]

The Scandal in Brody

A certain notorious event occurred in Brody, which created havoc among the scholars of the *kloiz* and shook public life in the city.[44] It

37. See below, n. 126.
38. [In the introduction to the responsa of R. Ezekiel Landau, his son, describing his father's role in Brody, tells us that] "there were, at that time, four separate groups of judges, each one serving a different week in the month, each with its own presiding judge ('*av bet din*), of whom all were distinguished for knowledge and wisdom, 'hating ill-gain and fearing the Lord'" (R. Yaakobke son of R. Ezekiel Landau, *Divrey Yedidut, Noda Bihuda*, pt. 2 [Prague, 1811]).
39. *Shivhey Habesht*, p. 2d [Ben-Amos, #8]. ["Our master, R. Gershon of Kuty (= Kutov), was head of a rabbinical court in the holy community of Brody . . . "] The first time the Baal Shem Tov visited in R. Gershon's house, two rabbinic courts were holding sessions before him. "He was presiding, examining the cases they were considering" (p. 3a [Ben-Amos, #8]).
The claim of Simhoni (cited in Horodezky, *Hahasidut Vehahasidim*, pt. 4, p. 135) that R. Gershon "was neither a distinguished scholar (*ga'on*), nor well-known (*mefursam*), nor a Brody rabbi" is unfounded.
40. *Mat'amey Yitzhak* (Piotrkow: Moses Elias and Eleazar Schonfeld, 1904) p. 13. Regarding rabbinic salaries in that period, see S. Assaf in *Reshumot* 2 (1922):278, and *Shivhey Habesht*, p. 10a.
41. See *Shivhey Habesht*, p. 10a [Ben-Amos, #55].
42. According to R. Abraham Benjamin Kluger (in '*Ohel Naftali* [Warsaw: Zeidman and Blemburg, 1910], p. 69), it was stated in the *pinkas* of the *kloiz* that "R. Abraham Gershon of Kuty became the leader of the weekday services in the Great *Kloiz* because of his pleasant voice." See Halperin, *The First Immigration of Hasidim to the Land of Israel*, p. 13, n. 15, quoting N. M. Gelber. Perhaps it was as "cantor" that R. Gershon went "to visit the well-to-do on holidays" (*Shivhey Habesht*, p. 24b [Ben-Amos, #151].)
43. According to *Shivhey Habesht*, p. 4a [Ben-Amos, #15], the Baal Shem Tov revealed himself first to one of R. Gershon's students who was spending the Sabbath with him and commanded him "to go to the group of great Hasidim [*kat hahasidim hagedolim*] in the city, and also to the rabbi of the community" and to tell of him. Apparently, this rabbi, before whom the Baal Shem Tov appeared, was R. Eleazar Rokeah.
44. *Noda Bihudah*, pt. 1 (Prague, 1775), *even ha'ezer*, # 72; '*Emunat Tzaddikim* (Brooklyn, n.d.), #33; Kamelhar, *Mofet Hador* (Piotrkow: Y. Kamelhar, 1934), pp. 6–7; Gelber, *Aus Zwei Jahrhunderten* [Vienna and Leipzig: Lowit, 1924], p. 18; [Gelber, "Pinkas," pp. 55–56;] and L. Levin in the *MGWJ* 70 (1926):77–78.

both accounted for R. Gershon's departure from Brody and demonstrates his position in the community. This is the tale:

Rumors began to spread in Brody concerning the promiscuity of a certain woman, a member of one of the wealthiest families in the town. Because her relatives, including her father-in-law, were influential and not above resorting to physical force, they succeeded at first in intimidating those who spread the story and in silencing them. Several years later, however, the woman's shameful behavior was exposed publicly.

The weeks immediately preceding Rosh Hashanah were a time for repentance. In Elul 1741 (?), several men appeared before the rabbinical courts to confess their sins and receive the penances of self-mortification or fasting prescribed by the rabbinical judges as being appropriate to the sins committed (*teshuvat mishkal ha'avonot*).[45] Each of these men confessed independently of the others. It was thus that the court learned that a number of people had been involved with this woman. After deliberations, the judges informed her father-in-law that night of the incriminating testimony. They had approached him in the most tactful manner, for he was known to be violent. Nevertheless, as soon as he heard of the

45. [*Teshuvat mishkal ha'avonot*.] The custom of public confession [i.e., before the court in our case] was uncommon among the Jews. At about the time of the incident in Brody, the practice was the subject of a responsum. The question had been asked: "If a man wished to repent and he is eager to confess his sin in public so as to shame himself, is he permitted to do so or not?" R. Meir Eisenstadt (d. 1744) rules "that it is forbidden to recount sins in detail. One should confess, rather, when one is alone. Even on one's deathbed, one should not recount one's sins in public; the confession should be made, instead, between the individual and his Creator. Only if the person does not know the appropriate penance for sin [*teshuvat mishkal ha'avonot*] is he permitted to consult a sage as to the proper penance . . . *However, of late, new-comers have arrived*, claiming that, on the contrary, one must publicly confess one's sins, and that this was never forbidden by law. *Such a practice is heretical!* [emphases A.J.H.] May the Lord lead me in the way of truth (*Panim Me'irot* [of Meir Eisenstadt (Sulzbach, 1733)], vol. 2, #178). See *BT* Yoma 86b; Maimonides, *Mishneh Torah*, "Laws of Repentance," 2:5.

Balaban (*Letoldot Hatenu'ah Hafrankit* [Tel Aviv: Dvir, 1935], pp. 71–72), who knew of a case of public confession in Brody in 1752, assumed that the introduction of the practice by the authorities of the Jewish community was in reponse to the Frankists who were notoriously lascivious [and the need to identify and isolate them]. "Those who recanted would tell of the sins committed by various Jewish women to the 'confessors.' As a result, their husbands or their mothers would abandon them and drive them from their homes. Thus not only did their marital life cease, but they were forbidden to set foot in their parents' homes. The regional council [*Va'ad*] of Lwów, which had ventured to condemn the activities of these straying women, suffered the most severe consequences, for the women who had been sentenced turned for help to the city's overlord, Count [Josef] Potocky, and he dispersed the council and inflicted severe penalties on its most prominent members." Balaban based this assertion on a manuscript in the Ossolinsky Library in Lwów. That the practice of public confession actually preceded the appearance of Frank is evident from the statement of R. Meir Eisenstadt quoted above.

[See p. 27 of the Hebrew edition. For information concerning the idea and practice of *teshuvat mishkal ha'avonot*, see A. Rubin, "The Concept of Repentance Among the Hasidey Ashkenaz," *Journal of Jewish Studies* 16 (1965), pp. 161–76. See also A. Rapoport-Albert, "Confession in the Circle of R. Nahman of Braslav," *Bulletin of the Institute of Jewish Studies* (London) 1 (1973):65–97.]

charges, he insisted that the judges disclose the witnesses' names to him
so that he could have them thoroughly beaten. The judges refused. The
man then threatened the entire community and, finally, managed, because of his considerable influence, to summon the witnesses before the
judges in a public hearing. The witnesses repeated their earlier state-
ments. When the woman's relatives saw that their threats were to no
avail, they came up with the scheme of bringing in judges from elsewhere
to accept fresh testimony and disqualify the first witnesses. The woman's
father-in-law and other of her relatives—"bullies, physically powerful,
who threaten mischief and carry it out"—went to the Gentile courts and
denounced the local *dayanim* and the first set of witnesses. The governor
of the town condemned both the judges and the witnesses and imposed
"horrendous punishments" upon them, financial as well as physical. He
issued a decree that anyone daring to speak ill of the woman would suffer
"an unbearably heavy penalty": either public lashing for insubordination
or a fine of 100 zloti.[46]

At this point, R. Ezekiel Landau entered the fray and composed a long
responsum in which he argued that the testimony of the original witnesses
was valid and that the woman was forbidden to her husband.[47] The
"scholars of the *kloiz*," enraged by this suppression of justice and the
brazenness of the rich, apparently supported R. Ezekiel. He, together
with R. Meir Margoliot, one of the most distinguished scholars of his
time, and R. Gershon,[48] volunteered to take up the fight for justice.
Gathering at the residence of the city rabbi, they publicly proclaimed
three times: "Know that this woman is wanton and forbidden to her
husband!" For this, R. Ezekiel, their spokesman, was made to pay the
fine which amounted to all his worldly possessions; R. Meir Margoliot,
who had not the wherewithal for the fine, was lashed for insubordination;
and R. Gershon, who likewise was unable to pay, took advantage of the

46. *'Emunat Tzaddikim*, #33.
47. [A woman who commits adultery is forbidden to her husband as well as her lover. See
BT Sota 27b.] *Noda' Bihudah*, pt. 1, *even ha'ezer* #72. This responsum was written in
Brody. He refers to it in the sermon for the Sabbath of Repentance in 1753, which he
delivered in Yampol: "It is almost *nine years* [emphasis AJH] since I answered that question
in a responsum I composed in Brody." See the note of the author's son in *Doresh Letziyon*,
#13 (Warsaw: Isaac Goldman, 1880), p. 119. R. Ezekiel Landau was there at the time, and
interrogated one witness himself ("and I asked the witness," *Noda' Bihudah*, p. 87d). The
author, whose son resided in Brody, was apparently apprehensive of involving the family so
that, in preparing his work for publication, he phrased the title thus: "A Question Directed
to Me by Ashkenazic Sages at the Border of a Foreign Land." His care in the whole matter is
reflected by his request to R. Gershon that the latter "write me and do not withhold any
further information; only see that it is delivered into my hands by a reliable man, and do not
permit strangers to get hold of it. There is nothing better [in matters such as these] than
discretion," as cited in the *Noda' Bihudah*, p. 88b; cf. n. 53.
48. [Composing the requisite of three for a rabbinical court.]

commotion to slip off and flee the city.[49] He headed for Miedzybórz, the residence of the Baal Shem Tov.

On his way to Miedzybórz, legend has it that a wondrous event befell R. Gershon, which, upon his arrival, the Baal Shem Tov explained: "Elijah, disguised as a Gentile, came to your aid." He also told him: "In Heaven it has been decided that the three who had sanctified the Lord's name in public will rise to eminence. R. Ezekiel will be appointed rabbi in Prague,[50] R. Meir will become rabbi in Lwów and Ostróg,[51] and R. Gershon will "preside over all appointments regarding holy matters" in the Land of Israel. And so it was.[52] According to another tradition, the rabbi of Brody, R. Jacob Yukel Horowitz, who joined the motion forbidding the woman to her husband, was dismissed from his post on this account by "ruffians" and was forced to leave Brody and settle elsewhere.[53] The departure of these scholars from Brody apparently took place in Heshvan or Kislev [late fall or early winter] of 1742.[54]

The woman's relatives again brought the matter before other rabbis; they, "the great luminaries," decided that she was indeed permitted to

49. Kamelhar, *Mofet Hador*, pp. 8–9. The details provided by Balaban (see n. 45) fit the description of the *Noda' Bihudah*. The material in Balaban deals with a similar event of 1752, but perhaps this is a typographical error, and should read 1742.
50. In *Mofet Hador*, pp. 8–9, it is told that R. Ezekiel Landau fled to Dubnów and stayed there for a time. In 1743/4, he was already serving as rabbi in Yampol (*Divrey Yedidut*, *Noda' Bihudah*, pt. 2). In the winter of that year, he visited Brody, and on the 9th of Adar, he wrote an approbation for the book *'Arugat Habosem*, signing it . . . "currently residing in Yampol." In the *Maggid Mishnah* on the *Mishnat Hasidim* (Zolkiew, 1745; I am quoting from the Lwów, 1878, edition), it is stated that R. Ezekiel "was accepted as head of the rabbinic court and rabbi in Yampol." The approbation is dated 11 Kislev 1744. According to a legendary account in *Devarim 'Arevim*, pt. 1, p. 6b, when R. Hayim Tzanzer and R. Ezekiel Landau met to excommunicate him, the Baal Shem Tov said, "I shall separate and scatter them in Israel" [Gen. 49:7], and R. Ezekiel was then rabbi in Yampol.
51. Our knowledge of R. Meir Margoliot in that period is scanty. I have only been able to learn that he signed an approbation for the *'Arugat Habosem* jointly with R. Ezekiel Landau on 9 Adar I 1745, as "the lowly Meir, residing in Horodenka."
52. *'Emunat Tzaddikim*, #33.
53. *'Ohel Naftali* [of Naftali Horowitz, (Lwów: Zeidman and Oisshnit, 1910)], #247. This family tradition is confirmed by several proofs: (a) the remark that the "*ga'on* and head of the rabbinic court" took part in R. Ezekiel's decision is noted in the *Noda' Bihudah*, p. 87b; (b) Friedberg, in *Toldot Mishpahat Horowitz* [Antwerp, 1928], #12, and Wurm both estimate that he left the Brody rabbinate in 1747; but on 6 Tevet 1742 we find him serving as rabbi in Gliniany (Glona), for on that date he issued an approbation for the book *Hukey Derekh* on the *'Even Ha'ezer* (Dyhernfurth, 1747). There, he is described as "formerly chief of the rabbinic court and principal of the yeshivah in Brody, currently chief of the rabbinic court and principal of the yeshivah in Gliniany"; and (c) Wurm, in *Z Dziejòw Zydostwa Brodskiego* (Brody: Nakladem Gminy Wyznaniowej Zydowskiej, 1935), p. 86, quotes an archival document that states, for some reason, that a certain rabbi was "expelled, and driven from the city" (*za swoy concept byl zaraz wygnany y wýswiecony z miasta*) and concludes, incorrectly, that this reference is to R. Nathan Netta. It is clear that this actually refers to R. Jacob Horowitz. Cf. also *Mat'amey Yitzḥak*, p. 13.
54. Cf. n. 53.

her husband. To invest this opinion with more authority, the family sent it
for approval to R. Hayyim Hakohen Rapoport, the rabbi of Lwów. He
composed a lengthy responsum which concluded with the following
words: "They have understood the matter and judged it well. They were
right in finding the woman innocent. . . . She is permitted to her
husband."[55] The family further sought the approval of R. Issachar Dov,
rabbi of Podhajce (Podheitz) and son of [R. Jacob Joshua Falk], the
author of *Peney Yehoshua*ᶜ. He concurred. In a responsum dated 24
Tishri 1743, he wrote: "The matter is as plain as can be, to the point
where extensive discussion is not appropriate. . . . For all aspects and
considerations [of the case] point toward . . . permitting this woman to
her husband."[56]

The controversy within the community and the dismissal of the rabbi
had caused a foul scandal. One document dated 12 Tammuz 1744,
complains: "Our eyes have witnessed the collapse of the rule of law in our
community, and no one is concerned to restore it."[57] The arrival of a new
rabbi, R. Nathan Neta son of R. Aryeh, formerly of Slutsk and Grodno,
was for some reason delayed. Since the rabbinical courts, located in
several places, were functioning during the interim without central authority, it was determined that they should conduct their sessions in the
house of R. Moses, son of R. Eleazar Rokeah, previously rabbi of
Zloczew and then a rabbinical judge in Brody, until the advent of the new
rabbi.

R. Gershon's Stay in Miedzybórz

R. Gershon may have intended not to settle in Miedzybórz, but
only to stay there for a while. His heart was set on the Land of Israel, the
land for which the ancients had yearned, the holiest of lands. Those in the
circle of the Baal Shem Tov, however, knew that the ascent to the Holy
Land was a matter not just of the heart's desire but also of the soul's
preparedness. The Land of Israel was not only a geographical location,
but a spiritual level as well, which could not be attained until one had shed
the polluting influence of one's own evil traits. Could this have been the

55. Rappaport, *Mayim Hayim* (Zhitomir: Shapiro, 1858), *even haᶜezer*, #9, p. 54b. In
this reponsum, the name of the city is absent. See, however, the following note.
56. R. Issachar Dov, rabbi of Podhajce (Podheitz), ibid., p. 108c, in a different responsum, specifically gives the name of the city as Brody. [See below, pp. 70–71, for the decision
of R. Isaac Bekhor David of Constantinople in this matter. R. Margoliot believes insufficient evidence was presented to sustain a conviction in his "To Remove Slander" (Hebrew), *Modia*ᶜ 7 (1938).]
57. [The passage is from the *Pinkas* of Brody, 12 Tammuz 1744, appointing R. Moses
Rokeah as judge and establishing the temporary headquarters of the rabbinical court in his
home. See Gelber, *History of the Jews of Brody*, p. 75, n. 116, citing *Reshumot*, 2:382.]

reason why R. Gershon delayed his immigration to the Land of Israel and chose to stay in the environs of the Baal Shem Tov for some three years?[58] The Baal Shem Tov had taught that there were seventy evil attributes in each individual and that "each [Gentile] nation [of which there were said to be seventy] has a [special] grasp of one.[59] When someone has corrected [all seventy of] his moral attributes, he need not fear any nation."

> Shmerl, a disciple of the Baal Shem Tov, said on one occasion: "Amalek is the evil attribute of anger." R. Gershon Kutover asked him: "How do you know this?" R. Shmerl replied: "It is written (Psalms 30:6) 'For his anger endureth but a moment.' The [letters of the Hebrew word] *"rega""* [moment] are the initials of the words [in the phrase (Num. 24:30)] 'Amalek was the first of the nations' (*reshit goyim 'amalek*)." When R. Shmerl wished to journey to the Land of Israel, he (the Baal Shem Tov? R. Gershon?) said to him: "What is the point of traveling this way to the Land of Israel? A person must first *be* a living analogy to "the *Land* of *Israel*" [*Eretz Yisrael*]. That is, out of one's own "earthiness" [*'artziyut*, from *eretz*, land or earth], one should become an "Israel."[60] That is to say, he should smash the evil within himself.[61]

It was the practice of Jewish moralists and preachers to direct their instruction chiefly at the masses. They would pour fire and brimstone upon the ignorant, simple folk as if they alone were to blame for having

58. Cf. above, n. 21.

59. It is remarked many times in the works of R. Jacob Isaac of Lublin in the name of the Baal Shem Tov, that the seven Gentile nations that resided in Palestine (before the conquest) correspond to the seven (evil) qualities (*midot*) in the *kelipot*; see his *Divrey 'Emet* [Zolkiew, 1828] to the *parashot* of *lekh lekhah* and *tetzaveh*. [The *kelipot*, literally "husks," represent the shards of the primordial vessels that burst in an ancient cataclysm within the godhead, and from which the sparks of holiness must be redeemed.] On the other hand, in the MS. HUC, "Writings of R. Pinhas Koretzer," p. 57a [= MS. Cincinnati ?], it is stated in the name of the Baal Shem Tov that "the sin of Amalek was that he interpreted all miracles in terms of natural history."

60. [*Mibehinat artziyut ye'aseh Yiśra'el.*]

61. This derives from a manuscript. However, R. Gedaliah of Linitz, in his *Teshu'ot Hen* to *parshat terumah* [Berdichev: Samuel Segal, 1816], wrote: "I have heard directly from the *Mokhiah* ("Admonisher") [R. Judah Lieb of Polonnoye], of blessed memory, in the name of the Baal Shem Tov, to the effect that the quality of forgetfulness is called Amalek." Cf. *BT* Nedarim 22b [where anger and forgetfulness are related]: "One who becomes angry forgets his learning." Generally, kabbalists found the roots of pride in the *kelipah* of Amalek, since the numerical value of the Hebrew name "*Amalek*," עֲמָלֵק, 240, is the equivalent of the numerical value of the Hebrew word for "haughty,"רם. In the book [of Samuel Lernowitz], *Kevod Hatorah* (Lwów, 1873), *parshat beshalah*, the Baal Shem Tov is cited as follows: "To destroy Amalek, the principal notion is to destroy the heavenly angel called the Haughty One (*Gas Ruah*)." According to the *Sihot Haran*, R. Nahman of Bratslav only succeeded entirely in uprooting the quality of anger from himself by traveling to the Land of Israel. [Cf. A. Green, *Tormented Master: A Life of Rabbi Nahman of Bratslav* (University, Ala.: Univ. of Alabama Press, 1978), chap. 2.]

driven God away and were holding back the redemption. The Baal Shem
Tov took the very opposite position. He argued: "What has been the sin
of these sheep?! If the mighty cedars were consumed by the flames, what
hope was there for the moss on the wall? The shepherds are guiltier than
the flock." He shifted the responsibility from the masses to the leadership—the elite, the rabbis and heads of the communities. The sole
purpose of his teaching was to purify man—especially the rare and select
few whom he had sensed to be "strong, devout, truthful, and incorrupt-
ible," and whom he elevated above the flock to be its faithful shepherds.
That R. Gershon held the same point of view is evident from one of his
homilies. He interpreted the verse in Isaiah (42:18), "O ye deaf, listen,
and O ye blind, look that ye may see," by posing the question: "If one is
deaf, how can one listen, and if one is blind, how can one see?"—and by
replying: "the deaf are the scholars . . . They should listen. The blind are
the masses, who see by looking up to the scholars. For if a matter is
worthy to the scholars, the simple man approves; but if not, etc."[62]

R. Gershon warmed himself at the glowing fire of the Baal Shem and
benefited from his wisdom and counsel. He testified that from Miedzybórz the Besht could observe what was happening in Jerusalem.[63] It is not
surprising, then, that R. Gershon, given to modesty in any case, recognized his own activities to be negligible in comparison with those of his
brother-in-law.

In the days when the Baal Shem Tov's fame was spreading and men of
eminence from many places were streaming to Miedzybórz to learn from
him, R. Yehiel, the rabbi of Kowel, sent

a certain man, both learned and wise, to scrutinize the Baal
Shem. On his way to Miedzybórz, the man fell ill; when he ar-

62. "In the name of our rabbi and teacher, R. Gershon Kitover [i.e., of Kutov] . . . and
the words of the sage are filled with grace," *Toldot Ya'akov Yosef* (Korzec: Abraham
Samson of Raszków and Abraham Dov of Khmelnik, 1780), pp. 198b and 187c.

[In] *Be'er Moshe* [Lwów, 1805], *parshat bereshit*, by R. Moses of Kozienice [we find a
fuller version of ". . . what was said in the name of the holy rav, our teacher and master,
Gershon of Kuty, may his memory be for a blessing. He explained the verse, 'O ye deaf,
listen, and O ye blind, look that ye may see.' Interpret 'O ye deaf' as 'O ye scholars.' (Since
the Hebrew consonants are identical, one can read *hehershim*, [= 'O ye deaf'] as *heharshim*
[= 'O ye scholars'], according to the rabbinic understanding of 2 Kings 2:16—'*veheharash
vehamasger*, the artisans and locksmiths,' see *Yalkut Shim'oni*.) The main thing is for the
scholars to turn their ears to 'hear' what they learn, that is, to pay attention to the words of
the Torah. Then everyone will follow their lead automatically, even the unlearned and
simple of the Children of Israel: they, too, will pay attention to the words of the Torah. And
this is what is meant: 'O ye deaf'—you scholars—'listen'—to the Torah. Then, of themselves, 'the blind'—the unlettered, simple people—'will see.' So far his holy words."]

According to the Baal Shem Tov, the repair (*tikun*) of a penitent is primarily accomplished by means of the leaders of a given generation (*Toldot Ya'akov Yosef*, p. 144a).

63. While he was living in Miedzybórz, he apparently heard the Baal Shem Tov's remarks
regarding the author of the *'Or Hahayim*, who died in Tammuz 1743. See below, n. 92.

rived, he took to bed at a local inn. The Baal Shem Tov sent
over his brother-in-law, R. Gershon. He sat with him and expounded words of Torah. Eventually, R. Gershon suggested that
they go together to the *bet midrash* for the afternoon service. As
soon as they were out of doors, the visitor suddenly recovered.
Mistaking his companion for the Baal Shem, he asked him, "Are
you the Besht?" Replied R. Gershon, "Ha! Ha! I, the master?
Would that my portion in the World to Come were equal to
that which our master gains just by smoking one pipeful of
tobacco'. . . !⁶⁴

Only a few of R. Gershon's own teachings have come down to us, but
his letters permit some insights into his character and interests. A manuscript in my possession has preserved a record of one of R. Gershon's
dreams. In that dream is a glimmer of the general outlook of this little-
known figure, as well as his attitude toward Miedzybórz, the center of the
movement.

From our master, the rav, R. Leib, of the community of Ladzien, grandson of the tzaddik, R. Gershon Kutover,⁶⁵ I heard this
story about his grandfather: Having decided to go to the Holy
Land, R. Gershon first visited his brother-in-law, the Besht.
When he arrived with his family, the Besht kept R. Gershon with
him—I believe it was for three years—and supported him. R.
Gershon and his entire household lived there at the Besht's expense. R. Gershon sat and studied until he was about to complete the entire Talmud. He invited the Besht and the *haverim*
(colleagues) to the meal celebrating his completion of the cycle of
study, and they promised to come. R. Gershon then proceeded to
study right through the night to [complete the last tractate and]
have the celebration on the next day. By morning, however, he
had no strength left. And after prayer, he thought: "Let me nap
a bit before I finish the last tractate." He lay on his bed and fell
asleep.

In his dream, he imagined that he had gone for a walk outside
the town of Miedzybórz, and lost his way. He wandered through
forests and over hills, unable to find the road back to the town.
He was especially anxious because he had invited the Besht and
his colleagues to the festive meal, and now he was not going to
be home in time to receive them. The thought tormented him for
what seemed to be three days during which he did not meet
another human being. When a man eventually came into view, he

64. *Shivhey Habesht*, p. 14c [Ben-Amos, #80].
65. According to Hasidic tradition, R. Leib of Ladzien was the son of R. Aaron, the son
of Gershon, and died in 1793; see Levi Grossman, *Shem Ushʾerit* [Tel Aviv, 1943], p. 58. It is
said that he was preacher in Ladzien.

was greatly relieved. He inquired after his destination and was told, "I am from Brody, which I left three days ago and have not been able to find again. I have been wandering about until I saw you." "Who are you?" R. Gerson asked.[66] "I am a *behelfer* for a rich man in Brody," he replied. That is to say, his work consisted of accompanying the wealthy man's sons to school and also tutoring them. Now R. Gershon told his companion of his own misfortune and his worry, how the Besht would be at the celebration and find his host gone. The man, in turn, related his own anxiety concerning the children who were neglected for three days and his employer's grievance against him which would inevitably result from this.

As they were going, they saw a large and beautiful castle. Drawing nearer, they heard the sound of the study of Torah. R. Gershon listened to the lesson in progress and was very pleased. They entered and saw the *rosh yeshivah* [the dean of the academy] studying with his pupils. When the class was finished, he and his companion approached the rosh yeshivah and asked him to show them the way back to the towns of Miedzybórz and Brody, for R. Gershon was upset at having to miss the celebration at his home, while his companion likewise told of his own worry. The rosh yeshivah said to them: "I think you dreamt up those towns, Miedzybórz and Brody. For there is no other world but this one!" And though R. Gershon protested, "but I know that I left Miedzybórz," it was to no avail. The rosh yeshivah insisted: "You must be dreaming that." They did not accept the rosh yeshivah's invitation to remain. When R. Gershon implored him for help, he suggested that they should go on to the neighboring yeshivah, as the people there might know the way back. R. Gershon and his companion went to that yeshivah and saw that the building was even grander than the first. They entered and heard a lesson which was superior to that taught at the first yeshivah. R. Gershon was exceedingly pleased. As they had done before, they approached the rosh yeshivah after the lesson, but they received precisely the same response as from the first one, namely, that there is no other world but this one! The head of the second yeshivah likewise invited them to remain, and R. Gershon's companion agreed. But R. Gershon implored the rosh yeshivah to show him the way back, explaining his torments. In vain. The rosh yeshivah could only say: "Go to the third yeshivah; there you might find what you are seeking."

R. Gershon and his companion went on to the third yeshivah, an overwhelmingly beautiful building, both massive and magnificent. They entered it. Once again the third rosh yeshivah in-

66. [While R. Gershon is addressed in the formal second-person plural, he himself uses the familiar singular.]

vited them to remain, but R. Gershon refused. (At this point his companion returned to the second yeshivah; he had merely been accompanying R. Gershon to the third.) R. Gershon said to the rosh yeshivah: "How can I bear not to be present at the festive meal when the Besht arrives?" As soon as R. Gershon mentioned the name of the Besht in that world, the head of the academy and all its members shook in awe. The rosh yeshivah repeated his invitation to R. Gershon to remain, and R. Gershon repeated his refusal, mentioning the Besht for a second time. Once again they trembled. At last, the rosh yeshivah was forced to ask that a map of all the worlds be brought before him. After studying the map, he said to R. Gershon: "True, there is a tiny and most corrupt world in which a town called Miedzybórz is located. If you follow my advice, however, you would remain here with us." R. Gershon refused. Then the rosh yeshivah instructed two of his pupils to take R. Gershon to his town. They opened a door and cast him through it. R. Gershon awakened and found himself lying in his bed.

The entire episode had taken approximately half an hour.

Just then the Besht and all the colleagues arrived for the festive meal. The Besht was silent. He immediately sent to Brody to inquire after the man [who had figured in the dream]. The report was that he had just died in his sleep. The Besht observed that the world was in need of that man, for he was apparently the soul of Joseph the Righteous, but he agreed to be there."[67]

During the period of R. Gershon's stay, the Besht entreated his brother-in-law to teach R. Tzvi, the Besht's only son, and R. Gershon agreed.[68] The Besht provided for him and his family, and R. Gershon immersed himself in study. We know that he had six sons and two daughters, one married[69] and the other a small girl.[70] Apparently, his two

---

67. MS. Uman. [Though no quotation marks confirm the story as being an exact copy of the MS, from other printed texts which Heschel refers to (e.g., *Shivḥey Habesht*) and which we can compare with the original, we know it was his custom to retell the original in a more felicitous style, using the source wherever possible though not necessarily quoting. One cannot so easily compare his version of this story with the MS. It would seem that here, too, despite the lack of quotation marks, this adaptation is close to the original.]

68. Years later, R. Abraham Gershon wrote to R. Tzvi, "You know how hard I labored. I came to Miedzybórz for your sake only and thank God I brought you along the way of Torah" (*Birkat Haʾaretz*, #326).

R. Gershon is also named as one of the Baal Shem Tov's circle in R. Meir b. Yavitz's responsum #27, in his collection of responsa entitled *Mayim Ḥayim* [Zhitomir: Hanina Lipa and Joshua Heschel Shapiro, 1857] which I think was written in 1744/5 or 1745/6. Dinur, in his "Origins of Hasidism" (Hebrew), *Zion* 10 (1945):174, fixes its composition at ca. 1744. I have discussed this elsewhere. [Again, if Heschel is referring to material he had already prepared, he never published it. See the Introduction, p. xl.]

69. His son-in-law's given name was R. Aaron (see *Birkat Haʾaretz*, #326), and his surname, according to the manuscript, Fradman (פראדמאן).

70. Her name was apparently Esther.

eldest sons[71] and his married daughter stayed in Europe; the younger ones[72] went with him to Palestine. Before leaving, R. Gershon secured the future marriage of his youngest daughter to R. Ephraim, the Besht's grandson, the future author of *Degel Mahaney 'Efrayim*. He seems to have promised to return to the Diaspora to give her in marriage.[73]

Sometime before Rosh Hashanah (1746),[74] R. Gershon set out from Miedzybórz. According to the story just quoted, he had stayed in Miedzybórz "about three years." If we are correct in assuming, therefore, that he had fled from Brody in Heshvan or Kislev of 1742 (5503), we must set the date of the beginning of his journey toward Palestine as the winter of 1745/6 (5506).

To the Holy Land

We have several documents which concern the period of R. Gershon's residence in Palestine from 1747 to 1757. According to his

71. R. Moses, the elder, and R. Isaac.

72. R. Yakir [Scholem, "Two Letters," p. 430, thinks the correct pronunciation of the name is "Yakar" and not "Yakir," but the name appears in contemporary documents as both "Yakir" and "Yakar." See Barnai, "Jewish community in Jerusalem," p. 219, n. 23. R. Yakir was the son-in-law of R. Moses of Ostróg.], R. Hayim Aaron, R. Ephraim Fishel, and R. Judah Leib.

73. [The mother of R. Ephraim was Edel, the daughter of the Baal Shem Tov.] Regarding the year of R. Ephraim's birth, there are four theories:

a. According to S. A. Horodezky, in *Hahasidut Vehahasidim*, pt. 3, p. 7, and R. Ezekiel Gutmann, R. Ephraim of Sudilkov was born "around 1747/8."

b. According to Isaac Avigri, writing in *Metzudah* 3–4 (1945):230, he was born "around 1743/4."

c. According to Kahana, *Sefer Hahasidut*, p. 305, he was born in about 1741/2.

d. According to Dubnow, *History of Hasidism* (Hebrew) (Tel Aviv: Dvir, 1930), p. 205, he was born close to 1736/7, because in 1750 the Baal Shem Tov refers to him in his well-known epistle [published by Jacob Joseph at the end of his *Ben Porat Yosef* (Korzec, 1781)] as "my grandson, the excellent young man, Ephraim, of extraordinary intellectual powers." [Cf. Rubenstein, "A Letter of the Baal Shem Tov to R. Gershon of Kutov" (Hebrew), *Sinai* 67 (1970):125–26.]

We can now confirm the date of this letter as 1750, thanks to the manuscript published by R. David Frankel in *Letters of the Baal Shem Tov*, p. 5. Avigri's hypothesis is thus refuted. The 1736/7 date is further supported by the addendum to the letter published by Frankel, from which we learn that, by 1750, R. Ephraim was already old enough to marry. His father, R. Yehiel [the son-in-law of the Baal Shem Tov], wrote to R. Gershon, "I have written already several times regarding my son Ephraim the groom, to learn if you plan to go abroad (i.e., to leave Palestine, to return to Poland), in which case, I shall await your arrival. If you do not plan to come, God forbid, then I can wait no longer. ["... tell me, and if not, tell me;] that I may turn to the right hand [or to the left," Gen. 24:49]. I only ask you to release me from the accords if you do not plan to come" (*Letters of the Baal Shem Tov*, p. 5).

74. The Baal Shem Tov informs him that "on the day of the New Year of the year 5507 (= September 1746) I engaged in an ascent of the soul, as you know I do." See *Letters of the Baal Shem Tov*, #1. [Cf. L. Jacobs, *Jewish Mystical Testimonies* (New York, 1977), pp. 148–50 for an English translation and exposition of the letter.]

own testimony of the 28 Iyar 1757, he had lived in Hebron for six years, "and it is now four years since I established residence in Jerusalem." By this account, he could not have arrived in Palestine later than 28 Iyar 1747.[75]

What was the purpose of R. Gershon's move to Palestine? The view that he went there to propagate the teachings of the Baal Shem Tov is incorrect.[76] In fact, R. Gershon was merely one in a continuous movement from the Diaspora of Hasidim and kabbalists of those generations who settled in the Holy Land.[77] Among them were many of the Baal Shem Tov's circle: R. Nahman of Horodenka and his son, who went before 1740/41,[78] R. Joseph "the truthful" of Pistýn, the father of R. Isaac of Drohobycz,[79] and both the father and the son of R. Jacob Joseph of Polonnoye.[80] One could add many others to the list.[81]

The longing for the Holy Land was not, however, confined to the circle of the Baal Shem Tov.[82] Some time before 1744/45, R. Benjamin Zev, son of R. David of Zamość (or his father?), had immigrated to Palestine. He described his feelings in the following words: "When I was there, it was almost as if I had acquired an additional soul in comparison to how I had been in the Diaspora, for the Land of Israel has the good quality of rendering its inhabitants more wise, more pious, and more righteous. Furthermore I observed that the people of the Land of Israel are truthful and compassionate. They are distinguished in rank, each of them as a

75. *Birkat Haʾaretz*, #332.

76. S. A. Horodezky, *ʿOley Tziyon*, p. 138, thinks that "the Baal Shem Tov wanted his brother-in-law to be his representative in Palestine and to spread his teachings there." Yitzhak Werfel (Raphael), in *Hasidism and the Land of Israel* (Hebrew) [Jerusalem: Hotzaʾat Hasefarim Haʾeretz Yisraʾelit, 1940], p. 15, writes, "Because the Baal Shem Tov himself could not go to Palestine, a goal of his life, he hastened to send his brother-in-law and disciple."

77. In 1745/6, "the emissary of Sidon, Kalonymous Kalman, called by the Sephardim Solomon Ashkenazi, son of the well-known Hasid, our teacher, R. Aaron, of blessed memory [who was author of *Markevet Mishnah* to the *Mishneh Torah* of Maimonides], and the grandson of the well-known R. Moses Harah of Zamość, published the *Seʾah Solet* of R. Raphael of Norcia in Zolkiew. [Cf. Tzvi Horowitz, *On the History of the Polish Jewish Communities* (Hebrew) (Jerusalem: Mosad Harav Kook, 1978), pp. 287–88.]

[The term "Hasidim" was used before and even during the time of the Baal Shem Tov to describe pietists who were not necessarily asociated with the movement he established. For example, the "group of great Hasidim in Brody," R. Judah the "Hasid," or the "Hasid" R. Elijah of Vilna, the most prominent opponent of Beshtian Hasidism.]

78. See below, Addendum: "R. Gershon's First Journey to the Holy Land," pp. 90–97.

79. I shall discuss him elsewhere. [See below, pp. 152–81.]

80. Cf. *Birkat Haʾaretz*, p. 63d.

81. This exceptionally long note appears in the Endnotes; see p. 188.

82. There were some who felt, in the wake of the Sabbatean unrest, "that they should not wreak havoc . . . by pressing for the final redemption . . . for indeed, the audacious [who sought to enter the Promised Land prematurely, in the days of the Bible] fell by the hand of Amalek" (*Ruah David Venishmat David* (Salonica: Betzalel Ashkenazi, 1747), p. 58b).

holy angel descending from Heaven, and their customs are like the customs of the ancients."[83]

R. Simhah b. Joshua, the maggid of Zalozce,[84] who was an admirer of R. Nahman of Kosów but not, apparently, a Hasid of the Baal Shem Tov,

83. *Shaʿarey Binyamin* [Zolkiew: Segal, Mann, and Segal, 1752], Introduction. From the style, it seems that the author was not born in Palestine. After the fire in Nicopolis, he traveled around in the name of that community to collect funds to rebuild the synagogue of R. Joseph Caro ("in which God had appeared to him") which had been destroyed. In the introduction to his book, he describes his efforts *to introduce the use of spoken Hebrew* [emphasis A.J.H.] into his congregation:

"When I lived there, I noticed with much consternation that they spoke only Gentile languages (*leshon ʿaga veʾaga*; cf. *BT* Sanhedrin 101b and the comment of Rashi there, s.v.),whereas the holy tongue was almost forgotten. If such was the situation with immigrants to Palestine, then how much the more so among the residents of the Diaspora! I myself saw this scandalous sickness spread to all branches of the Jewish people—to the point at which they would tell stories learned from the Gentiles, and say, with no shame, 'The Arabs certainly had a point when they said such and such . . .'; just as the Jews living in Germany or Greece say, 'Those German or Greek Gentiles certainly had a good point in saying such and such.' Even in the West, one hears such things. All this causes me great pain. I cannot fathom why they prefer the parables of Gentile sages to the holy parables of King Solomon or to those of the Talmud or to those of the other holy sages—this is all an insult to the daughter of Jacob! My own soul,on the other hand, cleaves to the daughter of Jacob, and therefore it saddens me that the Jews have permitted themselves the sacrilege of forgetting the language of the daughter of Jacob—which must never happen, especially because the disuse of the holy language prolongs the dispersion (i.e., of the Jews; [*galut*]), as is proven by the fact that the main reason for which the Jews were redeemed from Egypt was that they did not change their language. 'And the young man did not hesitate to do the deed, for he desired the daughter of Jacob.' [The author continues to lift most of his language from Gen. 34, portraying himself as Shekhem son of Hamor who circumcised himself and tried to convince his people to circimcise themselves so that he would be allowed to marry Dinah, the daughter of Jacob.] So I spoke to the hearts of the residents of our little town, (saying) 'These men are our friends; let them settle in the land and move about in it, for the land is certainly large enough for them.' There is only one condition for these men to dwell among us and become a single nation and speak a common language with us—that we circumcise the foreskins of our mouths to speak the holy language, just as we are (genitally) circumcised. I came to the city confident (see Gen. 34:25), and day and night I persisted in collecting and writing down material from the holy tongue . . . parables . . . to restore its holiness as it was of old."

84. R. Simhah was born in 1710. He wrote several books of *musar* and *ʾaggadah* ("ethics" and "legend"). On 27 Iyar 1764, he and his wife left Zalozce for Palestine. Ten days later, they set sail from Galati on the Black Sea and arrived in Constantinople [after two months] on 27 Tammuz. In his party were to be found R. Nahman of Horodenka, R. Mendel of Przemyślany, R. Leib of Lintz, R. Friedel of Brody, R. David son of Mendel of Przemyśl, R. Wolf, R. Israel, and R. Joseph. They arrived in Akko on 12 Tishri 1764. R. Simhah went to Safed for the winter and stayed there about seven months, until Iyar [1765], after which he was obligated to return to Poland, where he became the preacher of Brailov; he died there on the eve of Passover, 1768. A description of his journey was published under the name *Ahavat Tziyon*. As has already been proven (in the article "The Book 'Ahavat Tziyon': The Nature and Author of its Forgery" (Hebrew) *Yerushalayim* 4 (1892):137–52), part of this account was copied word for word from the travelogue of the Karaite, R. Samuel b. David, who made his journey to Palestine in the years 1640/1 and 1641/2. It is presumed that R. Simha's son-in-law, Solomon of Dubnów, published the book "either in the author's lifetime or posthumously . . . and in order to increase the size and quality of the book to promote sales, he added some stories . . . derived from the book of the Karaite traveler." [See Piekarz, *Beginning of Hasidism*, pp. 90–93.]

gives ample expression to the mood of the "pietists" and their attitude toward the idea of settling Palestine. At the end of his book, *Netiʿa shel Simḥah* (Zolkiew, 1763), in a chapter entitled, "The Destiny of a Jew Is to Go up to the Holy Land," he wrote the following:

> I cannot begin to understand God-fearing men who have it within their power to journey to the Holy Land but [prefer] instead to pass their lives and eventually die in the fetid air of this desolate country. Their bodies are buried in the defiled dust of the Diaspora,[85] the place of the worm and the maggot. Those who are drawn to the corporeal vanities of life do not surprise me, for how could they understand the advantages of the Land of Israel while they say: "The Land of Israel is here, in the Diaspora, where we are and where nothing is lacking." I am amazed, however, at those of the God-fearing for whom the fleeting moment and bodily pleasure are secondary to eternal life and the joys of the soul. For even should they observe the commandments and engage in study and prayer throughout their lives outside the Land, they could not achieve the eminence and perfection to be gained by just one year in the Land of Israel. He who serves the king in his palace cannot be likened to the king's servant in distant islands, even though the Lord, blessed be He, reigns everywhere. (And it is even more appropriate for those who are childless to journey to the Land of Israel, since, as it says in [the Talmudic tractate of] Yevamot: "It is possible that residence outside the Land has caused [their childlessness].[86] Their distant wanderings outside their homeland will count as the travails[87] which they should otherwise undergo after death, as it is written in the *Zohar* to the sections of *Bereshit, Noah, Lekh (Lekhah), Vayeshev, Mishpatim,* and to the book of *Ruth.*"
>
> The reason they are held back, no doubt, is what is written in the talmudic tractate of Sukkah (53a), "a man's feet are responsible for him." That is to say, since Providence has decreed that he will die outside the Holy Land, he has no desire to set out on a journey to it. This argument, however, should be refuted. Is he not free to pray that God should change his destiny and allow him to join his holy ancestors who are in the Land of Israel? Another factor which prevents [people from journeying to the Holy Land] is that they are not aware of its advantages which

85. [See *BT* Shabbat 14b–15b.]

86. Cf. *BT* Yevamot 64a, and the comment of Rashi there regarding Abraham and Sarah: ". . . perhaps they were barren because of the sin of residing outside of Palestine." The Maharsha explains, "Because in the Diaspora, he was not worthy to father children, but the merit (i.e., the intrinsic merit) of the Land of Israel . . . helped him." Cf. also the remarks of R. Elijah Mizrahi to *parshat lekh lekhah.*

87. [Heb.: *gilgul meḥilot . . .* the burrowing of the dead underground on their way to the Holy Land for resurrection at the advent of the Messiah.]

persist even during its desolation, like those fools who claim that
its only distinction now is that the flesh [of the dead] is consumed
there without being eaten up by worms. But the heart of him
who consults the book *Hesed Le'avraham* (by R. Abraham
Azulai) will be ablaze with excitement to go to Palestine . . .

Miedzybórz and Constantinople

The Jewish community in Palestine had from time immemorial
depended on financial support from the Diaspora. Money for the poor of
the Holy Land was collected in almost every spot to which Jewry had
been dispersed. In the eighteenth century, the Jews of Constantinople
distinguished themselves by the assistance they offered. Their concern
for the needs of the Palestinian Jewish community in the Holy Land and
its consolidation was greater than that of any other community. When the
Sephardic *kolel*[88] stood on the brink of bankruptcy, the wealthy Jews of
Constantinople assumed financial responsibility for it and undertook "to
pay all debts outstanding to Gentiles incurred by the *kolel*s of the holy city
Jerusalem." They sent a special emissary "to restore the devastated altar
of God."[89] In times of trouble, Jews who had won special favor with the
Turkish authorities would plead before the sultan on behalf of their
brethren in the Holy Land, often succeeding in averting trouble. As a
result of their considerable influence on the fate of the Sephardic settlement in Palestine, the communal leaders of Constantinople became the
custodians, as well, of the internal affairs of that community in the Holy
Land. They appointed its officials as well as the heads of its rabbinic
academies (*yeshivot*). Even the money raised in Poland for the Jewish
community in Palestine was administered through "the officers for Jerusalem, Hebron, and Safed" in Constantinople.[90]

Despite the fact that Turkish Jewry of the period was in a state of
decline, the Jewish community of Constantinople still enjoyed a splendid
reputation among the Ashkenazim, the Jews of Central and Eastern
Europe. They treated the Sephardic rabbis with special admiration.
Those who went on pilgrimage from Europe to the Holy Land would stop
over in the Ottoman capital, receive financial aid from the wealthy, and

88. [See pp. 102–6.]
89. See Shohet, "The Jews of Jerusalem in the Eighteenth Century" (Hebrew), *Zion* 1
(1936):405. Regarding the help extended by the Jewish community of Constantinople to the
Jews of Palestine in 1730, see the end of *Birkat Ha'aretz*. [Cf. Y. Barnai, "Pekidei Erez
Israel Bekushta," *EJ* 1974 Yearbook, pp. 248–49; for other sources see above n. 1.]
90. A rich assortment of material relating to the help extended to the Jews of Palestine by
the Jews of Constantinople is to be found in JTS MS. 4008 [*Pinkas* Constantinople (Barnai
refers to it as *Pinkas Pekidey Kushta*); see above nn. 1 and 81]. Regarding the seventeenth
century, see Israel Halperin, "On The Relationship Between the Jewish Councils and
Communities of Poland and Palestinian Jewry" (Hebrew), *Zion* 1 (1936):82.

leave impressed by the life of the Sephardim, their dignity, and their scholarship. A kabbalist from Nikolsburg, writing in 1750, had this to say: "While on the Lord's journey toward the Holy Land, Heaven itself instructed me to stop here in this very great city, filled with men of scholarship and understanding, princes and leaders, who support the students of Torah. They showed me the quality of their graciousness and goodness in all manner of kindness and stand prepared to do even more."[91]

In the winter of 1746/47,[92] we find R. Gershon, the kabbalist, who had served as second cantor in the *kloiz* of the "sages of Brody," suddenly appearing in the metropolis of Constantinople as a communal figure, consulted by leaders of the Jewish community. Acquainted with the internal affairs of the city and well-versed in the relationship between its Jewish leaders and the sultan's court, he attended to the needs of the Jewish settlement in Palestine.

R. Gershon was a retiring person. When later offered the chief rabbinate of the Ashkenazi community in Palestine, he refused, saying: "Why should I suffer the pride?" and regarded the call as an act of Satan "who hoped to capture him in the snare of pride." Knowing that the dignitaries of Jerusalem were coming to his house to pay their respects, he deliberately absented himself and could not be found when they arrived. Observed R. Gershon, "Thank God, I fled from [unwelcome] honor." "All my life I have shunned honor," he said of himself.[93] All those who

91. R. Abraham Hayim Cohen, son of R. Samuel, the grandson of the author of the *Meʾirat ʿEnayim*, immigrated to Palestine in 1749/50 or even later. H.Y.D. Azulai, in his *Shem Hagedolim*, book section, letter *ʾaleph*, #142, recounts, "In his old age, he came to Hebron, where he died . . . and I saw he was composing a commentary to the entire Bible and living a most pious life, by virtue of which he might be called 'holy.'" His commentary to the book of Psalms, the *ʾEretz Hahayim*, was published in 1750 in Constantinople, as he stopped there on his way to Palestine (see Appendix, document # 5). On the title page of the Lwów 1904 reprint, it is noted that R. Israel, the maggid of Kozienice, was especially fond of this book and used to recite psalms from it. [According to Yaari, *Emissaries*, p. 583, R. A. Cohen came to Israel in 1746, and evidence of his activity can be traced as late as 1763. He likewise composed liturgical poetry (*piyutim*) for the festivals found in *Mayim Hayim*, published in 1756 by his son, R. Abraham Benjamin.]

The Hasidim who went to Palestine in 1777 were also well received by the wealthy Jews of Constantinople; see the 1778 letter of R. Israel of Polotsk in *Likutey ʾAmarim* [by Menahem Mendel of Vitebsk (Lwów: Shalom Zwerling, 1911), pt. 2, pp. 31a–33a], letter #27.

92. Because of the details within the letter [from Hebron; see above p. 44 and Appendix, document 1], we can fix the time of its composition in the winter of 1747/48, after the month of Kislev. It is also stated there that "it is about four years since you told me" of the death of R. Hayim ibn Atar. It is usually thought that R. Hayim died in Tammuz 1743 (see the *History of the Sages of Jerusalem* (Hebrew) [by A. Frumkin (Jerusalem: Solomon Press, 1928–30)], pt. 3, p. 12). In Elul, R. Gershon left Constantinople. According to Yaari, *Letters of the Land of Israel*, p. 286, a ship left Constantinople at the beginning of Elul (according to *ʾAhavat Tziyon*, on 18 Elul) and arrived at Jaffa on the eve of Rosh Hashanah. [See below note 132.]

93. *Birkat Haʾaretz*, #326.

followed the Baal Shem Tov were distinguished by the same quality. The teachings of the Baal Shem were not to be passed on with ostentation; what was done by his disciples was accomplished quietly, out of the public eye: their wonderful vision was borne in private. What, then, made the retiring R. Gershon, who had never sought a career of eminence, accept the burden of communal responsibility?

It is clear that R. Gershon became involved with this work and remained in Constantinople not to advance his own ends but for the benefit of others—either the Jewish settlement already in the Holy Land or those whose move there could be facilitated.[94] This fact, when taken together with the breadth of R. Gershon's activity, sheds new light on the circle of the Baal Shem Tov's followers. Reading between the lines, it becomes clear that the Baal Shem Tov himself was in communication with important public figures of his time and that the links between Miedzybórz and Brody stretched as far as Constantinople and Jerusalem. Members of the Baal Shem Tov's circle were neither cut off from the world of practical affairs, nor was Miedzybórz some remote corner of the world; rather, it was the center of far-reaching activities.

How did R. Gershon find a place in the circle of Constantinople's dignitaries? Who prepared the way for him?

A major role would seem to have been played by his colleague from the *kloiz* in Brody, R. Ezekiel Landau. We know that R. Ezekiel, then rabbi of Yampoli, and R. Jacob Landau, the rabbi of Tarnopol, were chosen in 1749/50 to be "treasurers of the *kolel*s of the Four Lands, the lands of

---

94. Rosanes, *History of the Jews of Turkey* (Hebrew) [Sofia: Amichpat, 1937–38], pt. 5, p. 12, states that at that period there were no Ashkenazim in Jerusalem and that R. Gershon was "the first to attempt to settle there, but was unsuccessful because of the danger, indeed the impossibility, for Ashkenazim to make their home in Jerusalem." Therefore, he went to Constantinople, "to see if he could utilize the influence of Jews close to the government to obtain the necessary permission." Rosanes does not give a source, and I do not know whence he obtained this information. It is true that the situation of the Ashkenazim in Palestine was depressing, but there was an Ashkenazic community in Jerusalem, and in 1748 they wanted to accept R. Gershon as their "rabbi and leader [*nasi*], father and guardian [*patron*]." Also according to Gaon, *Oriental Jews in the Land of Israel* (Hebrew) [Jerusalem, 1938–48], pt. 1, p. 98, the community was "entirely Sephardic. In Jerusalem, there was a *minyan* of Ashkenazic Jews who existed clandestinely under the most arduous condition. The Moslems had claimed a large sum of money was owed them for years from the Ashkenazim, and every Ashkenazic Jew who wished to settle in Jerusalem had to do his part toward paying off this debt. For this reason, Ashkenazic immigrants were afraid to come to Jerusalem, or did so dressed like Sephardim to pass as members of that community. They did not open a synagogue of their own, lest it attract attention, and were thus obliged to be content with a small service organized in a Sephardic synagogue. On occasion, there were not enough Ashkenazim, and a Sephardic Jew was necessary to complete the quorum of ten (*minyan*)."

Halperin errs (in *The First Immigration of the Hasidim to the Land of Israel*, p. 15) when he says that R. Gershon was not "a public figure." [Cf. A. Yaari, *Emissaries*, pp. 520–34.]

Poland, in charge of the affairs of the Jewish settlement in Palestine."[95] It is possible that R. Ezekiel was already engaged in this work as early as 1746/47. In any case, by that time, he was already one of the most famous rabbinic authorities of the day, with a reputation which reached as far as Constantinople.[96] According to Hasidic tradition, R. Ezekiel was related to the Baal Shem Tov's wife and, thus, also to R. Abraham Gershon.[97] We have already seen that R. Ezekiel and R. Gershon were friends who had taken joint action during the notorious controversy in Brody when both were members of that city's *kloiz*. From R. Ezekiel's collection of responsa, *Nodaᶜ Bihudah*, it is evident that a relationship of mutual affection and respect was preserved between the two men. In his letter to R. Gershon, R. Ezekiel wrote: "The delight of my eye and my heart's desire, aristocrat and master, sage who is preferable to a prophet, lion, the scholar (*hakham*) who is complete in every way, light of Israel, right-hand pillar, mighty hammer."[98] R. Gershon kept up a regular correspondence with R. Ezekiel and wrote to him even from Constantinople.[99] In his letter to R. Isaac Bekhor David, R. Ezekiel described R. Gershon as "my beloved friend, the scholar (*hakham*) who is complete in every way, a holy saint."[100]

This relationship between R. Gershon and R. Ezekiel, which is important for a number of reasons, was known up to the present only from sources preserved in the *Nodaᶜ Bihudah*. Indeed, there were those who

95. Israel Halperin, *Pinkas of the Council of the Four Lands* (Hebrew) [Jerusalem: Mosad Bialik, 1945], p. 338. Cf. his article "On the Relationship between the Jewish Councils and Communities of Poland and Palestinian Jewry," p. 87; [Halperin, *Eastern European Jewry* (Hebrew) (Jerusalem: Magnes Press, 1968)]. The reading there of "R. Isaac Landau" seems suspect to me. In the *Pinkas* Constantinople manuscript, to which I have referred above, there are some letters from Constantinople to R. Jacob Landau of Tarnopol, who was a treasurer for funds for the Jews of Palestine; cf. the appended documents to this essay. It was R. Jacob Landau who served with R. Ezekiel Landau as a treasurer for funds going to Palestine. Was the name R. Jacob Landau, chief of the rabbinic court of Tarnopol, confused with his father's name, R. Isaac Landau, head of the rabbinic court and rabbi of the region of Lwów? [For biographical information regarding R. Jacob Landau, see Appendix, document 3, n. 249.]

96. "His reputation went forth in those lands and the lands of Ishmael and the grand city of Constantinople and as far away as the Land which is Crowned in Glory (Palestine). The greatest sages, elders, and scholars sought him out, as one would who sought the very word of God. All this is evident from his book, which includes numerous responsa he penned while still a youth . . ." (R. Yaakovke Landau, *Divrey Yedidut*, *Nodaᶜ Bihudah*, pt. 2).

97. Cf. *Bet Rebbi* [of H. Heilman (Berditchev, 1900; rpt. Tel Aviv: Leon Offset, n.d.)], p. 176. However, he does not address R. Gershon with the initials *shin-bet*, the title for a relative (i.e., *sheᵓer-besari* "flesh of my flesh").

98. *Nodaᶜ Bihudah*, pt. 1, *even haᶜezer*, #73. [See *BT* Baba Batra 12a and *JT* Peah 4b.]

99. Ibid. In his letter to the Baal Shem Tov, R. Gershon recalls that he sent "a letter (*ketav*) to the most excellent scholar (*gaᵓon*) our teacher, R. Ezekiel" (*Birkat Haᵓaretz*, p. 64a).

100. *Nodaᶜ Bihudah*, #74.

doubted whether the "R. Gershon" mentioned in that book was identical with R. Abraham Gershon, the Baal Shem's brother-in-law. They were justifiably skeptical that in Constantinople, a transient and an Ashkenazi to boot, unacquainted with Judeo-Spanish or even with [Sephardic] Hebrew "pronunciation, which would have been strange to an Ashkenazi in those days," could join the circle of the city's dignitaries and become engaged in the affairs of the Jewish settlement in Palestine. It has been suggested therefore, that the man called "*ḥakham* Avraham Gershon" in the *Nodaᶜ Bihudah* was a Sephardi.[101] However, the document in *Pinkas* Constantinople proves beyond any shadow of a doubt that the responsum in *Nodaᶜ Bihudah* was, in fact, addressed to the brother-in-law of the Baal Shem Tov. From the *Pinkas* we learn that R. Ezekiel Landau and R. Jacob, rabbi of Tarnopol, sent 100 ducats to Constantinople, "so that they be given to the rav, our master, R. Abraham Gershon Kutover."[102]

Having shown the persisting ties between R. Gershon and R. Ezekiel Landau, we are now in the position to reconstruct R. Gershon's acceptance by the Jewish leaders of Constantinople. R. Ezekiel Landau was well-known to the officers of [the charities for] Jerusalem, Hebron, Safed, and Tiberias in Constantinople. In a letter to him, they described him as "the eminent scholar, renowned as a crown of glory and a diadem of beauty."[103] R. Isaac Bekhor David, an officer of that charitable group[104] and one of the rabbis of Constantinople, must have been aware of R. Ezekiel's prominence, just as R. Ezekiel knew of the former's stature and was prompted to refer to him by such lofty titles as "eminence of eminences," "whose heart is like the heart of a lion and whose appearance is that of crystal."[105] It is possible that R. Ezekiel wrote to R. Isaac Bekhor

101. "I am utterly amazed how anyone could take the responsum in the *Nodaᶜ Bihudah* to be to R. Abraham Gershon Kutover, given that, in that responsum, the author addresses his questioner as 'the delight of my eyes and my heart's desire, the sage (*ḥakham*) who is complete in every way, the lamp of Israel, the right-hand pillar, the mighty hammer.' There can be no question that the author of the *Nodaᶜ Bihudah* would never have used the phrase 'lamp of Israel, the right-hand pillar, the mighty hammer' for R. Gershon, because (1) we know of [R. Ezekiel Landau's negative] feelings toward Hasidism; (2) the salutation, "the sage who is complete in every way" (*hehakham hashalem vehakolel*) was only in use among Sephardic rabbis, while the responsum immediately following is addressed to *Hakham Abraham Gershon*, and, although an Ashkenazic Jew could conceivably be called *hehakham*, the title *Hakham* [i.e., without the article] is strictly a Sephardic usage, and (3) in any case, nowhere does the text add 'Kutover' [i.e., from Kuty] to the name Abraham Gershon . . . There is therefore no doubt whatsoever that the responsum was written to a Sephardic sage named Abraham of the Gershon family living in Constantinople" (Jacob Goldman, in Rivlin's comments and addenda to Frumkin's *History of the Sages of Jerusalem*, addenda to pt. 3, p. 41).

102. See Appendix, document 3.

103. See Appendix, document 4.

104. Cf. the announcement regarding the village of Yasiv in Deinard, *Shibalim Bodedot* [Jerusalem: Lunz, 1915], pp. 34–35.

105. [Num. 11:7] *Nodaᶜ Bihudah*, 1st ed. ##73,74. R. Isaac Bekhor David died in 1755 according to Rosanes, *History of the Jews of Turkey*, pt. 5, p. 13.

David about his friend, R. Abraham Gershon, and his mission. The latter became friendly with the Constantinople *hakham*, discussed halakhic (legal) matters with him and may have told him the reason for his own and R. Ezekiel's flight from Brody. He may have actually conveyed to R. Isaac the contents of R. Ezekiel's sharp responsum on this affair, a copy of which he had. We know that R. Isaac Bekhor David examined the problem in depth. He composed a long responsum by himself in which he objected to a number of elements in R. Ezekiel's opinion. He gave the responsum to R. Gershon.[106] R. Ezekiel replied to all these criticisms in a letter to R. Gershon. Later, having received a personal communication from R. Isaac, R. Ezekiel wrote directly to him.[107]

R. Abraham Gershon and the Leaders of Constantinople

R. Gershon may have wished to avail himself of the support of a court favorite, R. David Sonago.[108] "A powerful man, the father of orphans and a shelter to the poor of his people,"[109] "he used to give alms both openly and anonymously, supporting scholars in every locality, old or young, even small children at the very beginning of their education."[110] R. David Sonago died in the winter of 1746/47[111] and was succeeded by his son, R. Jacob Sonago.[112] When R. Gershon wrote of this to his friend, R. Ezekiel Landau, the latter replied:

106. The communication is recalled in R. Ezekiel's sermon for the Sabbath of Repentance for 1752: "This problem was posed to me by the late, well-known scholar and Sephardic *hakham*, Isaac Bekhor David . . ." in *Doresh Letzion* [Prague, 1827], sermon #13; see his son's note.

107. R. Ezekiel notes that R. Isaac's critical observations reached him "this year in the month of Shevat via a letter from the Hasid, *Hakham* Abraham Gershon, and I have responded via R. Barukh, the brother of R. Nethaniel of Chotýn (Hattin). My words have already been received by his honor, so I shall not repeat myself," *Noda' Bihudah*, p. 58d, and cf. p. 59c, "and this is as I wrote last year via R. Barukh, the brother of R. Nethaniel of Chotýn."

108. [See index to A. Yaari, *Emissaries*, who reads the name "Sonano" or "Zonano."]

109. These are the words of the kabbalist, R. David son of Moses De Modena, in *Ruah David Venishmat David* (Salonica, 1747), Introduction; cf. also R. Judah Navon, *Kiryat Melekh Rav* (Constantinople: Reuben and Nissim Ashkenazi, 1751).

110. R. Isaac Bekhor David, *Divre 'Emet* (Constantinople: Reuben and Nissim Ashkenazi, 1760), sermon #10.

111. Ibid., sermon #8: ". . . that I preached in 1747 on the Sabbath before the beginning of the month of Nisan when the Torah reading was *Pekudey*, recalling the death of the exalted dignitary, R. David Sonano, may his soul rest in paradise." Cf. sermon #7: ". . . that I preached regarding the death of the exalted dignitary, R. David Sonano . . . on the Sabbath of *parshat beha'alotekhah*, in 1747."

112. In the manuscript of *Pinkas* Constantinople, he signed a letter dated 11 Nisan 1748; he signed in 1748 among the delegates of Jerusalem, Hebron, and Safed, according to Deinard in *Shibalim Bodedot*. His name is mentioned as well in H.Y.D. Azulai's *Ma'agal Tov Hashalem* [ed. A. Freimann (Jerusalem: Mekitzey Nirdamim, 1934)], pp. 46 and 47; cf. also *Pinkas* Constantinople, p. 46b.

I have received this letter of unsullied purity from him in whose
well-being and *honored status* I rejoice. I praised God Who has
not abandoned his pious one (*ḥasido*) and shall not abandon
him, but will guard the steps of His pious one and grant him all
manner of good. . . . I likewise rejoiced that God has remembered His people and has secured for them the compassion of the
mighty king of Ishmael [the sultan of Turkey], may his glory be
elevated, so that he has now established the son of the late well-
known noble, R. David Sonago, at his father's post. May God
secure him the compassion of the king and his ministers to enable
him to take his father's place and may he grow from strength to
strength.[113]

In Constantinople, R. Gershon gained the friendship of one of the
most prominent leaders of the community, a wealthy and well-known
philanthropist, R. Moses, son of R. Menahem Soncino (Tzontzin), a
member of the famous family of printers.[114] R. Moses Soncino was a
regular visitor at the sultan's court, "working salvation in the midst of the
land," "a prince among Jews," "the eminently wise and wealthy man, a
grandee who encompasses the entire range of perfection, accomplished
in all the virtues enumerated by the sages."[115] He was one of the patrons of
the period who poured very generous sums of money into underwriting
the publication of scholarly works[116] and whom we have to thank for
making Constantinople a place in which many Hebrew books were
printed. His house was always open to scholars.[117] At times he used to
"turn away from his business affairs and engage in the pursuits hallowed
by Heaven."[118]

According to a document which I found in *Pinkas* Constantinople, R.
Moses Soncino was "involved in receiving the funds" sent from Poland by

113. *Nodaʿ Bihudah*, pt. 1, *ʾeven haʿezer*, #73.

114. In *Birkat Haʾaretz*, his name is given as Tzinitz; according to Cahana and the
manuscript source: Tzontzin. He is referred to many times in *Pinkas* Constantinople.

115. *Responsa Masʾat Mosheh* (Constantinople: Jonah b. Jacob, 1734–42), Introduction
to pt. 2.

116. E.g., *Responsa Masʾat Mosheh* in three volumes. On the help extended by R. Moses
Soncino in the publication of books, see Abraham Yaari, "Biographical Miscellany," *Kiryat
Sefer* 13 (1936):127.

117. R. Abraham Israel, who published his father's book *Masʾat Mosheh*, "sits in his
[i.e., R. Moshe Soncino's] house and lacks nothing" (introduction to pt. 3). R. Hayim
Alpandri writes in his introduction to the book *Dina Dehayey* that "he [R. Moses] respects
and admires the sages and is himself a rabbinic scholar, in whose midst I dwell, in the very
palace of the king."

118. In the introduction of R. Samuel Amato to the *Masʾat Mosheh*, vol. 1, it is stated
"the resident brothers are 'two golden pipes' [i.e., important dignitaries: see Zech. 4:12],
the leaders of the minions of Israel, exalted grandees, most wise sages, R. Joshua Soncino
and R. Moses Soncino . . . may they be blessed . . . Who has heard of such a thing—that
[such a one] should abandon all his worldly affairs and deal rather with heavenly matters?
Surely, the very countenances of these men glow!"

R. Ezekiel Landau "for the Ashkenazim in Jerusalem, may it be rebuilt and established quickly in our days Amen, to whom he would forward the money."[119]

The extent of R. Gershon's reputation is apparent in the fact that he was among the scholars of Constantinople who supplied a letter of introduction to R. Hayim Yeruham Vilna, a native of Jerusalem and one of its prominent rabbis, who, together with R. Meir de Segura, was sent on behalf of the Jerusalem community to Constantinople, and from there to Vienna. This letter of introduction was published in Constantinople in 1747.[120] To free himself from charges of Sabbateanism, R. Jonathan Eybeschütz had provided R. Hayim Yeruham with samples of the former's amulets and in his book, *Luḥot ʿEdut*, had recorded R. Hayim's favorable opinion of them. To bolster the authority of R. Hayim Yeruham, R. Jonathan cited the letter of introduction given R. Hayim by the scholars of Constantinople. However, of the Constantinople dignitaries, R. Gershon alone is mentioned by R. Jonathan, although at that time many renowned authorities lived there, such as R. Isaac Bekhor David, whom we have mentioned earlier, and others. The full text of R. Gershon's letter was published in *Hapardes* by the well-known Hasid, R. Aryeh Lieb Epstein, rabbi of Königsberg. Historians of Hasidism have overlooked this letter because R. Gershon's name is only alluded to in the text. But the identity of its author becomes clear if one compares the Epstein text with the fragment published in Eybeschütz's *Luḥot ʿEdut*. R. Aryeh Lieb Epstein described R. Gershon as "one of the great men of the age" (ʾeḥad migedoley ʿolam).[121]

When R. Gershon was about to leave Constantinople, R. Moses Soncino asked him to write "from time to time." R. Gershon was truly fond of R. Moses and referred to him as "my most distinguished friend,"[122] while referring to R. Jacob Joseph, the Besht's noted disciple, only as "my friend." R. Moses Soncino remained involved with R. Gershon after the latter's removal to Palestine. He acted as intermediary in the correspondence between R. Gershon and the Baal Shem Tov. Indeed, one of the letters which has come down to us, the "Hebron Letter," was in fact sent to the Baal Shem through R. Moses who might have met the former during his stay in Constantinople on his aborted trip

119. Cf. Appendix, document 4.

120. In *Luḥot Haʿedut*, p. 57a, the date 1757 is given, but this is a typographical error since the book was only published in Altona in 1755, and the favorable letter concerning R. Hayim Yeruham is dated 1754. In the book *Hapardes*, the date [of R. Gershon's letter] is given as Nisan 1747. See Appendix, document 4. In his book *Shevirat Luḥot Haʾaven* (Zolkiew, 1756), R. Jacob Emden attacks R. Hayim Yeruham as a Sabbatean, and it is amazing that he does not assault R. Gershon as well . . .

121. See Appendix, document 2.

122. *Birkat Haʾaretz*, p. 63d.

to Palestine.[123] He also was entrusted by R. Gershon with money matters. R. Moses held a part of the estate left by R. Jacob Joseph's father who had passed away in the Holy Land. This consisted of the sum of 50 piasters which a certain Jew, Zusman, had borrowed from R. Jacob Joseph's father. R. Gershon eventually got the money back from Zusman's widow and sent it to R. Moses for transmittal to R. Jacob Joseph.[124]

After R. Gershon's arrival in Palestine from Constantinople, he received the news that R. Moses Soncino

> was at the threshold of death, (because of our many iniquities), for he was afflicted with the disease which is known here as *bek'an* . . .[125]
> It struck his heart and confused his limbs in the same way, apparently, as had happened to our master, R. Jacob Babad of Brody.[126]

123. [See Ben-Amos, p. 237, #231. Y. Yaari claims that the fuller record of the unfortunate journey is found in the Yiddish version of *Shivḥey Habesht*. "Two Basic Recensions" (Hebrew), *Kiryat Sefer* 39 (1964):559–61. See, however, Joshua Mondshein, *Shivḥei Ha-Baal Shem Tov* (Jerusalem: Hanahal, 1982), pp. 22–41.]

124. In an earlier letter (which I have been unable to inspect), R. Abraham Gershon explains why it was impossible to get the money from Moses Soncino.

125. In *Birkat Ha'aretz* and in the manuscript of the Hebron Letter, the name of the illness is missing. In the text given by Cahana, in the place of *shekorin beka'n* (בכא׳ן) = "which is known here as . . . ", we find *shekorin babak* (באבאק) = "which is known as *babak*."

126. In all of the other texts of the Hebron Letter the reading is R. "Jacob, a.b.d. mi-Brody" [*'av bet din*: "chief of the rabbinic court of Brody"]. The error is explained: While the name of the rabbi of Brody at about that time was a R. Jacob, that is, R. Jacob Yukal Horowitz, previously the rabbi in Brailov, who succeeded R. Eleazer Rokeah as the rabbi of Brody, had R. Abraham Gershon been referring to him in his letter, he probably would have used some such title as *ga'on*. Further, one would use the prefix *bet* before the place name to translate "of" in the expression "chief of the rabbinic court of . . . ", rather than the prefix *mem* (*mi-Brody*). From these observations, and from the psychological association evident in the letter, one may conclude that the person intended was not "Jacob a.b.d.," but "Jacob B. a.b.d.," which is to say, "R. Jacob *Babad* of Brody," a wealthy philanthropist and one of the leaders of Galician Jewry in his day.

According to the text of his tombstone as given by Kahan in *'Anaf 'Etz 'Avot* [Cracow: Kahan, 1903], § 90, R. Jacob Babad died on 27 Elul 1748; see also Gelber, "*Pinkas*," #75. In that city he founded the *kloiz*, one of the most important institutions in modern Jewish history. Scholars learned there day and night, and thence came forth for a few generations both halakhists and kabbalists known as the *Sages of the Kloiz*; see above, pp. 50–52. N. M. Gelber, the authority on Brody Jewry, once wrote that R. Hayim Segal Landau, "the venerable rabbi," was the founder of the *kloiz*; see his "*Pinkas*," #149, and also G. Scholem, "Baruchya, the Leader of the Sabbateans in Salonika," in *Zion* 6 (1940–41), p. 193. This cannot be, because R. Hayim died on Purim 1797 whereas the *kloiz* was founded seventy years earlier. Elsewhere (*Aus Zwei Jahrhunderten*, p. 18, n. 4), Gelber calls R. Jacob Babad the founder of the *kloiz* (on p. 38, correct 1758 to 1748), without giving his source. It is nonetheless so, that R. Jacob son of Isaac Babad, the father-in-law of R. Isaac Horowitz, later to become rabbi of the joint community of Altona, Hamburg, and Wandsbeck, was the founder. The proof for this is in the words of R. Ezekiel Landau, one of the sages of the *kloiz*, in his *Noda' Bihudah*, pt. 1, *yoreh deah*, #43: "the sages who sit in the study-house of the late great R. Jacob Babad." This responsum was written when R. Isaac Horowitz lived in Horochów, that is to say, before 1752, when he settled in Brody.

The husband of R. Jacob Babad's sister was R. Israel Halperin, chief of the rabbinic court

We have almost despaired of all hope of recovery. It is now two weeks since he left (Who? Someone close to R. Moses?), promising that he would let me know if he had any good news of him. He has written to me to say that, thank God, he has had good news, for he received letters from the eminent. . . . But I do not know whether he is now in good health or, God forbid, not. May the Holy One, Blessed be He, grant him complete recovery, speedily and in our days, Amen. Almost the entire [community in] the Land of Israel wept when they heard the sad tidings, for he was the central pillar of the community in this holy province and no one matched his meticulous observance of the commandments.[127]

Not too much later—apparently in the winter of 1749/50—R. Moses Soncino did die.[128] His brother, "The eminent prince, the glory of the generation, our honored master, R. Joshua Soncino,"[129] was already burdened with "the yoke of public office which rested upon him, for many people crowded at his door." He was therefore not asked to take

of Zaslaw, whose son, R. David Halperin, chief of the rabbinic court of Ostróg, became a noted disciple of the Baal Shem Tov. It is reasonable to assume that R. Jacob Babad heard of the fame of the Baal Shem Tov from his nephew. Finally, it follows from the style of R. Abraham Gershon's letter that the Baal Shem Tov knew R. Jacob Babad well and even knew of his illness; one only makes references to those who can understand the allusions. ["Illness struck his (R. Moses Soncino's) heart and confused his limbs in the same way, apparently, as had happened to our teacher, Jacob Babad of Brody."] In light of this, it becomes easier to understand the stories about the relationship of the Baal Shem Tov to the sages of the *kloiz*. [See Ben-Amos, index, under "Brody."]

127. According to the manuscript, *Birkat Haʾaretz*, p. 63d. He apparently recovered, because in 1748 he signed his name as one of the Constantinople representatives [*pekidim*] of the Jewish communities of Jerusalem, Hebron, Safed, and Tiberias, along with R. Joshua and R. Aaron Soncino on an approbation in favor of the village of Yasiv. See Deinard, *Shibalim Bodedot*, pp. 34–35. There is no question that this refers to R. Joshua's brother, Moses, and not to R. Moses, son of Joshua, because only the former was active in communal matters. Cf. document 4 in the Appendix. The text that appears on the tombstone of Rebecca, the widow of R. Moses Soncino, is printed in *Ḥelkat Meḥokek* [of A. Brisk (Jerusalem: S. Halevi Zuckerman, 1901–10)], § 2, p. 47.

128. [See, however, Barnai, "Jewish Community in Jerusalem," p. 200, n. 42. He cites two documents from the *Pinkas* Constantinople—the second, dated 8 Nisan 1752—in which R. Moses is mentioned. In both letters, the officials note that funds were usually transmitted to the Land of Israel via R. Moses Soncino, but that he had grown enfeebled and no longer recalled to whom precisely the monies were to go. The implication is that R. Moses survived, but probably retired from charitable work.]

129. On the help extended by R. Joshua Soncino in publishing books in 1748–57, see A. Yaari, "Biographical Miscellany," pp. 127–29. He also published the responsa and novellae of his great-grandfather, R. Joshua Soncino, under the title, *Nahalah Lihoshuaʿ* (Constantinople, 1731; see the introduction by R. Samuel Amato), and was helpful in the publication of kabbalistic books, e.g., *Sefer Ḥaredim* (Constantinople, 1757) and *Midrash Talpiyot* (Smyrna, 1736). He was the first to help in the publication of the *Sedey Yehoshuaʿ* on the Palestinian Talmud (to the orders of *Moʿed*, *Nashim*, and *Nezikin*; Constantinople, 1749), in which he is described as "the splendor and beauty of the generation, the magnificence of Israel, the nobleman and courtier . . . our tower and strength, crowned with elegance." Together with " . . . the exalted nobleman, R. Jacob Zonana," he aided R. Elijah Hakohen of Smyrna in publishing *Midrash Talpiyot* (Smyrna, 1736).

his brother's place as manager of the funds sent from Poland for the Ashkenazim in Palestine. The appointment fell, instead, upon the two "blessed brothers, wealthy and eminent, understanding and wise, our honored masters, rabbis Abrahan and Joseph Camondo."[130] The money received by them was sent on to the officers in Jerusalem, who distributed it to the Ashkenazim. The receipts were returned to the Camondo brothers. Sometimes the expected funds were late in arriving from Poland. The brothers would then instruct the officers in Jerusalem to advance the usual allotment to the Ashkenazim "to enable them to purchase their grain during the threshing season, and to secure their livelihood."[131]

In the summer of 1747,[132] R. Gershon left Constantinople.[133] He sailed to Palestine in the company of two rabbis whose friendship he had

130. Camondo was the family name of a wealthy and well-known Constantinople family from which stemmed R. Solomon (called "Jelibi") b. Abraham Camondo (1730–1810), the author of the books *Neharot Damesek* and *Ben Meshek* (Salonica, 1802), printed together with the volume of gaonic responsa, *Sha'arey Teshuvah*, the publication of which R. Solomon, son of Jacob Camondo, assisted; Abraham Camondo (1785–1873), a banker and philanthropist (see the *Jewish Encyclopaedia*, 3:521–22). The most important family member was Abraham Camondo, who was one of the richest men of his day, born in Constantinople in 1785 and died in Paris in 1873; see the article in the *Jewish Encyclopaedia* and also Rosanes, *History of the Jews of Turkey*, 5:103.

131. Cf. Appendix, document 4.

132. The Hebron Letter, which was published in *Birkat Ha'aretz* # 326, was written in Hebron after Kislev, 1747; [Barnai, "Notes on the Immigration of R. Gershon," pp. 113–14, suggests Tevet-Shevat, 1747/48. For a review of the dating of the letter by Cahana, Hordezky, Rivlin, Shohet, Bihovsky, and Yaari, see Halperin, *Hasidic Immigration*, pp. 52–53; Barnai, *Hasidic Letters*, pp. 33–34; cf. Katz-Shteiman (n. 1) pp. 303–5.]

From the letter we learn that R. Gershon's wife and children were in Hebron in Tishri 1747, and that he arrived in Jerusalem from Constantinople on the eve of Rosh Hashanah [i.e., 31 Elul, the last day of the year], 1746, after a journey of about a month. [The letter reads: "On r(osh) h(odesh) (the first of the month of Elul) on my journey to Jerusalem, I expended considerable funds on taxes and expenses and arrived in the Holy City . . . on the morning of ʿerev Rosh Hashanah." In his notes, Heschel questions whether he came to Jerusalem directly from Constantinople or after stopping in Hebron. Katz-Shteiman, "Concerning Barnai's Notes," 42:303, n. 14, emends "r. h. Elul," i.e., "1 Elul," to "kh. h. Elul," i.e., "28 Elul" (the Hebrew letters *resh* ר and *khaf* כ are similar). Accordingly, R. Gershon, after depositing his family, would have departed Hebron, some fifteen miles from Jerusalem, on 28 Elul, spending the night on the way, and reaching Jerusalem the following morning. Cf. Barnai, *Hasidic Letters*, p. 34.]

There is [in addition] a chronological problem. R. Gershon writes, "I arrived in the Holy City on Friday morning, ʿerev Rosh Hashanah." In 1746, however, ʿerev Rosh Hashanah fell on a Monday, and only in 1742 and 1749 did it fall on a Friday. [The suggestion of Katz-Shteiman (p. 304) that the Hebron Letter be consequently dated in the winter of 1749/50 is refuted by the discovery of the tombstone, dated 1747, of R. Abraham Kazis, whom R. Gershon says in his letter that he eulogized shortly before. See Barnai, "Notes on the Immigration of R. Gershon," pp. 311–13; and below, nn. 212, 213.] Neither 1742 nor 1749 is a feasible date in light of the events described in the letter. Apparently, we have a slight error in transcription which changed *bayom sheni* ביום שני, Monday, to *bayom shishi* ביום ששי, Friday.

133. Rosanes, *History of the Jews of Turkey*, pt.2, p. 12, writes that in Constantinople, R. Gershon became "friendly with the physician, Rabbi Isaac David (who supported with his

acquired:[134] R. Isaac Rosanes, chief of the rabbinic court of Constantinople,[135] and R. Abraham Rosanes.[136]

---

own funds the production of books, and who is not to be confused with R. Isaac Bekhor David), who apparently had ties to the royal court. But this friendship seems to have come to naught, except that as a result of the influence of this doctor, R. Gershon consented to travel with him to Palestine disguised as a Sephardic Jew. Unfortunately, he died almost immediately upon arriving in Jerusalem, and nonetheless, R. Abraham Gershon was unable to settle in Jerusalem except in disguise for many years." I cannot substantiate these claims.

134. In his letter to the Baal Shem Tov, he says that he found "great favor in their eyes," *Birkat Haʾaretz*, # 326. The names of the rabbis have become confused in the copies of the letter and have thus eluded the scholars who have dealt with this issue. They are referred to twice, and through comparison of both places in the various printed and manuscript sources of the "Hebrew Letter," one can identify the names with certainty. He recalls two Sephardic sages "who went with me on the boat," and they are:

> *Birkat Haʾaretz*: R. Abraham תיל"ש with the chief rabbi (*harav hakolel*) of Kanita
>
> Cahana: R. Abraham רייזילّש with the great rabbi (*harav hagadol*) of Kosta (Constantinople)
>
> Manuscript: R. Abraham רזל"ש with the chief rabbi (*harav hakolel*) of Kosta (Constantinople)

After that, we read that in that same year, there died "more than two hundred Jews, among them":

> *Birkat Haʾaretz*: The great rabbi, R. Abraham רייבעליש, and our teacher and rabbi, R. Isaac Rosen, chief of the rabbinic court of Kanita
>
> Cahana: The great rabbi, the sage R. Abraham רייזלש, and our teacher and rabbi, R. Isaac, the chief of the rabbinic court of Kosta (Constantinople)
>
> Manuscript: The great enlightened rabbi, R. Abraham רייזעלש, and Rabbi Isaac רייזעלש, the chief of the rabbinic court of Kosta (Constantinople)

The manuscript text allows us to identify the names, in which a single family name is given for both: רייזעלש, and this solves the riddle. From reliable sources, we know of two Constantinople rabbis of that period, R. Abraham b. Joseph Rosanes and R. Isaac Rosanes, both of whose dates match the story of R. Abraham Gershon. [See below n. 136.] The Ashkenazic scribe miscopied the Sephardic name (giving a *lamed* instead of a *nun*), and transformed it into an Ashkenazic one. He also copied Kanita for Kushta (i.e., Constantinople), cf. *Birkat Haʾaretz*, p. 64a,

135. R. Isaac Rosanes was, according to H.Y.D. Azulai (in *Shem Hagedolim*, letter *yod*, # 327), "well-known as a philosopher and as a talmudist; he died as a young man." He was a rabbinic judge in Constantinople. In 1737, he received testimony regarding a Jew who had been converted to Islam (Moses Cohen, *Kehunat ʾOlam*, pt. 1, # 46 [Constantinople: Jonah b. Jacob, 1740]; he is mentioned as well in § 24). According to Rosanes (*History of the Jews of Turkey*, (pt. 4, p. 200), "his last surviving text is his approbation for the Ladino *Meʿam Loʿez* to Exodus by Isaac Magriso, Constantinople, 1747." As I mentioned above, he issued an approbation in Iyar 1747 for the book *Nehpah Bakesef*, pt. 1. He issued joint approbations for both these books with R. Abraham, son of R. Joseph Rosanes. According to Rosanes, "A year later (i.e., in 1748) he (R. Isaac Rosanes) traveled to Palestine and settled in Jerusalem (see also Eisenstein, *ʾOtzar Yisraʾel* [New York: Jewish Encyclopaedia Publishing Co., 1906–13], 9:272) and died there in 1749. On his tombstone is engraved "The excellent rabbi, R. Isaac Rosanes," and next to it is his wife's, with the inscription "The *rabbanit* Madame Hanulah, the widow of the great rabbi, R. Isaac Rosanes." Both graves are on the Mount of Olives. R. Isaac left behind a son, R. Abraham, who was rabbi in Smyrna (see Rosanes, pt. 5, pp. 64–65). Here, too, Rosanes does not give any source, but the richness of his detail assures us he was working with a source before him. That source was not the letter of R. Abraham Gershon. Rosanes never refers to R. Abraham Gershon's journey in the company of these two Constantinople sages; it is clear he, too, did not identify the names of the rabbis in that letter. The only problem is that Rosanes gives 1749 as the year

of R. Isaac's death, whereas the letter of R. Abraham Gershon gives the year of R. Isaac's death as 1748. Possibly, Rosanes was working with an oral tradition and made a mistake of one year. It is interesting that the name of R. Isaac is mentioned neither by Frumkin in his *History of the Sages of Jerusalem*, nor by Gaon in his *Oriental Jews in the Land of Israel*. The letter of R. Abraham Gershon is apparently the only evidence of his stay in Jerusalem. After I wrote that, I found the document in *Sefer Hapardes* (see Appendix, document 2) in which the two rabbis of the Rosanes family are mentioned.

136. R. Abraham the son of R. Joseph Rosanes was the most important rabbi in Constantinople. Noted for his wisdom and long life, he was among the fiercest opponents of the Sabbateans. H.Y.D. Azulai (in *Shem Hagedolim*, letter ʾaleph, # 105) writes, "When I was young, I had the great fortune to meet this holy man and to be inspired with his Torah." He immigrated to Palestine with his wife and settled in Jerusalem. M. Rosanes (*History of the Jews of Turkey*, pt. 5, p. 18), fixes the year of R. Abraham Rosanes's immigration in 1742/43, without indicating his source. This cannot be accurate because in Iyar 1747 he issued an approbation to the book *Nehpah Bakesef* (pt. 1) (Constantinople, 1748) in Constantinople. The way the date is phrased indicates that both R. Abraham son of R. Joseph Rosanes and R. Isaac Rosanes intended to immigrate to Palestine, in that the year (A.M. 5507) is spelled out numerologically to form the words " . . . ʾaʿaleh ʾet [. . . if I raise not Jerusalem above my chiefest joy" (Psalms 137:6)]; the numerical value of the six Hebrew letters of those first two words is 507, i.e., 507 years into the sixth millennium, or 5507.

In 1747, R. Abraham signed a letter of recommendation on behalf of R. Hayim Yeruham Vilna (see Appendix, document 2), and he died, apparently on 18 Heshvan 1747 (according to the calculation of Wachstein, in Frumkin's *History of the Sages of Jerusalem*, addenda to pt. 3, p. 32; see pt. 3, p. 19; and cf. further, Rosanes, pt. 5, p. 18, n. 46). Rosanes had copied the tombstone as a young man and had written "5505" (1744) instead of "5508" (1747) [substituting the Hebrew letter "*he*" for "*het*"]. Cf. Gaon, *Oriental Jews in the Land of Israel*, pt. 2, p. 636.

I have found another hint that R. Abraham son of Joseph Rosanes arrived in Palestine in 1747. In his approbation to the book *Peri Haʾadamah*, pt. 1 (Salonica, 1752), R. Abraham Rosanes wrote, "I have not yet calmed down, nor have I rested because of fatigue of the journey . . . and I, the least in the Land of Israel, . . . moan in his heart at the sight of evil . . . this habitation of the Lord . . . how has it passed to aliens; in its gate apostates dance (Heb.: Ben Stada and Ben Talmiyon [cf. R.T. Herford, *Christianity in Talmud and Midrash* (London: Williams, 1903), pp. 35–39, 55–57, 345; D. Catchpole, *The Trial of Jesus* (Leiden: E. J. Brill, 1971), pp. 9–11, 29–31, 35, 42–47, 60–65]) . . . in the place in which plentiful prayer should be offered to the Lord our God, those cursed Gentiles worship, each one in his own way, an alien worship-service [see Isa. 28:21], containing the lies they have invented. Why do You watch betrayers prancing about in Your sanctuary?" The approbation has no date, but another one in the same work is from 1747. Even the text engraved on the tombstone of R. Abraham's wife confirms this supposition. It reads: ". . . wife of the illustrious rabbi, our honored master, Abraham Rosanes, *whose soul is in Eden* (emphasis AJH). She went to her eternal home on 27 Tishri 1748." See *Helkat Mehokek*, [of A. Brisk], # 4, p. 3.

[Because of the prominence of rabbis Abraham and Isaac Rosanes, Heschel's proof of their identification as the companions who accompanied R. Gershon on his trip to Palestine has facilitated the dating of that journey. The discovery by Heschel of an allusion to their imminent preparation for departure to the Holy Land in the approbation of the rabbis Rosanes to *Nehpah Bakesef* in Iyar 1747, and the evidence of R. Isaac Rosanes's arrival in his approbation to *Peri Haʾadamah* in 1747, confirm the letter R. Gershon himself wrote on 28 Iyar 1757, stating that he had spent ten years in Hebron and Jerusalem and consequently had departed Constantinople ten years earlier. (See above, pp. 62–63.) Further evidence supporting Heschel's dating of R. Gershon's trip with the rabbis Rosanes from Constantinople to the Holy Land during the last part of the month of Iyar 1747 is now supplied by Barnai in "Notes on the Immigration of R. Gershon," pp. 111–13, who has published two Ladino excerpts from the *Pinkas* Constantinople MS: one which can be dated 22 Iyar 1747,

The Rabbinate in Jerusalem

R. Gershon arrived "in the holy city of Jerusalem" on the eve of Rosh Hashanah and remained for two weeks. On his first Sabbath there, the scholars and dignitaries of Jerusalem gathered to welcome him. The extent to which he was respected is evident from the fact that all the Ashkenazim of the city looked to him to become their rabbi. R. Gershon described their appeal in the following words: "Stay with us and be our teacher, our leader and patron, to prevent us from going astray, and we shall furnish you with letters from all the Sephardic scholars [confirming your appointment]." They pleaded with him "intensely and repeatedly, for eight days." He refused, however, to accept the office of chief rabbi of the Ashkenazic community in Jerusalem, true to his claim: "All my life I have shunned honor. This now is surely the work of the one [Satan] who hopes to ensnare me in Jerusalem by pride."

The Sephardic scholars likewise pleaded with him to stay in Jerusalem, as they were very favorably impressed by him, especially R. Abraham Rosanes and R. Isaac Rosanes, the chief rabbi of Constantinople, who had sailed with him to the Holy Land. But he refused them all. R. Abraham Schwerzalk, the wealthy Jew of Brody, even offered to pay him 100 piasters (*'arayot*) if he accepted the rabbinate, but he refused this also.[137] They implored him with "heartrending words," so much so that he was moved and thought: "Master of the Universe, I know not whether this is the work of the Lord, blessed be He, or the work of 'that one', God forbid . . . In short, they pleaded with him so fervently" that he could no longer gainsay them and at last agreed. The people were overjoyed at this and began to shout: "Long live the king!" Without delay, the Ashkenazic scholars went and rented "a very fine dwelling" for him, in addition to a special *bet midrash*, and handed him the keys. They also hired a certain Jew to go to Hebron and bring R. Gershon's family to Jerusalem. R. Gershon began to compose a letter to his family, but after completing the first few words he was drained of all strength and could not put down another line. It was as if his hands were bound, so that he could no longer write. He then said to the people of Jerusalem: You see, it is not the

mentioning that R. Abraham Rosanes was expected shortly in Palestine and that he "and several other great men" (R. Gershon?) were en route from Constantinople; the second, dated 17 Av 1747, mentioning that a letter had already been received from Jerusalem which confirmed the arrival of R. Abraham Rosanes. Barnai, in fact, sets the date of arrival at "the beginning of the month of Sivan."]

137. [See above, n. 81. In the 1740s, two *gabai'im* (administrators) handled the allocating of charity funds from abroad within the Ashkenazic community. One of the *gabai'im* was R. Abraham of Brody. See Barnai, "Jewish Community in Jerusalem," p. 195, #16. In this section, Heschel is again paraphrasing the language of the Hebron Letter.]

desire of the Holy One, blessed be He, that I settle here. They implored him still further. When he tried to resume the writing of the letter, however, he was so struck by melancholy that he felt "as though the entire burden of Jerusalem, may it be rebuilt and established, were resting upon [him]." He was about to return to Hebron, when the people of Jerusalem "prevented the muleteers" from taking him. "They bribed them daily" to keep putting off his departure, in hopes that he might yet change his mind. But R. Gershon had decided to return to Hebron,[138] and so he did.

Several weeks later, R. Gershon realized that the Holy One, "may His name be blessed forever into eternity," had dealt miraculously with him. For, immediately after the festival of Sukkot, there was an outbreak of plague in the city.[139] In the ensuing two months, more than two hundred Jews died as a result, among whom were "many sages, and persons of eminence and accomplishment," including R. Abraham Rozanes and R. Isaac Rozanes, chief of the rabbinic court of Constantinople. Of those who had come to Palestine with R. Gershon, only three or four survived. And the survivors themselves "had reached the very gates of death. Now the city was of substantial size, containing about a thousand heads of

---

138. "*Veshiviti nafshi hadrana*" ["I was as one who repudiates his promise," is the reading of R. Gershon's words in the MS. of the Hebron Letter]. See *BT* Ketubot 53a. Both published editions of the letter give the incorrect reading *hadraga*.

139. There is a reference to the plague of 1747/48 in the book *Peri Ha᾿adamah* (Salonica, 1752), pt. 1, p. 42b: "That year brought several difficulties, among them plague and other troubles, and even though it is not customary to declare a public fast day on account of the plague, because the sickness ultimately derived from lack of rain . . . they agreed to proclaim a *ta῾anit geshamim* "fast for rain" . . . on 18 Kislev 1747. [The custom of fasting during a plague was proscribed because of the danger to life in such a weakened condition. See *BT* Ta῾anit 22b and *Shulhan ῾Arukh, orah hayim* # 576:2, *sha῾arey teshuvah*, citing R. Moses ibn Habib and R. Isaac Luria.] On the third fast [in the series of three consecutive fast days, Monday, Thursday, Monday], on the Monday of the week in which the Torah section *vayeshev* was read in the synagogue, their prayers were answered at about ten o'clock in the morning, and they [therefore] abandoned the fast. All the congregations here in the holy city of Jerusalem gathered together for the afternoon service and recited the *hallel* psalms of thanksgiving, with its closing benediction." Cf. *Sefer Nehpah Bakesef*, pt. 2, p. 36a: "In 1747/48 there was a gap of forty days between rains, and some of the rabbis of the Holy City wanted to proclaim a communal fast with all its stringencies." Finally, "the rains came, thank God, in great abundance, and there was no need to fast." In the book *Malki Bakodesh* (Salonica: Betzalel Halevi, 1749), p. 127a, I found that R. Moses Hagiz, a possible victim of the plague, died in 1747/48; this was not known to the historians. Rosanes, *History of the Jews of Turkey*, pt. 5, p. 256, fixes the year of his death in 1760/61, relying on Azulai in *Shem Hagedolim*; in my copy, however, there is no such reference. [In a private communication to A. Heschel, A. Yaari writes that while the date of 1760/61 for R. Moses Hagiz's death is not explicitly given by Azulai, it is implicit in his remark that R. Moses "arrived in Sidon in 1737/38, died in Safed, and lived nearly ninety years." Nearly ninety years from his birth in 1671/72 would be 1760/61. Yaari then refers to the problem he raised in his *Emissaries*, p. 371, namely, that according to this calculation, R. Moses would have resided for more than twenty years in Palestine, and "it is surprising that nothing is reported of him there," and concedes that Heschel's discovery of an earlier date of 1747/48 for R. Moses's death solves the dilemma.]

households." Said R. Abraham Gershon: "Praised be His Name forever. One who benefits from a miracle is never aware of it [at the time]."[140]

His Stay in Hebron

At that time, the Jewish community of Hebron, though important, was penniless. Poverty had compelled the Jews to borrow money from the Gentiles at exorbitant rates of interest, so that

> in time, their debts rose to an intolerable level, to the point where even the largest portion of the contributions coming from abroad was not enough to cover the interest and a small portion of the capital. The lay leader of the community, the *parnas*, who was the personal guarantor of these debts, saw no other means of handling the situation but to allocate all the monies raised abroad for the repayment of the debts. Thus the students and scholars of Hebron were robbed of their sole source of livelihood . . . The city's troubles were so notorious throughout the Near East that many refused to settle there.

The Jews lived in one block of houses (*ḥatzer*) surrounded by a wall.[141]

It is interesting that R. Gershon, who had come from Poland and knew what it was like there for a Jew, did not think so badly of life in Hebron. In his letter he writes: "The eminent Gentiles here love the Jews dearly. When there are circumcision feasts or other celebrations, they visit in the evenings, and make merry with the Jews, clapping and dancing with them, very much like the Jews themselves, so to speak."[142] R. Gershon was received in Hebron with great respect. When the most eminent Gentile of the city, the mayor, came to welcome him, R. Gershon presented him with a pipe (*tzibek*) he had gotten in Constantinople. The Gentiles grew fond of R. Gershon and told him that since the day he arrived in Hebron, he had brought them "good fortune." On *Simḥat*

140. [See *BT* Niddah 31a.]

141. Rosanes, *History of the Jews of Turkey*, pt. 5, pp. 307–8. All visitors to Hebron at that time had to pay a tax to the sheikh of the city, and because of that burden many did not go; see Gaon, *Oriental Jews in the Land of Israel*, p. 196.

The Jews of Hebron sent emissaries to distant lands. In 1753/54, they appointed the sage Raphael Carigal to travel abroad. He visited Constantinople and Turkey and was the first emissary from the Holy Land to visit America. He lived for a while in New York and Philadelphia, and became a friend of Ezra Stiles, the president of [Yale University; see Rosanes, *History of the Jews of Turkey*, pt. 5, p. 309; the *Jewish Encyclopaedia*, 3:593 [and the *Encyclopedia Judaica*, vol. 5, cols. 179–80]. Even R. Mordecai Tama, the translator of the responsa of Maimonides into Hebrew and their publisher, in his book *Pe'er Hador* (Amsterdam: Janson, 1765), was an emissary of the Jews of Hebron. [On the character of M. Tama, see Yaari, *Emissaries*, pp. 589–90, and on the conditions in Hebron at that time, pp. 569–607.]

142. *Birkat Ha'aretz, # 326.*

Torah [the Feast of the Rejoicing of the Law at the end of *Sukkot*] he was given the honor of being *Ḥatan Torah*.[143] On the evening after the festival all the Jewish scholars, as well as the Gentile officials, came to celebrate with him, "and they clapped and danced just like the Jews and sang hymns of praise [to God] in Arabic."

It was in Hebron, apparently, that R. Gershon became acquainted with R. Hayim Hakohen of Nikolsburg[144] and with R. Isaac Zerahiah Azulai,[145] father of the noted traveler and author, R. Hayim Joseph David Azulai, who reports in his own writings an opinion in the name of R. Gershon.[146]

Withal, R. Gershon was not happy in Hebron:

I am embittered and dissatisfied for I sit alone shut away in my study all the while with my young son.[147] No one comes to see me. Nor have I found [here] any man after my own heart, although the distinguished Sephardic scholars[148] love me dearly and treat me with great honor and perform all services for me,[149] [such that] I never even have to go out of the courtyard of the house. Still, our natures differ[150] and I have found no man after my own heart. I grieve for my [other] sons whom I have left behind like a flock without a shepherd. . . . Had I lived among the Ashkenazim I would not have had so many troubles.[151] I did not

143. [Lit., "bridegroom of the Torah." *Simḥat Torah* marks the completion of the annual cycle of weekly readings from the Pentateuch and its beginning anew. The last individual called to the Torah as its reading is completed is called "bridegroom of the Torah," and it is the custom for him to hold a reception for the congregation in his honor following services.]

144. See Appendix, document 5. Cf. above, n. 91.

145. He died on 23 Tevet 1765 in Jerusalem. See Azulai, *Shem Hagedolim*, letter ʾaleph, # 15, and Rosanes, *History of the Jews of Turkey*, pt. 5, p. 267.

146. Cf. Azulai, *Simhat Haregel ʿal Rut* (Livorno: Castillo and Saadun, 1782), the end of the book: "In checking some notes from my illustrious father and teacher, may his memory be a blessing, I see he puzzled over a comment of Rashi, and he quoted, in that regard, the pious rabbi (*harav hehasid*) R. Abraham Gershon Kutover, may his memory be for a blessing . . . " Some say (see *History of the Sages of Jerusalem*, pt. 3, p. 59) that it is to R. Abraham Gershon that the remarks in the ʾAmar Yosef of R. Joseph Alkalai (Salonica: Betzalel Halevi Ashkenazi, 1831), p. 94b, are making reference: "and the light of our eyes, R. A. Gershon, may God preserve him, gave a new interpretation based on that which R. Nissim and R. Meir Abulafia wrote . . . " R. Joseph Alkalai, however, died in 1818. [In a private communication to A. Heschel, A. Yaari writes that "the R. A. Gershon mentioned in ʾAmar Yosef was not our R. Abraham Gershon but a well-known Sephardic ḥakham, who is mentioned in the literature of the time."]

147. In the manuscript [*Birkat Haʾaretz*]: "our honored teacher and rabbi".

148. In the manuscript: "who are here".

149. According to the manuscript.

150. Manuscript: "Neither is there a common language." On the good relations which the Sephardim had with the Ashkenazic Jews, cf. Rosanes, *History of the Jews of Turkey*, pt. 5, p. 285.

151. In the manuscript: "sadness".

expect to be so unhappy here. But I realize that the Holy One, Blessed be He, does not wish me to live among the Ashkenazim.[152]

Despite all this, he loved the Holy Land passionately. When he was forced to leave it, he wrote: "My departure from the Land is as difficult for me as the departure of the soul."[153]

Among the Kabbalists in Jerusalem

Around the first of Iyar 1753, R. Gershon left Hebron and settled in Jerusalem. He remained there for several years, and was still there on the first of Iyar 1757.[154] In Jerusalem he became especially close to the circle of the kabbalists. Already during his visit in Jerusalem in 1748, it is known that he prayed on the High Holidays in the *bet midrash* of R. Gedaliah Hayyun,[155] called "master of the pious." R. Gedaliah "gave himself completely to the 'true science' [Kabbalah] of our master, the Ari [R. Isaac Luria], of blessed memory, meditating upon all the *kavanot* of the master (Luria), of blessed memory, when fulfilling commandments or in prayer . . . in holiness, seclusion, and asceticism."[156] R. Gedaliah was the founder of the well-known *bet midrash*, Bet El, attended by men of spiritual accomplishment who had "abstained from all the pleasures of this world and, in prayer, practiced all the *kavanot* of the Ari, of blessed memory." In Bet El, R. Gedaliah himself used to lead the service.[157] After his death in 1750/51, R. Gedaliah was succeeded by the famed Yemenite kabbalist, R. Shalom Sharabi, the distinguished commentator on the writings of Luria. R. Shalom died in 1751/52.[158]

---

152. *Birkat Ha'aretz*, # 326. According to Gaon, *Oriental Jews*, p. 98, there were no Ashkenazic Jews at all in Hebron at that time.

153. *Birkat Ha'aretz*, # 327. The author of the *Shivhey Habesht*, p. 10c [Ben-Amos, # 58], tells that he heard R. Pinhas teach about "when R. Gershon was in the Holy Land. It is the ancient custom there to strain both drinking and cooking water because their water is not fresh, but is rather well water, and one regularly finds worms and mosquitoes in it. R. Gershon's wife was unaware of this and did not strain her water, since that was not the practice in Poland, whereupon the women composed a song of mockery and sang it in the synagogue. She returned home in tears, crying, 'Why have you brought me to a place where I am mocked?' R. Gershon tried to comfort her, saying, 'Show me the woman who composed the song,' and so she showed her to him walking from the synagogue. He spat and said in amazement, 'What? That woman can speak?'"

154. *Birkat Ha'aretz*, # 332.

155. Ibid., # 326.

156. Azulai, *Shem Hagedolim*, personalities, letter *gimel*, # 6.

157. Frumkin, *History of the Sages of Jerusalem*, pt. 3, pp. 18–19.

158. Ibid., pp. 116–19. [While R. Gershon moved to Jerusalem only a year or so after R. Shalom's death in 1753, the short distance to Hebron, where R. Gershon lived, permitted frequent visits.]

The meeting between the representatives of two mystical movements—the brother-in-law of the Baal Shem Tov, founder of Ashkenazic
Hasidism, and R. Shalom Sharabi, founder of a parallel fellowship
among the Sephardim—was one of profound significance. The small
fellowship of Bet El laid the foundations for the community of kabbalists
in Jerusalem which, for several generations, exerted immense influence
on the life of Palestinian Jewry. The two movements began almost
simultaneously—the former in Miedzybórz, the latter in Jerusalem's Bet
El. Both are characterized by love of one's fellow Jew and a devotion to
the mystical teachings. Although Bet El admitted both Hasidim and
Mitnagdim [i.e., the "opponents" of Hasidism], it is known that the
Sephardic kabbalists saw themselves much closer to the former group.
The Hasidim were viewed as "men of eminence who stood on a higher
rung of the ladder of understanding than did the others." The Mitnagdim, on the other hand, were called "*Pashtanim*," "literalists," by the
circle of Bet El. By this designation it would appear that they were seen
not as worthy antagonists of Hasidism but as individuals still on the
bottom rung of the ladder of understanding, [that of "literal meaning,"
peshat], aspiring, like the kabbalists themselves, to ascend to the fourth
rung of "mystical meaning," *sod*, but without success.[159]

Of the remarkable kabbalist, R. Shalom Sharabi, who reestablished
Bet El and expanded its activities, it was said that he was "the messiah of
Israel."[160] He must have heard of his contemporary, the Baal Shem Tov.
In a letter to the latter, R. Gershon said that the name of the Baal Shem
was known in Jerusalem:

> My beloved brother-in-law, allow me to tell you something.
> When I was in your holy presence, you said to me once that you
> had a vision of a scholar arriving in Jerusalem from a country of
> the West [North Africa] and that he was a spark [*nitzotz*] of the
> Messiah without being aware of it himself. He was a great scholar
> of both the revealed and hidden realms of study and given to

159. Uriel b. Zion, *Sar Shalom Shar'abi* [Jerusalem, 1930], p. 29. In 1777, R. Abraham
of Kalisk wrote in Safed, "though aware of all the [local] calumnies (of the Mitnagdim
against the Hasidim) as well as the stories that were current abroad, the Sephardim humble
themselves before (R. Mendel of Vitebsk [d. 1788, the leader of the Hasidic migration to
Palestine]), and, through the mercy of God, this contemptuous mockery [of the Hasidim] is
repellent to all [the Sephardim] because it smacks of lust" (according to the manuscript in
my possession, which has certain deviations from the text of *Likutey 'Amarim*, letter #29).

160. He "revealed all that could be revealed, as the observer will see, regarding '*Adam
Kadmon* (Primordial Man) and his four supernal worlds [i.e., the world of emanation
comprising the supernal *sefirot* laid out in the highest heaven in an anthropomorphic shape,
and their lower projections], even regarding the Ancient One of '*Adam Kadmon* (MS. JTS
0425). [R. Shalom Shar'abi's mystical eminence is thus testified to, in that he penetrated to
the secrets of the Ancient One of '*Adam Kadmon*, the most recondite manifestation of the
godhead in the world of emanation.]

weeping. Later on, you said that you do not see him any longer
and that you thought that he has passed on. When I arrived here,
I investigated the matter and was told the most extraordinary
things of this man. His name was R. Hayim ben Atar. He was
exceedingly pious, sharp-witted, and master of both revealed and
secret teachings. Compared with him, all the scholars of Israel
were as monkeys are to men. They sang his praise to me. He
came to Jerusalem accompanied by a number of his disciples and
great scholars. In short, he was truly pious, saintly, and holy. But
because of our numerous iniquities, he did not last long in Jerusalem—just a year—before dying some four years ago at the
very time when you spoke [of it] to me. When I told the scholars
here of the words you had used in speaking of him, they were
astounded. In short: *Your name is known in the gates of Jerusalem*, and the local scholars have asked me to write to you,
urging you to come and take up residence here, for they long to
see your face.[161]

R. Gershon joined the circle of Bet El and, in a document dated Iyar
1758, was listed among those who studied in the "conventicle of the
pietists."[162] He was famed for his piety. According to one account, "on 9
Av, while facing the site of the Temple and reciting the dirges of lamenta-
tion, he fainted several times and could hardly be resuscitated so great
was his anguish."[163]

Once there was a drought in the Holy Land. R. Shalom Sharabi
proclaimed a fast in Jerusalem, ordered everyone to gather in a certain
synagogue, and appointed R. Gershon to lead the service. Now, in
Jerusalem it was customary for the person leading the service also to say
words of admonition to the congregation. R. Gershon reviewed his
address all through the night; by early morning, his throat was parched.
He sent his son, R. Leib, to tell R. Shalom that someone else must take
his place, since he could not lead the service. However, during the
service, while the "Song of the Sea"[164] was being recited, R. Shalom
realized that R. Gershon had regained his voice. Immediately after the
silent prayer,[165] he ordered that the cantor step down and R. Gershon
take his place. R. Gershon recited aloud the "Eighteen Benedictions"[166]
[which had already been said in silence] and began the penitential

161. *Birkat Ha'aretz*, § 326. Cf. R. Abraham Kalisker: "Our holy master (R. Ber of
Miedzyrzec) and the rav, Baal Shem Tov, were respected by all of the Sephardim" (*Kiryat
Sefer*, 1:147).
162. *Hama'alot Leshelomo* [of S. Hazan (Alexandria: F. H. Mizrahi, 1894)], letter *tav*.
163. *Hibat Yerushalayim*, p. 43a.
164. [Exod. 15:1–19.]
165. [The *'amidah* is first recited silently by everyone and is then repeated aloud by the
cantor.]
166. [See *BT* Berakhot 34b.]

prayers. But after the introductory section, he stepped down and refused to continue. His son inquired why he had done this. R. Gershon replied: "The words of the introductory section of the penitential prayers came so easily from my mouth that had I gone on, it would have started to rain immediately. As I feared that I might grow arrogant [at my instant success], I stopped, for I know that it will rain for two of three consecutive days. And so it did."[167]

At that time there lived in Hebron "the extraordinary rabbi, the holy saint"[168] R. Mordekhai Robio, head of the yeshivah *Hesed Le'avraham Ve'emt Leya 'akov*, and head of the yeshivah *Keneset Yisra'el*.[169] He came to Palestine from Smyrna, apparently, where he had studied in his youth with R. Isaac Hakohen[170] who served as chief rabbi of that city for forty years[171] and had ordained him.[172] R. Mordecai is the author of *Shemen Hamor*.[173] He settled in Hebron in 1740/41,[174] taught there, and raised up many disciples. Around 1742/43, he went abroad to solicit funds for his community.[175] When he returned in that year to Hebron, he was appointed chief rabbi.[176] Around 1756/57, R. Gershon's daughter, Esther, became engaged to the son of R. Mordecai Robio.[177] R. Gershon described the groom as "a very worthy man, learned and highly regarded by people." The date of the wedding was set for Hanukkah, 1757.[178]

167. *Shivhey Habesht*, p. 10a [Ben-Amos, #55; Heschel is paraphrasing this story, as he often does elsewhere].

168. Azulai, *Shem Hagedolim*, s.v. *Shemen Hamor*; see Rosanes, *History of the Jews of Turkey*, pt. 5, p. 261.

169. *Shemen Hamor* (Livorno: Rovio, 1793), author's son's introduction.

170. Ibid., *'Even Ha'ezer*, # 2.

171. Rosanes, *History of the Jews of Turkey*, pt. 5, p. 62. He wrote the book *Batey Kehunah* (Smyrna, 1736).

172. The text of his ordination (*semikhah*) is printed in *Batey Kehunah* [Smyrna: Jonah Ashkenazi and David Hazan, 1736–41], *'Even Ha'ezer*, p. 31d.

173. Livorno, 1793. His book *Har Hamor*, containing novellae to the code of Maimonides and sermonic material (Salonica, 1835), is mentioned in *'Otzar Hasefarim* (letter *hey*, # 492), but I have been unable to examine a copy.

174. R. Abraham Gershon writes in 1756: "He has been a resident of Hebron about sixteen years."

175. He visited Amsterdam and cites in his book *Shemen Hamor, yoreh de'ah*, p. 21a, what he heard from R. Saul, the chief of the rabbinic court (apparently, the reference is to the author of the *Binyan 'Uri'el* [(Amsterdam: Y. and A. Proops, 1778), R. Saul Loewenstamm (1717–90), who was rabbi of Amsterdam from 1755–90]), and he also recalls some homilies in the name of R. Jonathan Ashkenazi.

176. According to Gaon, *Oriental Jews*, p. 196, he began to serve in 1783/84, but this is incorrect.

177. *Birkat Ha'aretz*, # 327. R. Mordecai had a son, R. Abraham Rovio, who was a rabbi in Hebron from 1804 to 1807. In 1793, when he was "the emissary of the holy city of Hebron," he published his father's book, *Shemen Hamor*, in Livorno, which included some of his own sermons (e.g., a sermon from 1757 in his father's honor). In Smyrna, he received the money for the publication of the book. Cf. A. Ganar (Malakhi), "The History of the Jewish Settlement in Hebron" (Hebrew), *Hator* (Jerusalem), (1929):19.

178. R. Mordecai died, apparently, in 1757: cf. *Shemen Hamor*, sermon #1: "a sermon which I gave in honor of my father and teacher, after the first month following his death,

During his residence in Jerusalem, R. Gershon was one of the leaders of the Ashkenazic community and was much respected by the "*gevirim*."[179] On a letter, dated 5517 (i.e., 1756/57), sent by the Ashkenazic rabbi of Jerusalem to the leaders of the Jewish community of Metz,[180] R. Gershon was the first signatory.[181] In this letter, they complain of their difficult plight. They argue that although the Sephardim in the Holy Land derive the greater part of their income from funds given their emissaries by the Ashkenazic communities of Poland and Germany, the Sephardic administrators (*gabai'im*) in the Holy Land who receive these funds do not apportion to their Ashkenazic brethren enough to secure their livelihood. In 1756/57, they had received a letter from R. Berman Shpeyer, who had contributed 600 *litras* to the emissary Shneur Feivish for the poor of the Ashkenazic community. They thank him for his generosity and plead with him to continue to support them in the future. They describe the calamity which had befallen them since they had not received any money for some time. The condition of the Ashkenazim was worse than that of the Sephardim, for the latter spoke the language of the land and could earn a little through commerce. The major complaint of the letter is against the Sephardic emissaries who discriminate against them in the allocation of alms, and they ask that money earmarked for the Ashkenazic poor be given to Ashkenazic emissaries.[182]

---

may he rest in peace . . . in 1757." In the *Pinkas* Constantinople MS, I found two Ladino letters (dated 15 Heshvan 1751 and 12 Kislev 1751), to "the perfect sages, the exemplary judges, the excellent rabbis, those emissaries of God [*meshulaḥim*], R. Mordecai Rovio and R. Abraham Israel." This solves the problem raised by Rosanes, *History of the Jews of Turkey*, pt. 5, p. 324. The identity of the letters from 1775 which were signed by R. Mordecai Rovio is suspect; cf. *HUCA*, 5:412. [A. Yaari, however, in *Emissaries*, pp. 498–99, and in a private communication, believes that 1757 is the year not of Rovio's death but of that of his father, that R. Mordecai died in 1782, and that the letters signed in 1775 are authentic.]

179. The Baal Shem Tov requests that R. Gershon write to the *gevirim* [i.e., the *pekidim* or representatives of the Land of Israel in Constantinople, who dispersed all funds] on behalf of R. Jacob Joseph Hakohen, author of the *Toldot Ya'akov Yosef*, "to support him generously" [see *BT* Ketubot 111a–b; *Ben Porat Yosef*, the end].

180. A. Lunz, "Dovev Siftey Yeshenim," *Yerushalyim* 2 (1887):148–51. The letter was addressed to the wealthy men of Metz and to its rabbi. It is interesting that the rabbi in Metz at that time was R. Samuel Heilman, who supported the side of Emden in the Emden-Eibeschütz controversy, regarding which, see *Revue des Études Juives* 12 (1886):289. [See Barnai, *Hasidic Letters from the Land of Israel*, pp. 46 and 49.]

181. After R. Abraham Gershon, someone from the city of Szydlow signed his name, but the name is erased. Judging from the lists of support (see above, n. 81), it seems that this was R. Joshua of Szydlow. The other signatories, e.g., R. Aryeh Judah son of Alexander of Opatów, R. Mordecai Petahia son of R. Judah Leib, R. Yakar son of R. Abraham Gershon, and the emissary Shneur Feibush, were mentioned in those lists. It is interesting to note that R. Abraham Gershon received the largest sum.

182. See Appendix, document 3. [Further research has confirmed the significant role played by R. Gershon. He had become the Ashkenazic representative for funds raised in the Diaspora to support those in the Holy Land. "During the 1750s, R. Gershon of Kuty was at the head" of those who distributed funds for the Ashkenazim. The dissension between the Ashkenazim and the dominant Sephardic community over the distribution of funds col-

On the day of the Fast of Gedaliah (3 Tishri), 1756, R. Gershon's wife Bluma died.[183] "The world became dark for me; she departed into [the World of Eternal] Rest and left me to my sorrows," he wrote to his brother-in-law, noting also the great respect paid her at the funeral. He decided not to marry again, but the rabbis in Jerusalem overcame his reluctance by arguing that he was bound "by the Torah" to take another wife.[184] They wanted him to marry a local woman, but on this point he refused to accede. There were few Ashkenazic Jews in Palestine at the time, and he did not want to take a Sephardic wife, "for our attitudes, customs, and temperaments differ." For that reason, he decided to return to his country of origin to find a suitable wife;[185] he planned to be with the Baal Shem in the summer of 1757. He asked the latter to find him "a suitable woman, one forty years of age, not of a certainty able to bear children, wise, of some financial means, and willing to leave with him for Jerusalem, may it be rebuilt and established speedily in our days, amen, before the festival of Sukkot."[186]

Apparently, R. Gershon did leave Palestine at that time.[187] He passed

lected in Europe for the Land of Israel continued after the time of R. Gershon, and increased. "His sons, who were then among the leaders of the Ashkenazic community in Jerusalem," were involved in this trying matter. Indeed, one son, R. Hayim Aaron, was at the very center of the controversy, and traveled throughout Central and Eastern Europe in the latter part of the 1760s representing the Ashkenazim of Jerusalem. The records of the Furth community (1770), for example, indicate that he had appeared before them and brought "numerous ordinances (takanot) of previous authorities from the years 1694 and 1729 . . . to the effect that all monies collected . . . in all communities in Poland and Germany . . . should go to the Ashkenazic community of Jerusalem." The ire aroused by R. Hayim, when he himself proclaimed similar takanot in these communities, was temporarily assuaged by the joint efforts of the pekidim in Constantinople and other leading figures, such as R. Ezekiel Landau, who nullified his decrees and gave the Sephardim permission to collect in these areas. The immigration of Hasidim, beginning in the latter 1770s, strengthened the Ashkenazic cause and contributed to the continuance of the agitation. See Barnai, "The Jewish Community in Jerusalem," p. 197, pp. 202–5, nn. 17 and 18; and "Pekidei Eretz Israel" (English).

183. *Ben Porat Yosef*, end.
184. [See *BT* Yevamot p. 62b.]
185. Regarding the question of whether it is permitted to leave the Land of Israel in order to marry and settle abroad, cf. Maimonides, *Mishneh Torah*, laws of Kings 5:9, and the *Kesef Mishnah*; and also, the opinion of the author of the *Shema* *Ya'akov* [R. Israel Jacob Algazi], and R. Yom Tov Tzahalon in *Birkat Ha'aretz*, ## 52 and 308. See the book *Kiryat Melekh Rav*, # 13, regarding one who came "from a distant land, from the cities of Germany, to dwell in our land, the city of God, and conducted himself in holiness, abstinence, and fear of the Lord. About a year after he had settled there, however, he knew that he could bear it no longer without a wife . . . and therefore desired . . . to marry."
186. *Birkat Ha'aretz*, # 327.
187. Hasidic legend supports this theory. It is told that once during the recitation of the Shema during the Friday evening service, the Baal Shem Tov approached his brother-in-law, shook his hat, and cried out, "Ah!" After the service, R. Gershon entered the private room of R. Ber of Miedzyrzecz and wept before him. The students went to the Baal Shem Tov and told him, "R. Gershon is weeping." The Baal Shem Tov answered, "When I saw, during the recitation of the Shema, that R. Gershon had [succeeded in] taking leave of all

away several years later. According to some, he died in Palestine,[188] while others claim that he died abroad and was buried in Kuty.[189] In 1762/3, clearly, R. Abraham Gershon was no longer alive.[190]

---

bodily awareness (*hayyetah lo hitpashtut hagashmiyut*), I feared that he might become proud." This story is told by R. Saul Bick of Miedzybórz. As is known, R. Ber only became a follower of the Baal Shem Tov a few years before 1760, during which time R. Gershon would have been in Poland. Cf. above p. 16.

[Later scholars have taken up Heschel's theory that R. Gershon returned at that time to Poland. A. Rubenstein, in "An Unpublished Portion of *Shivhey Habesht?*" (Hebrew), *Tarbiz* 35 (1965):180–82, relates an episode in the name of the *mitnaged* R. Israel the preacher of Slutsk which places R. Gershon and R. Mendel of Przemyślany as colleagues, together with the Baal Shem Tov. Since R. Gershon left Poland for Palestine before 1747 and R. Mendel was born in 1728, the latter would have been hardly nineteen at the time, while R. Gershon would have reached a mature fifty. If R. Gershon returned to Poland, however, one could posit a later date for this incident and solve the discrepancy in age. Rubenstein takes this as additional evidence that "between the fall of 1757 and the spring of 1760, the death of the Besht, R. Gershon departed Palestine for Poland." Barnai, "Notes on the Immigration of R. Gershon Kutover," believes the date was between the fall of 1758 and the spring of 1760. See Scholem, "Two Letters," p. 430, n. 4.]

The fact that in Iyar 1758 R. Gershon's name is listed among the fellows of the *Midrash Hasidim* (see above, n. 162) does not prove he was then in Palestine, because as a regular scholar, he could have been recorded even though he had gone abroad for a while.

188. Lunz, "Kivrey Eretz Tzvi," *Yerushalayim*, 1 (1882) 125: "His grave is on the slopes of the Mount of Olives, but his tombstone has fallen victim to the ravages of time." See *Hibat Tziyon*, p. 43a, "and in the cemetery, there is the grave of R.G.K. (R. Gershon Kutover) . . . and, at his feet, the grave of his grandson." According to the residents of Jerusalem, many have searched for his grave, but none has found it.

[With the return of the cemetery on the Mount of Olives to Jewish hands in 1967, the grave of R. Gershon was located by Jacob Gepner who described it, with photographs, in his *'Or Ki Tov* (Jerusalem: Mifal Helkat Mehokek, 1968), pp. 17, 68, 77–86. The tombstone reads " . . . Abraham Gershon Ashkenazi," the meaning of the last word of which has been debated: Rubenstein claims that it simply distinguishes the deceased from the mostly Sephardic members of the kabbalists of Beth El who are buried next to him ("On the Manuscript of the Letter of the Baal Shem Tov to R. Gershon of Kutov," in *Sefer Margaliot*, ed. Y. Raphael [Hebrew] [Jerusalem: Mosad Harav Kook, 1973], p. 188); Bauminger, on the other hand, argues that it is a surname used during R. Gershon's lifetime ("More about the Letter of the Baal Shem Tov to His Brother-in-Law, R. Gershon of Kutov," *Sefer Margoliot*, p. 359, n. 61, and is supported by evidence which Barnai supplies from a manuscript dated 4 Adar 1754 in which he is called " . . . Abraham Gershon Ashkenazi."]

189. According to Joel Mastboim, *Galicia* (Warsaw: Farlag Jacobson-Goldberg, 1929), p. 106, in the 1920s R. Gershon's grave could be seen in Kutov. The tombstone was in poor condition and was repaired thanks to the author's efforts.

190. *Birkat Ha'aretz*, # 333. [The gravestone in Jerusalem uncovered by Gepner gives the date of R. Gershon's death as "21 Adar I 1761 (5521)." Through analysis of documents from the Eliacher collection pertaining to R. Gershon's son, R. Yakar, Barnai, "Notes on the Immigration of R. Gershon Kutover," p. 116, has established the authenticity of that date.]

Addendum

R. Gershon's First Journey to the Holy Land

Much has been written about the immigration to Palestine by Hasidim from the Baal Shem's circle, but the matter has still not been properly clarified. Several important facts have either escaped the attention of scholars or have been misinterpreted. It is generally accepted, for example, that R. Gershon first journeyed to the Land of Israel in 1746/47. I am inclined to the supposition that this was not his first trip there. There are four pieces of evidence:

(1) *Shivḥey Habesht* records the following:[191]

> I heard this from R. Falk. . . .[192] When R. Gershon of Kuty went abroad from the Land of Israel to arrange a marriage for his son, he decided, as an afterthought (*ʾagav ʾurḥa*): "Now that I have crossed the sea, thank God, I shall go to my brother-in-law, the Baal Shem Tov (of blessed memory)." He came to him on the eve of the holy Sabbath. The Baal Shem Tov arose to recite the afternoon service and lingered in prayer until the stars appeared. Now, R. Gershon, like the Baal Shem Tov, had been using the prayer book of the Ari[193] of blessed memory. [Waiting for the Baal Shem Tov to finish, he had enough time] to review the weekly Pentateuchal portion, studying the original Hebrew twice and also going over the Aramaic translation (Targum);[194] he then asked for some cushions and lay down to rest. Later, during the Sabbath Eve meal, R. Gershon asked his brother-in-law, the Baal Shem Tov:
>
> "Why did you linger so at prayer? Like you, I, too, prayed with *kavanot*, [but I finished so much before you that I had time] to review the Pentateuchal portion, reciting the Hebrew text twice and the Targum once, and [still was waiting so long for you that] I had to lie down and rest, while you were yet standing and shaking your body."
>
> R. Gershon [was caustic because he] wanted the Besht to explain himself, but the latter was silent and would not say a word. R.·Gershon went over again what he had said and repeated his question.
>
> Then the Baal Shem Tov replied:

191. *Shivḥey Habesht*, p. 8b [Ben-Amos, # 46].
192. The famous Hasid of Titshilnik, *Shivḥey Habesht*, p. 7a [Ben-Amos, # 34], R. Falk, is mentioned several times; he was "exiled to the Crimea with R. Joseph Ashkenazi, the cantor of the Baal Shem Tov, during the time of the flight" [from the Haidamaks; see above pp. 34–40], p. 7b [Ben-Amos, # 40].
193. [R. Isaac Luria of Safed, the foremost Jewish mystic of the sixteenth century, whose kabbalistic meditations to parts of the liturgy (*kavanot*) were incorporated into some of the later prayer books.]
194. [See *BT* Berakhot 8a.]

"When [in the second blessing of the *ʿamidah*] I read the words 'quicken the dead' (and R. Falk was not sure whether the Besht was referring to the words 'Thou quickenest the dead' or to 'quickenest the dead with great mercy') and I . . . concentrate upon the *kavanah* of *yiḥudim*,[195] then the souls of the dead come to me in their thousands. I talk to each one of them, and find out why he had been rejected from his portion of heaven . . . I repair each one, pray for him, and raise him. I deal with them in order of their importance. There are so many that if I wished to raise them all I would have to stand reciting the *Shemoneh ʿEsreh*,[196] for three years. But when I hear the [heavenly] herald proclaim, 'It [the Sabbath] is sanctified. It is sanctified,'[197] and it is impossible to elevate any more souls, I conclude the *Shemoneh ʿEsreh*."[198]

Said R. Gershon mockingly (*bederekh seḥok*): "Why do they not come to me?"

The Baal Shem Tov replied: "Stay here with me over the coming Sabbath, and I shall give you the *kavanot* in writing, so that they come to you. And so he did.

On the following Sabbath eve (i.e., Friday afternoon), when the Baal Shem Tov finished reciting the Kaddish just before [the *ʿAmidah*] prayer, R. Gershon, like him, stood up to pray. But the Baal Shem did not begin his prayer, for he knew that R. Gershon would not be able to bear it and would be terrified. He adjusted his watch and sniffed snuff, waiting for R. Gershon to get to the passage which had that *kavanah*. When [R. Gershon] reached it, he saw the dead converging upon him like a vast herd of sheep, and he fainted. The Baal Shem Tov then roused him and ordered him to his house. That night, at the table during the meal, the Baal Shem asked R. Gershon: "Why did you faint?"[199] R. Gershon replied, "When I applied myself to the *kavanah*, the dead came to me like herds. . . ."

[Then the Besht said to his followers jokingly: "Strike him, so he will not mock the Besht."][200]

---

195. ["Unions": a mystical term for an intention (*kavanah*) to unify God with the *Shekhinah*.]

196. ["Eighteen Benedictions," or the *ʿamidah*, i.e., the "standing" prayer, of which "the quickening of the dead" is a part.]

197. ["On the Sabbath eve there is a veritable commotion of souls coming and going, ascending and descending. . . . All the souls are full of joy and eagerness to become crowns for the holy people on earth, for the righteous in the lower Paradise. At last comes the moment when a voice proclaims throughout all the spheres: 'It is sanctified! It is sanctified!' Then there is peace everywhere, perfect peace, even to the wicked in Gehenna, and all the souls crown themselves, some above, and some below." (*Zohar, parshat terumah*, 135–6a; English trans., Sperling and Simon [London: Soncino Press, 1933], 3:386–89)]

198. [In the Hebrew text, the Baal Shem Tov addresses R. Gershon in the formal third person while the latter uses the familiar second person in speaking to the Baal Shem Tov.]

199. [The Baal Shem Tov now shifts to the familiar second person.]

200. [Heschel does not quote the conclusion of the story.]

When did all this happen? On 17 Heshvan 1756, R. Gershon wrote the
Baal Shem Tov from Palestine, reporting that his wife had died and that
since a Sephardic woman was unacceptable to him, he intended to return
to his country of origin to find a suitable wife, adding: "If God grants me
life, I shall be with you at your holy residence by next summer, (may it
[that season] come to us for good tidings)."²⁰¹ However, the visit in
Miedzybórz mentioned in *Shivhey Habesht*, which we have quoted here,
took place when R. Gershon had gone abroad not to find a wife for
himself but "to arrange a marriage for his son." During the visit—paid
only "as an afterthought" (²*agav* ²*urha*) to the main purpose of the
journey—he slighted the Baal Shem by speaking to him "mockingly."
Such a visit must be dated back to a time when R. Gershon had not yet
come to recognize the Baal Shem's eminence, i.e., prior to his journey in
1746/47. For by 1747/48, he was already bound to him with bonds of love
and reverence.²⁰²

(2) R. Pinhas of Korzec told his disciples the following tale:

> R. Gershon was in the Land of Israel, and when R. Nahman
> Horodenker arrived there, the two of them met on the Sabbath
> and rejoiced greatly. On the eve of the Sabbath they lingered so
> long at the table that the light was on the verge of extinguishing,
> for the oil had run out. R. Gershon shouted: "What is this?!"
> *Vos iz dos*? And the light continued to burn throughout the Sab-
> bath. When R. Gershon returned from the synagogue at the end
> of Sabbath, he ordered: "You! Stop!" *Die! Hayde!* And the light
> expired.²⁰³

When did this meeting between R. Nahman and R. Gershon take
place? According to the tradition recorded in *Shivhe Habesht*,²⁰⁴ R.
Nahman traveled to Palestine three times. His third journey was in
1763/64²⁰⁵ at which point neither the Baal Shem Tov nor R. Gershon was
alive.²⁰⁶ From another account, however, we can assert that R. Nahman
first arrived in Palestine before [fall] 1740, left it, and then returned in
1741. [This time, his absence from the Holy Land is the clue.]

The author of *Shivhe Habesht* relates having heard the following tale
from R. Yehiel Mikhel, the maggid of Zloczew: R. Eleazar of Amsterdam went to the Holy Land "because of R. Nahman of Horodenka, for
he said, 'When both of us are in the Holy Land, we shall bring the

201. *Birkat Ha²aretz*, # 327. [The most formal third-person plural is used here.]
202. [See above, pp. 148–49.]
203. MS. Uman. R. Pinhas told of this at a Hanukah feast, at which time there was seated
before him R. Zalman Vilner from Palestine.
204. *Shivhey Habesht*, p. 21b; cf. p. 26d [Ben-Amos, ## 129, 169].
205. According to the ²*Ahavat Tziyon* of R. Simhah son of R. Joshua of Zalozce.
206. *Birkat Ha²aretz*, # 333 [see n. 190 for the date of R. Gershon's death].

Redeemer.' To herald his [R. Eleazar's] arrival in the Holy Land, all his fellow townsmen came to [meet] him. And when he saw R. Samson, the son of R. Nahman, and asked him, 'Where is your father?,' he replied, 'He has gone abroad.' Said [R. Eleazar] '*Vey! Vey!* It is because of him that I have come.' When R. Nahman heard that R. Eleazar had journeyed to the Holy Land, he hurried back there, but before he arrived R. Eleazar was dead—because of our many sins.''[207]

There is no doubt that this "R. Eleazar" is the eminent talmudist and kabbalist, R. Eleazar Rokeah, who was rabbi of Brody from 1713/14 to 1735. He became rabbi of Amsterdam in 1735 and left the city on 10 Sivan 1740, for "he was accepted as a *nasi* (notable) in the Land of Israel." He traveled there and settled in Safed during the Intermediate Days of Sukkot [early fall], 1740. In the following year, he became the subject of the enmity of a number of kabbalists in Safed whom R. Eleazar had tried to prevent from studying the book *Hemdat Hayamim* [which was suspected of being a Sabbatean work]. Because of this furor, he passed away in the fall of 1741.[208]

R. Nahman of Horodenka [in other words] came to the Land of Israel three times: (1) before [fall] 1740 [and the arrival of R. Eleazar of Amsterdam], (2) in 1741 [soon after R. Eleazar's death], and (3) in 1763/64 [when R. Gershon was no longer alive]. The account by R. Pinhas of Korzec, a friend and admirer of R. Nahman, [about a meeting in Palestine between R. Gershon and R. Nahman] cannot be sustained unless it is assumed that on his first visit, R. Nahman found R. Gershon already there. Like many other scholars of his generation who had tried to settle in the Holy Land, R. Gershon, apparently, returned to Europe. By 1742, at any rate, he was in Brody, and involved in the controversy there [see pp. 52–56].

(3) According to *Shivhey Habesht*, R. Gershon lived in Safed for a certain time. He became friendly there with the rabbi of the city, the *hakham* of the Sephardim, "a very good man" who grew quite fond of R. Gershon. Once, however, on "a very cold" day, it so happened that the

207. *Shivhey Habesht*, p. 26a [Ben-Amos, # 169]. R. Yehiel Mikhel lived many years in Brody and certainly knew R. Eleazar who was rabbi there at that time. [See above, p. 51.]

208. These dates are mentioned in the Yiddish book *She'erit Yisra'el* (Amsterdam, 1771) by the grammarian R. Menahem Mann son of Solomon Halevi, a contemporary and resident of the same city as R. Eleazar. R. Jacob Emden writes in his *Shevirat Luhot Ha'aven*, p. 46, about the cause of his death. From the context in *Shivhey Habesht*, p. 11c [Ben-Amos, ## 63, 64] one can deduce that the anger felt by R. Eleazar regarding the *Sefer Hemdat Hayamin* [for its suspected Sabbatean origins; see Yaari, "Who Wrote the Book Hemdat Yamim?" (Hebrew), *Ta'alumat Sefer* (Jerusalem: Mosad Harav Kook, 1954)] was known in the Baal Shem Tov's circle. We also learn there about the Baal Shem Tov's negative feelings about that book. On the other hand, we know that the Palestinian kabbalists venerated the work; cf. *'Etz Hayim*, pt. 3, *nehar shalom* (Warsaw, 1891), p. 31b, and the *Kevod Hakhamim* [of M. M. Halperin; Jerusalem, 1896].

ḥakham simply misunderstood what R. Gershon had said and suspected that something was being kept from him. Sephardim being "very strict in regard to falsehood," the *ḥakham* accused R. Gershon of lying. R. Gershon replied, "I have spoken the truth." Furious, the *ḥakham* rushed to the Holy Ark and declared by oath that R. Gershon was lying! Enraged in turn, R. Gershon at once "proclaimed a ban (*ḥerem*) against the *ḥakham*!" The *ḥakham* removed his shoes,[209] walked home, gathered the congregation, and told them of what had happened to him. They went to R. Gershon and asked him, "Why did you put our *ḥakham* under the ban?" Said R. Gershon, "Because he swore a false oath." Eventually, the *ḥakham* pacified R. Gershon who then withdrew the *ḥerem*.[210]

The narrator added the following:

A letter arrived from the Besht to R. Gershon in which was written, "I saw that you were being tried in a heavenly palace [*heykhal*] and that the intention was, God forbid, to sentence you to death. Why were you disrespectful of the city's rabbi? Now, I wanted to go to that palace and plead on your behalf, but the gates were closed before me and I could not enter there. Then I said: "Master of the World, whatever he did was for Your sake!" A voice proclaimed: "Let him be, since he did it for the Lord's sake! Nevertheless, let his sentence be one month of blindness, a blind man being considered as dead (*BT* Nedarim 64b)." And so, from now on do not be so harsh. . . ."

R. Gershon replied to the Besht: "I do not know what to make of you. The story is true, but it amazes me that you 'saw' them judging me before the incident even occurred."

For the date which the Baal Shem had written his letter preceded the event!

This story, mentioned also in a work by R. Menahem Mendel of Lubavitch,[211] should be put together with another piece of information. In

209. [As does the mourner, for that is the class into which one who is excommunicated falls.]
210. *Shivhey Habesht*, p. 10a [Ben-Amos, # 56]. "And it seems to me that this occurred in Safed." Cf. *BT* Nedarim 7b, and Maimonides, *Mishneh Torah*, laws regarding oaths 12:9: "One who hears a vain usage of the divine name from his fellow, or a false oath . . . is obligated to excommunicate the speaker, and if he fails to do so, then may he himself be excommunicated." About that time a mild dispute broke out between two worthies of the city Liter, and both parties became angry and excommunicated each other. See the *Sama' Dehaye* (Amsterdam: Joseph Dayan, 1739), *yoreh de'ah*, # 21, and also *Sefer Tashbatz* (Amsterdam: Naftali Levi and Ziskind Levi, 1738), pt. 1, # 55, p. 28c: "If we were actually to excommunicate all liars, there would be no one innocent, and all the world would be *ḥerem*" [which means both "excommunication" and "desolation" (Josh. 6:17)].
211. M. M. Shneurson, *Derekh Mitzvotekhah* (Poltava: Elijah Akiba Rabinowitz, 1911), p. 59a:
"And thus is understood the story of how the Baal Shem Tov foretold at Rosh Hashanah what was to transpire (later in the year), in the well-known story about his brother-in-law R.

his [Hebron] Letter of 1747/48, R. Gershon mentions the death in Safed of R. Benjamin Kazis.[212] This scholar was a native of Adrianople who, "because of the hardship which he suffered in that city," had moved to Constantinople, and became one of its rabbis and teachers.[213] In his old age, in 1745/46, he journeyed to Palestine and served as the chief rabbi of Safed.[214] R. Benjamin did not live long in Palestine. After two years, he died in an epidemic.[215] R. Gershon records: "I delivered an extensive eulogy over him (in Hebron), for the local scholars had invited me to do so, since I knew him to be one of the greatest men in all Israel."[216] Clearly, they would not have invited R. Gershon to eulogize the Sephardic *hakham* had they not known that R. Gershon was well-acquainted with him. When and where could R. Gershon and R. Benjamin have become acquainted? One can only assume that R. Gershon lived for some time in

---

Gershon Kutover and the sage in the Holy Land. In that instance, the Baal Shem Tov had predicted to him in writing the entire incident before it came to pass in reality. Even if his soul's ascent did not reach the most recondite manifestation of the godhead in the world of emanation (*'Adam Kadmon,* "Primordial Man") but merely the palaces (*heykhalot*) of *Yetzirah* (i.e., the third-highest world of emanation), he could yet see fifteen years ahead at a glance. Thus at Rosh Hashanah, when he received his portion of vitality for the entire year (that is why it is called *rosh* [head], just as the head contains the vitality for the entire body), he could include the whole year in a single look." This detail, that the Baal Shem Tov foretold the event at Rosh Hashanah, is not included in the *Shivhey Habesht.*

[This excerpt from *Derekh Mitzvotekhah* derives from a discussion of time in which the author develops the theme that the higher one goes in the spiritual worlds the less differentiation one finds there, until one reaches the ultimate Unity. This applies to time as well. The upper worlds are beyond time, because there is no differentiation between past and future. Thus one who is able to ascend to these upper worlds can see the future in the present. Moreover, Rosh Hashanah, the beginning of the New Year, is the source of all happenings in the year, as the head is the source of all movement in the body. Therefore, on Rosh Hashanah one is able to see all future events in one glance, because it is beyond the differentiation of time.]

212. The manuscript version of the letter: "The rabbi of Safed was R. Kozes, may he rest in peace." In Cahana's text, the reading is Kizes. The name is lacking altogether in *Birkat Ha'aretz,* # 326. R. Benjamin died, apparently, in the fall of 1747, possibly in the plague that moved from Jerusalem to Safed. His book, *Megilat Setarim,* on the first part of the *Sefer Mitzvot Hagadol* of R. Moses of Coucy, was published posthumously in Constantinople in 1750. Rosanes, *History of the Jews of Turkey,* pt. 5, p. 293, estimates that he settled in Safed in 1740. In our estimation, he arrived in 1746.

[Heschel's supposition as to R. Benjamin's date of death has been confirmed by the recent location of R. Benjamin's tombstone in Safed by Gepner; it reads "8 Tevet 1747." Since in the Hebron Letter R. Gershon mentioned that he recently had eulogized R. Benjamin at his funeral, and we can now establish the time of R. Benjamin's death, the dating of the Hebron Letter in the winter of 1747/8 is confirmed. See M. Yizraeli, *The Letter of 5508* (Jerusalem, 1978), and Barnai, "Notes on the Immigration of R. Gershon Kutover," p. 311.]

213. Cf. R. Jacob Abraham Ghiron's introduction to the *Megilat Sefer* of Benjamin Kazis (Constantinople: Reuben and Nissim Ashkenazi, 1750).

214. H.Y.D. Azulai, *Shem Hagedolim,* personalities, letter *bet,* # 24.

215. *Megilat Sefer,* introduction of R. Hayim Modai: "God took him . . . after two years . . . and he rested in the land." [For the date of his death, see above nn. 188, 189.]

216. *Birkat Ha'aretz,* # 327. [". . . *tzaddik hador vegadol beyisra'el.*"]

Safed between 1745/46 and 1746/47.[217] This would account for the spread
of his reputation to Jerusalem to the point where, in Tishri 1747, the
scholars of the Ashkenazic community wished to accept him as "rabbi
and leader, father and guardian."[218] These scholars must have known him
from the years he had spent in the Holy Land before 1747/48.[219] Furthermore, in the winter of 1747/48 we find R. Gershon active in Constantinople on behalf of the Jewish community of Palestine. It is hard to
imagine that a man who had never been there would have been permitted
to present the case of its needy residents before the leaders of the
Constantinople community. A final point: If we assume that R. Gershon
had arrived in Palestine only for the first time in the late summer of 1747,
on the very eve of Rosh Hashanah, it would be difficult to understand
how he could possibly have installed his family in Hebron while he
himself went to Jerusalem for the High Holidays.[220] This becomes more

217. The story in *Shivhey Habesht* [p. 25b] [Ben-Amos, # 193] about R. Gershon
attending a circumcision in Akko where he spent the Sabbath suggests that he lived
somewhere near Akko, e.g., Safed. The story is mentioned by a firsthand witness, the Baal
Shem Tov's grandson, R. Moses Hayim Ephraim of Sudilkov: "And God saw the light that
it was good" [Gen. 1:4]. "The Midrash teaches: 'that it was good, means good to store up for
the righteous (tzaddikim) who use it in every generation' [*BT* Hagigah 12a]. My revered
grandfather [the Baal Shem Tov], may he rest in peace . . . asked, 'Where is that light
hidden?,' and answered [his own question], 'God has hidden it in the Torah. Thus the
righteous in every generation use that light, that is, by studying the Torah in which that light
is hidden they can see from one end of the universe to the other,' *as I myself have observed*
[emphasis AJH] on many occasions. [For example,] he [the Baal Shem Tov] once wrote my
great-uncle in Palestine, the late R. Gershon Kutover, that he had "seen" him one Sabbath
outside the Holy Land and wondered what he was doing there? My great-uncle answered in
a letter that on that Sabbath a wealthy man was planning a circumcision for his son just
outside the boundaries of the Land of Israel [the border of the Holy Land, according to
rabbinic definition, ran through Akko] and had sent for R. Gershon to act as the circum-
siser. And so on and on, for there are more examples than I can quote of how he [the Baal
Shem Tov], in fact, saw from one end of the universe to the other, all of which was
accomplished with the light hidden in the Torah." See *Degel Mahaneh 'Efrayim* (Korzec,
1810), *parshat bereshit*. [Other theories have been proposed as to R. Gershon's meeting
with R. Benjamin. A. Yaari, in a private communication to A. Heschel, was of the opinion
that R. Gershon never resided in Safed, since there is no mention of it in the voluminous
correspondence from the city at that time, that he met R. Benjamin in Constantinople
where the latter was a rabbi and may even have come to Israel with him on the same boat.
Katz-Shteiman, "Concerning Barnai's Notes on the Immigration of R. Gershon on Kutov,"
pp. 302–3, also believes that the two met in Constantinople and that they may have renewed
their acquaintance in Safed where R. Benjamin was rabbi. Thus he could have been the
Safed rabbi who was the "admirer of R. Gershon" mentioned in *Shivhey Habesht*, p. 10a
[Ben-Amos, # 56]. Barnai ("Notes on the Immigration of R. Gershon," p. 115), on the
other hand, argues that R. Gershon stayed in Akko for a while after he arrived in Sivan
1747, explaining the story of the circumcision in *Shivhey Habesht*, and then traveled to
Safed, where he met R. Benjamin, and then on to Hebron, where he left his family, arriving
directly in Jerusalem just before the New Year.]
    218. [See above, p. 79.]
    219. [However, see Barnai, "Notes on the Immigration of R. Gershon," p. 311.]
    220. [See above, n. 132.]

plausible, however, if having lived in Safed for a time, R. Gershon transferred his family to Hebron before leaving for Constantinople.[221]

Perhaps R. Gershon chose to live in Safed because it had been the city of the fathers of kabbalah, R. Moses Cordovero, R. Isaac Luria, and R. Hayim Vital, and later of R. Isaiah Horowitz, author of *Sheney Luḥot Haberit*. R. Eleazar Rokeah, rabbi of Brody and Amsterdam, whom R. Gershon must have known from his days in Brody, also chose to live in Safed. R. Hayim ben Atar and his group considered settling there.[222] R. Pinhas of Korzec, likewise, yearned to live in Safed.[223]

We know that Safed was dear to the Jews abroad, who looked after its residents well. From the four corners of the earth they sent generous financial support. However, between the years 1740 and 1750 the Jewish community of Safed went into a severe decline. Conditions there had deteriorated and were in many ways worse than those of the Jerusalem community. The authorities oppressed the Jewish residents of Safed by heavy taxation and harsh laws. They suffered especially from their neighbors who would raid their homes periodically. The roads were unsafe to the point that Jews could hardly travel beyond the city limits for fear of their neighbors. A contemporary complained of this: "The city, said to be 'of perfect beauty,' 'a joy to the whole earth,' 'a most precious stone,' has become a nightmare . . . We were forced to flee to the high mountains and hills to seek shelter from the wickedness of the Gentiles.[224] In 1742 catastrophe struck the city, bringing death to a large section of its population.[225] Some left Safed and moved to Egypt or to nearby cities like Tiberias, Akko, and Jerusalem.

(4) The letter discussed in the Appendix, document 1, proves that R. Gershon had visited Jerusalem before 1746/47.

221. Rosanes, *History of the Jews of Turkey*, pt. 5, p. 12, tells, without giving a source, that R. Abraham Gershon lived in Safed for five years, from 1742 to 1747, "and after he tried unsuccessfully to move to Jerusalem, he traveled to Constantinople, to see if he could use the influence of Jews close to the court to obtain permission to settle there, or at least a royal decree to the rulers of Jerusalem ordering them (to allow him to settle there)." Rosanes was, perhaps, basing his information on the forged letters published in the *Ginzey Nistarot*. [See above, nn. 94, 133.]

222. Yaari, *Letters*, p. 247.

223. "When the late rabbi [R. Pinhas] planned to travel to Palestine, he intended to settle in a biblical city of refuge because such a city provides refuge to murderers, and one might hide there. He heard that Safed, the holy city, may it be rebuilt speedily and within our days, was none other than Kadesh, the city mentioned in the Book of Joshua [20:7] as being a city of refuge" (MS. HUC) [= MS. Cincinnati? Cf. above, pp. 34–35, n. 179.]

224. Ezra b. Raphael Malki, *Malki Bakodesh* (Salonica: Betzalel Halevi, 1749), Introduction.

225. See Gaon, *Oriental Jews*, p. 172. Cf. the pamphlet about the poor of Safed that circulated at the Council of Tyszowce (Tishvitz) in Elul 1742, cited in Halperin, *Pinkas of the Council of the Four Lands* (Hebrew).

Appendix

Document 1: An Unknown Document about the Baal Shem Tov

In the letter he wrote during the winter of 1747/48—commonly referred to as the "Hebron Letter"—R. Gershon described his arrival in the Holy Land in the fall of 1746, on the eve of Rosh Hashanah.[226] This epistle reflects nothing of the upheaval of spirit one would expect from a Jew privileged to set foot for the first time on the soil of the Holy Land. In the first letter a pilgrim would send to his brethren in the Diaspora, it was the accepted practice generation after generation to describe the landscape, especially that of Jerusalem, and to express one's grief over the desolation of Zion.[227] While the "Hebron Letter" was the initial one R. Gershon wrote from Palestine after having returned there from Constantinople,[228] this was clearly not his first time in the Holy Land. In fact, a brief passage from another letter by R. Gershon, preserved in a different source, has the telltale characteristics of being a fragment of a letter which R. Gershon had written during his very first visit in Palestine.

This passage was published in *Nofet Tzufim* by R. Meir Teomim. R. Meir was "a maggid in the holy community of Lubartów for some ten years and was later appointed maggid and rabbinical judge in the holy community of Lwów,"[229] where he died in 19 Tammuz 1773.[230] *Nofet Tzufim* was printed as part of the book *Rav Peninim* published in 1782 in Frankfurt a.M. by R. Meir's son, the well-known author of *Peri Megadim*, R. Joseph Teomim.

Commenting on the *haftarah* associated with the weekly Pentateuchal portion of Noah, R. Meir wrote:

> I have seen a letter from the Holy Land, written by the Hasid, our master, the rabbi, R. Gershon, may his light continue to shine, to his renowned (hamefursam) brother-in law, Baal Shem Tov, may his light continue to shine, in which he said as follows [emphasis AJH]:

---

226. Cf. Abraham Yaari, *Letters of the Land of Israel* p. 278; Israel Halperin, *The First Immigration of Hasidim to the Land of Israel*, p. 52. This date is confirmed via a comparison of the names of the rabbis who died in 1747/48; see above, nn. 132 and 134.

227. Cf. the remarks of R. Abraham Rosanes, the companion of R. Gershon, in the former's approbation to the book *Peri Ha'adamah*; see above, n. 136.

228. R. Gershon recounts what happened to him from the day he arrived in Jerusalem. This was not, however, his first letter home, because in it he refers to the fact that he had written to his family "several times" from Hebron and Constantinople.

229. *Rav Peninim* (Frankfurt a.O.: Joseph Teomim, 1782), title page.

230. The text of the tombstone is published in S. Buber's *'Anshey Shem* (Cracow: Y. Fischer, 1895), p. 136.

"When I arrived in the holy city of Jerusalem and saw that it was
well built-up, I prostrated myself and wept, saying: 'How is it, O
Jerusalem, that you, who are compared to a widow, should wear
such fine clothes during the days of your widowhood? Oh that I
had witnessed your desolation!'"[231]

Besides indicating that R. Gershon's first arrival in the Holy Land
antedated the journey described in the "Hebron Letter," this source is
important for another reason. It is one of the few documents which
mention the Baal Shem Tov by name during his lifetime.[232] Furthermore,
the citation in *Nofet Tzufim* refers to him as *"hamefursam,"* "the renowned." This refutes the claims by certain scholars that the founder of
Hasidism lived in some remote corner of the Jewish world and was
unknown during his lifetime to all but a very small circle.

It is generally accepted among Hasidim that R. Meir Teomim, father of
the author of the noted halakhic work, *Peri Megadim*, was an intimate of
the Baal Shem Tov. This tradition is supported to some extent by the text
we have just cited. From his book *Birkhat Yosef Ve'eliyahu Rabba*,[233] it
emerged that he knew and admired R. Nahman of Kosów, the Baal
Shem's well-known colleague.[234] Other early figures of the Hasidic movement are either cited by R. Meir or cite him. Elsewhere he wrote: "I
heard from the Hasid and eminent rabbi of Kowel (Kovli), who toward
the end of his life was appointed chief of the rabbinic court of the holy
community of Horodna, the venerable master and teacher, R. Yehiel
Mikhel, of blessed memory."[235] R. Meir is also quoted by R. Benjamin of
Zalozce.[236]

Between the years 1740–47, R. Meir was without a permanent position
as maggid, so he became an itinerant preacher in a number of communi-

---

231. This letter was also known to others, and reference is made to it in the *Peri
Megadim*, *'orah hayim*, # 561, and also by R. Joseph Moses, the maggid of Zabarov (who
died in 1815), in his book *Berit 'Avram* (Brody, 1875), p. 135b. [Cf. Scholem, "The
Historical Figure of the Baal Shem Tov (Hebrew)," *Devarim Bago* (Tel Aviv: Am Oved,
1975), p. 300.]

232. [The blessing, "May his light continue to shine," is conferred on the living.]

233. This rare book is in my possession. It contains an approbation dated 1741, but was
only printed in Zolkiew in 1747. According to the approbation of the rabbinic judges of
Lwow, R. Meir was the head of the yeshivah in Lwów, where "rich and poor alike, his
friends and comrades, all drank together of his learning and erudition."

234. R. Meir calls him "the great chastiser, the eminent late R. Nahman, may his
memory be for a blessing." This an important source for determining the date of R.
Nahman's death. He refers to R. Nahman again in his *Me'irat 'Enayim* to the Torah section
of *vayikra'*.

235. *Me'irat 'Enayim* to Torah section *shemini*. In another manuscript from the circle of
the Korzec Hasidim that is in my possession, it is mentioned that R. Meir taught Torah in the
name of R. Yehiel Mikhel, the chief of the rabbinic court in Horodno [that is, R. Yehiel
Mikhel Margoliot. Cf. Y. Alfasi, *Hahasidut* (Tel Aviv: Zion, 1969), p. 52].

236. *Torey Zahav* (Mogilev: Asher Zelig, 1816) to Torah section *ki tavo'*: "After God
graced me with this explanation, I heard the great maggid of Lwów, R. Meir, who gave
precisely the same explanation."

ties. In 1740/41, he preached in Ostróg and in 1746/47 in Bar,[237] near
Miedzybórz. It is possible that during this period he visited Miedzybórz,
where the Baal Shem resided.

Document 2: A Letter of Recommendation [written by R. Gershon Kutover] for R. Hayim Yeruham and R. Meir de Segura[238]

From the *Sefer Pardes* (Königsberg, 1759) by R. Aryeh Leib
Epstein, who writes:

[The following is] a recommendation for the distinguished rabbis,
emissaries of the Land of Israel from Safed and the Galilee,
which is in Judah, printed in the holy community of Constantinople, in the month of Nisan 1747, addressed to all the inhabitants
of the earth . . . and written by *one of the most esteemed of men*
[*'eḥad migedoley ha'olam*]. It reads as follows:
"When I passed through this holy community of Constantinople I witnessed the glorious sight of the two commanders of
Israel's hosts [*tzeva'ot*], like unto the splendors of the mirrors
[*mar'ot tzov'ot*] from which Betzalel fashioned the laver for the
tabernacle, standing in front of me. These were the scholars,
accomplished in all the virtues and qualities enumerated by our
Sages of blessed memory. They are both sharpwitted [*ḥarif*] and
learned [*baki'*] in the books *Sifrey* and *Sifra* as well as in the
Tosefta and the entire Talmud.
"One of them is the perfect and most erudite scholar, a veritable 'Sinai,'[239] a holy kabbalist, 'a mouth speaking wondrous
things,' an established member of the community, whose words
impress his listeners profoundly and permanently. [His wisdom]
'hath hewn out her seven pillars.' He draws down from [heaven]
above light for the lamp. This is our honorable master and
teacher, R. *Hayim Yeruham*, may his light shine,[240] son of that
righteous man, our master and teacher, Jacob. He is one of the
notable members of the holy community of Vilna, whose renown
and praise in his generation have reached as high as the shoulders
of 'the long-faced one' (*'Arikh 'Anpin*), drawing down to 'the
short-faced one' (*Ze'ir 'Anpin*),[241] 'four minds included in three.'

237. According to the book, *Birkat Yosef Ve'eliyahu Rabba.*
238. [See above p. 73.]
239. ["Sinai" = a scholar of mountainous erudition.]
240. See *History of the Sages of Jerusalem*, pt. 3, p. 64, and above, n. 7. He and R. Meir
de Segura traveled together as emissaries of the Jews of Safed, not as the author of the
aforementioned history would have it.
241. [Kabbalistic terms denoting divine moods of forbearance and impatience. See
Scholem, *Kabbalah* (New York: Quadrangle, 1974), pp. 140–43).]

He has revealed profound mysteries and concealed them in the book *Ya'ir Netiv*,[242] composed by this righteous and saintly man of blessed memory.

"The second, like the first, is the perfect and erudite scholar, a veritable 'Sinai of holiness' [Psalms 68:18]. 'He shall be called holy [Isaiah 4:3].' This is our honorable master and teacher, *Meir de Segura*, who is crowned with the crown of wisdom."

Signed on this document in praise of these two rabbis, [in the same way in which] Mar, R. Ashi's son (head of one of the Babylonian academies in Amoraic times) [used to sign], are the distinguished and eminent scholars of the above mentioned holy community of Constantinople, all of whom are as strong as lions, and more so. These are the following: the great and celebrated rabbi, the perfect scholar, our honorable master and teacher, *Abraham*, son of our master and teacher, *Joseph Rosanes*, may God guard him,[243] (grandson of the eminent scholar *Judah Rosanes*, author of the book *Mishneh Lamelekh*, as well as the great rabbi, our master and teacher, *Isaac Rosanes*,[244] may God guard him[245] and the great rabbi, our master and teacher *Isaac Bekhor David*, may God guard him.[246] "Four kings against three." These four were joined by the following three noblemen of the land and its protectors, the wealthy lords, the treasurers, the perfect and renowned scholars: the celebrated master and perfect scholar, our honorable master and teacher, *David Kimhi*, may God guard him, the celebrated lord, the perfect and erudite scholar, our honorable master and teacher, *Aaron Soncino*,[247] and the celebrated master, the eminent scholar, our honorable master and teacher, rabbi *Ezra Bassan*, may God guard him. Equally excellent, these scholars are the finest of all the scholars of the Jews [emphases AJH].

242. See Frumkin, *History of the Sages*, pt. 2, pp. 85 ff.
243. See above, n. 136.
244. See above, n. 135.
245. In 1744/45, he signed a pamphlet decrying the high price of clothing in Jerusalem. See *History of the Jews of Turkey*, pt. 5, p. 440.
246. See above, pp. 69–73.
247. He was one of the Constantinople rabbis who signed the pamphlet on behalf of the town of Yasiv (see Deinard, *Shibalim Bodedot*, p. 134), and was also one of the officials (*pekidim*) overseeing the funds for the communities of Jerusalem, Hebron, and Safed (p. 35.) He helped publish the *Nehpah Bakesef* (Constantinople, 1748) and is referred to on the title page of that work as "combining Torah and worldly success, a complete sage, a renowned judge, chosen of the God." In 1747/48, he signed a pamphlet about the price of clothing in Jerusalem; see Rosanes, *History of the Jews of Turkey*. See A. Yaari, "Biographical Miscellany," p. 129, and Gaon, *Oriental Jews*, pt. 2, p. 586.

Document 3: A Letter from Constantinople

This document, from the *Pinkas* Constantinople of the library of
the Jewish Theological Seminary (MS. 4008), was apparently composed
in 1749/50. [The date is tentative, as it is expressed by means of literary
allusions. It is directed to two leading rabbis of Europe, R. Ezekiel
Landau of Prague and R. Jacob of Tarnopol, who had written a letter
regarding the distribution of funds collected from Ashkenazi communities outside of the Holy Land to support the Ashkenazi Jews in the Holy
Land. They had raised the following questions: (1) Why were Ashkenazic
funds turned over to the Camondo brothers in Constantinople? (2) Why
had they in Europe not yet gotten receipts of the money's delivery in the
Holy Land?

Document 3 responds to these questions: (1) The Camondo brothers
are highly qualified for this responsibility, especially since their business
affairs make it easier for them to be in touch with Europe. The exact role
of the Camondos is as follows: money coming from the European Ashkenazic communities goes to the Camondos in Constantinople, then to the
Constantinople *pekidim* (officials), then to the Holy Land *pekidim*, there
to be distributed (presumably by Ashkenazic leaders such as R. Gershon,
etc.) to Ashkenazic Jews in the local communities. Receipts, correspond-
ingly, go from the Ashkenazim of the Holy Land to the Holy Land
pekidim, to the Constantinople *pekidim*, to the Camondo brothers, to the
Ashkenazic representatives in Europe. That, essentially, had been the
content of a previous letter from Constantinople to the above rabbis,
which was lost, and is now repeated. (2) While receipts have already been
received from the Ashkenazim of Jerusalem, those from the remaining
communities in the Holy Land were lost and "hopefully will be replaced
with new ones."

The letter further assures the Ashkenazic leaders that the money sent
to the Holy Land will "be distributed there according to your excel-
lencies' instructions. It is our responsibility according to instructions that
whatever will be sent to us in the future for the Ashkenazim of the Holy
Land we shall distribute among them exclusively, without benefiting the
Sephardim even by one small coin. Furthermore, even out of our own
(Sephardic) charitable funds, we allocate a certain proportion . . . to the
Ashkenazic poor."

This letter, which described the nature of financial support for the Holy
Land and the tension between the Ashkenazim and the Sephardim,
associates R. Ezekiel Landau with R. Abraham Gershon Kutover, and
indicates the communal role which the latter played.]

To the mighty foundations of the earth, the two great men of
the generation, the leaders, learned in Torah, the distinguished

rabbis: our honorable master and teacher, R. *Ezekiel*,[248] may God protect and perserve him, and our honorable master and teacher, R. *Jacob*,[249] may God protect him and preserve him, who is firmly established in the city of *Tarnopol*—may the Lord preserve it. May both your names be freshly remembered forever, Amen.

Since the sound of prayer has been raised to the "one who is wondrous in deeds" from your lofty and eminently learned throne, as we have learned upon receiving your lucid letter delivered by the eminent R. *Isaac Elsafan*, may God guard him, we realize that your excellencies are querying the matter of the money sent to the Holy Land by the eminent R. *Abraham Camondo*,[250] may God guard him. You claim that you do not know who has authorized him to take the money. We would like to remind you that we have already discussed the matter in a previous communication in which we explained to you that, since the burden of administering the accounts of Jerusalem—may it be rebuilt and reestablished—is already resting upon us, we cannot bear another yoke. It seemed, therefore, appropriate to us to appoint these two highly respected persons who desire nothing but the grace of God, the honorable and blessed brothers, the eminent R. *Abraham* and R. *Joseph Camondo*, may God guard them, to carry out this important task. They receive the contributions which come from the Ashkenazic communities [outside of the Holy Land], which are made for the Ashkenazim of the Holy Land, and then they pass them on to us. We in turn send the money to the Holy Land, to be distributed there according to Your Excellencies' instructions. It is our responsibility to hand the receipts promptly and regularly to the brothers Camondo,

248. This is clearly R. Ezekiel Landau who lived in Yampol at that time. See above, n. 50, and document 4.

249. R. Jacob Segal Landau, the chief of the rabbinic court of Tarnopol and Podolia, was the son of R. Isaac Landau, the chief of the rabbinic court of Opatów, Zolkiew, the Lwów region, and Cracow. He died in 1767/68. According to *Da'at Kedoshim* (St. Petersburg: Behrman, 1897–98), p. 119, it was he whose approbation, written in 1723/24 at the Jaroslaw council, of the book *Yefey Mar'eh 'Im Kevod Hakhamim* on the Midrash Rabbah, was signed "Jacob Landau, currently residing in Tarlow." This signature is lacking in my copy. Friedberg, in *The Families Landau* (Hebrew) [Padgorza, 1905], p. 18, and also Halperin, *Pinkas of the Council of the Four Lands* (Hebrew), p. 303, think that this R. Jacob was the rabbi of Tarlow in 1725/26. In 1741/42, he was rabbi in Tarnopol (see Halperin, *Pinkas*, p. 334) and signed the pamphlet on behalf of the poor Jews of Safed that was issued at the Council of Tyszowce (Tishvitz). He died, apparently, in 1757/8, after 10 Heshvan, since in the book *Bat 'Eni* by R. Issachar Dov of Zloczew, # 2, a responsum of his dated 10 Heshvan 1757 is cited. At the time of the publication of the *Korban Reshit* (Frankfurt a.O.: Judah Leib b. Asher Zelig, 1778), he was already deceased. There he is called "the venerable scholar" [*haga'on hagadol vehayashish*]. His father was the brother of R. Ezekiel Landau's father, R. Judah Landau. R. Jacob was very respectful of R. Ezekiel and called him "the holy one of God, his honor, my cousin" in the introduction to the *Korban Reshit*. His remarks were cited in the responsa of R. Hayim Cohen, *'Even Ha'ezer*, # 63. [See above, n. 95.]

250. See above, n. 130.

and they in their turn will send them on to Your Excellencies.
They are well qualified to carry out this task as they have good
connections in the Ashkenazic communities.

This was the essence of our previous letter to Your Excellencies. It would appear that you never received it. But we still
feel that, as far as we can see, there are none more suitable for
this task than these two honest and trustworthy men. Accordingly, we proceeded last year in this manner.

The sum of 100 ducats which was sent from the Ashkenazic
communities to be delivered to our master and teacher, R. *Abraham Gershon Kutover*, may God guard him, was so delivered.[251]
We handed over the receipt for it to the eminent R. *Abraham
Camondo*, may God guard him. Likewise the 92 ducats sent by
means of R. *Isaac Elsafan* were received here through the above
mentioned R. Camondo. We in turn transferred this money to
the Holy Land where it was distributed appropriately, and we received receipts from the Ashkenazim of Jerusalem. Unfortunately, the receipts from all remaining communities in the Holy
Land have been lost on the way, together with other letters belonging to us. With God's help, they will send us fresh copies and
we shall pass them on to Your Excellencies. We are prepared to
let our trustworthiness rest in their hands.

Whatever will be sent us in the future for the Ashkenazim of
the Holy Land we shall distribute among them exclusively, without benefiting the Sephardim even by one small coin . . . For we
are well acquainted with the principle whereby "whosoever acts
against the wishes of the host" etc.[252] Furthermore, even out of
our own [Sephardic] charitable funds we allocate a certain proportion which we instruct our officers in Jerusalem to give to the
Ashkenazic poor, that [our officers] might extend their concern to
them also, for we are all brothers, sons of the living God.

May your academy of learning prosper in accordance with the
desires of your eminences . . . and the desire of your beloved
friends, the officials for the holy city of Jerusalem—may it be rebuilt and reestablished—who reside here . . . [in] Constantinople—may the Lord preserve it. The undersigned, on the third
week of the month of Nissan, in the year 5510 (1750). [Emphases
AJH]

251. [To R. Gershon who, apparently, was in Palestine.] In the well-known letter of 1750
[which appeared at the conclusion of his disciple R. Jacob Joseph's book *Ben Porat Yosef*],
the Baal Shem Tov writes to R. Gershon, "Do not be annoyed that I have sent you no
support. Because of this treacherous time of plague and famine in our land, as well as other
lesser matters that depend on me for their resolution—e.g., the support of our family, let
alone other poor Jews—I have no more money. In fact, *we have nothing left but our bodies*
[emphasis AJH], and, the Lord willing, should God grace us, etc., then certainly, etc.
    252. [See *BT* Pesahim 86b.]

Document 4: A Letter by R. Gershon Kutover from Constantinople to R. Ezekiel Landau

The end of the second month of Adar, 1750. To those . . . learned in the Torah, taken into the counsel of rulers, elders, princes and commanders, men of renown, . . . men of . . . , leaders of the holy community of Yampol, may the Lord preserve it. And to him who is raised above them all, "as the color of electrum (Ezek. 1:4)," like a divine being, paragon of the generation, the learned master, the leader, famous as a crown of beauty and a wreath of glory, our honorable master and teacher, R. *Ezekiel*,[253] may God protect and preserve him. To all who are there with him, may God guard them and surround them with goodwill as a shield. May they thrive as corn and flourish as the vine and enjoy great prosperity. So be it. May this be Thy will.

Now that we have extended all these many greetings to you, O kings and governors, let us come to the point. While the late eminent master, the honorable rabbi, *Moses Soncino*,[254] may he rest in peace, was still alive, he used to receive from Your Excellencies, may God guard you, all the money raised for the Ashkenazim of Jerusalem, may it be rebuilt and reestablished speedily in our own day Amen, and send it on to them. Now the above-mentioned deceased has departed to his eternal rest . . . while his brother, the lord, the eminent prince, the glory of the generation, our honorable master and teacher, *Joshua Soncino*,[255] may God protect and preserve him, is too occupied with the worthy burden of public office which rests upon him, for many people flock to him daily, and he is not able to take on the above-mentioned task. Therefore, we have searched and found these two trustworthy men, the honorable and blessed brothers, the eminent lords, understanding and wise, our honorable masters and teachers, R. *Abraham* and R. *Joseph Camondo*, may God protect and preserve them,[256] to assume the burden of receiving from Your Excellencies the money raised for the Ashkenazim of the holy city of Jerusalem, may it be rebuilt and reestablished. Upon receiving the money they will hand it over to us, and then it shall be our responsibility to send it to our officers in the holy city of Jerusalem—may it be rebuilt and reestablished speedily—so that they may distribute all of it among the Ashkenazim of the holy city. These officers will also collect the receipts and then forward them to the above-mentioned eminent brothers. Thus the money would

253. That is, R. Ezekiel Landau; see above, n. 50.
254. See above, pp. 72–75.
255. See above, n. 129.
256. See above, n. 130.

reach the Ashkenazim of the Holy Land in time to purchase their wheat during the threshing season and to secure their livelihood there. For even though there may not always be ready means of transporting the money to the Holy Land, through the activities of the above-mentioned eminent brothers, the money will at least be received here, awaiting the opportunity of a secure passage to the Holy Land. This will enable us to write to our officers in the Holy City and to instruct them to pay out the cash available to them there in order to provide for the current needs of the Holy City. This will certainly be carried out.

Let us now conclude by sending you our kindest regards and blessings, and by wishing you whatsoever good Your Eminences desire.

Those who love you faithfully and seek your well-being and prosperity, the undersigned officers for the holy city of Jerusalem—may it be rebuilt and reestablished speedily in our own days, Amen. (Signed) here, in Constantinople, may the Lord preserve it, With warmest greetings.

We have written similarly to the leaders of the holy community of Tarnopol, headed by the great rabbi, our honorable master and teacher, R. *Jacob Landau*, may God guard him.[257] [Emphases AJH]

Document 5: A Letter by R. Gershon to R. Tzvi the Scribe

[The following responsum written by R. Gershon to R. Tzvi, the scribe of the Baal Shem Tov, deals with the problem of the inversion of the Hebrew letter *nun* [נ] in the Torah scroll. The law requires extreme care in the way in which a Sefer Torah is written. It must be copied in the exact manner in which it was handed down in the Masoretic tradition. The slightest deviation may render it unfit for public Torah reading. Extra letters or missing letters disqualify it from use. Moreover, even if a single letter is written in a form which deviates from that prescribed by the tradition, the scroll may not be used.

Among the laws regulating the writing of a Sefer Torah are those of the inverted *nun*. The Talmud (Shabbat 116a) states that Heaven decreed that two verses in the Book of Numbers (10:35–36) be separated from the other verses by distinguishing signs. These two verses were considered so significant that they merited being treated as a book unto itself. Tradition

257. See above, document 3, n. 249. [According to Barnai, *Jewish Community in Jerusalem*, p. 213, nn. 7–8, document 3, is to be dated not 1750 but 1753, and would therefore be preceded by document 4. Document 4, which records R. Moses Soncino's death and the Camando brothers' succession to his position, as well as the manner in which the moneys of the Ashkenazic Jews were handled, would then be the so-called lost letter which document 3 mentions.]

has it that the signs the Talmud refers to are the inverted form of the letter *nun* in the Hebrew alphabet. One of these signs is to be placed at the beginning of the section and one at its end. Different customs have arisen with regard to these inverted *nun*'s. (1) Some scribes used to invert only the upper part of the *nun*, some inverted the lower part, and some inverted it completely. (2) Likewise, there arose different practices with regard to the placing of these inverted *nun*'s. Some scribes placed these *nun*'s in the empty spaces preceding and following these verses; others inverted the *nun*'s found in words at the beginning and end of these verses. As a result of these divergent customs, a halakhic controversy ensued over which is correct. Among the many responsa written on this subject is the one by R. Gershon to the scribe of the Baal Shem, R. Tzvi. This responsum, the only extant sustained exposition by R. Gershon, reflects his rabbinic authority and his use of both talmudic and kabbalistic sources in reaching a halakhic decision.]

The responsum below was copied by R. Shabbetai of Raszków, a disciple of the Baal Shem Tov, who introduced it with the following words:

I returned and considered.[258] I, the copyist, Shabbetai of Raszków, the son of our master and teacher R. Tzvi, have realized that it is necessary for all those who wish to know how to write a Torah scroll according to the Law to be informed about the inverted *nun* in the word "*binso‘a*" ("*vayehi binso‘a ha’aron*"— "And it came to pass when the ark set forward." Num. 10:35). All scribes used to follow the practice of inverting the *nun* in the middle of the word "*binso‘a*" and the word "*kemit’onenim*" ("as murmurers," Num. 11:1). This matter has already been noted by the R. Solomon Luria (the sixteenth-century talmudist) and other halakhic authorities. I would like to report in this connection, however, what I have found in a letter from the talmudic and kabbalistic scholar, the man famous for his piety, our master and teacher, *R. Gershon Kutover*, who wrote from the holy city of *Jerusalem* and supplied conclusive proofs for his view from the Talmud and the Zohar. He argued that the two inverted *nun*'s should stand by themselves (i.e., not in the middle of the words ["*binso‘a*" and "*kemit’onenim*"]). One [inverted *nun*] should precede the words "*vayehi binso‘a*"; and the other [inverted *nun*] should precede the words "*vayehi ha‘am kemit’onenim*." He wrote further that in the Torah scrolls belonging to the author of the book *Ḥesed Le’avraham* and to R. Isaac Aboab he found the two inverted *nun*'s standing by themselves, as prescribed above, [and not in the middle of words]. Even the famous and pious

---

258. [שבתי אני וראיתי אני, "I returned and considered" (Eccles. 4:1). The first Hebrew word has the same letters as the copyist's name, שבתי 'ר.]

master and teacher Hayim of the holy community of Nikolsburg
wrote the *nun*'s in this way in his own Torah scroll. All this was
indicated by this famous, pious man, our late master and teacher,
the above-mentioned R. Gershon.

Subsequently, I had the opportunity to examine the collection
of Responsa entitled *Laḥmey Todah* by a certain member of the
holy community of Venice (R. Isaiah Basan; Venice, 1741). He
discussed the question in great detail, supplying other proofs from
the Gemara Rosh Hashanah [17b, where it says] "[The Psalmist]
inserted signs here," etc., "having the same force as the 'buts'
and 'onlys' of the Torah," etc.; as well as Rashi's comment on
the Psalm [107, which begins with the words] "Give thanks,"
where [in verse 17] he refers to the inverted *nun*'s etc. Consult
those passages. He adds other proofs to the effect that the inverted *nun*'s should each stand by itself, in the way mentioned
above. Also in the book *Ta'amey Torah* (published in Zolkiew in
1742) by the deceased author of the book *Siaḥ Sefunim* (Zolkiew,
1751/52), our master and teacher, R. Eliezer, of our own community, discusses the matter at some length, and he draws the *nun*'s
essentially in the way advocated by the Hasid, R. *Gershon*, who
found from the two Torah scrolls mentioned above that the two
nun's should be drawn in this way   and not in any other way.
Anyone wishing to understand the matter properly should consult
the Zohar in the section on the Pentateuchal portion of
beha'alotekhah. Make sure, however, that the above-mentioned
nun's should not interfere with the order of the "closed sections"
of the Torah [i.e., those parts separated from each other by a
space in the middle of the line], but rather that the prescribed
amount of space for the "closed section" and the "open section"
should exclude the *nun*'s. Understand this well and be exact.

I wish to comply with the wish of the person who asked me to
copy out the text of the responsum composed by the pious kabbalist, the perfect and renowned scholar, the late R. *Gershon
Kutover* of the holy city of Jerusalem, may it be rebuilt and reestablished soon in our days. The following, therefore, are his
own words, as pure as gold.

R. Gershon's letter was written after 1749/50, the year of R. Hayim of
Nikolsburg's migration to Palestine. From which city was it written? R.
Gershon notes that to clarify the matter of the *nun*'s he examined three
Torah scrolls, those of R. Abraham Azulai, R. Isaac Aboab, and R.
Hayim of Nikolsburg. We know that R. Abraham Azulai lived in Hebron
and later in Gaza (according to the Introduction to *Ba'al Berit
'Avraham*); concerning R. Isaac Aboab we know that a Torah scroll of his
was at "R. Isaac Aboab's prayer house" in Safed, as described in the
book by R. Simhah of Zalozce, *'Ahavat Tziyon*, p. 24.

The letter, first published in the book *Mishneh 'Avraham* by R. Abraham, son of R. Tzvi (Zhitomir, 1868), has escaped the attention of scholars of Hasidism. Since it is of considerable importance, I have published it here again.

To my beloved friend, closer to me than a brother, the honorable, learned, and pious master, R. Tzvi Hirsch, may his light continue to shine, scribe in the holy community of Miedzybórz.[259]

You may take my word for it that even at this hour, as I am writing this letter to you, I have been checking on this matter of the inverted Hebrew letter *nun*. In the most precious Torah scrolls, belonging to kabbalists and the noblest men of the generation, such as the scroll which was the possession of the eminent scholar and kabbalist, author of the book *Ḥesed Le'avraham*,[260] who wrote it with his own hand, as well as the scroll of the eminent scholar and kabbalist, R. Isaac Aboab,[261] I have found that the *nun*'s are [inverted] in between sections [of the Torah] but not in the middle of the words. They are shaped so that the top of the letter is straight; only the bottom part is inverted, as is customary both in the books of the Sefardim and among the Ashkenazim   like this   even though the opinion of the author of *'Or Torah*[262] is that, according to the meaning in the Zohar it should be inverted in this way   Now, these great scholars had examined the book *'Or Torah*, which was before the author of the *'Asarah Ma'amarot*,[263] which was published earlier than the former volume, and, nevertheless, even they wrote their *nun*'s in this way   and they did not invert the entire letter thus   Nor did they follow the third method, the one advocated by the *'Or Torah*   to write it thus   Now, even the *'Or Torah* allowed that, "Those who invert the bottom part of the *nun* only   thus   are not at fault."[264] And he harmonized this method with the intention of the Zohar. Since both these great men [i.e., R. Abraham Azulai and R. Isaac

---

259. He is mentioned many times in the *Shivhey Habesht* [see Ben-Amos, Index].

260. R. Abraham Mordecai Azulai, the grandfather of R. Hayim Josef David Azulai, immigrated from Fez to Palestine, lived in Hebron and Gaza, and died in Hebron in 1643. Aside from the *Ḥesed Le'avraham*, he wrote *Zoharey Ḥamah*, *'Or Haḥamah*, *Ba'al Berit 'Avraham*, and other books.

261. Perhaps the reference is to the rabbi of Toledo who lived at the time of the expulsion from Spain and who is mentioned on occasion in the *Bet Yosef* with the honorific title, "our great rabbi." He wrote a supercommentary to Nahamanides (Constantinople, 1525), *Nehar Pishon* (sermons on biblical themes) (Constantinople, 1538), and others. Nothing is known about his living in Palestine.

262. R. Menahem de Lonazno. The text was printed first in his book *Shtey Yadot*, in Constantinople, and thereafter printed as a separate book (Amsterdam, 1659, and Zolkiew, 1747).

263. By Menahem Azariah of Fano, published several times.

264. [The blank spaces are blank in Heschel's manuscript.]

Aboab] wrote the *nun*'s in this way in their own Torah scrolls and
in their own handwritings, we should rely upon them. As for
those who invert the *nun* in the middle of the words "*binso^a*",
and "*kemit^onenim*," their scroll is disqualified in my opinion.
(For in the words, "*vayomer vaya^amod*"—"For he commandeth,
and raiseth"—and in the verse "*vayitz^aku ^el YHVH*"—"and
they cry unto the Lord"—in Psalm 107 [vv. 25, 28], there is no
nun at all. Therefore the inverted *nun*'s which appear there must
indicate nothing other than the separation between the verses.
This proves that inverting the *nun* in the middle of the words
["*binso^a*" and "*kemit^onenim*"] cannot substitute for the proper
nun. And a Torah scroll in which this is permitted would be de-
ficient and thus disqualified from use.)

At the same time I consulted also a Torah scroll from Germany, brought here by the kabbalistic scholar, our master and
teacher R. Hayim Cohen of the holy community of Nikolsburg,
author of a commentary on the book of Psalms.[265] He commis-
sioned a scribe to write this Torah scroll for him in Germany, but
he wrote all the divine names in it himself, according to a special
kavanah. When I examined them, I realized that he had inverted
the *nun* even in the middle of the word. I went to see him and
gave him my opinion on the matter, as stated above, and he immediately corrected his scroll accordingly.

I have further proof from the Talmud to the effect that the *nun*
should be inverted only as a mark of separation between the
verses. For our rabbis have taught: "God marked this section [by
the inverted *nun*'s which appear] above and below it" (that is,
immediately before and after it).[266] If we are to take this as referring to the *nun*'s in the middle of the words "*binso^a*" and
"*kemit^onenim*," this raises difficulties, whichever way you look
at it. For if by "above" they meant the inverted *nun* in the middle of the word "*binso^a*," which is in the middle of the [first]
verse [of this special section], "*vayehi binso^a ha^aron*"—"And it
came to pass, when the ark set forward" (Num. 10:35), then the
second inverted *nun*, the one "below," should have likewise
appeared [somewhere] in the middle of the verse, "And when it
rested," etc., [which concludes the especially marked section
(Num. 10:36)]. For the intent of the word "below" should be
comparable to that of "above." Alternatively, if by "below" they
meant [the inverted *nun*] in the middle of "*kemit^onenim*"
[Num. 11:1], which is the verse immediately following the especially marked section, then the mark [of the inverted *nun*] signify-
ing "above" should have appeared [not in the first verse of the
specially marked section, viz., "*binso^a*" (Num. 10:35), but]

265. See above, n. 91.
266. *BT* Shabbat 115b.

somewhere in the middle of the verse [immediately preceding
that section, "And the cloud of the Lord was upon them by day]
when they went out of the camp" [Num. 10:34], namely, the *nun*
of the word *"bamaḥaneh"* ("the camp") should have been inverted so that the marking referred to as "above" is comparable
to that of "below." [Since this is not the case, one must conclude
that the inverted *nun*'s] surely should appear [only] in between
the verses.

I have further proof from the Zohar against inverting the entire
letter [*nun*], as it was inverted in the above-mentioned book, *'Or
Torah*. The Zohar (3:155a–b) says as follows: "'And when the
Ark rested,' the *nun* turned its whole face away from Israel, back
toward the Ark etc." (Consult the passage.) It is important to
specify exactly what is meant by "turned its whole face." If, when
the Zohar says "the *nun* turned its face toward Israel," it means
that the whole letter turned round, thus   , then it follows as a
matter of course that when it turned back toward the Ark the
whole letter turned round again. There is further difficulty in R.
Simon's query [regarding R. Eleazar's view, which the Zohar reports first and which is quoted in part above]. For why did R.
Simon say that if this was so (namely, if the *nun* turned its whole
face away from Israel when the Ark rested), then the second *nun*
should be straight, not inverted? First of all, R. Eleazar really did
suggest that the second *nun* should be straight. But surely, both
[R. Eleazar and R. Simon] must have realized that it should be
inverted. R. Eleazar himself implies this when he says earlier on
in the passage: "What is the meaning of the inverted letter *nun*
introduced here twice?" But it is hard to harmonize this with
what he says subsequently, for how could he have suggested that
the letter *nun* turned back toward the Ark (as this would seem to
suggest that by turning back it straightened itself out and ceased
to be inverted)? And later on R. Eleazar says: "What I said I
found in the Book of R. Yeba the Elder who said that the *nun*
returned either to one or the other side [of the Ark]." It may be
understood from this that the second *nun* returned straight! One
may further ask, how could R. Simon have said [to R. Eleazar]
"What he [R. Yeba the Elder] said is rightly said, "for his own
opinion was that the *nun* is straight, as if a letter has been added
to the Torah? It follows that the meaning of, "the *nun* turned its
face toward Israel," cannot possibly be that it was completely inverted, but rather that it was [partly] inverted in one of two ways,
either thus   or thus   . Therefore, when R. Eleazar says
that the *nun* turned back toward the Ark he has to state that it
turned its whole face back, lest one should understand the words
to mean that it turned back only its bottom part, as in the first
drawing, or only its top part, as in the second drawing, in which
case [as a result of turning back only that part of the *nun* which

had been inverted previously] the *nun* would become straight. This would contradict R. Eleazar's own view [that both *nun*'s should be inverted] implied in his saying that it is inverted twice, as quoted above. This is why he said that the *nun* turned its whole face back. It means that if the *nun* first appeared thus   when it turned back its whole face it appeared thus   and vice versa. All this is to prevent the appearance of a straight *nun* which would count as an additional letter in the Torah. This is why R. Simon queried R. Eleazar's view by saying, "If this is so, then the second *nun* should be straight, etc." And this is why R. Eleazar quotes R. Yeba the Elder as saying that the *nun* returned either to one side or to the other side [of the Ark]. And as I have explained, this is why R. Simon could have said of this that it was rightly said, for both methods share the same intention. But all that I said above to resolve these difficulties is to make sure that the letter *nun* should not be inverted in full (i.e., at both ends, top and bottom). For both these eminent scholars of the generation [i.e., R. Abraham Azulai and R. Yitzhak Aboab] wrote the *nun*'s with their own hands and in their own Torah scrolls, in the shape which I mentioned above. We should rely upon them entirely, as stated above.

Three

Rabbi Nahman of Kosów: Companion
of the Baal Shem

T HE RELATION OF RABBI NAHMAN OF KOSÓW (KOSOV), ONE OF THE founders of the Hasidic movement, to the Besht was not that of disciple to master. Indeed, in the early years of the Baal Shem's ascendancy R. Nahman had been among the opposition; even after joining the group, he retained his independence.

The details of R. Nahman's life, as well as the role he played in establishing the movement later to be known as Hasidism, are still unclear. In this essay I shall attempt to portray the man on the basis of sayings attributed to him and information about him which I have garnered from both published sources and from the manuscripts I have been fortunate to discover.[1]

R. Moses and the "Society of Hasidim" in Kuty

R. Nahman was the most prominent member of the "society of Hasidim" [*hevrah shel hasidim*] of Kuty (Kitov), from which the first disciples of the Besht were drawn. At the head of the "society" was R. Moses of Kuty.

The leading community in that area of Eastern Europe where the Besht was born, grew to manhood, and achieved fame, Kuty had as its rabbi at this time, R. Moses, a figure of note and a distinguished kabbalist esteemed by his colleagues.[2] Even the Besht addressed him with titles of high honor: "Flaming torch, profusely yielding olive,[3] juice of the pomegranate, the rabbi, the great light whose teaching is clear and pure as the

1. [For other treatments of R. Nahman, see M. Piekarz, *Bimey Tzemihat Hahasidut* (Jerusalem: Mosad Bialik, 1978), pp. 23–30; J. G. Weiss, "A Circle Of Pneumatics in Pre-Hasidism," *Journal of Jewish Studies* 8 (1957):199–213. Footnote numbers in this chapter are not consistent with those in the Hebrew version because of the division of the latter into chapters, each with its own set of notes, and because of the rearrangement of certain passages.]

2. In a letter to R. Moses, his brother, R. Hayim of Horodenka, paid him the ancient compliment of "from Moses until Moses none has arisen like unto Moses." *Letters of the Baal Shem Tov and His Disciples* (Hebrew), ed. David Frankel [Lwów: Frankel, 1923], p. 6. [See Appendix A to this chapter for biographical data on R. Moses of Kuty.]

3. "*Zayit shifkoni*," an olive that gives forth abundant oil. See *Mishnah* Peʾah 7:1.

sun."[4] Only R. Moses of Kuty is described as *harav hagadol*, "the Great Rav," by R. Jacob Joseph of Polonnoye, the foremost disciple of the Besht and chief recorder of his teachings.[5] The kabbalist, R. Barukh of Kosów, quotes him by name as "my uncle, the distinguished Rav and noted Hasid."[6]

R. Moses engaged in *kavanot*[7] and *yihudim*.[8] R. Jacob Joseph of Polonnoye writes:

> Once when the great rabbi, our master and teacher, Moses of Kuty, was overseeing a *get* [writ of divorce], he was asked the following question: We understand the passage, "Know him in *all* your ways" (Prov. 3:6), to indicate that we must seek to bring about a *yihud* through each act we perform. [The word "know" implies unification], as in the verse, "And Adam knew [i.e., was intimate with] his wife" (Gen. 4:1). But how can we bring about a *yihud* through a divorce, which separates rather than unites?
>
> [R. Moses] replied . . . that before one brings about a *yihud*, one must first remove the *kelipot* [the "husks" which surround the nut, i.e., evil] . . . Divorce is the act of detaching these *keli-*

4. From a letter of the Besht published by R. Israel Halevi Kitover of Piltshin, grandson of R. Moses of Kuty's son-in-law, R. Jonah. See the end of *Shevil Ha'emunah*, R. Israel's commentary to Saadia's *Sefer Ha'emunot Vehade'ot* (Józefów: [Setzer,] 1885). The letter was also printed at the end of *Butzina Dinehora* by R. Barukh of Miedzybórz (Lwów: Karl Bodvisser, 1880).

5. *Toldot Ya'akov Yosef* [Korzec: Abraham Samson Katz of Raszkow and Abraham Dov of Khmelnik, 1780], p. 84b.

6. *Nehmad Vena'im* (Józefów: Setzer, 1883), pp. 25, 32, 38, 45, 47, 93. The quotations cited here and in Barukh's other volume, *'Amud Ha'avodah* (Jósefów: Setzer, 1883) are largely explanations of Rashi's commentary on the Torah, and include one explanation of an obscure midrash (ibid., p. 37). It is strange that R. Barukh does not cite any of R. Moses's teachings relating to Kabbalah. [R. Barukh, objecting to the restraints the Polish rabbinic authorities imposed upon the study of the kabbalistic writings of R. Isaac Luria, composed his important work as a true gateway to the study of Kabbalah. "These two books," writes A. Yaari, "are the most significant literary response to the Frankist movement (*Mehkarey Sefer* [Jerusalem, 1958], p. 453)." Despite approbations from leading rabbis, the publication of R. Barukh's writings was nevertheless delayed until more than fifty years after his death in about 1795. Some confusion exists regarding the names and arrangement of the works. Heschel gives the title of one volume as *Nehmad Vena'im*, referring to the Józefów edition (1883). The first Cernăuţi (Tchernovitz) edition (1853), however, knows it simply as *Yesod Ha'emunah*. Further, while the other volume, *Amud Ha'avodah*, is subtitled in its first Cernăuţi edition (1854) as Part 2 of *Yesod Ha'emunah*, Piekarz's research leads him to conclude that material in *Amud Ha'avodah* actually precedes the other volume and suggests further problems to which the printing postponement may have contributed. See Piekarz, *Bimey Tzemihat Hahasidut*, pp. 55–57, and Index, and S. Porush, *Encyclopedia of Hasidism: Books* (Hebrew) (Jerusalem: Mosad Harav Kook, 1980), cols. 408–11.]

7. ["Meditations," usually associated with specific prayers recited before performing *mitzvot*.]

8. ["Unifications." The method is described in the *Sha'ar Hayihudim* of R. Isaac Luria. One fills one's mind with the letters of two or more divine names and then combines them, bringing about a "unification" of the forces associated with these names. In a more general sense, as here, the term denotes a unification of divine forces.]

pot and driving them away so that the *yihud* might take place, which is the marriage of each partner to a proper mate.

This was the reason [he said] that [at the time a *get* is administered] they recite [the formula:] "for his sake (*lishmo*), for her sake (*lishmah*), for the sake of divorce." [The words, "For the sake of divorce," are recited to drive away the *kelipot*, after which there can be a proper *yihud* (for each partner)].[9]

The extent of R. Moses's fame as a wonder worker is demonstrated by the fact that as late as 1908 the then-rabbi of Kuty wrote: "We have heard of the marvels which 'Moses performed in the sight of all Israel' . . . According to a tradition handed down to us, he promised on his deathbed that if ten men would pray at his grave in periods of trouble, he would intercede on their behalf. And many times [as rabbi of this community], I have received letters of request, enclosing charity for ten poor men, and they visited his [R. Moses's] grave to pray that God might answer His people Israel at the time of their sorrow."[10] There still existed in that year, an "amulet about a cubit in length and breadth which was written in a fine hand on parchment in square Hebrew script [used in the writing of a Torah], apparently the single surviving amulet [given by R. Moses]. And I know that great and holy men had provided large sums of money to the one who showed it to them, for they recognized that the amulet had proven effective, a wondrous charm and an excellent safeguard."

In Kuty "and in two localities nearby, it was the custom, unlike anything we have heard in our time in all the 'cities of Judah and Israel,' not to bury a Jew in a *talit* [prayer shawl] which had *tzitzit* [fringes] on it." This practice was established by R. Moses "because of an incident in Kuty on the eve of Yom Kippur when the people stood crowded together in the synagogue so tightly that their holy rav commanded that they remove their prayer shawls to allow for more room. [When the dead, who also visit the synagogue on Yom Kippur, removed their prayer shawls, they were exposed in their shrouds and fled. Therefore] a decree was issued from then on that no one was to be buried in a proper *talit*." [The dead, not wearing a proper *talit*, i.e., one with fringes, would then be

9. *Toldot Ya'akov Yosef* [p. 84b]. [The formula recited by the witnesses, "*lishmo, lishma, leshêm gerushin*" (*Shulhan Arukh*, 'even ha'ezer 154:59), confirms R. Moses's thought that *yihud* is the purpose even of divorce. One part of the formula, "for the sake of divorce" (*gerushin*), is given the meaning of driving away (*garesh*) the *kelipot*. The other part of the formula—"for his sake" (*lishmo*), which can be read, "for the sake of the Hebrew letter *vav* (*le-shem vav*)," and "for her sake (*lishmah*)," which can be read "for the sake of the Hebrew letter *hey* (*le-shem hey*)"—brings into *yihud* two letters of the Divine Name *YHVH*.] Compare the observations of R. Gershon of Kuty on the meaning of the *get*. See my essay, "R. Gershon Kutover," *Hebrew Union College Annual* 23 (1950–51), pt. 2, Hebrew section, p. 20 [4] [this volume, pp. 44–112].

10. [R. Hayim Gelernter,] *'Oneg Hayim Lashabbat* [Munkács, 1908; rpt. New York, 1973], Introduction.

discouraged from coming to the Kol Nidre service, since they could be easily identified.][11]

R. Moses of Kuty was the leader of the "society of Hasidim,"[12] also called the "holy society,"[13] which existed at that time in Kuty. Ascetics who removed themselves from worldly temptation, these Hasidim delved into the mysteries of the Torah, and undertook the task of bringing about *yihudim.* "This was their constant concern: How to serve the Lord." A sign of the dizzying heights which they reached was the contract they found it necessary to enter into *"that none of them would prophesy."*[14] They would gather by R. Moses in the afternoon for the third Sabbath meal, "and remain until the middle of the night," listening to "words of the living God." They engaged in practical kabbalah, "in dream analysis, and were able to discern holy or evil signs in people's faces."[15]

The beginnings of the emerging Hasidic movement can be traced to this society from which the Besht attracted his earliest followers. Reference to this body is discerned in the salutation of the Besht's letter to R. Moses:[16] "Abundant peace to that great and dear man, noblest of those mighty tamarisk trees, profusely yielding olive, juice of the pomegranate, is this not the rav, the great light, whose teaching is clear and pure as the sun." In talmudic usage, "mighty tamarisk trees" (*'ashley ravrevey*) is an idiom for great sages.[17] The Besht thus honored R. Moses as the leader of a group of important scholars. Among the members of the "holy society" led by R. Moses of Kuty were: R. Nahman of Kosów, R. Abraham Gershon of Kuty and his brother, R. Aaron, R. Judah Leib, known later as the *mokhiah* of Polonnoye,[18] the ritual slaughterer of Kuty whose name is not known to us,[19] and R. Alexander, the first scribe of the Besht and the father-in-law of the author of *Shivhey Habesht.*

There was a tradition among the people of Kuty that the Besht had lived in that city and in its neighboring villages during the early period of his life, when he still dwelt in seclusion and had not yet disclosed himself.

11. Ibid., Introduction; [S. Kahana,] *'Anaf 'Etz 'Avot* [Cracow: Kahana, 1903], p. xxxiv. The basis of the story is the common belief that the dead attend the synagogue at the time of the recitation of the *Kol Nidrey* prayer [appearing in the clothing in which they were buried. (Cf. *Be'er Hetev* to *Yoreh De'ah* 352:1)]. Among the people of Kuty, there also circulated the legend that R. Moses had created a golem!
12. *Shivhey Habesht* [Ben-Amos, ## 116, 20].
13. [Ibid., # 209.]
14. Ibid.
15. [Ibid., ## 209, 116.]
16. See above, n. 4.
17. *BT* Betzah 27a. [Cf. *Torah Shelemah, vayera'* (New York: Shulsinger, 1949), pp. 862–63, ##131, 134.]
18. *Shivhey Habesht* [Ben-Amos, #209].
19. His brother was R. Moses, "a marvelous tzaddik," leader of the worship service (*shaliah tzibbur*) in the house of study in Bar and a *mohel* (*Shivhey Habesht* [Ben-Amos, ##200, 202, 209].)

R. Moses, "his elder by some years, was his teacher and the revealer of his true character."[20] That it was R. Moses who revealed the Besht is also attested to by a genealogical manuscript which was in the possession of R. Samuel Zanvil Kahana.[21] In support of the notion that R. Moses knew the Besht before his emergence is the tale which the author of *Shivḥey Habesht* quoted in the name of his father-in-law, R. Alexander, the student and scribe of the Besht: The Besht had married the sister of R. Gershon of Kuty,[22] who served for a short while as a judge in the court of R. Moses.[23] R.Gershon looked down on his brother-in-law, the Besht [for the latter, still in his self-imposed anonymity, went about as an ignorant simpleton]. R. Gershon apparently asked "the rav, the Hasid . . . the great light, our teacher, Moses," to present the Besht to a deranged woman in Kuty who had the power to "disclose to people both their evil and good qualities . . . It was hoped that [the Besht] would learn something from her rebukes and change for the better."[24]

Further evidence of the close relation between R. Moses and the Baal Shem Tov is the fact that R. Moses's brother, R. Hayim, the preacher of Horodenka,[25] married the sister of R. Nahman of Horodenka, one of the leading disciples of the Besht.[26] A letter of the Besht has been preserved, an answer to R. Moses's request that the Besht "travel [to Horodenka] and cure the child of [R. Moses's] brother, the Rav, R. Hayim, who had fallen ill." The content of the letter reflects the ongoing exchange and the mutual admiration between R. Moses and the Besht. The Besht writes: "Behold, I descend and ascend according to your wish. I set out as you instructed and pressed myself in the urgent journey to the community of Horodenka and used your method in solving the matter satisfactorily."[27]

---

20. *'Oneg Ḥayim Lashabbat*, Introduction. If this evidence is correct, then one may conclude that the Besht was born a number of years after 1688. [The birthdate of R. Moses was 1688 (see Appendix A). It is further asserted that the Besht was "revealed in his thirty-sixth year." Since this must have been before R. Moses' death in 1738, the Besht's birth has to be put prior to 1702.] It is said that "the grandchildren of R. Moses Kitov stuttered because his children had shown disrespect to the Besht" (*Mikhtavim Mehabesht Vetalmidav*, p. 7).

21. MS. *Megilat Yuḥasin*; *'Anaf 'Etz 'Avot*, #103.

22. See my essay, "R. Gershon Kutover" [this volume, pp. 44–112].

23. From an oral source. Compare *Miktavim Mehabesht Vetalmidav*, p. 7. According to a family tradition, R. Moses was also R. Gershon's brother-in-law. See Samuel Noah Gottlieb, *'Ohaley Shem* (Pinsk: Glauberman, 1912), p. 149.

24. *Shivhey Habesht* [Ben-Amos, #20].

25. R. Hayim was the father-in-law of R. Meir Margoliot, author of *Me'ir Netivim* and a disciple of the Besht. Cf. M. M. Biber, *Mazkeret Legedoley 'Ostraha* (Berdichev: Sheffel, 1907), p. 200.

26. See my essay, "Unknown Documents in the History of Hasidism" (Yiddish), *YIVO Bleter* 36 (1952):115 ff.

27. See above, n. 4. The Besht does not call him "my beloved," as he does when addressing letters to his student, R. Jacob Joseph of Polonnoye, and to his brother-in-law, R. Gershon. The author of *Shem Hagedolim Hehadash* (*Gedolim*, #144) and A. Kahana

R. Nahman and the Besht

Data about R. Nahman's life are sparse. We are indebted to R. Jacob Joseph of Polonnoye, whose books have preserved some of his sayings, and to the author of *Shivhey Habesht*, who recorded scattered incidents of his life.

R. Nahman held no religious office. He was neither rav nor maggid, but a man of some wealth who leased an estate near the city of Kuty.[28] As a prosperous grain dealer, he traveled with his merchandise throughout the cities of Galicia and Podolia.[29] He was not the typical landowner, however, who gloried in his possessions and was preoccupied with money. Always uppermost in his mind was the fear of the Lord whose mercy extends even to the animals. Once, seeing R. Nahman labor under a heavy load of straw fodder for his animals, one of his friends exclaimed: "Fool! Why must you bother yourself with this? Order one of your servants to haul it for you." "You are the fool," countered R. Nahman, "The Torah teaches: 'I will give grass in the field for the cattle, and thou shalt eat and be satisfied' (Deut. 11:15); which is to say: first the animals are to be fed, only then may we eat. And you want me to give away the honor of doing this mitzvah to a servant?"[30]

It is reported that R. Nahman paid "a fixed amount weekly to a certain person to remind him of the name of God (YHVH) when he was in the company of others, lest he forget, so that God's name might constantly be before him."[31] This custom is known to us from the circle of the kabba-

---

(*Hahasidut* [Warsaw: Die Welt, 1922], p. 72) are incorrect in asserting that R. Moses was a disciple of the Besht. [For further biographical information on R. Moses, see below, Appendix A.]

28. "I have heard from the rav of our community" that R. Nahman "controlled [the produce] of the whole village" (*Shivhey Habesht*, p. 29a [Ben-Amos, #209].) That R. Nahman, who served neither as rav nor as maggid nor was dependent on others for his livelihood, was occasionally referred to as *mokhiah* ("rebuker") does not mean that he held a communal office. (He was called by the name *Hamokhiah* only by R. Meir Teomim (*Birkat Yosef Ve'eliyahu Rabah* [Zolkiew, 1747], Introduction). The title was accorded him probably because he traveled widely, admonishing people. R. Nahman lived for some time in the city of Vladmir-Volynski, where he "built a house of study adjacent to the water with a bathhouse nearby." (*Shivhey Habesht* [Ben-Amos, #109].)

29. Ibid. [and #111]. "He went by way of the holy community of Zalrave." "He was in the holy community of Vladmir-Volynski."

30. Ibid. [Ben-Amos, #209].

31. *Toldot Ya'akov Yosef* [p. 186b]. The source is the verse, "I have set the Lord before me always" (Psalms 16:8–9). According to R. Shimon Hasida, "One who prays should always consider himself as if the Shekhinah is before him, as it is said: 'I have set the Lord before me always'" (*BT* Sanhedrin 22a). This requirement is only for the time of prayer. [Cf. *Midrash Tehilim* 16:8, ed. Buber, p. 122: "Rav taught: In making a blessing a man is required to say, 'Blessed art thou, O Lord,' for a blessing wherein the Lord's name is not mentioned is no blessing; as Scripture says, 'I have set the Lord before me always'" (Psalms 16:8).] The phrase, "always," is explained by Rashi as, "in every act," and by Ibn Ezra as, "day and night." The words, "I have set . . . before me," mean, according to Rashi, "I have

lists. It is said of R. Isaac of Drohobycz—who like R. Nahman, at first opposed the Besht—that while he ate he would gaze at the tetragrammaton (YHVH) engraved upon a silver tray, which was supported by his thumb.[32]

It was in that generation that the Baal Shem "revealed himself" and that his fame spread throughout the region. At first R. Nahman was quite opposed to him—so much so that the Besht is supposed to have made the following strange statement: "The rav, R. Nahman, seeks to kill me, but, with the help of God, he will not succeed!"[33]

In the opinion of the author of *Shivhey Habesht*, the discord between the Besht and R. Nahman was "for the sake of Heaven," a disagreement about "matters which stand upon the heights of the world and which common people are unable to grasp."

---

set the fear of the Lord before my eyes"; according to Maimonides, "I do not turn my thoughts from Him, as if He were my right hand which one does not forget for even the slightest moment"(*Moreh Nevukhim*, pt. 3, chap. 51). R. Isaac Luria, however, is cited as having explained, "One should always imagine the letters of the tetragrammaton before one's eyes, and this is the mystery of 'I have set the Lord before me always'" (*Be'er Hetev* to *'Orah Hayim*, 1:3). [See Hayim Vital, *Sha'ar Ruah Hakodesh*, *twenty-first yihud*, ed. Ashlag, p. 142).] R. Isaiah Horovitz writes, "And behold in my time in the holy community of Safed—may it soon be fully rebuilt—there was a very old sage, noted for his piety, and unique in his generation. It was common knowledge that he had never come to sin. Before his death he revealed his secret—that throughout his life he would always imagine the letters of God's name, as if they were written out in front of him so that his eyes beheld them. He would not depart from this practice even for one moment, thus literally fulfilling the verse, "I have set the Lord before me," even while eating and other daily actions." (*Sheney Luhot Haberit*, p. 239b) [See Piekarz, *Bimey Tzemihat Hahasidut*, pp. 23–24; cf. below, n. 80.

32. M. H. Kleinman, *Zikhron Larishonim* (1907; rpt. Brooklyn: Moriah, 1976), p. 15. [See below, chap. 4, R. Isaac of Drohobycz, p. 169.]

33. In *Shivhey Habesht* [Ben-Amos, #228], R. Nahman is alleged to have used a special *kavanah* in the *Tahanun* prayer [which requires prostration (*nefilat apayim*)] for the destruction of one's enemies. Where did the author of *Shivhey Habesht* get this peculiar notion? The *Zohar* (3:176b) states that the [*Tahanun* prayer, involving] prostration is the "Tree of Death." Based on this, R. Hayim Vital (*Sha'ar Hakavanot*, '*inyan nefilat 'apayim*, homilies 2 and 3) writes that the intent of such prostration is to throw oneself down from the Universe of '*Atzilut*, where one stands during the *Amidah*, to the bottom of the Universe of '*Asiyah*, "like a person casting himself from a rooftop to the ground below," so as to choose among and gather up the [divine] sparks. This is an admission to mortality, according to the mystery of the verse, "Her feet go down to death" (Prov. 5:5), a descent into the [realm of the evil] husks (*kelipot*). "Our sages state that after one recites *Tahanun* with devotion, his enemies fall before him. This is measure for measure, since he causes himself to fall for the sake of the above-mentioned restoration (*tikkun*)." Though I have not found this statement explicit in the Talmud, it is probable that R. Hayim Vital meant the tale of Imma Shalom (wife of Rabbi Eliezer b. Hyrcanus) in *BT* Baba Metzia 59b which suggests that Rabbi Eliezer's *Tahanun* prayer resulted in the death of his wife's brother, Rabbi Gamliel. R. Israel ben Aaron Jaffe of Shklov (*'Or Yiśra'el* [Frankfurt a.O.: M. Gottschalk, 1712], p. 92d), in his commentary on the verse, "And [Moses and Aaron] fell on their faces" (Num. 16:23), puts it quite clearly. He writes, "Through reciting *Tahunun* one can exact vengeance against one's opponents. Therefore, when Moses and Aaron fell on their faces (i.e., said *Tahanun*, including the prostration), Korah, who had opposed them, was swallowed up by the earth." [Cf. Tishby, *Mishnat Hazohar*, 3d ed. (Jerusalem: Mosad Bialik, 1971), 2:275–76.]

It happened that the disciples of R. Nahman expressed a desire to join him against the Besht.

Incensed, he responded with a parable:
"It happened that two mighty princes had a crown made for the king, on which they spent a vast sum. When the crown was almost completed, an argument broke out between them as to how to set the precious stone in the diadem. One advised this way, the other that way. Both, however, had the glory of the king at heart. At the heat of their quarrel, a commoner, passing by, took the side of one of them. Both turned upon him in anger: 'How dare you insinuate yourself into a matter which has nothing to do with you? If we argue, it is because we recognize the glory of the king whose very greatness prompts our disagreement over the setting of the jewel.'

"Our argument," said R. Nahman, "is likewise the ancient controversy of Saul and David, may he rest in peace, which was afterward that between Hillel and Shamai. How dare you poke your heads into such a concern!"[34]

Once R. Nahman's students approached their master and teacher with the query: "Why is it that everyone travels to the rav, the Besht, and praises him so highly? Why do you not decide to go there and find out what he is really like so that we will know where the truth lies? For why should he be a snare to us?"

Taking the suggestion, R. Nahman traveled to the holy community of Miedzybórz to the rav, the Besht, who received him graciously. Later the two of them entered a special room and requested that they be left alone. One fellow, however, managed to hide himself there [and it was he who reported the following conversation]:

The rav, our master, R. Nahman, spoke:
"Israel, is it true that you say you know people's thoughts?"
"Yes," he replied.
"Tell me, then [said R. Nahman], what I am thinking about at this moment."
The [Besht] answered: "It is well-known that thought is not static, but flits among many objects and constantly changes its form. However, if you focus your mind on one thing, then I will know."
The rabbi, our master, R. Nahman, did so.
The Besht said: "The name YHVH is in your mind."
R. Nahman said: "You would know this is any case. For I must always think that thought, as it is written, 'And I have set the Lord (YHVH) before me always.' It is obvious, therefore, that if I put aside all other thoughts and concentrate my mind on only one, it must be the name YHVH."

34. *Shivḥey Habesht* [Ben-Amos, #230].

The Besht answered: "But there are many holy names of God, and you could have concentrated on any one of them."

At this, R. Nahman admitted that it was as the Besht had said. Afterward, they discussed the mysteries of the Torah.[35]

From that time forth he drew close to the Besht and would travel to him. The *Shivḥey Habesht* records that once he and R. Jacob Joseph, "the rav of the holy community of Polonnoye," went together "from the holy community of Nemirov to spend the Sabbath with the Besht."[36] The Besht cherished R. Nahman. According to one source, the Besht described him as "the Hasid, beloved and chosen of the Lord."[37]

The Besht taught that man's eye could scan the entire world from end to end and his ear could discern the heavenly voices, but for the weakness of the flesh which blocks the senses like a curtain. "It is proven fact," said R. Jacob Joseph of Polonnoye," that my teacher [the Besht] saw from afar and heard from above."[38] Once, so it is said, R. Nahman asked the Besht, "I know within myself that I am a tzaddik. Why, then, do I not see and hear as you?" To which the Besht answered, "If you wish it, I shall bestow this capacity on you." Something happened which made R. Nahman request that the Besht take the power away from him. "For there are some souls who have no need to see from one end of the world to the other!"[39]

"R. Shmerl related that each day during the month of Elul [which precedes the high holidays of Rosh Hashanah and Yom Kippur], R. Nahman used to pray with mystical meditations (*kavanot*). The Besht ordered him to desist, because [these *kavanot*] must be reserved for the battle of Rosh Hashanah [to counter Satan's charges against the people of Israel], and even though one never knows in advance whether one will indeed use these *kavanot*—for to the Lord belongs the battle—nevertheless, one must take all necessary precautions. For we dare not rely upon miracles!"[40]

It is possible that the Besht had R. Nahman in mind when he offered the following interpretation of the verse: *'ashrey 'adam lo' yaḥshov Adonai lo 'avon*, "Fortunate the man to whom the Lord ascribes not sin" (Psalms 32:2).

One is obliged to meditate constantly on the tetragrammaton (YHVH), never turning one's mind from it irrespective of what

35. Ibid. [Ben-Amos, #228].

36. Ibid. [Ben-Amos, #142].

37. Y. Hager and Y. Berger, *'Ateret Ya'akov Veyisra'el* (Lwów, 1881), p. 53b.

38. Jacob Joseph of Polonnoye, *Tzafnat Pa'neyaḥ* (Korzec: Abraham Samson Katz of Raszków and Abraham Dov of Khmelnik, 1782), p. 18d.

39. R. Yitzchak Isaac of Komarno, *Netiv 'Emunah*, # 5, #14.

40. M. Gutman, *Mitorat Hahasidut*, bk. 1 (*Torat Rabenu Pinḥas Mikoretz*) (Bilgorey, 1931; rpt. Tel Aviv: Mosad Harav Kook, 1953), #71.

one may be doing or saying, as it is written, "I have set the Lord (YHVH) before me always (Psalms 16:8)." While people generally do not take this obligation seriously, Psalms 32:3 praises those who do take it to heart. The Hebrew can be homiletically repunctuated to read *'ashrey 'adam lo yaḥshov' Adonai—lo 'avon*, "Fortunate the man who, when he does not commune with the Lord, considers it a sin for himself!" The verse would then be speaking of one who acknowledges his sin in turning his mind away from constant contemplation of God and, failing to fulfill the commandment, "I have set the Lord before me always," immediately regrets it![41]

R. Nahman died at about the age of forty.[42] The supposition that he passed away before the Besht (d. 1760) is supported by the legend, cited later in this chapter,[43] regarding the temporary ascent of the Besht's soul into Heaven in the year 1756/57, as well as by the story we shall soon present about R. Nahman's widow having visited the Besht. In my opinion, one must fix the date of his death as having been before 1746.[44]

It appears that R. Nahman's first wife died and that he was survived by the woman he remarried. "After the demise of her husband, we are told, she traveled once to the Besht, may his memory be for a blessing, who

41. *Divrey Moshe* by R. Moses of Dolina, *beshalah* (Zolkiew: S. P. Stiller, 1865), p. 36d. R. Gedaliah of Linitz, *Teshu'ot Ḥen* (Berdichev: S. Segal, 1816), passim.

42. " . . . concerning the rav, may his memory be for a blessing, who said of R. Nahman of Kosów, may his memory be for a blessing, that he did not live long, for he died about forty years of age." From a MS.

43. Cf. pp. 144–45.

44. In that year, when the book *Mishmeret Hakodesh* was published, he is referred to as already deceased. "And I heard in the name of the Hasid, R. Nahman, may the memory of the righteous be for a blessing" (R. Moses of Satanów, *Mishmeret Hakodesh* [Zolkiew, 1746], p. 47a). I am convinced that the reference here is to R. Nahman of Kosów (a city not far from Satanów), for he was the only one of that generation well-known as "the Hasid, R. Nahman." Cf. p. 122 [Heschel, Hebrew text].

Putting the year of R. Nahman's death before 1746 is not consistent, however, with a statement by R. Uziel Meisels (*Tif'eret 'Uzi'el* [Warsaw: N. Schriftgiesser, 1863], p. 24a), who writes: "I have heard . . . *from the mouth of* [emphasis AJH] that holy and pure man, R. Nahman Kosover, may his memory be for a blessing" [i.e., he and R. Nahman were apparently contemporaries]. But if R. Nahman did indeed die before 1746, R. Uziel could not have heard directly from him. For we know two things about R. Uziel: He was still alive in 1786 (since he eulogized R. Yehiel Mikhel of Zloczew who passed away in that year [p. 54]). And, furthermore, R. Uziel "was not forty-two years of age" when he died (see his brother R. Isaac's introduction to R. Uziel's posthumously published *Tif'eret Tzvi* on Tractate Betzah [Zolkiew: Gershon Litteris, ca. 1803], p. 180c. Therefore the earliest possible year of R. Uziel's birth would be after 1740 [1786 − 42 = 1744], only a few years before R. Nahman would have died! Perhaps the words "I heard from the mouth of . . . R. Nahman Kosover" are not to be taken literally. In *Tif'eret 'Uzi'el* we find: "I have heard from the mouth of . . . R. Israel Besht, may his memory be for a blessing." [According to the above, R. Uziel was born in 1744 at the earliest, while the Besht died in 1760 (see Alfasi, *Temirin* [Jerusalem: Mosad Harav Kook, 1972], 1:298).] The matter requires further study.

[According to a source quoted by Piekarz, *Bimey Tzemiḥat Hahasidut*, p. 26, R. Nahman was buried in Miedzyrzecz.]

treated her with great honor. When asked whether the rule that 'A scholar's wife is to be treated like the scholar himself' applies to the second wife, he replied: 'Since she merited to lie next to so holy a body for some years, she herself is worthy of respect.'"[45]

From his first wife was born a son, Moses, who is known in Hasidic writings as "the Great Rav" (*Harav Hagadol*).[46] R. Nahman's second wife also bore him a son whose name is unknown to us.[47] Nor have the names of R. Nahman's students been recorded.[48]

45. From a MS.
46. "The custom of calling the day following Yom Kippur, "God's Name" [Yiddish = *Gott's Nomen*], was explained by R. Pinhas of Korzec in the name of *the Great Rav*, our master, R. Moses, the son of the rav, our master, R. Nahman, may his memory continue into the future world. According to the Talmud in Kritot [25a]: 'They said of Baba the son of Buta that he would contribute an *'asham talui* [a sacrifice brought when the commission of a sin was doubtful] each day, except for the day following Yom Kippur.' The reason for this is that on the day after Yom Kippur everyone is [free of sin and therefore] in a category of a tzaddik. Furthermore, the Talmud [Baba Batra 65b] says that, 'In the future world, the tzaddikim will be called by the name of the Holy One, blessed be He.' [Hence the day following Yom Kippur, when everyone is a tzaddik, is called 'God's Name.'] Understand this." (R. Pinhas of Korzec, *Nofet Tzufim* [Piotrkow: H. Palman, 1911], p. 14, #110.)

A further teaching of R. Moses is in a manuscript in my possession from the circle of R. Pinhas of Korzec: "I heard from him [R. Pinhas?] in the name of the rav, R. Moses, the son of R. Nahman, may his memory be for a blessing, that it is written in the *Tikunim* or in the *Zohar*, 'Despair and sneering come from the spleen.' Despair, which is depression, has its source in the spleen, as does biting humor. He then related that he had seen a man who was said to be a great wit and recognized that, in fact, he was depressed and very melancholic. Know, he added, that when people speak to one another on the Ninth of Av [which is the day of sadness] humor gets mixed in with their words and oddly enough the *bon mot* is frequent and people laugh, for at this time [the spleen] rules. Therefore, I am careful not to speak at all with others on Tisha B'av." [According to the Talmud, "the spleen laughs," *BT* Berakhot 61b; cf. *Zohar* 3:132b, *Tikuney Zohar* 21 (49b), 32 (76b), 48 (85a).]

The importance of R. Moses can be measured by the fact that he is cited both by R. Pinhas of Korzec and R. Jacob Joseph, the maggid of Ostróg. "I heard directly from the rav, R. Moses, son of R. Nahman of Kosów, may his memory be for a blessing, in reference to the remark of our sages that when Sarah conceived, other barren women conceived with her." (*Rav Yevi: hidushim 'al tehilim*, Psalm 24 (Slavita, 1792), p. 67b.) Regarding his life, we know only that about the year 1760 he visited Ostróg. It was the custom in that city to honor an important visitor to the city with a gift of mead or wine. And in the communal register it is written, "One barrel mead for the son of R. Nahman Kosover" (M. M. Biber, *Mazkeret Lagedoley 'Ostraha*, p. 216). [The text has the abbreviation "a.p.," which can be taken for the Yiddish, *ein fas*, (one barrel).]

47. One elder from Korzec said that "he heard [the following explanation] from another son of R. Nahman Kosover—not from R. Moses but from another son whom he had with the second wife . . . in the name of his father: 'Guard my soul [says King David in Psalm 86:2], for that I am pious.' The Talmud (Berakhot 4b) raises a question: 'Was David, then, so immodest as to call himself pious?' [The Talmud replies that] David meant, 'And am I then not pious? For while all the kings of the East and the West sleep late, I rise at midnight [to study the Torah].'

"But how does this answer the question [about King David's apparent immodesty]? The explanation, however, is that King David prayed, 'Guard my soul'—from the evil impulse that makes me arrogantly believe—'that I am pious.' And regarding this it was asked: 'How could David have even suspected that he might hearken to the evil impulse, so that it was necessary for him to pray that he be spared?' The Talmud explains that since he would rise at

The veneration with which R. Nahman was regarded both by his contemporaries and by later Hasidim is evident from their references to him. R. Jacob Joseph of Polonnoye wrote: " . . . which I heard from the mouth of the noted Hasid (*heḥasid hamefursam*), our master, R. Nahman, may his memory live on in the world to come."[49] Also, "from the deceased, our master, the rav, R. Nahman";[50] "from the deceased, the Hasid, our master, the rav, may his memory continue in the world to come";[51] "which I heard in the name of the Hasid, our master, the rav, Nahman Kosover";[52] "in the name of the deceased Hasid, our master, the rav, R. Nahman";[53] "in the name of the deceased Hasid, our master, the rav, R. Nahman Kosover."[54] R. Joseph, chief rabbi of Olesko, refers to him as "the rav, the noted Hasid";[55] R. Benjamin of Zalozce calls him "the distinguished and marvelous Hasid" (*heḥasid hamuvhak hamufla'*);[56] R. Moses of Stanov and R. Simhah of Zalozce have him as "the Hasid."[57] R. Meir Teomim used the words "the great mokhiah" (*homokhiaḥ hagadol*);[58] R. Uziel Meisilish calls him "a holy and pure man" (*'ish kadosh vetahor*);[59] in *'Ohev Yiśra'el* by Abraham Joshua

---

midnight, the evil impulse tempted him to feel pride over it. So he prayed that he might be delivered from such temptation. 'And the words of the wise are full of grace.'" (*Pe'er Layesharim* [Jerusalem: Rosenstern, 1921], p. 126b.)

The author of *Shivḥey Habesht* relates a story about R. Nahman which he heard from R. Shneor, the grandson of R. Nahman (*Shivḥey Habesht* [Ben-Amos, #109]).

48. One of his intimates was R. Yudil of Tshidnov, the son of the *mokhiah*, R. Joseph, who was also related to R. Nahman and was with him in Vladmir-Volynski (Ludmir); see this chapter n. 28 and p. 135). An iron merchant, R. Yudil, followed the way of R. Nahman in not wishing to benefit from the labor of others. The Besht said of him that he was the transmigration of the soul of Samuel the Prophet.

It was the custom of R. Yudil to be very careful "to have fish on Sabbath." This was once achieved by way of a miracle (*Shivḥey Habesht* [Ben-Amos, #108]).

49. *Toldot Ya'akov Yosef* [p. 166d].

50. Ibid. [p. 137b].

51. *Zafnat Pa'neyah* [p. 22b].

52. *Toldot Ya'akov Yosef* [p. 98d].

53. Ibid. [p. 99d].

54. *Ketonet Pasim* (Lwów: A. J. Heshel b. Judah Gershon, 1866), p. 7d.

55. *Ginzey Yosef* (Lwów, 1792), p. 3d.

56. *Torey Zahav* [Mogilev: Asher Zelig, 1816], p. 90c.

57. *Mishmeret Hakodesh*, p. 46a.

"I heard from the Hasid, our master, R. Nahman of Kosów, may his memory live on in the world to come, this explanation of the passage from *The Ethics of the Fathers* (6:1); 'He who studies the Torah merits many things . . . he is called friend, beloved, lover of God and man . . . and he becomes humble . . . ' [Reading 'and he becomes humble,' not 'and be you humble.'] That is to say, because of his study of Torah, he will be humble and forgive those who shame him" (*Netia' shel Simḥah* of Simhah b. Joshua; Zolkiew, 1763).

58. *Birkat Yosef Veliyahu Rabah*, Introduction; *Rav Peninim* (Frankfurt a.O.: 1782), p. 54b.

59. *Tiferet 'Uzi'el*, p. 64.

Heschel of Opatów, R. Nahman is referred to as "the holy rav (*harav hakadosh*), the man of God, who is called holy." [60]

R. Levi Isaac of Berdichev reported that when R. Nahman would hold the *pe'ot* or curls on either side of his head, his mind dwelt upon *yir'ah*—the right *pe'ah* standing for the awe of God's majesty and the left curl standing for the fear of His punishment. And when he held his beard, his mind dwelt upon *hesed*. [61]

Legend recounts that R. Nahman repaired many souls. He taught "the proper way" to "genuinely pious persons who had not achieved the true understanding of God"; restored "noted talmudic scholars" who had become heretics, to the true belief; and turned "thorough scoundrels, sinners, and lascivious ones" toward the correct way by preaching to them "in a respectful manner, without scorn." [62]

Considered the ranking personality among the circle of the Besht, R. Nahman's name is accounted among the most highly esteemed. A later writer observes that "It was in this generation that the Besht revealed himself. He possessed the 'holy spirit,' experienced revelations of Elijah, and achieved other exalted spiritual rungs. He disclosed, as well, the mysteries of the Torah to his holy disciples who also possessed the "holy spirit," such as his brother-in-law, R. Gershon Kutover, R. Nahman Kosover, and the other famous followers." [63]

---

60. *'Ohev Yiśra'el, parshat toldot.*
Teachings of R. Nahman are also quoted by R. Pinhas of Dinovitz, *Śiftey Tzaddikim, parshat hayey sarah.*

61. *Toldot 'Aharon*, R. Aaron of Zhitomir, *parshat lekh lekha.* "*Yirah*" is from the divine name, "*Elohim*" (*Peri 'Etz Hayim, sha'ar hatefillin*, chap. 2, p. 20d). The difference between the two types of *yir'ah*—awe of God's majesty and fear of God's punishment—is well-known. See *Zohar* 1:11b. The Hebrew word *pe'ah*, has the same numerical value—86—as the Hebrew word *'Elohim*. See *Peri 'Etz Hayim, sha'ar haselihot*, chap. 7, p. 59d. See the *Likutey Torah* (Zolkiew, 1775), *parshat beshalah*, p. 56b. [The thirteen attributes of mercy are said to be derived from the thirteen tufts of the beard of *Arikh Anpin*. See *'Etz Hayim, sha'ar arikh anpin*, chap. 9; *Sifra Detzeni'uta*, chap. 3.]

62. *'Ateret Ya'akov Veyisra'el*, p. 53b.

63. *Vikuha Raba* [of Jacob Bakhrach; 5th ed. (Munkács, 1894; rpt. Warsaw: M. Kleinman, 1913), p. 32a].
According to Jacob Emden (*Sefer Hit'avkut* [Lwów, 1877], p. 80b), R. Ezekiel Landau supported a certain "Nahman Kosov, who was an especially offensive heretic (Sabbatean) and a worthless vulgarian, and sent him to the city of Opatów to contaminate that holy community. But when the Jews of proper belief there recognized him, they revealed his true identity. Now, the family of R. Ezekiel Landau made a great issue over this, igniting fires of controversy in his defense . . . as a reliable source has told us." Wthout any proof, Simon Dubnow (*Toldot Hahasidut*, p. 102) identifies the person whom R. Jacob Emden accused of being a Sabbatean with our R. Nahman of Kosów. Since idle suspicions have a way of gaining currency, the opinion has spread that R. Nahman was a Sabbatean.
To refute this allegation it is appropriate to consider a statement that has been preserved in the name of R. Nahman, which testifies to his determined opposition to the false messiah and his awareness of the disaster which belief in him brought about.
"The Hasid, our master and teacher, Nahman of Kosów, may his memory be for a

126   Chapter Three

R. Nahman's Way in Hasidism

Excitable and enthusiastic, a man of many troubles, R. Nahman
struggled not only with others but with himself as well. To remain fixed in
the rut of habit, spiritually at ease, was loathsome to one who longed to
reach the summit of soul and mind. He explained the scriptural verse,
"These are the generations of Jacob, Joseph . . . " (Gen. 37:2), to
mean: Each day Jacob "would add" to his completeness (reading the
name, Joseph [Heb. = *Yosef*] as the verb, "he would add"). The tzaddik
must continually move from one rung to another.[64]

blessing, explained the verse [of the Psalm of exile], 'By the waters of Babylon' (*Bavel*)
(Psalms 137:1), to mean, 'Concerning the heavenly lights which have become confounded'
(*nitbalbelu*). In the future, however [the lowly world will be elevated, and all the more the
upper worlds, as it is said, '*All* the worlds will be as on the Sabbath day.' And this is the
meaning of [the verse of the Psalm of redemption], 'A song of ascents' [*ma'alot*] (Psalms
126:1): for then there will be singing from the upper regions [*ma'alot*] and also from the
lower ones. And when will they sing? 'When the Lord will have brought back [from exile]
those who return to Zion' (ibid.) i.e., when the Lord Himself brings *the true Messiah*, and
not, as at the time of catastrophe [i.e., 'by the waters of Babylon'], *when the kelipah* ('*husk
of evil*' [= Shabbetai Tzvi?]) *misleads the people with lies and brings not deliverance but
destruction!*" [emphasis AJH]
    This passage is found in a rare volume, *Netiya' shel Simhah*, p. 31a, by R. Simhah the son
of R. Joshua of Zalozce. R. Simhah is also the author of '*Ahavat Tzion*, a description of his
journey to the Holy Land in the year 1764 with a group of Hasidim from Galicia, the
Ukraine, and Lithuania. See Hayim Lieberman, "Chasidic Research—A Reappraisal," in
Bitzaron 33 (1955):114. [See now Lieberman, '*Ohel Rahel* (Brooklyn: Empire Press, 1980),
p. 13. M. Braver, "On '*Toldot Hahasidut*,' " in *Hahêd* 8, no. 6 (1933):29–30, also disagreed
with Dubnow's identification of Emden's allegedly Sabbatean Nahman of Kosów with our
Nahman of Kosów, and argues that Emden's subject was someone else, namely, an in-law of
R. Jonathan Eibeschütz.]
    [Piekarz *Bimey Tzemihat Hahasidut*, p. 29, asserts that R. Jacob Joseph brings the same
interpretation of Psalm 137 in the name of R. Mendel of Bar (*Toldot Ya'akov Yosef*, p. 35b)
and therefore questions its identification with R. Nahman. A comparison of the two
passages, however, shows that only the one in the name of R. Nahman spells out the
reference to the Messiah.]
    64. *Toldot Ya'akov Yosef*, pp. 98d, 99d, 194d, 197d; *Ben Porat Yosef*, p. 44b; *Tzafnat
Pa'neyah* [p. 24a].
    [Piekarz (*Bimey Tzemihat Hahasidut*, pp. 26–27) argues that Heschel's protrait of R.
Nahman is marred by the fact that some of the passages brought in his name as characteristic
of him are only "commonly used expressions of the time." The first example Piekarz offers
is the above passage which, though cited frequently by R. Jacob Joseph in the name of R.
Nahman, is also quoted once by R. Jacob Joseph in the name of R. Judah Leib of Pistýn, an
important member of the circle of the Besht. "Furthermore," writes Piekarz, "this teaching
is an innovation of neither R. Nahman of Kosów nor R. Judah Leib of Pistýn, but was
frequently found among the circles of the pious, for example in the passage mentioned in the
Sheney Luhot Haberit, "In the fellowship of the Hasidim who met together im simplicity and
piety . . . and added (*hosifu*) holiness without measure each day and night to Torah, *mitzvot*,
and *Hasidut*" (*Sheney Luhot Haberit*, hilkhot teshuvah, 2, p. 190b).
    Piekarz confuses "origin" with "validity," as well as "characteristic" with "unique."
Though a particular teaching may not be "unique," that is, an innovation of a certain
thinker, and though one may even uncover earlier "origins" of that teaching, it may still be
considered a "valid characteristic" of him. This is the case here. The fact that this teaching is
quoted six times in R. Nahman's name in R. Jacob Joseph's books, comprising almost

Ascent demands daring, the willingness to stake one's life. And none dares except from resolute determination. The problem is that man is trapped between two jurisdictions. "Just as strife divides one nation from another and separates an individual from his fellow, so, too, at times, within the heart of man." A net is stretched out to entangle the feet of those who would climb the mountain of the Lord; some mysterious force incites the Good Impulse (*yetzer hatov*) to subdue the Evil Impulse (*yetzer hara‹*). Man struggles upward, mounting from rung to rung, and then, of a sudden, midway, it is as if the ladder were reversed. Instead of rising, he finds that he was actually falling, as if each ascent seems first to require a descent.

Change is not only the law of nature, it is as well the law of time and of man. There are moments when one is thrust from one's rung and falls to the level of *katnut* [constricted consciousness]. But one can avoid calamity by joining oneself to "the tzaddikim who are on the rung of *gadlut* [expanded consciousness]. Consequently, by virtue of a bond with them, one can experience *gadlut* even while on the level of *katnut*. This is a cardinal principle." [65] Attachment to the tzaddikim is especially necessary for the common man. For "the common people are in the category of *katnut*, while the tzaddikim are in the category of *gadlut*. When the common people join themselves to the [tzaddikim], they also experience the mystery of *gadlut*." [66]

R. Nahman, like Shamai of talmudic times, was known to have had a temper and appeared to deal despotically with others. He was not remembered for his gentle nature, nor did he emulate the consideration displayed by the Lord who, according to the Midrash, spoke at Sinai according to each person's ability to hear. [67] His words were like the lash of a whip.

> I have heard about the Hasid, our master and teacher, R. Nahman, may his memory be for a blessing: A merchant once galloped through his prayers at full speed. After he finished, the *mokhiah* [rebuker, i.e., R. Nahman] approached and spoke to him just as rapidly. "Madman!" the merchant screamed. "Who

---

twenty percent of all the teachings of R. Nahman which R. Jacob Joseph brings, makes it, *ipso facto*, "characteristic" of his outlook, regardless of whether that same teaching is brought once by the same author in the name of a contemporary (who may have heard it from R. Nahman, may have been misquoted by R. Jacob Joseph, or may, in fact, have taught it along with R. Nahman).]

65. *Toldot Ya‹akov Yosef*, p. 166d [quoting the Hasid, R. Nahman].

66. *Tzafnat Pa‹neyah*, p. 37b. R. Nahman said: "The reason that one cannot get the Lord to respond to prayer is that we are far from Him on account of our sins. The only alternative is for all Israel to join together as one, each man to his neighbor, one neighbor to the next, until they reach [Him] . . . " (M. Y. Gutman, *Mitorat Hahasidut*, bk. 1, #72).

67. See *Midrash Tehilim* 31:7.

can grasp what you are saying?" To which R. Nahman replied: "And who do you think can understand *your* prayers? What is more, should you argue that the angels perceive the thoughts of man [however unintelligibly they may be uttered], you know only too well that when you prayed you did not have a single holy thought in your head!"[68]

R. Nahman apparently did not engage in dialogue with the community. His strength lay in his relationship to the individual. He sought to conquer young minds; to teach them, for example, to disdain perfunctoriness in the performance of *mitzvot*. While his admirers praised him with the title "Hasid," the title of maggid (preacher) was never accorded him. Perhaps the following remark reflects some of the impatience he felt when he had to speak in public. "If the wise man, who wishes to teach Torah and reproof finds himself surrounded by fools—for it is written, 'fools scorn wisdom and reproof' (Prov. 1:7)—*then his tongue turns heavy . . . unable to speak*. As Moses said: 'I am heavy of tongue. . . . How can I approach Pharoah,' that is, the stiffnecked people [the Hebrew letters for "Pharoah" (FaR'O) and "neck" ('OReF) are similar] who spurn rebuke."[69] "Being heavy of tongue was not his [Moses's] fault but that of others," for when the wise man speaks to "those who are deaf to wisdom and reproof, it is then that his tongue turns heavy."[70] He complained that the people "turned away from him and shut their ears to wisdom and reproof."[71] The wise man who falls in with fools is held in contempt by them. It is better "in such a situation to play the fool himself, for then he will be honored by them."[72]

Bar Kapara taught, "When a man loses his temper, nothing ascends to his hand [i.e., is achieved] but anger."[73] R. Nahman explained why the term, "to his hand," was used. "It is known that every night, when the souls ascend to heaven, each person records in his own hand [upon the Heavenly record book] every sin he has committed that day. Should he have lost his temper that day, however, then the *hand* only writes down the sin of anger. To write more is unnecessary, for anger, since it leads to all other sins, embraces all other sins. This is the meaning of the words, 'nothing ascends to his hand.' [No angry soul ascends on high to write with his hand] anything other than the sin of his anger."[74]

68. R. Joseph Teomim, *Rav Peninim* (Frankfurt a.O., 1782), p. 54b.
69. *Ben Porat Yosef*, p. 65c.
70. Ibid., p. 67d.
71. Ibid.
72. *Ketonet Pasim*, p. 45c.
73. *BT* Kidushin 40a.
74. R. Pinhas of Dinovitz, *Siftey Tzaddikim, parshat matot*; *Yismah Lev* to *BT* Berakhot [of Menahem Nahum Twersky; Slavuta, 1798].

It is characteristic of a *mokhiaḥ* to dwell upon the failings of others, pointing to the flaws of the congregation and the corruption of the individual. Interpreting the verse dealing with the law of Passover: "Neither shall there be leaven (*ḥametz*) seen with *you*" (Exod. 13:7), our sages say, "Your own (*ḥametz*) you do not see, but you see that of others and of the Most High!"[75] R. Nahman reads the statement as an exclamation: "Your own [sins] you do not see,[76] but you do see [the sins] of others! Indeed, you pursue an investigation into the sins of others . . . and even 'of the Most High!'"[77]

"It is a cardinal principle," R. Nahman taught, "that one should not hold himself in low esteem. Rather should he believe that it is as if the entire world were created only for his sake. If he were alone in the world, he would hold himself to be a tzaddik and a hasid, just and true. This is not the case now, however, for when he sees an ugly trait in his neighbor he should understand that some portion of it resides in himself."[78]

A comtemporary writes: "I have heard in the name of the Hasid, R. Nahman, may the memory of a tzaddik be for a blessing: 'Should you wish to praise, praise God; and should you wish to find fault, find fault with yourself.'"[79]

Amiability was not one of R. Nahman's salient features. By nature a rebel, his demands were numerous, severe, and not to be compromised. He went so far as to admonish others for failing to fulfill the verse, "I have set the Lord before me always" (Psalms 16:8), even when they were engaged in their daily work. And when they objected in astonishment, "But how is that possible?," he would answer: "If you can think of your business while you pray to God in the synagogue, why not the reverse?!"[80] Though the people were not prepared to accept his demands,

75. *BT* Pesahim 5b. [". . . of the Most High" refers to what has been consecrated for use in the Temple. This is excluded by the phrase 'with you,' since consecrated items do not belong to 'you.'" Literally, the passage from Pesahim means that one may "see," i.e., have in one's possession, leaven which is not one's own, i.e., which belongs to "others" or is consecrated to "the Most High."]

76. "A person sees all faults other than his own."*Mishnah* Nega'im 2:4.

77. *Tifʾeret ʿUziʾel*, p. 64. [I.e., When something bad happens to you, you do not blame your own shortcomings, but see a shortcoming in Divine Providence!]

78. *Toldot Yaʿakov Yosef*, p. 29a.

79. *Mishmeret Hakodesh*, see above, n. 57. R. Jacob Joseph of Polonnoye brings a similar epigram in the name of the Besht. "For I have heard Musar in the name of my master which can be taken as a lesson for all: If one wishes to speak ill of another creature or person, let him speak ill of himself; and if he wishes to praise another person, let him rather praise God" (*Toldot Yaʿakov Yosef* [p. 29a]; Cf. *Ben Porat Yosef*, p. 59b).

80. *Toldot Yaʿakov Yosef*, p. 17d. [Piekarz points out that R. Nahman's assertion that one should meditate on God's presence even when doing business "is not characteristic of R. Nahman alone, but is an echo of the authors of the Musar literature such as R. Isaiah Horowitz, author of the *Sheney Luhot Haberit* (Piekarz, *Bimey Tzemihat Hahasidut*, pp. 23, 27). He cites a similar passage from a contemporary writer, Peretz ben Moses (*Bet Peretz*

he nevertheless stood firm. It was as if he had upended the passage from the Ethics of the Fathers (2:1) to read: "Which is the way that one should choose for himself? That of which others do *not* approve." The rule of thumb is to be contrary; to reject what the average man esteems; to hold fast to that which people discard. "As a general rule," R. Nahman taught, "one should seek not the approbation of his neighbor, but rather his opposition!"[81]

The joyous worship of the Hasidim was like a briar piercing the flesh of those emasculated of spirit who ridiculed the peculiar ways of the disciples of the Besht. R. Nahman cautioned the Hasidim not to be intimidated by such mockery. He compared their plight "to a king who invented a marvelous musical instrument, one which possessed within it

---

[Zolkiew, 1759], p. 20b), and refers to older Musar and homiletical sources, and Maimonides. Heschel himself, however, writes that "the custom of meditating on God's name during daily affairs is known to us from the circle of the kabbalists," and brings the example of a contemporary, R. Isaac of Drohobycz, giving sources from Midrash, Maimonides, the *Sheney Luhot Haberit*, and Isaac Luria. (See above, pp. 118-19, nn. 31, 32.) The passage from *Bet Peretz*, while most helpful, is in a more didactic context and contains neither the power nor the vividness of that of R. Nahman, "who *admonished* people who did not fulfill the verse, 'I shall set the Lord before me always,' even when engaged in their daily work, etc. . . . " Furthermore, we know of the personal habit of "the Hasid, R. Nahman Kosover who paid a fixed amount weekly to a certain person to remind him of the name of God, when he was in the company of others, lest he forget, so that God's name might be constantly before him" (*Toldot*, p. 186b). The association of this teaching with R. Nahman is clear and adds a significant dimension to the understanding of his personality. Cf. above n. 64.]

81. This explains the story which relates that "[Once on Purim] Raba 'slew' Rav Zera, and on the next day prayed for him and revived him" (*BT* Megilah 7b [read *ve'ahyai* instead of *ve'atasi* in *Tzafnat Pa'neyah*, p. 15c]). We know that Rav Zera had wanted to emigrate from Babylonia to the Land of Israel and that he had hidden himself from R. Judah, his master, who taught that "one who emigrates from Babylonia to the Land of Israel violates a positive commandment of the Torah" (*BT* Ketubot 110b). And since Raba helped Rav Zera to emigrate [to the more peaceful environment of Palestine], it was as if he "slew" him. "For it is a general rule [continued R. Nahman] that a person should seek not the approbation of his neighbor but rather his opposition. [R. Eleazar had taught] 'be in opposition (*kabel*), and you will endure.' (R. Nahman interpreted the word '*kabbel*' to mean 'in opposition.' [The Targum for *kenegdo* ('opposite him' in Gen. 2:21) is '*lekabbley*.' In other words, one should seek not acclamation but opposition.] The Talmud then says that 'Raba prayed for Rav Zera and revived him' [R. Nahman explains this to mean that at first it was felt that Rav Zera was wrong in leaving Babylonia] since true 'opposition' is found principally in the study of Torah, and [such opposition is strongest among] the scholars of Babylonia who are called "biters" (*BT* Sanhedrin 24a). [Discussions were carried on far more energetically in the Babylonian academies than in the Palestinian.] In the Land of Israel, however, [the Talmudic scholars] were at peace with one another. [The Jerusalem Talmud contains less controversy than the Babylonian.] Prayer on the other hand, requires harmony. Raba, therefore, came to agree with Rav Zera [since for prayer, the Holy Land is a better environment. I.e., he felt that the lack of "opposition" enhanced the opportunity for successful prayer]. . . . He asked mercy, which is prayer, and revived [Rav Zera]." (*Tzafnat Pa'neyah*, p. 15c). [Before R. Zera departed for Palestine, he fasted for one hundred days to forget the Babylonian method of dialectic study (*BT* Baba Metzia 85a). Perhaps R. Nahman understood this as a further indication that it was for prayer not study that R. Zera had gone to Palestine.]

the sounds of all instruments. The king commanded his servants to demonstrate this instrument before the other monarchs. His servants went forth to do his bidding. They came first to the court of a king who, shrouded in mourning, drove them off. [They journeyed on] until they found a king who needed what they had. The wicked are like those in mourning, because of which the joy of the *mitzvah* is like a thorn which pains them."[82]

R. Nahman neither apologized to his critics nor sought to justify his ways before them. He gloried in serving the Lord and held in contempt those provincials who, out of ignorance, had the audacity to criticize the Lord's elect. He compared the situation to a king who sought an artist

> to paint frescoes in the royal palace. Artists from all the provinces of the king assembled to compete. One artist drew a field in which there was a stalk of wheat with a small bird perched on it. Everyone marveled at the man's skill, except for one ignorant peasant who said with disdain: "In a field, stalks wave, but this painted one stands still!"
>
> The artist then proceeded to paint another picture, this time depicting a plow and several plowmen. The king and his nobles liked the picture. Once again, however, this peasant was critical: "What's supposed to go on the right is drawn on the left." In this manner the painter was shamed several times. Finally, he drew a young lady-in-waiting, serving and adorning the queen in her private chamber. This time, when the same fellow found fault, the king had him thrashed, exclaiming: "How dare you criticize the king's maidens in the innermost chambers upon which you have never in all your life laid eyes!"[83]

The Midrash to the Book of Lamentations interprets the phrase "many in number" from the verse "How does the city, many in number, dwell alone?" (Lam. 1:1), to signify "many in opinion." Quoting R. Nahman, the *mokhiah* of Polonnoye explains this Midrash to mean that the prophet is lamenting the destruction of the people of Israel who were blessed in understanding that the service of God, which is one at its root, divides into many branches. "Each man serves the Lord according to his own understanding, though his neighbor may differ from him."[84]

Once, on his way through the city of Zalrave (?) on a business matter at the time of the morning services, R. Nahman halted his

---

82. *Ketonet Pasim*, p. 20c; *Toldot Ya'akov Yosef* [p. 137b].
83. *Ketonet Pasim*, p. 7d [cf. *Tosefta* Megillah 2:17].
84. *Teshu'ot Hen*, *parshat vayehi*. R. Gedaliah of Linitz adds: "And his holy words are reasonable, indeed unassailable. For it is not possible for two men to serve the Lord in one way, just as no two prophets prophesy in a single style." See R. Pinhas of Dinowitz, *Siftey Tzaddikim*, *parshat vayikra*.

coach opposite the *bet hamidrash*, took his *talit* and *tefillin*, and
entered. He wrapped himself in his *talit*, put on his *tefillin* and,
without asking permission, simply began leading the worshipers in
prayer.

Although offended at the stranger's arrogance, the congregants
were moved despite themselves and listened with silent pleasure,
for the words that came from his mouth were sweeter than
honey. Still, they were annoyed. And so, when after the *Kaddish
Derabbanan*, he began to recite *Hodu* ("O give thanks") before
saying *Barukh She᾽amar* ("Blessed be He who spoke") [contrary
to the Ashkenazic pattern of prayer which places *Barukh
She᾽amar* first],[85] the entire congregation was outraged and
thought to remove him forcibly from the cantor's lectern. They
could not bring themselves to do it, however, so strong was their
desire to listen to his chanting. All the while he prayed, they debated the matter, but the moment he finished they leaped upon
him with a harangue:

"How dare you lead the congregation without permission and,
what is more, how dare you alter the rite of worship from that of
our fathers and their fathers, who were great scholars in their
generation (*gedoley hador*)?"

"*And who tells you*," he countered, "*that they are in Paradise?!*"

At his reply the congregation writhed.

Now, among those present was the author of *Toldot Ya῾akov
Yosef* (?) who had given over his position as community preacher
to one of his students, R. Zalman. This R. Zalman attacked R.
Nahman even more sharply than the others, until R. Alexander,
a disciple of R. Zalman, came and said: "Let the man be. He is
ever with the Lord."[86]

85. [This was an example of the controversies which led to the establishment of separate
Hasidic synagogues. The Hasidim adopted the Lurianic-Sefardic rite in contradistinction to
the prevailing Ashkenazic rite. See H. J. Zimmels, *Ashkenazim and Sephardim* (London:
Jews College Publications [N. S. 2], 1958), p. 120, and L. Jacobs, *Hasidic Prayer* (New
York: Schocken, 1973), chap. 3. Cf. I. Elbogen, *Hatefilah Beyisra᾽el* (Tel Aviv: Dvir, 1972),
pp. 65–66; S. Baer, *Seder ῾Avodat Yisra᾽el* (Berlin: Schocken, 1936), p. 59; A. Z. Idelsohn,
Jewish Liturgy (New York: Holt, 1932), p. 81.]

86. *Shivhey Habesht* [Ben-Amos, #111].

[Heschel's two question marks (after "Zalrave" and after "the author of *Toldot Ya῾akov
Yosef*") point to problems which this passage presents: (1) The author of *Toldot Ya῾akov
Yosef* was R. Jacob Joseph of Polonnoye and not Zalrave or, as the following MS version
suggests, Zolkiew; (2) he was the city's rabbi and not its "community preacher," which
position, as is well-known, was held by R. Aryeh Leib, author of *Kol Aryey*. Nor do we
know of any successor to R. Jacob Joseph by the name of R. Zalman. Further, if this was R.
Jacob Joseph's synagogue, why would the people object to the rite of the Besht, and why did
R. Jacob Joseph himself not take a hand in the matter? And what was his connection to the
city in which the episode occurred?

In a recent publication (*᾽Ohel Raḥel* 2 (1981):434–36), H. Lieberman raises these and

R. Nahman's understanding of the claims of Hasidism required that one repudiate serving God in a manner which merely imitated the ways of former generations. A favorite byword of his was *"Pay no heed to the fathers!"* (*ʾal tifnu ʾel haʾavot*).[87] When people complained about some new religious practice introduced by the Besht and his circle, "But my father and my father's father did not do this," he would answer: "Pay no heed to the fathers! . . . And moreover, did [your father] bring the Messiah? . . . "[88] Only Lot's wife looked backward!

Respect for one's elders and their practices was an accepted rule among the Jewish people. This principle is reflected in such rabbinic passages as: "Keep the customs of your fathers" (*BT* Betzah 4b); "If the elders say 'Tear down' and the children say 'Build,' tear down and do not build, for the very tearing down advocated by the elders is building" (*BT*

---

other questions, which he answers with reference to a manuscript copy of *Shivhey Habesht* in which a different version of the story appears:

"Once, on his way through the city of Zolkiew [not "Zalrave"] . . .

"Now, among those present was the author of *T. Sh.* (= *Tevuʾot Shor* [not *Toldot Yaʿakov Yosef*], who had given over his position as community preacher to one of his students. This R. Zalman attacked R. Nahman even more sharply than the others, until R. Alexander *T. Sh.* (= *Tevuʾot Shor* [the master and not "a disciple" of R. Zalman]) came and said: . . . "

In summary: the city was Zolkiew instead of Zalrave; the person was R. Alexander Shor, the author of *Tevuʾot Shor* (Zolkiew, 1733), instead of R. Jacob Joseph; and R. Alexander Shor was the master instead of a disciple of R. Zalman.]

87. This is a paraphrase of Leviticus 19:31, "Pay no heed to ghosts (*ʾovot*)," vocalizing *ʾovot* (ghosts) as *ʾavot* (fathers); thus, "pay no heed to the fathers." The same play on words is quoted from another source by R. Israel Jaffe, *ʾOr Yisraʾel* (Frankfurt a.O.: M. Gott-schalk, 1702), Introduction, p. 5c: "I have heard the following repeated in the name of the distinguished *gaon*, my in-law, the rav, our learned master and teacher, R. Moses, the son of R. David, who toward the end of his life taught Torah in the holy community of Vilna. Reprovingly, he would say: 'Pay no heed to the *ʾovot* [ghosts], i.e., Don't listen to those who justify things by harking back to their fathers (*ʾavot*).'"

This stance is in opposition to exaggerating the value of *minhagim* that continued to multiply from generation to generation. Compare the remarks of Rabenu Tam: "You have also argued that one should not change a *minhag* [custom] because of mockery. This particular custom, however, is not a *minhag*; it is *gehinom* (Hell) spelled backward! If fools behaved so, wise men did not. And even a proper *minhag* does not overtake a *halakhah*. You have erred greatly already in doing this and, I fear, will continue to entertain similar foolish ideas" (*Shiltey Giborim* to the *Mordekhai*, *BT* Gitin 85a). See my essay, ["Toward an Understanding of Halakhah,"] in the *Yearbook of the Central Conference of American Rabbis* 63 (1953), p. 406, n. 8. [In this essay Heschel brings other supporting sources, among which is the following: "And as to their claim, namely, that they have followed this practice for many centuries and that the *minhag* takes precedence over the *halakhah* . . . ; when you examine this argument closely, you will see that they have constructed an edifice on a tottering foundation . . . If we are dealing with a *halakhah* which is already fixed in the Talmud, certainly no one has the power to annul or change customary practice in opposition to the *halakhah*. Only if *halakhah* is uncertain, are you permitted to follow the *minhag* (which differs from the *halakhah*)—not the reverse, namely, to introduce a new *minhag* in opposition to a *halakhah*. For such a *minhag* is in reality *gehinom*"(R. Jacob Riecher, *Shevut Yaʿakov* [1860; rpt. Brooklyn: M. J. Finkelstein, n. d.], vol. 2, resp. 6, p. 2a)].

Megillah 31b, Nedarim 40a); "As a bird cannot fly without wings, so Israel cannot endure without the elders" (*Vayikra Rabbah* 11:8, *Tanhuma, shemot* 29). In contrast, R. Nahman accorded honor to the young. The times demanded that a war be waged for the Lord, and it was clear to him that in the ways of war "the aged are not expert."[89] "In the academy none excels the elder; on the battlefield none excels youth."[90] The elders had become so at home in this world that their souls had forgotten what they once beheld in the higher world before they descended into their bodies. Young people, however, still recall the higher world. Once he said to a young man: "You have not yet forgotten the ways of heaven . . . !"[91]

Prayer

R. Nahman strove to fortify the pillar of prayer. He would travel from city to city to teach people how to pray. From time immemorial, there had been preachers who rose up from the people Israel and sought to influence the congregation by the force of their teaching. The Besht and R. Nahman broke a new path. They moved people with the power of their prayer, as well. It was R. Nahman's custom when he came to a city to go to the synagogue and lead the congregation at prayers, sometimes even without the permission of the synagogue officials. *Hitlahavut*, the burning fervor which characterized Hasidic prayer, was not common then. "But the words that came from his mouth were sweeter than honey."[92] The author of *Shivhey Habesht*, R. Dov Ber, the son of R. Samuel, said that just "to hear R. Nahman sigh in prayer is to have one's heart broken."[93]

R. Nahman demanded *hitlahavut* in prayer. He encouraged even those who prayed with the congregation not to hide their fervor, but to make whatever "gestures their *hitlahavut* requires." In criticism of the practice, he was once reminded that the Talmud relates that Rabbi Akiba distinguished between public and private worship, shortening his prayers "when worshiping with the congregation so as not to burden them," and only when he "prayed alone [*beyahid*], would he roam from corner to corner because of his agitated motions."[94] To this objection R. Nahman answered: [The expression *beyahid* means "alone" or "as a single unit."] "If a man prays with companions among whom there is love and unity,

88. *Toldot Ya'akov Yosef*, p. 44b.
89. *BT* Shabbat 89b.
90. *BT* Hagigah 14a.
91. *Toldot Ya'akov Yosef*, p. 156c.
92. *Shivhey Habesht* [Ben-Amos, #111].
93. Ibid. [Ben-Amos, #110]. In the name of his father-in-law, R. Alexander Shohet, for many years the Besht's scribe.

then the whole congregation *is* like one and each individual 'prays [at one with his fellow] *beyaḥid*.'"[95]

What is the content of prayer? The elect do not pray for things of this world, such as bread or clothing. They pray for spiritual matters. Only the multitude pray for wordly things. How, then, do the elect ever attain the necessities of life? They obtain them from the prayer of the multitude. "For when the common man prays for food or clothing . . . , clothing and food also are given to the elect who pray only for spiritual sustenance . . . "[96]

R. Nahman apparently possessed the gift of song.[97] The impact of his musical talents is reflected in the following tale. Once, on the morning of the Sabbath, R. Nahman and one of his intimates (?) , R. Yudel, went to the bathhouse next to the house of study. "R. Nahman went about his business very quickly, but R. Yudel followed a more leisurely pace. While the latter was still removing his clothes in the *mikveh*, R. Nahman [had already finished, departed, and had commenced] leading the congregation in worship. When R. Yudel emerged from the *mikveh*, he heard R. Nahman singing the prayer, *Haʾaderet Vehaʾemunah*. This inflamed him so that he raced to the house of study while still in his undergarments and danced there for some two hours!"[98]

R. Nahman was among the first who introduced the custom of praying according to the Sefardic rite, the pattern of prayer which in those days in Poland was restricted to kabbalists.[99]

---

94. *BT* Berakhot 31a.

95. "I have heard in the name of the rav, the distinguished Hasid, our teacher, Nahman Kosover, that if a man prays with his companions among whom there is love and unity, this is called 'praying *beyaḥid* ["alone," because he is "at one" with his fellows],' and it is then permissible to make whatever movements are in accord with his *hitlahavut*, whereas that is not permissible in another situation." *Ginzey Yosef* (Lwów, 1792), p. 3d.

96. *Ben Porat Yosef*, p. 20d; *Tzafnat Paʿneyah* [p. 22b].

97. According to a manuscript, his son, R. Moses, knew his melodies, among them the melody for *ʾOr Panekhah*, the liturgical poem for *Shabbat Shekalim*.

98. *Shivḥey Habesht* [Ben-Amos, #109. *Haʾaderet Vehaʾemunah* is from the Sefardic rite of the morning service and is found in *Heykhalot Rabbati*. See I. Davidson, *Thesaurus of Medieval Hebrew Poetry* (New York: Jewish Theological Seminary, 1925), 2:116.]

99. For example, he would recite *Haʾaderet Vehaʾemunah* in the morning Sabbath service. *Shivḥey Habesht* [Ben-Amos, ##109, 111]. [It was the Lurianic Sefardic rite which the early Hasidim adopted. The first *sidur* which was published for Hasidim was that of the R. Shneor Zalman of Lady (Shklov, 1803). Other early prayerbooks used were the *Sidur of R. Asher* (Lwów, 1787) (with the approbation of the scholars of the *kloiz* in Brody) and the *Sidur Kol Yaʿakov* by R. Jacob Kopel Lifshitz of Miedzyrzecz (Slavuta, 1805) (with the approbation of R. Asher Tzvi of Ostróg). R. Asher Tzvi mentions that according to a report, the Besht saw and approved the book. Cf. A. Wertheim, *Halakhot Vehalikhot Bahasidut* (Jerusalem: Mosad Harav Kook, 1961), pp. 94–96; Y. Alfasi, "A New Source for the Nusaḥ Ari of the Hasidim" (Hebrew), *Temirin*, ed. I. Weinstock, (Jerusalem: Mosad Harav Kook, 1972), 1:227–302. Alfasi claims to have discovered "the first *sidur* in which the customs of the Besht are mentioned by name and which was written during the lifetime of the Besht" (d. 1760). According to Alfasi, the manuscript was written by R. Abraham

In the course of his many journeys, R. Nahman taught countless Jews by the example he set that the nature of prayer is a consuming flame. In the words of the Besht: *"Wherever R. Nahman has traveled, people know what prayer is, and wherever R. Nahman has not traveled they do not know what prayer is."* [100]

In earlier times the question had already been raised: Since God knows the thoughts of men, as well as their needs, why is it necessary to put them into words when one prays? R. Nahman suggested an answer: "By means of the organs of physical speech, vessels are formed through which divine grace can flow to the physical world." This would not be so if one silently prayed with thought alone, in which case the flow would also descend only in a spiritual form. [101]

Yetzer Hara[c]

The Musarists held that good and evil are two separate kingdoms. The Holy One, blessed be He, they argued, delimited the one to *mitzvah* and the other to sin. The Good Impulse (*yetzer hatov*) draws man to *mitzvot*, while the Evil Impulse (*yetzer hara[c]*) entices one to sin. The ways are clear, the borders fixed, and the domain of the one does not impinge upon the domain of another. "The Evil Impulse has no power over him in whose heart the Torah resides. It can neither rule him nor touch him." [102] "The Evil Impulse cannot enter the house of study . . . it may accompany one along the way, but when it reaches the door of the house of study, it is forbidden to enter." [103]

In the school of the Besht, however, they recognized that the boundaries overlap; that good and evil stood opposite, but also within, one another. They saw not only evil in its defilement and good in its holiness, but also the mixture of the two, the confusion of mitzvah and sin. What endless gyrations the *yetzer hara[c]* performs to drive a man from this world; how subtle its approach, enticing man to do a mitzvah which is, in fact, a sin disguised as a mitzvah! And, contrariwise, sometimes "from the bitter comes the sweet."

The sages have taught: "If you meet that scoundrel (the *yetzer hara[c]*), draw him into the house of study." [104] R. Nahman was astonished at the

---

Samson of Raszków, the son of R. Jacob Joseph of Polonnoye. Scholem confirms the authenticity of this manuscript. (Scholem, *Devarim Bago* [Tel Aviv: Am Oved, 1975], p. 295, n. 3a.) Cf. above pp. 131–33 and n.85.]

100. The author of *Shivhey Habesht* in the name of his father-in-law [Ben-Amos, #110].
101. *Ben Porat Yosêf* [p. 17d], p. 41b; *Ketonet Pasim*, p. 28d.
102. *Midrash Tehilim*, 119:7.
103. Ibid., 119:64.
104. *BT* Sukkah 52a, Kiddushin 30a.

conditional expression, "if," as though to say that one is not perpetually confronting the Evil Impulse. "There is certainly no single moment when one does *not* meet that scoundrel. Of course," he went on to explain,

> if everyone recognized him as the *yetzer hara*ᶜ, they would beware of him. But he is shrewd, disguising his clothing and his language, even going so far as *to act the part of the yetzer hatov, the "Good Impulse,"* urging [man] to do a mitzvah! Then one has no recourse except to drag him into the house of study, and learn and pray with fear and trembling. If it was in fact the "Evil Impulse," it will then be crushed and unable to maintain the pretense. If, nevertheless, it continues to tempt, he will know that this is not the Evil Impulse.[105]

> The Evil Impulse entices man to grievous sins. Should a man be righteous enough to subdue the *yetzer hara*ᶜ time after time, *it may then devise to subvert him, by enticing him to heinous sins disguised as mitzvot.* It may mislead him, for example, by persuading him that it is a mitzvah to inform on another to the Gentile authorities or to shame another, or the like. It may suggest *an ulterior motive for doing a good deed, a motive so slight that he hardly notices,* unless he probes his conscience thoroughly. Therefore the tzaddik should not turn his attention from the *yetzer hara*ᶜ even for a moment, as the saintly [R. Bahya][106] puts it, "While you sleep, he lurks for you; if you hide, he watches you. He acts without warning to drive you from this world and the next."[107]

Evil, however, need not be considered as that which brings only guilt and shame to man. Man possesses the power to conquer the Evil Impulse by understanding that with every

> assault of the Evil Impulse, some ultimate good emerges. As the sages have taught . . . "Both Satan and Penina had a pious purpose [in acting as adversaries. Satan let Job show his true mettle, and Penina caused Hannah to fret, pray, and thus conceive

---

105. *Toldot Yaʿakov Yosef*, p. 73a.

106. See Bahya, *Hovot Halevavot, shaʿar yihud hamaʿaseh*, chap. 4.

107. Quoted in the name of "the marvelous and famed Hasid, our master and teacher, R. Nahman Kosover." He goes on to relate this thought homiletically to the Mishnah: [Zevahim 5:1]: "The most holy sacrifices are offered *betzafon*, toward the north side of the altar. Sacrifices of lesser holiness are slaughtered everywhere in the courtyard!"

"By 'the most holy' is meant the most righteous ones, whom the *yetzer hara*ᶜ 'slaughters *betzafun*' [the Hebrew can be vocalized as *tzafon* (north) or *tzafun* (hidden)], i.e., in hidden, deceptive ways . . . for it knows that such people would refuse to commit an obvious sin.

"Those of 'lesser holiness' are the common people of lesser religious seriousness. They 'are slaughtered everywhere,' that is to say, the *yetzer hara*ᶜ can destroy them even with obvious sins" (R. Benjamin b. Aaron [preacher of Zalozce], *Torey Zahav* [Mogilev: Asher Zelig, 1816], p. 90c; see also *Tzafnat Paʿneyah*, p. 36d [?]).

Samuel. When R. Abba b. Jacob gave this exposition] . . . Satan came and kissed his feet."[108]

Likewise, whenever anything negative befalls a man through the actions of the Evil Impulse, good may come of it. Take the spilling of blood, e.g., when one is publicly shamed and turns pale, which is as if his blood were spilled. This may benefit him both physically and spiritually. Physically, it is a remedy for an overabundance of blood . . . Spiritually, the benefit is obvious. The same is true in matters of sexual misdeeds. From bodily experience one may draw spiritual lessons, and from physical lust one may learn to come to spiritual desire, as I have written in another place.[109]

We find a similar idea in the interpretation of the verse, "Also a fool, when he is silent (maharish), is counted wise" (Prov. 17:28). R. Nahman raised the following question: "The word maharish is actually in the causative, indicating not that one "keeps silence," but that one "silences" others.[110]

Likewise [R. Nahman observed], it is dificult to understand the talmudic teaching, "In all his years, David never dreamed a good dream."[111]

But the answer lies in the fact that *foolishness is occasionally beneficial for man.*[112]

We find this to be the case in regard to David who fell into the hands of Achish, king of Gath, and acted the madman (1 Sam. 21:14). Thinking him someone else, they released him. The Talmud [Avodah Zarah 18b], similarly, reports that R. Meir escaped

108. *BT* Baba Batra 16a.

109. *Tzafnat Pa'neyah*, p. 38a; *Toldot Ya'akov Yosef*, p. 12b. Just as R. Jacob Joseph uses the expression "the spilling of blood" [yet intends it to be taken not literally but only as an allusion] to mean shaming a person in public [in accordance with the Talmud; cf. *BT* Baba Metzia 59a], so he uses the expression "sexual license" to mean matters related to sexually tinged misdeeds. Actual sexual license, according to *BT* Sanhedrin 75b, is in the category of those prohibitions for which one should die rather than transgress. R. Nahman meant actions like those discussed by some medieval authorities, e.g., R. Jonah Gerondi's assertion in *'Igret Hateshuvah* that the Torah forbids one even to look at a married woman. Cf. *Sefer Haredim*, Negative Commandments, chap. 2: "An indication of the admonition not to look at a married woman is found in the verse 'Thou shalt not follow after the desires of thy heart.'" Cf. the words of R. Simon ben Lakish: "You shall not say that only one who commits adultery is called an adulterer, but one who commits adultery with his eyes is also called an adulterer,"*Leviticus Rabbah* 23:12. [For a discussion of sexuality and erotic symbolism in early Hasidism, see Heschel, *Kotzk* (Tel Aviv: Hamenorah, 1973), 1:235–43, an English summary of which is found in Dresner, "Hasidic Truth," *Shefa* 2:4 (1981):23–25.

110. [The verse, as it stands, could be read, "Also a fool, when he silences others is counted wise."] If the verse wished to indicate that the fool himself was silent, it should have used the word *shotek* or *harash* instead of *maharish*.

111. *BT* Berakhot 52a.

112. See *BT* Ketuvot 17a [cf. *Zohar* 3:47b].

his pursuers by entering a house of ill repute, leading his enemies
to believe that the man they were chasing was not he.[113]

It is for this reason that in his dreams a tzaddik occasionally
enters into the realm of the *kelipot*, so that they should not be
envious of him [and attack his piety]. For a similar reason, improper thoughts may enter his mind during prayer. It is very
much like the case of Caleb, who joined the other spies, acting as
if he were one of them, so that he would be able to silence
them.[114]

This, then, is the meaning of the verse (Prov. 17:28): "Also a
fool, when he silences others [*maharish*], is counted among the
wise."[115]

"Also a fool," i.e., when he pretends that he, too, is a fool.
Such a one is then able to "silence others," like Caleb, regarding
whom it is written, "and Caleb silenced the people" (Num.
13:30). He is therefore "counted wise." For with regard to Caleb
[versus those who feared to conquer the Promised Land], it is
written, "And my servant Caleb because he had a different spirit
[and hath followed Me fully, him will I bring into the land . . .
and his seed shall possess it"]. (Num. 14:24)[116]

---

113. [Both David and R. Meir escaped punishment by acting out of character. The latter
incident refers to the story in the Talmud (Avodah Zarah 18b), which is here quoted in full.
"Beruria, the wife of R. Meir, was the daughter of R. Hanina b. Teradion. Said she to her
husband, 'It is a disgrace that my sister is condemned to a brothel.' So he took a *tarkab* full of
dinars and set out. If, thought he, she has not been subjected to anything wrong, a miracle
will be wrought for her, but if she has committed anything wrong, no miracle will happen to
her. Disguised as a soldier, he came to her and said, 'Prepare yourself for me.' She replied,
'The manner of women is upon me.' 'I am prepared to wait,' he said. 'But,' said she, 'there
are here many prettier than I am.' He said to himself, that proves that she has not committed
any wrong; she no doubt says this to every comer. He then went to her warder and said,
'Hand her over to me.' He replied, 'I am afraid of the government.' 'Take the *tarkab* of
dinars,' said he; 'one half distribute (as a bribe), the other half shall be for yourself.' 'And
what shall I do when these are exhausted?' he asked. 'Then,' he replied, 'say, "O God of
Meir, answer me!" and you will be saved.' 'But,' said he, 'who can assure me that that will be
the case?' He replied, 'You will see now.' There were there some dogs who bit anyone (who
incited them). He took a stone and threw it at them, and when they were about to bite him
he exclaimed, 'O God of Meir, answer me!' and they let him alone. The warder then handed
her over to him.
Finally, the matter became known to the government, and (the warder), on being brought
(for judgment), was taken up to the gallows. When he exclaimed, 'O God of Meir, answer
me!' they took him down and asked him what that meant, and he told them the incident that
had happened. They then engraved R. Meir's likeness on the gates of Rome and proclaimed
that anyone seeing a person resembling it should be brought there. One day (some Romans)
saw him and pursued him. He escaped by entering a harlot's house. . . . 'Heaven forbid,' said
they (the Romans). 'Were this R. Meir, he would not have acted thus!'"]

114. *BT* Sotah 35a.

115. *Tzafnat Pacneyah*, p. 62b, c [Cf. Dresner, *The Zaddik*, pp. 199–207].

116. "And now Israel, the Lord your God asks what of you? (Deut. 10:12)." R. Nahman
read this verse thus: "God asks of you to be in the category of 'what,' so that you will say,
'After all, what are we?,'" like Moses, who said to Israel, "What are we that you complain
against us?" (Exod. 16:7) (*Toldot Yacakov Yosef* [p. 18c]). Humility and reverence are a

Self-Interest

Many are the pitfalls along the path of one who strives for truth.
Yearning to serve the Creator with his whole heart, man is beset with
self-interest (*peniah*), that smallest trace of selfish benefit which taints the
soul. *Peniah* distorts man's path, drives him into error, and, in the end,
brings him to a halt. The gate is slammed in his face and the way toward
the light is closed.

More than all the wise men of past generations, those of the Besht's
school were aware of this danger. It is written, "He who walks on the way
alone [*baderekh yehidi*], and turns his heart to vanity, is guilty of
death."[117] R. Nahman observed: [Proper Hebrew style requires that] "it
should have been written in the reverse order: 'He who walks alone on
the way [*yehidi baderekh*] and turns his heart to vanity, is guilty of death.'
Then he explained the statement as referring to a just and blameless man
who 'walks in the way of the One of the world' [*baderekh Yehido shel
'Olam*], but 'turns his heart to vanity,' that is to say, while he performs a
good deed he feels some small *peniah*—such a one 'is guilty of death.'"[118]

How frail is man. Beloved of God, fashioned in His image, man seems
bent on defacing that likeness. Yet, even before sickness strikes, Heaven
provides a cure. The Mishnah says: "If a man lost his 'seal' [tokens
purchased in return for sacrifices to be offered in the Temple], they made
him wait until the evening."[119] R. Nahman gave this explanation to the
passage: "Whoever, through the darkness of his deeds, Heaven forbid,
has lost 'his seal,'—that is to say, his Divine image—'they make him wait
until the evening'—that is to say, until the eve of the Sabbath, which is the
focal point of the week, or until the eve of the New Month, which is the
focus of the month, or until the eve of Rosh Hashana, which is the focal
point of the entire year."[120]

---

single rung (ibid. [p. 42a]. "Moses our teacher, may he rest in peace, was 'more humble than
any man on the face of the earth' (Num. 12:3). He cleaved so completely to the Lord that he
forgot that there were other people in the world less worthy than he [thus reverence led to
humility]" (*Ketonet Pasim*, p. 47c). [A further teaching of R. Nahman.]

117. *Mishnah* Avot 3:4.

118. *Toldot Ya'akov Yosef*, p. 73a. See *Toldot Yitzhak* by R. Isaac of Niesuchojeze
(Nezkizh), pt. 2, p. 33, which quotes from a manuscript in the name of R. Nahman of
Kosów: "R. Simon answered his followers in regard to the question of the *shofar* with the
phrase '*bereyro demilah*.' [R. Nahman is referring to the passage from the *Zohar*, 3:99a: 'R.
Abba, as he was once studying with R. Simon (bar Yohai), said to him: "Many times have I
inquired concerning the meaning of the *shofar*, but I have never yet received a satisfactory
answer." R. Simon replied: "This is *bereyro demilah*, the true explanation of the matter
... "'] [R. Nahman] interpreted this phrase to read *milah berurah ladonai*, which is to say,
the [sound of the properly blown] *shofar* is the pure word to the Lord."

119. *Mishnah* Shekalim 5:5. The seal is the image in which man was created. "The Holy
One, blessed be He, marked every man with the seal of the first man" (Sanhedrin 38a).

120. R. Pinhas of Dinovitz, *Siftey Tzadikim, parshat hayey sarah*. Cf. the words of Bar
Kapara: [God says], "I have set the likeness of mine image on them, but because of their sins
it has become distorted" (*BT* Moed Katan 15b).

Like the kabbalists of that generation, R. Nahman practiced self-mortification and spoke about the need for fasting from Sabbath to Sabbath.[121] He also concerned himself with undoing the harm of involuntary nocturnal seminal emission [*keri*], which so disturbed the conscience of the kabbalists. It is reported that once after such an incident, he fasted from Sabbath to Sabbath until he destroyed the *kelipah* which was created from it. Nevertheless, he was told in a dream that a trace of the sin had remained, i.e., that the purification was not complete.[122]

The preachers of that generation taught that man should live as if Hell (*gehinom*) itself were stretched out beneath him, waiting. R. Nahman too was reviled at his own sinfulness, knowing that he would be judged in the future world. He stood in dread not only of *she'ol*, but of punishments even more severe. "I have heard from the deceased, the distinguished *mokhiah*, our master, the rav, R. Nahman, may his memory be for a blessing: 'Let not your *yetzer hara'* lull you into the false hope that *she'ol* will be a refuge into which you flee and have done with it all. But know what suffering will befall you before you ever arrive there!' "[123]

"My children," R. Nahman used to say to his family, "as we ingest them, so (when, after death, our souls enter into the bodies of animals) they shall ingest us."[124]

"All Israel has a share in the world to come."[125] This statement can easily become the slogan of fools, for if our portion in the world to come is guaranteed, why should one labor to serve God in this world? R. Moses explained in the name of his father, R. Nahman, that the intent of the above passage from the Mishnah is not "as people commonly understand it," that everyone will just parade into paradise. The accurate analogy is "to a prince who had many poor servants to whom he distributed portions of the land that they might work and seed it. If they do not work, they do not eat. But in the case of a stranger, even if he wanted to work it would be of no avail, because he never had a portion in the first place. And this is the meaning of 'All Israel has a share in the world to come'—if they work it!"[126]

121. "I have heard in the name of R. Nahman Kosover: 'The wise physicians have written that if man fasts seven successive days, tasting nothing, he must certainly die [see Maimonides, *Mishneh Torah*, *hilkhot shavu'ot* 1:7]. He (R. Nahman) said that our sages alluded to fasting from one Sabbath to the next, which is six days. That is why they also said: "Repent one day before you die" ('Avot 2:10), which is to say, go so far in repentance (fasting) that you reach the "one day before you die" [which is the day before] the seventh day of fasting, when one inevitably dies.' These are the words of the Hasid, R. Nahman of Kosów" (R. Barukh of Kosów, *Amud Ha'avodah*, *derush sheni leteshuvah*).

122. *Shivhey Habesht* [Ben-Amos, #209].

123. R. Meir Teomim, *Birkat Yosef Ve'eliyahv Raba* (Zolkiew, 1747), Introduction. [*She'ol* is the biblical term for Hell.]

124. From a manuscript quoting R. Raphael of Bershet.

125. *Mishnah* Sanhedrin, chap. 10.

126. From a manuscript.

Man dwells in a world of lies and filth. Does he have the power to set straight what he has distorted? Can the prisoner, unaided, free himself from the jail? This was a question which agitated R. Nahman, in whose name the following parable was told by R. Raphael of Bershet.

A bird, with long legs and beak, became mired in a swamp and could not pull her legs free. She considered the dilemma. Did she not have a long beak? She thereupon sank her beak into the mud, leaned upon it and extracted her feet. What happened? She had managed to get her legs free, but now her bill remained in the mire. She thought for a moment, set her feet into the mire once again, and retracted her bill. She rejoiced over her solution, but now her feet were stuck. R. Nahman concluded: It sometimes happens that while a man seeks to put one place right, he sets another awry. It is only the Lord who can ultimately make straight what we distort. We ruin in so ugly a fashion, while His way of restoring is so fine![127]

Death: Fear and Longing

There are two fundamentally opposed approaches to understanding the world of time and space, represented by the talmudic sages R. Akiba and R. Ishmael.

According to the school of R. Akiba, the world to come is all beauty and light and goodness; this world is all ugliness and darkness and evil. The verse, "And thou shalt live by them" [the commandments] (Lev. 18:5), refers to the world to come. From this, it would appear as if R. Akiba's school had concluded that the people Israel have no share in this world. According to the school of R. Ishmael, however, if one is worthy, he may inherit both worlds, this world and the world to come. The Holy One, blessed be He, set in the heart of man a love for this world, which he should labor to build. "Thou shalt choose life" (Deut. 30:19), Scripture teaches. "'And thou shalt live by them' [the commandments] (Lev. 18:5), and not die by them."[128] "Live by them"—in this world.

Many went in the way of R. Akiba. Even Maimonides could write: "Desolation of the soul is found in the perfection of the body; perfection of the soul is found in the desolation of the body."[129] Later, however, he rejected this view and affirmed that of R. Ishmael.

R. Nahman felt that all the goods of this world, except those of the spirit, are vanity. In this he agreed with the words of the sage: "Divorce in

127. From a manuscript.
128. [*BT* Yoma 85a.] Cf. A. J. Heschel, *The Theology of Ancient Judaism* (Hebrew) (London and New York: Soncino, 1962–65), 1:127 ff.
129. Maimonides, *Introduction to Commentary to the Mishnah*.

this world—marriage in the world to come."[130] To R. Nahman, sin and pain mark this world, from which death is a refuge which tolls salvation for man. All his life the *tzaddik* struggles with the Evil Impulse which entices him to sin. So dread was R. Nahman's fear of falling into transgression that he longed for death. Longing for death? Is such a concept not quite foreign to the teachings of Judaism? Investigation will show, however, that R. Nahman was not alone in his yearning for death, and that the matter depends upon two differing points of view.

One view is the following: "And God saw everything which He had made *and behold it was very good*" (Gen. 1:30). "In the name of R. Samuel it was said: The words ' . . . behold it was very good,' denote the Good Impulse. The extra word 'and,' in the beginning of the phrase, denotes the Evil Impulse [which is also 'very good'] . . . But for the Evil Impulse, no man would build a house, take a wife, or beget children."

The opposing view is revealed in the tradition that in the copy of the Torah of R. Meir, the student of R. Akiba, "it is written: 'And behold it was very [*me᾽od*] good': Behold death [*mot*] was good."[131] "Death was good for the righteous in that they would find peace for their souls and good for the wicked in they would no longer sin."[132] R. Judah the Prince, who follows the views of R. Ishmael in matters of the *᾽agadah*, holds that the death of the righteous is "evil for them and evil for the world."[133] But other sages say that "death takes the righteous because of the generation,"[134] that is, because of the *sins* of the generation. According to R. Ami, "As the red heifer atones [for the sins of the people], so does the death of the righteous atone"; and, similarly, R. Eleazar taught, "As the vestments of the priests atone, so the death of the righteous atones."[135] R. Nahman could not bring himself to say that the death of the righteous was bad for them. [To the contrary,] "The tzaddik who dies to atone for the sins of the generation, receives [in return] the merit of the generation."[136]

"R. Nahman Kosover did not live to an old age . . . for he served the Lord with exceeding fervor and would pray that God should take him

130. *Ben Hamelekh Vehanazir*, ed. A. M. Haberman (Tel Aviv: Mosad Harav Kook, 1950), p. 102.

131. *Genesis Rabbah*, 9:7, 9:5 [In other words, in the copy of R. Meir, who was himself a scribe, the word *mot* (death) was in place of *me᾽od* (very)].

132. *Midrash Agadah* to Genesis, ed. Buber, p. 5.

133. *Mishnah* Sanhedrin 8:5.

134. *BT* Shabbat 33b.

135. *BT* Moed Katan 28a. According to *Leviticus Rabbah* 2:1, the death of the righteous is among the ten things that are called precious.

136. *Ben Porat Yosef*, p. 68d. R. Nahman explained the verse, "He that hateth gifts shall live" (Prov. 15:27) to mean: "The tzaddik who dies to atone for the sins of the generation receives [in return] the merit of the generation. But he who desires not the merits of the community—i.e., 'he that hateth gifts—shall live.'"

from this world before he grew feeble and no longer had the strength to serve Him as he was accustomed." And, indeed, according to R. Pinhas of Korzec, R. Nahman died when he was but forty-two years of age. The son-in-law of R. Pinhas, the rav of Kalinblat, added, "that R. Nahman used to scream so loud it could be heard in the street:

"Sweet Father, I want to go home!" "*Tatenyi, ikh vil a-heim!*" According to others, he would shout:

"Take me home lest I spoil!" "*Nem mikh aheim, varim ikh hob mora ikh zol nit kalya veren!*"[137]

A tale:

> "For how many years [after R. Nahman's death, said the Besht], did I yearn to see my beloved friend, the chosen of God, R. Nahman of Kosów, in the higher world. I searched but did not find him whom I love. Through *yihudim*, I prayed that my soul be elevated to the place where he reposed, but I was not given permission."

(Toward the end of the story the Besht at last reached R. Nahman who said to him:)

> "If you wish to join me in this supernal world of eternity, hand over your soul to the angel who is known to you and let your body die in the world below. Perhaps through you, we shall merit that the Higher Will will be moved to deliver the exiles of our people, for how long must it yet be before the final redemption? And, furthermore, in this way you will benefit in never having to encounter the angel of death nor feel the taste of death. Remain with me. Then I and the souls of the other *tzaddikim* will take you to that place which is prepared for you, and we shall remain colleagues in the eternal world as well."
>
> "And I replied: 'But it was always my desire to be buried in the land of Israel, for from there the soul has a great ʿaliyah (spiritual ascent), as is known.'

137. From a manuscript. R. Shmariah, the son of R. Elijah Haʾikriti, a fourteenth-century sage of Crete, in his commentary to the Song of Songs (a manuscript of which is in the possession of R. Joseph Lis), explained the words of Solomon—"Draw me after you" (Song of Songs 1:4)—as the soul's yearning to be separated from the body: "My only love is to depart my body and cleave to You . . . for the soul so despises the body that it longs for its liberation." The perfect soul "desires death more than hidden treasures and yearns to be divorced from the body." He explains "how Solomon would stand in prayer before God, that with a divine kiss the Lord might take the spirit from his body and join it to Himself. 'For I am lovesick' (ibid. 2:5)—For what love is he sick? . . . that God should take me from this world." According to R. Elijah de Vidas, "Death for the Jew is the higher mercy in that it purifies his soul" (*Reyshit Hokhmah, shaʿar haʾahava*, chap. 6).

Compare the words of pseudo-Maimonides: "Know, my son, that in this lowly and despicable world, unfortunate man has no rest. Happy the one whose days are brought to an end speedily and without undo hardship" (*Kovetz Teshuvot Harambam Veʾigrotav*, ed. Lichtenberg [Leipzig, 1859], pt. 2, p. 40a).

"And he said to me: 'Know, that it is decreed that you will die outside the Land of Israel, for so I have heard many times in the Academy on High. I am not permitted to reveal the reason to you as long as your soul is bound to your body. For it was decreed that I, too, would die outside the Land of Israel, for a reason that is hidden. But if you will hand over your soul as I have described, then I will reveal everything to you.'

"When I heard the words that came from his holy mouth, I longed to give my soul to the angel. But I was troubled over abandoning my only son and my only daughter without leaving a will in which I could prepare them for the days to come. A conflict ensued within me, whether to act as had been suggested or to die at my natural time as all men do, rather than suddenly as befalls the impious. And I keenly regretted to be separated from my peers without leaving them a plan and a course of action for the future.

"When the Hasid [R. Nahman] heard my response, he entreated me so fervently that I lamented bitterly over my impending separation from my wife, my son, and my daughter and my grandchildren, and, particularly, from my peers. My soul, however, was still in my body at that moment, and were it not that my wife roused me from my sleep, I would have acquiesced to the advice of the *tzaddik* [R. Nahman] and fulfilled his request. But because of her cry, my soul [fully] returned to my body."[138]

Judgment and Mercy

The way of R. Nahman of Kosów was different from that of the Besht. Although they shared many of the same principles, they disagreed on many details.

R. Nahman, who was a part of the circle in Kuty, surely believed, as did other kabbalists, that kabbalistic teaching belonged to the select and should not be widely disseminated. One of the innovations of the Besht's teachings was his desire that the way of Hasidism be spread among the people. The Besht used to travel throughout the land—a fact which remained in the memory of the inhabitants of Miedzybórz for many generations afterward—and sought to transform the Hasidic way, until then the province of the elite, into the possession of the people.

While the Besht faced the world with love, with joy, and with compassion, R. Nahman approached it with tension, bitterness, and revulsion. The Besht's demeanor was pleasantness. R. Nahman used to be harsh and authoritative with his disciples, as if he had come to pronounce

---

138. Jacob and Israel Berger, *'Ateret Ya'akov Veyisra'el* (Lwów, 1881), pp. 53–54, according to "the old manuscript, written in 1799."

judgment. The Besht was patient, sought to understand the way of each man, loved peace, and preached it; R. Nahman was short-tempered, waging a constant war for the conquest of men's hearts. Greater, he believed, is the power of opposition than that of conciliation.[139]

The Besht spoke gently and asked from the people only what they were able to accept, while R. Nahman was all aflame, raging and demanding that they stake their lives uncompromisingly. By his extreme manner, he sometimes gave the impression of being a wild man, as the prophet said, "Mad is the man of spirit" (Hos. 9:7). At times even his friends called him to his face, "*Meshugener* (crazy) Nahman."[140]

While R. Nahman followed the olden custom of holy men to fast all week long "from Sabbath to Sabbath,"[141] the Besht taught "that it is better to serve the Lord joyously without self-mortification."[142] The face of the Besht shone; R. Nahman's face was sullen. The Baal Shem, who beheld the bright side of the world, was saddened at the humiliation of man and his despair, and taught the way of compassion. R. Nahman, who saw the dark side of the world, man's trivial needs and crude passions, sought to distance himself from communal tumult. He longed to depart this life.

Said the Besht: "Serve your Father in Heaven willingly out of love."

Said R. Nahman: "You serve God only because you are compelled to do so."

R. Nahman broke with accepted ways. Everywhere he struck hard. Like the Besht, he sought to exalt prayer and demanded the mobilizing of all the forces of the spirit into one's worship. Of course, it was to be expected that the laggards and the vulgar opposed him; indeed, there were even some among them who urged him "not to pray"! How should one reach those who refuse to accept the proper way of prayer? The Besht assumed that the Torah had been accepted freely, that the children of Israel stood at Sinai with one heart, declaring, "We will do and we will hearken," and that, in the end, truth and peace would prevail. R. Nahman, however, held the contrary: Israel took the Torah only because the Lord lifted up Mount Sinai and held it threateningly over their heads. For the sages of the Talmud explained the verse "And they stood beneath the mountain" (Exod. 19:17) to mean that "God raised the mountain over them like a barrel and said: 'If you accept the Torah, good, but if not, this will be your grave!'"[143] "*One must compel man to*

---

139. See above, p. 130.
140. R. Judah Leib, the *mokhiah* of Polonnoye, said to him: "*Meshugener Nahman*" (crazy Nahman), *Shivḥey Habesht* [Ben-Amos, #209]; *Rav Peninim*, p. 54b. See above, p. 127–28.
141. See above, p. 141.
142. *Tzava'at Harivash* (Warsaw, 1913), p. 6.
143. See *BT* Shabbat 88a.

pray and serve the Lord," said R. Nahman, "for [in any case] all things come from God, may He be blessed. And he expounded upon this doctrine in detail."[144] Only if one plants the vines and does the required work will the vineyard flourish; otherwise there will be no grapes.

R. Nahman justified his harsh method of reproof by interpreting the passage "In the presence of the dead, one says only the words of the dead"[145] to read: "In the presence of the dead," that is, the wicked (for "the wicked are considered dead even during their lifetime" [*BT* Berakhot 18b]), "one speaks only of death" [that is, reminding them of what awaits them beyond the grave]. To a tzaddik alone is it proper to say "that he should cleave to the Lord."[146]

Keri

In examining closely the issues that preoccupied many of the moral teachers in the eighteenth century, one finds an extreme sensitivity to problems relating to sexual desire, as if this were a foundation of the entire doctrine of Musar. The range of this sensitivity continually expanded, introducing all manner of restrictions and ramparts against this urge. Concern reached such a degree that a minor infraction was taken to be horrendous sin that would delay the redemption and bring calamity to the world.

Even an involuntary seminal discharge during one's sleep (Hebrew: *keri*) brings down "a holy spark—a holy soul of the supernal treasure house of the King, one of the sons of the living God"—to be seized and tormented by the *kelipot*. Whole books were written on the severity of this sin and various remedies proposed for forgiveness and atonement.[147] People were seized by this problem out of apprehension regarding a desire over which there was no final mastery and a failing which was extremely difficult to correct. In the wake of apprehension came deep feelings of guilt, self-condemnation, and depression.

R. Nahman also raged against this enemy which dared to invade his life. According to the story which the author of *Shivhey Habesht* "heard from the rabbi of [his] community," R. Nahman experienced "an involuntary seminal emission [*keri*]—may heaven save us—and because of

---

144. *Ketonet Pasim*, p. 40b.
145. See *BT* Berakhot, 3b.
146. *Toldot Ya'akov Yosef*, p. 197c, and *Ben Porat Yosef*, p. 41a, where no source is given, only, "as I have heard the adage . . . "
147. R. Joseph, son of R. Solomon Darshan of Posen, *Yesod Yosef: Musar and Remedies for the Sin of Nocturnal Emission* (Hebrew) (Frankfurt a.O., 1679); R. Moses Graf, *Zera'Kodesh: Penitential Remedies for the Impairment of the Sign of the Covenant* (Hebrew) (Fürth, 1696); cf. *The Sign of the Holy Covenant* (Hebrew) of R. Joseph Kanafi (Livorno, 1884); and the *Toharat Yom Tov* of R. Hananya Yom-Tov Lipa Deutsch, in 9 volumes!

this fasted from Sabbath to Sabbath to slay the *kelipah*. Nevertheless, a residue of the sin still remained. He said it must be corrected and began to weep . . . ''[148]

The Besht opened the way to compassion. He taught that one should not measure life with too short a rod, that every experience offers man the opportunity to perform countless commandments, and that this should be his primary concern. He dare not check himself at every moment, lest he become soiled with the very sins over which he repents. It is forbidden to despair because of the weakness of the body over which one has no absolute control.

The Besht said:

> One should not worry over the unclean accident, an involuntary *keri*. Worry more over an impure thought than over the *keri*, which, had it not happened, could have meant death. [For the *keri* expels an evil "spark" that must be extinguished one way or the other.] "Dear [*yakar*] in the eyes of the Lord is the death of his pious" (Psalms 115:15), [means] *yakar*—which has the same consonants as *keri*—is good for his pious ones. That is to say, if it comes about not because of any prior lustful thought, then it is good. For otherwise the person might have died. Consequently, one should only worry about purifying one's thoughts. And when an evil thought comes to a man, heaven forbid, he should see how he might purify it by raising it to join with the Creator, may He be blessed . . .[149]

Appendix A

Biographical Data on R. Moses of Kuty

Born to his father, R. Solomon, on 26 Tevet 1688 (*'Oneg Ḥayim Lèshabbat*, Introduction), R. Moses died in Kuty on 17 shevat 1738. The inscription on his tombstone is recorded in Samuel Zanvil Kahana's *'Anaf 'Etz 'Avot* (Cracow, 1903), p. xxxiv: "Moses ascended to God. He is the rav, our master and teacher, Moses, son of our master and teacher, Solomon, who died on Friday, 17 Shevat 1738."

R. Moses's wife was Sarah Sasi, the daughter of "our master and teacher, Menahem Mendel." H. Z. Teomim (*Zikaron Larishonim* [Kolomyja, 1914], p. 32) conjectured R. Moses's father-in-law to have been R. Menahem Mendel of Kolomyja, "rav, *ga'on*, and holy one, disciple and friend of our teacher the Besht, may his memory shield us," as he is described on the minutes of the Society of Circumcisors in the

---

148. *Shivhey Habesht* [Ben-Amos, #209].
149. This exceptionally long note appears in the Endnotes; see p. 189.

holy community of Bar, Russia, on 28 Elul 1755. Sarah Sasi died on 4 Tishri 1763. Cf. the inscription on her tombstone, *ʿAnaf ʿEtz ʾAvot*, ibid. Concerning R. Moses's children, we know of two sons-in-law. One "was the noted, pious and humble rav," R. Jonah, the son of Abraham Halevi, who later succeeded R. Moses as rabbi of Kuty. R. Jonah died on the last day of Passover, 1774 (*ʿOneg Ḥayim Lėshabbat*, Introduction). R. Israel Kitover, editor of Saadia Gaon's *Emunot Vedeʿot* and author of a commentary to it, *Shevil Haʾemunah* [Jozefów, 1878; rpt. Jerusalem, 1945], was R. Jonah's grandson. See the introduction to the latter book.

Another of R. Moses's sons-in-law was R. Ephraim, who also served as rabbi of Kuty and was the son of R. Hayim, rabbi of Belaya Tserkov (Sedey Lavan).[150] R. Ephraim died on Shevat 1784 (*Oneg Ḥayim Lėshabbat*, Introduction; *ʿAnaf ʿEtz ʾAvot*, #2, 5). [His family was well-connected in Hasidic circles.] The son-in-law of R. Ephraim, the wealthy R. Eliezer Lipman Halperin of Leszniów, was the son of R. Joel Halperin of Leszniów, who was the father-in-law of R. Pinhas Halevi Horovitz [a disciple of the maggid of Miedzyrzecz, the rabbi of Frankfurt-am-Main, and] the author of the *Haflaʾah* (*Haflaʾah*, *shêvetʾ aḥim*; *ʿAnaf ʿEtz ʾAvot*, #19). R. Joel Halperin was the brother of R. David, chief rabbi of Ostróg and Zasláw, a disciple of the Besht. See my essay, "Letoldot R. Pinhas Mikoretz" (*ʿAley Ayin*, p. 244; this volume, p.1–43).

As has already been noted in this chapter (p.117), R. Hayim of Horodenka—R. Moses's brother—was the brother-in-law of a prominent disciple of the Besht, R. Nahman of Horodenka. R. Moses was also the uncle of R. Barukh, the son of R. Abraham, maggid of Kosów and author of *Yesod Haʾemunah*.

Appendix B
R. Jacob Joseph's Use of Titles

R. Jacob Joseph of Polonnoye was quite precise in the use of titles. R. Nahman of Horodenka, who was apparently younger than he, he called "*harabani havatik Moharan* (the scholarly and distinguished . . . R. Nahman"),[151] or "*harabani Moharan* (the scholarly . . . R. Nahman").[152] In some places, the title "Moharan," without any further appellation, means R. Nahman of Kosów.[153] Support for this view is

150. [*Sedey Lavan* (= White Field) was the Hebrew name given by the Jews to Belaya Tserkov, which means "White Church" and which was called in Yiddish "*Shvartze Tumeh*" (Black Impurity).
151. *Toldot Yaʿakov Yosef*, [p. 201b].
152. *Ketonet Pasim*, p. 40c.
153. On the other hand consider the passage in *Toldot Yaʿakov Yosef*, p. 199a, where the author writes, "I heard in the name of Moharan" [= Morenu Harav Rabi Nahman = Our

found in the fact that a teaching ("The purpose of uttered prayer") which he quotes from "Moharan,"[154] is later mentioned in the following words: "I have already written, in the name of the Hasid Mohraran, may his memory live on in the world to come."[155] The passage which is quoted as "that which I heard from the mouth of Moharan, may his memory live on in the world to come,"[156] is introduced in another place as "that which I heard from the mouth of the distinguished Hasid, Moharan, may his memory live on in the world to come."[157]

The exposition on the verse, "the history of Jacob-Joseph," is cited: in the name of "The Hasid Moharan Kosover,"[158] "the Hasid, the deceased Moharan,"[159] and "the deceased Hasid Moharan."[160]

---

teacher, the rav, Rabbi Nahman]. The teaching referred to regards God's command to Moses at Sinai, that "No man shall ascend with you (Exod. 34:3)," a verse which was paradigmatic for R. Nahman's manner of worship. "One should imagine that he prays before God in solitude with no one else there before whom he might want to display himself." Now this same idea is found in *Degel Mahaney 'Efrayim, parshat matot*: "I have heard [this] from my in-law, the deceased, faithful rav, our master, the rav, R. Nahman Horodenker, may his memory be for a blessing." Here, then, is a case where "Moharan" alone is not Nahman of Kosów, but Nahman of Horodenka. Further, at the end of *Toldot Ya'akov Yosef* we find: "I have heard from the scholarly and distinguished Moharan" [i.e., Nahman of Horodenka (p. 201b)]. And shortly after [p. 202a]: "I have heard from the above-mentioned Moharan" [i.e., Nahman of Horodenka]. However, without the expression "above-mentioned" Moharan, we might think he meant R. Nahman of Kosów.) See also [p. 19b], ["As I have recorded in the last section (of this book) in the name of Moharan"], which is an allusion to a later statement [p. 201b, "from the scholarly and distinguished Moharan," i.e., Nahman of Horodenka.] Cf. S. Dresner, *The Zaddik*, pp. 310, n. 41; 311, 312, n. 52 [see Piekarz, *Bimey Tzemihat Hahasidut*, pp. 260–65].

154. *Ketonet Pasim*, p. 28d.
155. *Ben Porat Yosef* [p. 17d].
156. *Tzafnat Pa'neyah* [p. 37a].
157. *Toldot Ya'akov Yosef* [p. 166d].
158. Ibid. [pp. 98d, 197d: "Moharan Kosover"].
159. Ibid. [p. 99d].
160. Ibid. [p. 194d].

[The existence of two R. Nahmans in the circle of the Besht, R. Nahman of Kosów, the subject of this chapter, and R. Nahman of Horodenka, an equally fascinating figure (see Heschel, "Unknown Documents," *YIVO Bleter* 36 (1952):115–18), is at times confusing. R. Jacob Joseph quotes both of them frequently and in a variety of ways. When the place names Kosów or Horodenka are added ("Nahman of Kosów" or "Nahman of Horodenka") the identity is clear. In addition, research has enabled us to distinguish between them even without the above place names, if certain other appellatives are provided. (To this extent Piekarz agrees with Dresner [*Zaddik*, p. 310, n. 41; p. 312, n. 52] and Heschel.) Thus when R. Nahman is qualified as "*Hehasid*" (the Hasid) or "*Hamanoah*" (the deceased) or both, it is R. Nahman of Kosów who is intended; and when it is "*Harabani*" (the scholarly) or "*Havatik*" (the distinguished), it is R. Nahman of Horodenka. Joseph Weiss was unaware of this rule of thumb. E.g., he quotes the following passage thus: "'I have heard from the deceased Hasid *Moharan* . . . ' [R. Nahman Horodenka]." The brackets were supplied by Weiss, who is incorrect. (Weiss, "The Beginnings of Hasidism," *Zion* 15 (1951):51. See Piekarz, *Bimey Tzemihat Hahasidut*, p. 24.)

Which R. Nahman is meant, however, when the source is simply *Moharan* alone without any further qualification? Heschel argues that "in some cases" "Moharan" alone refers to

R. Nahman of Kosów. Piekarz, on the other hand, suggests that "many passages brought by Heschel in the name of Moharan are by R. Nahman of Horodenka" (p. 30) and follows the "assumption" that "'Moharan' (alone) is R. Nahman of Horodenka" (pp. 260–61). The problem is not easily resolved. Heschel was aware that at times "Moharan" alone refers to R. Nahman of Horodenka; he gives three examples of this in n. 153 above, where in each case the same passage is quoted once in the name of "Moharan" alone and again where the place name Horodenka or the identifiable appellatives "*Vatik*" (distinguished) or "*Rabani*" (scholarly) are given. Furthermore, when using material he ascribes to Nahman of Kosów, Heschel seeks to alert the reader to the general problem of identification by providing in his footnotes to the original Hebrew edition the exact form in which the name is quoted (e.g., "Moharan Kosover," "the *Hasid* Moharan," "Moharan" alone, etc.), thus enabling the reader to be aware of which passages are in the name of Moharan alone without appellation. The problematic passages can be reduced by noting, as in the case of R. Nahman of Horodenka, which passages quoted in the name of "Moharan" alone are again quoted in a way to be identified with Nahman of Kosów, such as "Nahman of Kosów," "Nahman the Hasid," etc. See, for example, the following parallel passages in the Hebrew text, where the exact form of the quotations ascribed to R. Nahman is preserved: p. 124, nn. 2 and 3; p. 130, n. 40; p. 132, n. 51; p. 140, nn. 4, 5, 6, and 7. English text: nn. 101, 116; Appendix B, nn. 154 and 155, 156, and 157. In these cases, at least, Piekarz's "assumption" that "Moharan" alone is "Nahman of Horodenka" would not seem to hold.

All the above examples provide some help in identifying unclear passages. Most difficult are those times when the source is "Moharan" alone, without place name or other appellation such as "Hasid," "deceased," or "scholar," and without association with the same or a similar passage quoted in a fashion to be identified with Kosów or Horodenka. Piekarz, *Bimey Tzemihat Hahasidut*, pp. 260–65, and Heschel differ in their identification of these passages, Piekarz especially relating those dealing with "the redemption of evil" to Nahman of Horodenka (nn. 109, 115). The questioned passages are a small percentage of the approximately fifty citations used: Hebrew text: p. 125, nn. 5, 6, 7, 8, 14; p. 131, n. 46; p. 132, nn. 50, 51. English text: nn. 69, 70, 71, 72, 78, 109, 115, 116.]

Four

Rabbi Isaac of Drohobycz

WITHIN THE BAAL SHEM TOV'S CIRCLE WERE SEVERAL REMARKABLE personalities, who, though not by tradition numbered among his disciples, became his colleagues, were close to him in spirit, and struggled with the same problems that were central to the Baal Shem's doctrine. These individuals occupy an important place in the early history of Hasidism. Men of stature in their own right, their inclination toward or actual submission to the Baal Shem contributed significantly to the propagation, as well as the character, of Hasidism. To a certain degree they can be considered among the movement's founders.

One such figure was R. Isaac of Drohobycz. Though Hasidic literature reveres his name, the historical personage has remained clouded in legend. The facts concerning his life and character have yet to be established. What sort of person was he, and what was his "way"? This essay constitutes a first attempt at reconstructing an answer. Meager though the historical data be, they suffice to transfer the name of R. Isaac of Drohobycz from the realm of legend into that of history.

His Ancestors

Family tradition has it that R. Isaac was the scion of distinguished ancestors, of the line of R. Isaac Hayyut [Hayyes], author of ʾApey Ravrevey.[1] The "Seraph," R. Uri of Strzeliska, reputedly said of him, "R.

Footnotes for this chapter are not consistent with the Hebrew text.

1. See the title page of ʿAtzey Besamim, a work composed by the rabbi of Praga (near Warsaw), R. Isaiah Muskat. R. Isaiah was the son-in-law of R. Isaac of Radvil, son of R. Yehiel Mikhel of Zloczew [son of R. Isaac of Drohobycz]. The same information recurs on the title page of DaʿatTorah by R. Shalom Mordecai Hakohen [Schwadron], rabbi of Berzan.

ʾApey Ravrevey is included in PeneyYitzhak (Cracow, 1591), written by "the illustrious sage, the gaʾon, our teacher and master, the rav, R. Isaac, may he live forever, called R. Isaac Hayyut [Hayyes]." It is an abridged legal compendium in poetic format, containing two commentaries, ʾApey Ravrevey and ʾApey Zutra. The introduction notes that the author is of "the stock of the Hasidim (the pious ones) of the Provence." It also contains a eulogy of R. Isaac's young son, R. Samuel, who had "taken in marriage the daughter of our

152

Isaac Drobitcher was the ninth generation of those with the Holy Spirit."[2] R. Yosef of Yampol [R. Isaac's grandson], it is said, went even further. He claimed that the Holy Spirit had been with R. Isaac's family uninterruptedly for seventy-two generations.[3]

R. Isaac's mother was called, "Yente, the prophetess." It is reported that once, while cleaning house, she stopped to recite the *kedushah* prayer. Asked for an explanation, she answered that she had heard the angels uttering the words, "Holy, holy, holy is the Lord of Hosts" (Isa. 6:3), and had joined in.[4]

His father was R. Joseph Wirnik of Pistýn, famous as "R. Joseph the honest." Even the Gentiles honored him for his honesty and referred to him as "*sprawidliwi*," a "man of truth." Hasidic tradition has it that, at the end of his life, R. Joseph went to Palestine. We are told he sent his son, R. Isaac, a copy of the Pentateuch from the Holy Land, with the flyleaf inscription, "Him do I bewail, my father, R. Moses, murdered for the sanctification of the Holy Name."[5] R. Joseph's father was R. Moses of Pistýn, rabbi of the Galician community of Swierze[6] (near Przemyślany), who had died a martyr's death. R. Moses, it is said, is the subject of the following tale recorded by R. Barukh of Kosów:

noble master, the rav, R. Eliezer of Roptshi" [Ropshitz = Ropczyce?] . . . but in the Hebrew month of Tevet, during which the joyful day of his wedding had been arranged, his coffin lid became his permanent bridal canopy."

In addition to the laws and their sources, the book provides an occasional "*hidud* (wit-sharpener), *hiluk*, and a good, timely Ashkenazic *pilpul*, which are fine for illuminating souls and kindling hearts." Notable is the author's complaint that "the modes of penetrating yeshivah study have changed, and weakened is the voice of Jacob. As to *pilpul* . . . it is now diminished in the schools of learning, and no longer do brilliant mental stratagems well up from all hearts." This casuistry was not universally popular, however. According to S. Y. Fünn (*Kenesset Yisra'el* [Warsaw: Boimritter and Ganskar, 1886], p. 612), it was R. Hayyut who was intended by the seventeenth-century scholar, R. Yair Hayim Bacharach, when he wrote, "whoever reads the hairsplitting nonsense ["*hiluk u-biluk*," a pun on the phrase in *BT* Sanhedrin 98b, which includes the two proper names "Hilek and Bilek"] which is in his preface, will come to realize how sadly he had erred, may God help us" (*Havat Ya'ir* [Frankfurt a.M.: Johannes Wüst, 1699], #123).

[For a recent discussion of *pilpul* and *hiluk*—modes of talmudic study in the *yeshivot* of Eastern Europe from the fifteenth through the eighteenth centuries—see H. Z. Dimitrovsky's article, "On the Nature of Pilpul" (Hebrew), in the *Salo Wittmayer Baron Jubilee Volume* (New York: American Academy for Jewish Research, 1974, 3:111–81.]

The Author of *Tzemah David* mentioned R. Isaac as "the great rabbi, famous throughout the Jewish Diaspora, who made many disciples and propagated the study of Torah in Israel."

2. The encomium of Shalom Mordecai Hakohen, rabbi of Berzan, to *Mayim Rabbim* [see n. 3], by the rabbi of Kalbiel, R. Nathan Nata Hakohen, p. 4; *Zikaron Larishonim* [of Moses Hayim Kleinman; Piotrkow, 1882], p. 37.

3. *Mayim Rabbim* [Warsaw, 1903; rpt. Jerusalem, 1964], p. 137.

4. *Darkey Shalom*, p. 17b.

5. *Mayim Rabbim*, *megilat yuhasin*, p. 7.

6. [*Shem Ush'erit* of Joseph Cohen-Tzedek; Cracow: Y. Fischer, 1895], p. 30.

I have heard tell that in our generation the Gentiles fabricated
a blood libel against a certain saintly man. He was killed for the
sanctification of the Blessed Holy Name.

A wooden spike was forcibly driven through his lower parts
into his body, piercing through his entrails, with the spike-head
finally emerging near his ear. This happened close to the onset of
the Sabbath. During the entire preceding week not a morsel of
food had passed his mouth, for R. Moses was wont to fast on
weekdays. Close to the time of the Friday evening *kiddush*, the
benediction over the wine, they killed him.

Until death took him, he kept singing praises to the Lord with
a fervor born of intense love. Asked whether he felt pain, he replied that it was only now when the question had been put to him
that he had experienced any pain at all. This was so because of
the ardent concentration together with intense love with which his
soul clung to the Creator, blessed be He. His physical senses
were numbed by the great joy he felt in anticipation of the bliss
that would soon be his in Paradise. That his life left his body was
not because they had killed him, as the Gentiles believed. He
had, in a sense, brought on his own death by the intensity with
which he cleaved to the Lord, blessed by He.[7]

How did R. Joseph, son of the martyr and father of the tzaddik, R.
Isaac of Drohobycz, reach Palestine? The legend of his voyage and what
befell him exists in three versions:

(1) I have heard from R. Gedaliah of Barivke in the name, I
believe, of R. Abraham, descendant of the tzaddik, R. Isaac
Drobitcher, a tale that this same R. Abraham had heard from the
tzaddik, R. Isaac Radwiller, concerning his grandfather, the tzaddik, R. Joseph, known among the Gentiles as "*Yossi Sprawid-
liŵi*":

When news reached R. Yossele [the diminutive form of
Joseph] that the Baal Shem Tov, blessed be his memory, planned
to go to the Land of Israel with his *minyan* of Jews, R. Yossele
traveled to the Besht so as to be part of the group of voyagers.
All that he brought with him, however, were his *talit* and his *tefillin*, with nothing toward the expense of the journey.

At first the Baal Shem was agreeable to taking him. But those
in the Besht's entourage objected, saying: "We shall be unable to
accommodate him. For since he, too, is a person of importance
we shall have to cater to him as well; moreover, he lacks the
wherewithal for the voyage." They succeeded in persuading their
leader. But he said nothing to R. Yossele. It was only, I believe,

7. *'Amud Ha'avodah*, constituting the second part of *Yesod Ha'emunah, derush hamah-
shavah* [Cernăuti: Eckardt, p. 179a; Józefów: Setzer, 1883], p. 210c. [Cf. above p. 114, n. 6]

at the third meal of the Sabbath that he informed R. Yossele that
he could not travel with them.

Pounding on the table with his fists, R. Yossele warned the
Besht, "You who journey to the Land of Israel will not arrive
there, while I, who do not embark, will surely arrive there!"

Acquiring a horse and wagon, he traveled to Galatz[8] accompanied by his only son, R. Isaac Drobitcher. Upon arriving, the
townspeople suggested that he stay with them until ships put into
port and the weather was propitious for travel. He, however, refused and made his way outside the town, where he encountered
the harbormaster. The harbormaster also suggested that R. Yossele postpone his trip until conditions improved. Again, R. Yossele did not heed him and rode on until he reached the Tina
River. Here he handed over horse and wagon to the driver and
bade a final farewell (*gezigint*) to his son, R. Isaac, saying,

"Know that on the day after the festival you will say the
mourner's *kaddish* for me. My *tefillin* will reach you from the
Land of Israel."

After his son, R. Isaac, had gone, R. Yossele sat himself down
upon the sand, far from the port, wrapped in his *talit* and *tefillin*.
Now, it happened that a certain queen from a far-off land—Ire-
land, I believe it was—had embarked on a sea voyage to visit the
Turkish sultan. In the course of a tempest, her vessel was tossed
into the harbor of Galatz. As they neared the quay, she decided
on a stroll on the deck and saw R. Yossele wrapped in his *talit*.
Believing that what she beheld was some species of animal—
perhaps because she had never previously seen a Jew [at wor-
ship]—she summoned the ministers in her retinue to dispose of
the beast with their firearms. All went to do her bidding. There
was, however, one among them who had served as commissar in
the town where R. Yossele had lived. Upon approaching him, he
recognized the sage.

"What are you doing here?" he asked.

"I wish to travel to the Land of Israel," R. Yossele answered.

The minister at once advised the queen, "Be assured, if you
take this man on board, you will travel in safety and will find
favor with the sultan."

Although the queen agreed, R. Yossele refused to travel on
the same ship with her, so the queen, realizing that he was of
some special importance, had him transferred to a small vessel
which was towed by the larger one. Upon arriving in Istanbul,
the queen was received by the sultan with the greatest honor and
found favor in his eyes. She then said to her host, "I shall not

8. [Galatz is probably the modern Galati (Galatz, Gallacz) in Rumania, the only port of
Moldavia and about eighty-five miles from the Black Sea near the delta of the Danube
(Duna), no doubt the "Tina River" of this tale.]

budge from my ship until a vessel is provided for this Jew to make his way to Palestine." And so it was. R. Joseph was immediately sent on to Palestine. On the day following the festival,[9] he died. Like the Joseph of old, what R. Joseph had foretold did indeed come to pass.

As for the Baal Shem Tov, when he reached Istanbul not the slightest attention was paid him, nor was he shown the least deference, although everyone knew who he was. (For this was Heaven's way of deterring him from the voyage to Palestine.) He now found himself in abject poverty, having reached the point where he lacked provisions for even a single meal.

It so happened that at the same time the daughter of one of the city's wealthy Jews was undergoing a difficult childbirth. The woman's father was advised to call on the Besht for his help. He refused to do so, however. Not until the woman had reached the very threshold of death did he send for the Besht. The moment he entered the woman's house, she gave birth. Whereupon the Besht said, "*Az der bohur hat mikh derzehin, iz er taikef arois gespringen!*" (When the young fellow spotted me, he jumped right out!) The Besht was much honored by the wealthy father, who guided him through his palatial residence, showed him his treasures, and said: "Take whatever your heart desires." At that very moment, however, a ukase from the sultan arrived which declared that, owing to certain false charges made against the rich man, his assets were herewith frozen. And so the Baal Shem remained as poverty-stricken as before.

Following this incident, the fount of the Besht's wisdom dried up. Once he understood that all of these events were Heaven's way of preventing his trip to the Land of Israel and resolved to turn back home, his fame blossomed forth through all Istanbul.

May we be privileged by the blessed Lord to witness the coming of the Messiah soon in our own days, Amen."[10]

(2) When R. Joseph reached old age, he desired to go up to the Holy Land. He heard that our master, the Besht, blessed be the memory of the holy tzaddik forever, was of a similar mind. So the holy rabbi, the aforesaid R. Joseph, traveled to the Besht and asked that he take him too. The Besht, fearing the dire consequences of R. Joseph's well-known temper which was sure to explode on the long voyage, kept putting him off. The holy rabbi, the aforesaid R. Joseph, sensed this and said to him, "You will travel like royalty but will fail to reach your destination, while I, traveling like a *betler* (beggar), will get there, with God's help."

And so it was. The Besht embarked upon his journey, but his vessel was shattered and he was compelled to return home. The

9. [Apparently Shavuot; see below, n. 10.]
10. From a MS. Tradition has it that the anniversary of R. Joseph's death is the seventh day of the Hebrew month of Sivan.

aforesaid holy rabbi, on the other hand, sat himself down on the seashore, a book of holy writ in his hand, and studied. It so happened that at the same time a wealthy matron passed by in her ship and saw from afar someone seated on the shore. A servant, dispatched to inquire who this was, returned to inform her that it was the rav, R. Joseph, called *"Sprawidliwer."* She ordered that he be brought aboard the vessel, which then transported him to the Holy Land. And there he lies in honored rest.[11]

(3) This is the tale of the holy rav, R. Yossele, may the memory of the righteous be a blessing, known by all—Jew and non-Jew alike—as a man of truth (the Gentiles called him in their language "Yossele *Sprawidliwer"*). In his old age he decided upon making for the Holy Land, but the passage was beyond his meager means. So he sat himself down on the seashore, hoping that the good Lord would provide him with a vessel. And a miracle, indeed, occurred. The captain of a passing ship spotted him on the shore, alighted, and called out to him by name. The captain explained that he recognized him. When the captain was young, he had been in R. Yossele's town, poverty-stricken, without enough money for so much as a loaf of bread, and at the point of starvation. The rabbi had taken pity on him and cited the verse, "Cast thy bread upon the waters, for thou shalt find it after many days" (Eccles. 11:1). Having now recognized him, the captain took him aboard his ship and transported him to the Holy Land. This aforementioned holy rabbi was once asked by his son, the righteous rav, R. Isaac of Drohobycz, may his memory be for a blessing, how he would know the day of his father's ascent to his heavenly reward.

R. Joseph replied, "I assume you will be notified by Heaven."

And so it was. A year or two later, in midday, the righteous rav, R. Isaac, suddenly rose to his feet, took off his shoes, seated himself on the floor [as signs of mourning], and announced that his father, the holy rav, had just passed away and ascended into Heaven. Some months later, a letter reached R. Isaac from the Holy Land that his father, the holy rav, may his memory survive into eternity and his merit protect us, had indeed expired on that very day.[12]

His Life

On the basis of other traditions, one is led to the conclusion that R. Isaac was born prior to 1700.[13] He was a *maggid meysharim*

11. *Mayim Rabbim*, p. 137. [Spravidliver is spelled slightly differently in some texts.]
12. *Darkey Shalom*, p. 17b.
13. He was old enough for his son, R. Yehiel Mikhel, to have studied under R. Isaac Horowitz, who is said to have been born in 1715 (*Berakhah Meshuleshet* [Przemyśl, 1939],

(preacher), in which capacity he was said for a time to have served in Drohobycz,[14] hence his renown throughout Jewry as "R. Isaac Drobitcher."[15] It was his wont to travel far and wide, reproving his fellow Jews and returning them from the paths of sin. Although he lived in Galicia and Vohlynia, he was known to have traveled on one occasion as far as Slutsk in Lithuania.[16]

He spent a number of years (1727/8–1738/9) in the city of Brody,[17] then the most important community in Galicia and a celebrated Torah center. Brody was the seat of the *kloiz*, among whose "sages" were such renowned savants as R. Ezekiel Landau, author of the famed legal work, *Noda' Bihudah*, and R. Isaac Horowitz, later to occupy the rabbinical post in Hamburg, as well as R. Abraham Gershon of Kuty, brother-in-law of the Besht.[18]

We know that R. Isaac resided for some years in Ostróg, where there lived "the famous leader of his generation and mainstay of the Volhynia district," R. Joseph Yospe, known as "R. Yospe Ostraher." During this period, there existed in a number of cities (Hamburg and Brody, for example) institutions known as the *kloiz*.[19] Such a *kloiz* was organized in Ostróg by the wealthy and charitable R. Yospe. He "put up a building which had a synagogue on the lower level and a house of study on the upper level." No less than ten persons[20] were always present there, immersed in Torah study day or night; they were supported by R. Yospe. From these study houses emerged rabbis, extraordinary rabbinic judges, and well-known preachers, one of whom was the "righteous rav, the holy man of God, our master, the rav, R. Isaac of Drohobycz, may the

---

p. 101.The date seems reasonable, considering that R. Horowitz's friend, R. Ezekiel Landau, was born in 1714.

14. Rabbi Shalom Mordecai Hakohen (*Da'at Torah*, title page) calls him "maggid of the Horochów and Drohobycz communities." See also his encomium in *Mayim Rabbim*.

15. This is how he is called in R. Yospe Ostraher's will, dated 1762 (M. M. Biber, *Mazkeret Lagedoley 'Ostraha* [Berdichev: H. Y. Sheftel, 1907], p. 345).

16. *'Emunat Tzaddikim* [of Isaac Dov Ber b. Tzvi Hirsch, Warsaw, 1900], #52. While in Slutsk, R. Isaac arranged a match for his daughter, Bassil, with Nahman, later known as R. Nahman Litvak, the son of R. Yeruham Fishel. R. Nahman studied with his father-in-law until the latter's death. His son, R. Yehiel Mikhel, praised his brother-in-law's remarkable power of prayer. R. Nahman died in 1796. (Ibid.)

17. R. Isaac of Drohobycz resided in Brody during R. Isaac Hurwitz's first stay there. The story (*Ramatayim Tzofim*, *'Eliyahu Zuta* [Warsaw: Levin-Epstein, 1908], chap. 4, #116) that he lived in Brody during R. Horowitz's tenure there as rabbi is inexact. The latter was not accepted to the post until 1754 when R. Isaac's son, R. Yehiel Mikhel, was no longer "a youngster," as he is described in the story below [see p. 00]. R. Isaac of Drohobycz apparently passed away in 1744. [See N. M. Gelber, *History of the Jews of Brody* (Hebrew) (Jerusalem: Mosad Harav Kook, 1956), p. 115.]

18. See my essay, "R. Gershon Kutover: His Life and Immigration to the Land of Israel" (Hebrew), *Hebrew Union College Annual* (1950–51), pp. 22 ff. (this volume, pp. 44–112.

19. Cf. *Hokhmey AHW* [Altona, Hamburg, Wandsbeck], (Hamburg: Goldschmidt, 1908), p. 20.[See above, p. 51.]

20. ["*Batlanim*," people who had no occupation other than Torah study. Cities were expected to support at least ten such full-time scholars. See *BT* Sanhedrin 12b.]

memory of the righteous and the holy be for a blessing."[21] He was esteemed by the people of Ostróg. R. Isaac's son, as well, was later treated with special friendship by R. Yospe.[22]

A particularly colorful tale about R. Isaac has been preserved by the community of Ostróg:

> The daughter of the communal leader, R. Yospe, once took ill. During the night her condition worsened and brought her to the verge of death. At the break of dawn, her father repaired to the house of study, distributed alms to all the scholars, and asked them to fast and entreat the Almighty with their prayers for his daughter's recovery. It was only natural that all the scholars sympathized with their longtime benefactor. All day long they abstained from any food and immersed themselves in passionate recitation of the Psalms.
>
> The saintly R. Isaac, however, took the alms given him by R. Yospe and had them conveyed to his own wife with instructions to prepare a full breakfast for him: fish and meat and all the delicacies that go with a typical Sabbath repast! Having completed his prayers, he went home, ate heartily, washing down his meal with mead, and later returned to his duties in the house of study.
>
> The learned and pious men, on being informed of all this, were very upset. The eminent R. Yospe also heard about it but said nothing. When the girl later recovered, R. Yospe held a feast of celebration for the scholars of his *bet midrash*, with the rav and the tzaddik, R. Isaac, presiding; and there, during the banquet, R. Yospe put the question to him: how could he have dared enjoy food and drink while his colleagues fasted and prayed at such length in behalf of his mortally ill daughter?
>
> Said R. Isaac: "Were I to have fasted and prayed the day long, this would have been no novelty; nor would it have left any impression in the Upper Spheres, for the ordinary occasions no surprise. But when, on a regular weekday, I partook of meat and fish as though it were the Sabbath meal—this caused a great stir in the Heavens. It was then that they inquired there of one another: "How did Isaac come by such money, this being neither Sabbath nor the New Moon?"[23] Word then went forth that R. Yospe's daughter had taken sick and that her father had distributed alms to those scholars in the *bet midrash*. Owing to this study of the Torah and this charity, the girl was compassionately redeemed from the brink of the grave![24]

21. Biber, *Mazkeret Lagedoley 'Ostraha*, pp. 145 f.
22. R. Yehiel Mikhel is the only one not of R. Yospe's family mentioned in his will: "One hundred *zehuvim* (zloty) to the scholarly R. Mikhel, son of the late scholar, the renowned preacher, Master Isaac Drobitcher" (*Mazkeret Lagedoley 'Ostraha*, p. 345).
23. [Cf. 2 Kings 4:23.]
24. *Mazkeret Lagedoley 'Ostraha*, pp. 148–49.

R. Isaac left Ostróg to assume the position of preacher in Horochów. According to the stories in *Shivḥey Habesht*, R. Isaac took up his post as *maggid* and perhaps that of *dayan* (judge of the rabbinical court)[25] in the town of Horochów in Vohlynia's Ludmir district[26] sometime after the year 1739/40.[27] Resolute in his views, he did not fear to take issue with even the greatest scholars of his generation. The story is told, for example, of a dispute on one occasion between him and Rabbi Hayim Hakohen Rappaport,[28] the rabbi of Lwów. While in Brody and later in Horochów, quarrels flared up between R. Isaac and the communal rabbi, R. Isaac Horowitz. These tales of friction reflect the tension at the time between the *mokhiḥim* (preachers) and the rabbis, a tension which was to become a significant factor in the history of the Hasidic movement.

R. Isaac Horowitz

[In R. Isaac Horowitz, whose rabbinical career included important positions in Horochów, Gliniany, Brody, and Hamburg, our R. Isaac had as his antagonist one of the preeminent talmudists of the age, as well as a figure of remarkable piety.]
  R. Horowitz was born in 1714/15(?) to R. Jacob (Yokl) Halevi, who served as rabbi of Brody after 1774/75.[29] At the age of thirteen, he was married to Reitze, daughter of Brody's well-known communal leader, R.

25. *Berakhah Meshuleshet*, p. 102.
26. This information is authenticated by R. Abraham David Wahrmann, rabbi of Buczacz. See n. 28.
27. According to *Shivhey Habesht* [Ben-Amos, #67], R. Isaac's arrival in Horochów took place after R. Isaac Hamburger's service had commenced there. The latter is known to have assumed his office in about 1739/40. See *Berakhah Meshuleshet*. Serving there at the time as second *dayan* (judge) was R. Raphael Meizelesh, author of *Tosafot Shabbat* (Frankfurt a.M., 1767).
28. R. Abraham David, rabbi of Buczacz, writes in his *'Eshel 'Avraham*, #115: "From the maggid, famed for his good name, R. Tzvi Hirsh—whose honored resting place is in Nadwórna, may the Lord protect it—I heard of a dispute of sorts between the leader of all Diaspora Jewry, the well-known and popular master, R. Hayim Katz, may he rest in peace—or perhaps it was his equally illustrious late father, our master, the rav, R. Simhah Katz-Rappaport, may he rest in peace—and the rav and *mokhiah*, famed for his good name, our master, the rav, R. Isaac, may he rest in peace, of the holy community of Drohobycz, may the Lord protect it. When [R. Isaac] was maggid of Horochów, the rabbi [Simhah or Hayim], in the course of a discussion, asked him: 'What does one say [in the *honen hada'at* prayer of the Amidah]: "Oh, Favor us" or simply "Favor us"? Do you know?' [Responded R. Isaac,] 'I have heard that the two versions are essentially no different' [or, following another reading, 'This was the gist of what I heard,'] 'but at the moment I don't have before me Maimonides' *Mishneh Torah* [his legal compendium] to check this point.'" ['*Eshel 'Avraham*, ed. Wurmann (Buczacz: Dratler, 1906).]
  The debate appears to have been with R. Hayim, as his father, R. Simhah, rabbi of Slutsk, died in 1717; see S. Buber, *'Anshey Shem* (Cracow: Fischer, 1895), p. 216.
29. According to R. Tzvi Horowitz, *Berakhah Meshuleshet*, p. 101f. [See Gelber, *History of the Jews of Brody*, in regard to the Brody community.]

Jacob Babad,[30] and joined the *kloiz*[31] founded by his father-in-law.[32] A particularly close friendship developed between R. Horowitz and R. Ezekiel Landau, who would later write of him, "my most erudite friend . . . closer to me than a brother."[33] From 1724/25 to about 1739/40, he remained in Brody;[34] in 1739/40(?),[35] he assumed the rabbinic post in Horochów, which at the time was "a large and important community, replete with outstanding scholars."

In 1755, R. Horowitz replaced his father as the rabbi of Gliniany in Prussia. Owing to the disputes there with the *dayan*, R. Asher Lemil Halevi Segal,[36] R. Horowitz left his post after six years; in 1760/61, he returned to his native Galicia and reestablished his residence in Brody, where he was welcomed by R. Hayim Rappaport. He was later appointed rabbi of Brody and officiated in that capacity for three years. With the death of R. Jonathan Eybeschütz, the leaders of Altona, Wandsbeck, and Hamburg invited R. Horowitz to accept that tricommunal rabbinical position. Early in 1765 (the 23d of Shevat), he embarked on his term of leadership there.[37]

Even while still quite young, R. Horowitz was considered one of the major talmudic luminaries of his age; many were the rabbis who consulted him on matters of religious law. Even the highly respected authority, R. Ezekiel Landau, writing on a complex legal question involving the menstrual period (*nidah*), concluded his responsum with the following qualifications. "Under the above conditions, I now give my assent on the matter of this woman, but only if my honored relative by marriage and by blood, the distinguished rabbi and gaon of the holy community of Horochów, will concur with my ruling."[38]

The scholarly contemporaries of R. Horowitz had enormous respect for his sharp intellect.[39] Original, incisive, and authoritative in his deci-

---

30. Edward Duckesz, *'Iva Lemoshav* [Cracow: E. Gräber, 1903], p. 53.

31. Kamelhar, *Mofet Hador* [1934; rpt. Jerusalem: Yam Hatalmud, 1968], p. 5; see n. 11.

32. See [above, pp. 51 and 126.]

33. *Noda' Bihudah II*, *'even ha'ezer* [Prague: M. Katz, 1776], #112.

34. According to *'Emunat Tzaddikim*, #41, he was a *rosh yeshivah* in the *kloiz*.

35. According to *Berakhah Meshuleshet*, but I have failed to find any support for this. In 1748/49 he composed an encomium to *'Eyn Ya'akov*, Berlin of the same year. We know that in 1749/50 he had not as yet left Horochów. At the time, he participated in the Volhynia district commission (*Va'ad*) which assembled in Konstantynów "on 10 Tevet 1751"; he was among those who granted approval for the printing of the Talmud in Amsterdam. On the famous prohibition (*herem*) proclaimed in Brody in Elul 1751 against the use of amulets, he signed himself, "resident of the holy community of Horochów but whose authority extends over the Ludmir district": see *Hashahar* 6 (1975):341.

36. Later rabbi of Eisenstadt; died in 1790.

37. See *Berakhah Meshuleshet*, pp. 103–11. On "27 Sivan 1765" (erroneously printed "1768") he wrote an encomium to *Tosefot Shabbat*, which was published in Frankfurt am Main in 1767.

38. See *Noda' Bihudah I*, *yoreh de'ah*, #43.

sions, he yielded to no one: not to the most famed of rabbinical authorities,[40] not even to the Tosafists themselves [the thirteenth-century school of French-German talmudists] against whom he was known to have passed contradictory judgments. R. Landau was thus prompted to write to him: "I am highly surprised at my distinguished relative. Is this, then, the way of a sage, to reject the authority of the Tosafists? Can we allow ourselves to dispute their ruling in a case where we have found no contemporary of theirs differing with them? Even with the best of textual evidence on our side, we dare not reject their opinions, let alone with mere contentions such as yours."[41]

His contemporaries also esteemed him for his saintly character, as witnessed by the abundance of legends which have been preserved concerning him. It is related that he was of a tearful mien and practiced extreme asceticism. "His bushy brows tended to cover his eyes; when someone had flouted his will, he would brush his brows back and glare at the person, who would then soon be punished [by Heaven[42]]. His face, with its awesome air, resembled that of an angel of the Lord. Whoever saw him . . . would be seized with fear and trembling."[43]

The Baal Shem once said of R. Isaac: "I want you to know that from the New Moon Festival of Elul through the month of Marheshvan, the Holy Spirit rests upon him more than upon me." During those three months [which include the High Holy Days], R. Isaac would speak only in Hebrew, give himself up more to the study of ethical and kabbalistic works than to the Talmud, and weep freely as he recited Psalms before the Creator.[44] According to another legend, the Baal Shem said of R. Isaac that "from the New Moon Festival of Elul through the month of Heshvan, he was not in this world and that, during this quarter of a year, he [the Baal Shem] held him in especially high regard."[45]

39. R. Jonathan Eybeschütz, for example, was known to have engaged in talmudic correspondence with him. *Sefer Yehoshu'ah* (Zolkiew: Meyerhoffer, 1828), *orah hayim*, #17.

40. In reference to the opinions by the authors of *Turey Zahav* and *Magen Avraham*, he writes that "these latter-day authorities were in error" (*Mat'amey Yitzhak*, #1). "We cannot accept the decision presented by the author of *Mishneh Lamelekh*" (see *Noda' Bihudah I*, *'even ha'ezer*, #76).

41. *Noda' Bihudah*, *'even ha'ezer*, #77.

42. [Compare the talmudic legend of R. Yohanan and R. Kahana, *BT* Baba Kamma 117a.]

43. [Heschel supplies no source for this.]

44. *Berakhah Meshuleshet*, p. 111. According to Menahem Mendel b. Joseph, the author of *'Ateret Menahem* (Bilgoraj: Lifschitz, 1910), p. 64, the Baal Shem said of R. Isaac that "from the New Moon of Elul onward he literally spoils the pages of the *Reshit Hokhmah* [a sixteenth-century Palestinian work of Kabbalah] with his tears."

45. *'Ateret Menahem*, p. 64. "The Holy Spirit dwells within him from the New Moon Festival of Elul until the time of the fair at Krasna, when he is diverted from his spiritual endeavors by investments he would make during the fair with the Jewish merchants."

R. Isaac Horowitz won this respect from the Baal Shem, a man whom, at least initially, he opposed and derided. When the Besht's disciples asked him why he did not repay R. Isaac for his abuse, the Baal Shem responded, "What can I do? He is of a stock whose descendants are heard when they weep before the Lord."[46]

Several tales have been preserved concerning the relationship between the two rabbis Isaac. Behind the fictional elements one can discern the historical truth of the friction which no doubt existed between them.

The two were apparently colleagues even before their stay in Horochów. R. Isaac of Drohobycz had been a judge in the rabbinical court of Brody during the period when R. Isaac Hurwitz lived there. R. Simhah Bunim of Przysuche, who spent some years in nearby Lwów, related the following tale:

> In the course of a certain case concerning debts accruing to an estate, the heirs produced a promissory note to back their claim for payment due them. The note's signatory maintained that he had repaid his debts before the man's death. R. Horowitz ruled, however, that the heirs, upon oath, could collect the money they claimed as their due.
>
> At this point, R. Isaac Drobitcher rose to his feet. "The deceased himself," he argued, "stands before us, pleading that we tear up the note and asking that this be "a *tikun* [repair] for his soul!"
>
> R. Horowitz refused to heed these remarks. Whereupon his colleague opened R. Horowitz's eyes so that he too "saw" the dead man. Unmoved even by this demonstration, R. Horowitz declared, "It is not in Heaven (Deut. 30:12); we do not pay attention to heavenly voices."[47] He then proceeded to have the heirs swear to their statements and to inscribe his verdict. The Drobitcher, however, refused to append his signature to the decision, and a quarrel flared up between them.[48]

Another incident related by R. Simhah Bunim of Przysuche concerned

a holiday when pouring rain kept R. Isaac Horowitz from observing the commandment of having his meal inside the *sukkah*. He learned that his adversary, the aforesaid *dayan* and *mokhiah* (R. Isaac Drohobycz), was seated with his circle of adherents in his own sukkah, into which it was not raining. R. Horowitz re-

---

46. [N. Horowitz], *'Ohel Naftali* (Lwów: Zeidman and Oisshnit, 1910), pp. 73, 138; Responsa *Imrey David*, Introduction, #14.

47. [See *BT* Baba Metzia 60a.]

48. *Ramatayim Tzofim, 'Eliyahu Zuta*, chap. 4, #116. See another version in *Zikaron Larishonim*, p. 11. Interestingly, another legend relates that R. Isaac Horowitz was the one who conjured up a man from his tomb to testify before the rabbinical court; see *'Ateret Menahem*, pp. 65–66.

paired to the other's sukkah and took his meal there. Although
convinced of the justice of his case [against R. Isaac Drohobycz],
when it came to honoring the Lord [by observing the commandment to dwell in the sukkah], R. Horowitz put his own honor
aside, even though his actions might reflect favorably upon his
adversary.[49]

According to R. Simhah Bunim, circumstances were such that both
rabbis Isaac were forced to take leave of Brody.[50] R. Isaac of Drohobycz
was accepted as maggid (and, perhaps, as *dayan*, as well) in Horochów
sometime during R. Horowitz's tenure there as the communal rabbi. It is
certain that without the authorization of the rabbi (the head of the *bet
din*) one could not have been appointed to this juridical post.

Shivḥey Habesht has preserved two other stories about the stay of R.
Isaac of Drohobycz in Horochów:

> Just several weeks after R. Isaac Drobizner (*sic*) had been
> accepted as maggid of the community of Greater Horochów, the
> following incident occurred: It happened that a butcher owed
> money to the community's collector of taxes on kosher meat
> (*taksa*). While the tax collector was away his wife confiscated all
> the butcher's possessions—down to the very bedding—as surety
> for the debt. The butcher's wife came in tears to the aforesaid
> R. Isaac to complain. R. Isaac sent for the tax collector's wife,
> ordering her to return everything. She refused. Whereupon
> R. Isaac cursed her. Soon afterward her infant died.
>   When her husband returned from his trip, she poured out the
> story, saying: "A maggid, only recently appointed, has cursed
> me. Soon afterward our boy died!"
>   Now, the aforesaid R. Isaac had already left for his home in
> Ostróg where he had been serving as maggid for R. Yospe [for
> he had not as yet moved his family and possessions to Horochów.
> To facilitate the move,] the Horochów community had sent
> wagons to bring him and his family to their city.
>   What did the tax collector do but send a special emissary to
> Ostróg with a letter of warning: "If he (R. Isaac) has not yet de-
> parted, let him stay; if he has already left, let him return home.
> For even should he come here, he will be forced to leave."
>   R. Isaac wrote in reply: "I shall return (to Horochów) at the
> very moment your bier is borne toward me!"
>   And so it was. As R. Isaac entered the city gate, the deceased
> tax collector's body was about to be carried out the gate but was
> held up [to allow R. Isaac to pass through].

49. *Ramatayim Tzofim*, *'Eliyahu Zuta*, chap. 4, #116.
50. There may be some confusion of characters here, however. As I demonstrated in my
article on R. Gershon of Kuty, p. 26 (this volume, p. 55), R. Jacob Yokl Horowitz—
R. Isaac's father—was compelled to leave Brody in 1742.

The tax collector had a large family. Owing to their fear of the maggid, hatred for him simmered below the surface for a time. "Strife," however, the Talmud tells us, "is an opening made by a rush of water which widens as the liquid presses through it."[51] The dispute ultimately reached major proportions. But all who tried to harm the maggid were struck dead.

Among his antagonists in the feud was the rabbi of Horochów [R. Isaac Horowitz], who later became famous as rabbi of Brody and Hamburg. Peace was finally established between the two only through the intervention of R. Ezekiel, rabbi of Tomaspol,[52] who was a relative of R. Itsik. He wrote him that for God's sake he should come to terms with R. Isaac [of Drohobycz] who is like "a consuming fire."[53] So he proceeded to make peace with him.

On another occasion, a bolt of lightning hit the synagogue during the *minḥah* prayers. Two worshipers were struck dead, one near the synagogue's east wall and the other in the middle of the room.

The townspeople approached R. Isaac: "Master, you killed the people of the Lord!"[54]

He replied: "The one near the eastern wall died because of the feud. The other died owing to a false oath he took in Brody. During prayers he was holding the three ʾ*adumim* [ducats] which were paid him to swear fraudulently and was jiggling them."

Three ducats were found in the corpse's hand![55]

A further event is recounted.

Two litigants appeared before R. Isaac [of Drohobycz]. He ruled that one of them was obliged to take an oath on his claim. The plaintiff was about to do so when the second litigant, upset by the knowledge that his adversary had lodged a false claim, began to press that the other hurry up and take the oath.

Interjected R. Isaac, "Why are you so eager that he take the oath? With me anyone who lies will suffer one of his progeny to die."[56]

R. Isaac of Drohobycz and the Baal Shem Tov

It was at this time that the curtain of history was raised upon the Besht. [As is well-known, he was both suspect in the eyes of his contem-

51. [*BT* Sanhedrin 7a.]

52. Read "Yampol." This reference is to R. Ezekiel Landau, author of *Nodaʿ Bihudah.* [Cf., Mondshein, *Shivḥey Ha-Baal Shem Tov*, p. 37, n. 29.]

53. [See Isa. 30:27; the image applied to scholars is elaborated in *Pirkey ʾAvot* 2:15.]

54. [A reference to Num. 17:6.]

55. *Shivḥey Habesht*, p. 11d [Ben-Amos, #67. Cf., Mondshein, *Shivḥey Ha-baal Shem Tov*, p. 37, n. 28.]

56. Ibid., p. 12a [Ben-Amos, #68].

poraries, who had just passed through the travails of the Sabbatean movement, and open to ridicule. Whatever the disagreements between R. Isaac of Drohobycz and R. Isaac Horowitz, they shared at first a certain contempt for the so-called miracle worker of Miedzybórz.]

Hearing tales of the marvelous deeds of the Besht and how he helped barren women, it is said that R. Isaac Horowitz and his close friend, R. Ezekiel Landau, would deride the Besht publicly. When this was reported to the Baal Shem, he cautioned his disciples: "Be careful with these two honored sages, for half of the earth rests upon their merits—the swarthy Itzik and the thin Ezekiel! (*Oif dem schwartzen Itzik un dem daren Yeheskel shteht a halbe velt.*) Therefore I command you not to rush off and speak ill of them."

As the Sabbath would draw to a close, with the "Third Meal" already over and the time not yet come for the evening prayer, R. Isaac would enjoy listening "to some tale of the Baal Shem such as his activities among the womenfolk, or the way in which he was accustomed to distribute the leftovers of his meal (*shirayim*) to those who were at his table, the majority of whom were ignorant villagers. At such times, a faint smile of scorn would play about R. Isaac's lips. Told of this, the Baal Shem ordered two of his own people to go to R. Isaac's home late on the Sabbath day and tell him stories about the Besht, just to make that saintly man happy."

R. Isaac apparently caused the Baal Shem much pain. Although on one occasion, during the holiday of Sukkot, R. Isaac witnessed the Besht performing "a most awesome act" in the *sukkah*, he remarked, nonetheless, "His way is not mine. His soul works out its special fate and my soul works out mine." Legend has it that the Baal Shem once paid a visit late one night to R. Horowitz in Brody, asking for elucidation of a certain kabbalistic matter—"the joining of three letters." R. Isaac could not answer the question, and from that time on, he ceased his persecution of the Besht.

[The story of the relationship between R. Isaac of Drohobycz and the Besht follows somewhat similar lines. At the onset, R. Isaac opposes him, but the Besht—patiently and even reverently—refuses to do battle. There is, finally, some reconciliation of the two.] It is impossible, however, to produce a clear picture of R. Isaac's real relationship with the Baal Shem. There would seem to be some historical truth behind the legendary tales concerning the desire of R. Joseph (the father of R. Isaac) to accompany the Baal Shem to Palestine, as there is also in those tales which tell of R. Isaac's opposition to the Baal Shem. No foundation, however, exists for the claim that R. Isaac was a disciple of the founder of Hasidism.[57] It is, of couse, true that R. Isaac's son, R. Yehiel Mikhel of

57. As, for example, in *Shem Hagedolim Hehadash*, p. 34b, letter yod, #234; Rodkinson, *Toldot Ba'aley Shem Tov* [Königsberg: Petzall, 1886], p. 35; [Gelber, *History of the*

Zloczew, was among those who spread the Besht's teachings. Perhaps he joined the Besht's circle after his father's death.

According to tradition, at any rate, R. Isaac of Drohobycz was among those who at first cast derision upon the Baal Shem.

It was the practice of R. Isaac to go to sleep immediately at night after having uttered the Psalmist's words, "Into Thy hand I commit my spirit." [58] When he did not fall asleep quickly, however, he inferred that it was because he had sinned during the day and that Heaven was refusing to receive his spirit until he repented. Once when he could not fall asleep, he reviewed his day's deeds, but could find nothing amiss. Finally, he recalled that earlier in the day people had poked fun at the Baal Shem in his presence. Not only had he done nothing to stop them, but he had himself also joined the chorus. Arising from bed at once, he ordered his coachman to harness the horses and drive him straight to Miedzybórz so that he could apologize to the Besht. Upon his arrival, R. Isaac made directly for the Besht's house of study (*bet midrash*), where, in a corner, he recited his morning prayers along with the congregation. In the course of the service, the Baal Shem called him by name—"Our Master, R. Isaac, son of R. Joseph"—to the reading of the Torah. When prayers were over, he was greeted by the Baal Shem with the following words: "Peace upon you, our master and teacher. You have driven all this way to ask my forgiveness for your having ridiculed me. I herewith forgive you with all my heart." [59]

Though R. Isaac was initially opposed to the Besht, the latter was ever striving for closeness between them. The story goes that the Besht once even went to R. Isaac so as to serve him. The Besht brought him coffee and later returned the empty cup to the kitchen. Asked to explain why he had gone to the lengths of taking the empty cup back, he replied that [serving R. Isaac was like serving in the Temple on the Day of Atonement. For] "the returning the empty ladle [which had held the incense] on the Day of Atonement was also considered a part of the Temple service." [60]

There is a popular tale among the Hasidim about R. Isaac's rapprochement with the Baal Shem:

> When R. Isaac of Drohobycz heard of the remarkable powers of the Baal Shem's amulets, it occurred to him that this was most certainly accomplished by means of the sacred Names written in

Jews of Brody, p. 115; and Sholem, "the Historical Figure of R. Israel Baal Shem Tov" (Hebrew) *Molad* 18 (1960):19.

58. Psalms 31:6. This phrase is at the end of the 'Adon 'Olam prayer with which R. Isaac concluded his devotions before sleep.

59. Isaac J. J. Safrin, *Netiv Mitzvotekhah, shevil hayiḥud* [Jerusalem, 1947; rpt. New York: Sefarim Kedoshim, 1970], #4.

60. According to *Shivḥey Habesht*, ed. Horodetzky, pp. 200–201. See *BT* Yoma 32a.

them. So he decreed, "Because of improper use of the Name of God, the power of the amulets must pass away."[61] And that, indeed, is what happened. The talismans issued by the Baal Shem were now unavailing, having lost their special potency.

This state of affairs kept up for twelve months.

When the Baal Shem finally realized that his amulets were no longer providing any benefits, he sought the reason. It was eventually revealed to him that it was because of the tzaddik R. Isaac's pronouncement.

The Baal Shem thereupon wrought a remarkable feat by means of a kabbalistic combination of the words in the prayer *Ana Bakoah*. As a result of the Baal Shem's feat, R. Isaac, who was on a journey at the time, confused the days of the week and got himself one day behind—i.e., Monday was mistaken for Sunday, etc. Thus R. Isaac was a day off throughout the week. On what was a Thursday according to his reckoning (in fact Friday), he reached Miedzybórz. He had planned to spend the Sabbath in a neighboring town, but thinking the day to be only Thursday, he was in no hurry to press on since he believed he still had two days at his disposal. So he went about his stay at the local inn at a leisurely pace. He said his prayers, ate, and lay down to rest after the tiring trip, thinking all the while that a full day was still ahead of him for the remaining short journey.

When he arose from his nap, he was surprised to see the inn table set with the Sabbath tablecloth, two *halah* breads, and candelabra with candles affixed ready for the Sabbath-eve lighting. Astonished, R. Isaac tried to fathom the meaning of the scene. He approached the innkeeper and asked him to explain why everything was already prepared as if for the Sabbath, when it was only Thursday.

"But it's already Friday afternoon!" he was told.

His heart sinking, R. Isaac could not bring himself to believe them. Hastening outside, he saw Jews rushing here and there, some with their Sabbath vestments tucked under their arms heading for the ritual bath, others returning from their ablutions. Only then was he struck with the fact that what he had been told was in fact so, and he made his way back inside the building to prepare himself for the Sabbath.

As he was busy with these preparations, the Besht arrived and insisted that R. Isaac be his guest for the Sabbath meal. At first, R. Isaac declined the invitation, saying that since the innkeeper had prepared for him all sorts of delicacies, it would not be fair to have caused him this bother needlessly and to have wasted all that food.

---

61. [A play on *Pirkey 'Avot* 1:13, " . . . and he who makes (worldly use) of the crown (of Torah) shall pass away."]

The Baal Shem replied, "I have already asked the man, and he has agreed to waive both the loss and the privilege of having you as his guest."

R. Isaac, however, kept coming up with further pretexts, until he said finally, "The main reason for my refusing your invitation is that I am a voracious eater, and your honor simply will not be able to provide all I require."

The Baal Shem responded, "I have reserved sufficient quantities for my honored guest," and refused to relent until R. Isaac at last give his consent and went along to spend the Sabbath with him. They sat down for the Sabbath meal.

Now, it was R. Isaac's custom to fast from Sabbath eve to Sabbath eve [which left him famished]. On the Sabbath itself, therefore, he would have placed before him his own special silver tray, engraved with the Lord's name, which he loaded down with food.[62] The contents were then devoured as by a flame. After the *kiddush* was recited, R. Isaac arranged the tray before him in his usual manner, supported by his thumb so that he was able to see its reflection as he ate. After he had consumed every bit of all the food which had been placed before him at the start of dinner, he said to the Baal Shem, "Did your honor not assure me that he would provide all I require? Yet here I am hungry still, with nothing left to eat." Replied the Baal Shem, "I did indeed anticipate the arrival of angels, but not of *serafim* [fiery angels]!"[63] [A pun on the verb *saraf* (to burn up), in this case to consume the meal, as was R. Isaac's wont.] At that, R. Isaac removed his tray from before him and could eat no more.

Saturday night at the *melaveh malkah*, the post-Sabbath meal, the Baal Shem confronted R. Isaac. "Why has your honor taken from me the power of my amulets—amulets which I dispense to help people?"

Said R. Isaac, "It is forbidden to make personal use of the Holy Names."

---

62. [A. Kahana (*Sefer Hahasidut* [Warsaw: Lewin-Epstein, 1922], p. 64, n. 1) suggests a mystical numerical equation of the word for "food" and the name of God. The version of this story in Bodek's *Mif'alot Hatzaddikim* (Lwów, 1857), pp. 34–35, reads: "It was his holy custom to place the tray before himself whenever he put food into his mouth. He would gaze at its reflection during the entire meal . . . " According to this telling, the food was not necessarily put on the tray, which served only to remind him of the Lord during the meal and could have been smaller in size, even a medalion "hung on"—instead of "supported by—his thumb." Further examples of R. Isaac's habits in regard to food are found in the story above on p. 159, and in *Hiddushey Harim' al Hatorah* (Jerusalem: Nahaliel, 1967), p. 277; and Tzvi Hirsch Rosenbaum, *Raza De'uvda, sha'ar ha'otiyot* (Kiryat Sighet: Mefitzey Hasefarim Levet Kretshnif, 1971), pp. 25–26.]

63. ["*Af malokhim hoben mir zikh gerisht, ober af serofim hobin mir zikh nisht gerisht.*" See the version of this tale in B. Ehrman, *Devarim 'Arevim* 1 (Munkacs: Ehrman, 1903), pp. 10b, 11a, # 29. Angels are traditionally believed to call on every Jewish home with the advent of the Sabbath (cf. *BT* Shabbat 199b).]

"But there are no oaths nor any Names in my amulets,"
argued the Besht, "save my very own, 'Israel, son of Sarah, Baal
Shem Tov.'"

R. Isaac, unwilling to believe this, said that it was not possible
for the Baal Shem's name alone to possess such awesome powers.
Upon opening several amulets which were brought for R. Isaac's
scrutiny, he became convinced of the truth of what he had been
told. Then he uttered the following: "Lord of the Universe, if a
man earns his livelihood through the power of his own name,
what do You care? Restore to him the potency of the amulets
bearing his name."

And so it was. From that time forth, the Baal Shem again
worked mighty and awesome deeds by means of his amulets.

Those who witnessed these events were astonished at R. Isaac's
capacity to contravene the Baal Shem's express will.

Said the Besht, "What can I do? R. Isaac is now the tzaddik of
our generation, and all the worlds do his bidding. Certain things
about his conduct are not to my liking, but I must, perforce, be
quiet. And when he ventures the explanation of a passage in *Peri
ʿEtz Ḥayim*,[64] though I know a truer one, I am compelled to
silence."[65]

His Ways and Teachings

R. Isaac, venerated by his contemporaries, was no stranger to
miracles. A number of stories have survived about his marvelous powers:
One tale recounts that

R. Yitzhakel [the diminutive form of Isaac] of Drohobycz was
once traveling with the holy rav, R. Meir of Przemyślany, who
lived at the time of the Baal Shem.[66] They were on a mission to
redeem some Jews who had been seized and were being held for
ransom. Here it was Friday, and already for several hours now
they had been wandering lost in the thickness of a great forest.
Noon came, and it was their custom never to be on the road on
the afternoon before the Sabbath. They performed a certain act
which evoked the forest spirit (*sar*) who thereupon showed them
the way out and told them to spend the Sabbath at the home of
the holy rav, R. Mordecai Peshe, for he was a "prince of the
Torah" in that generation. Thus it happened that they came to
spend the Sabbath with him. At once aware of their great holiness, he treated them with the utmost respect.

64. [A kabbalistic work by R. Hayim Vital, the major disciple of R. Isaac Luria of Safed.]
65. *Zikaron Larishonim*, pp. 14–15; Kahana, *Sefer Hahasidut*, pp. 63–65; according to
Kamelhar, *Dor Deʿah* (Bilgorey: Kamelhar, 1933), 1:28, the incident occurred during R.
Yitzhak's residence in Ostróg.
66. [R. Meir died in 1773. A disciple of the Besht, he is not to be confused with his
grandson of the same name, a prominent tzaddik who died in 1850.]

In the early afternoon of the Sabbath day, R. Isaac went to the *bet midrash* to deliver a sermon on the need for moral rectitude. The townsmen, though great scholars, were *mitnagdim* [opponents to the way of the Baal Shem] and had contrived to contradict and embarrass the speaker. R. Mordecai, sensing this even as he sat at home, called to the group around him, "Come, let us all go to hear the sermon of the holy and eminent R. Isaac," and off he went. The assembled scholars, awestruck by his presence, turned dumb as stone. R. Mordecai sat through the sermon, then escorted his guest home, asking that drink be brought him as well. At the close of the Sabbath, R. Mordecai himself went about collecting a goodly sum for R. Isaac and also arranged a banquet for his guests.

When the time for parting came, the holy R. Isaac said to him, "None of the townspeople accorded us any respect except you. Therefore let me give you this blessing: May a son be born to you who will become as eminent a scholar and as great a tzaddik as I."

And so it happened. In that very same year, a son was born to R. Mordecai and was named Samuel Zeinvil.

It was after this that the holy R. Mordekhai departed this world. But his grave disappeared, and "no man knoweth of his sepulcher unto this day." His grandson and my grandfather, R. Judah Tzvi of Stretin, said that the grave had removed itself to the Land of Israel.[67]

This same R. Samuel Zainvil was rabbi of Zawalów, "and the disciple of the holy rav, R. Mekhele of Zloczew, may his memory be for a blessing. On R. Samuel Zeinvil's first visit to the latter, he was received with the greatest of respect. R. Mekhele then said to members of his inner circle. 'Be not amazed that I have accorded him such honor, for his birth was attendant upon my father's blessing that he become an illustrious scholar and tzaddik, and this assuredly will come to pass.' "[68]

R. Isaac was a great kabbalist, performing wondrous acts by means of the divine names. A story, told about him by R. Issachar Ber, the rabbi of Zloczew,[69] goes as follows: The late Hasid, our master, the rav, R. Isaac Drobitcher, may his memory be an eternal blessing, had once lost his way and found himself in a vast forest as night fell. With a certain formula of the divine Name, he performed a special favor for the forest *sar* who then led him in a twinkling of an eye to the town toward which he had been

67. [*Degel Mahaney Yehudah*, ed. E. Brandwein (Jerusalem: Bros. Brandwein, 1957), p. 3, #6.]

68. *Degel Mahaney Yehudah* [pp. 3–4, #8].

69. He was the brother-in-law of R. Levi Isaac of Berdichev and pupil of the maggid of Miedzyrzecz. R. Issachar Dov was the author, as well, of two works, *Bat 'Eynai*, a talmudic treatise, and *Mevasser Tzedek*, a Hasidic work on the Torah.

traveling."⁷⁰ What was the nature of this "special favor" that R. Isaac rendered the forest *sar*? According to R. Isaachar Ber, the angels are "fixed" into their individual heavenly stations.⁷¹ Only the tzaddik can elevate them to a loftier rung and thus to greater proximity to the Holy One, blessed be He. As the verse says: "And, Jacob dreamed; and behold a ladder set up on the earth, and the top of it reached to heaven; and behold the angels of God were ascending or descending by means of him (Jacob)"⁷² This is to say, it is through the efforts of the tzaddik that the angels are able to go up or down!⁷³

While residing in Brody—so goes the tale—R. Isaac himself instructed his young son, R. Mikhel. Angry with his father on one occasion, the boy went off to study at the local yeshivah of R. Isaac Horowitz, where the latter's students were delighted to receive him. After only three days there, however, the youngster apologized to his father and asked him to study with him once again. Irritated that he had abandoned their company, his former classmates came to the home of the maggid, R. Isaac Drobitcher, and waited outside for R. Mikhel. When he appeared, they accosted him: "Before you had the opportunity to study under our rabbi and were unaware of his acuity, it was not surprising that you did not join us. But now that you have spent three days in his presence—and surely you realize that his mind is sharper than your father's—why did you leave the yeshivah to return to him?"

R. Mikhel replied, "I had never before studied under any teacher save my father, who taught me all I know, from the alphabet onward. Whenever he studies with me I see the very letters floating forth from his lips. Now, after sitting for three days at the feet of R. Isaac Horowitz and seeing nothing similar, I was forced to apologize to my father and ask for his instruction once again."⁷⁴

R. Isaac was held in high esteem by the Hasidic masters, the tzaddikim. R. Benjamin, the maggid of Zalozce, referred to him as "the venerable and wondrous Hasid, man of God,"⁷⁵ while R. Abraham David of Buczacz called him "the rav and *mokhiah*, famed for his good name."⁷⁶ Attention has already been directed to the complimentary remarks of R. Issachar Ber of Zloczew.⁷⁷ R. Joseph Bloch, rabbi of Olesko and rabbi and maggid of Stanov, described R. Isaac as "the celebrated Hasid."⁷⁸

70. *Mevasser Tzedek* [of Issachar Dov; Berdichev, 1817], *parshat korah*.
71. [See Zech. 3:7: " . . . and I will give thee places to walk among these that stand by (i.e., the angels."]
72. Genesis 28:12 [Heb. *bo* = "on it," i.e., the ladder, or "by means of him."]
73. [The tzaddik, then, is the "ladder" between earth and heaven.]
74. *Kevutzat Ya'akov* [of Jacob Margoliot; Przemyśl, 1897], p. 67b.
75. Benjamin b. Aaron, *Torey Zahav* (Mogilev: Asher Zelig, 1816), *parshat pinhas*.
76. *Hamefursam beshem tov*. See above n. 28.
77. See above, and also n. 70.
78. *Ginzey Yosef* (Lwów, 1792), *parshat aharey*.
Kol Aryeh by R. Aryeh Leib, the preacher of Polonnoye, was published (Korzec, 1798) by

When R. Isaac's son, R. Yehiel Mikhel, paid his first visit to the Baal Shem, the latter ordered his disciples to treat him with deference. "You should know," he said, "that this man is the son of the saintly R. Isaac Drobitcher. Let me tell you about his father. At birth he received from Heaven the tiniest imaginable soul. Yet he elevated it to the height attained by that of R. Simon Ben Yohai." [79]

Very few of R. Yitzhak's teachings have come down to us. [From among them, the following give one a sense of his constant self-scrutiny:]

(A) R. Tzvi Hirsh of Zydaczów, quotes the following from R. Isaac of Drohobycz:

> Before preaching to the children of Israel one must be sure that at least one of three conditions is being satisfied:
> The speaker himself is benefited by what he says;
> all Israel is benefited by what he says;
> the teaching is transmitted only after the instructor has heard it from the mouth of the Almighty Himself." [80]

(B) R. Isaac said:

> Each time I plan a journey during which to reprove the children of Israel and uplift straying souls the *yetzer hara*ᶜ (Evil Impulse) pounces upon me, arguing: "Isaac, stay home and continue with your study of Torah. Why trouble yourself to travel from place to place? Why interrupt your studies?"
> So I say to him: "But my travels and lectures are intended only to earn a little money, which I am badly in need of."
> "Oh," replies the Evil Impulse, now encouraging me. "If it is only money that you're after," he says, "then go in peace."
> And he no longer troubles me.
> However, once I reach the place where I am to preach, I put aside all thoughts of reward. I preach and reprove only for the sake of Heaven. [81]
> . . . For no great *mitzvah* is without an admixture of *yetzer hara*ᶜ at its inception. For when an individual intends to perform a *mitzvah* for its own sake, he is always set upon by the *yetzer* and consequently frustrated from implementing the act. But, if

---

"R. Israel, son of the wondrous scholar, our master and teacher, R. Yehiel Mikhel Segal, and grandson of the rabbi and preacher, our master, the rav R. Isaac of Drohobycz" (from the encomium of R. Levi Isaac of Berdichev). The encomium of R. Asher Tzvi, rabbi of Ostróg, refers to him as " . . . grandson of the rav, the great luminary, the keen-witted master, R. Isaac, the maggid of the holy community of Drohobycz." Is this our R. Isaac Drobitcher?

79. *'Igra Depirka*, by R. Tzvi Elimelekh of Dynów [Lwów, 1858], #29.
80. R. Zev Wolf Leichter of Lwów, *Zeved Tov* (Lwów: A. Salat, 1911), p. 5b.
81. Here the author provides the following proof-text:
"In so doing, I fulfill the commandment (When coming across a mother bird with her young), "thou shalt in any wise let the mother bird go" [Deut. 22:7]—that is, abandon the original intent—"and the young thou mayest then take unto thyself"—that, is, the *mitzvot* and good deeds [which are generated by the original plan].

one embarks on his mission with a selfish motive in mind, the *yetzer* is outwitted and is no longer an obstacle. One can rid himself of his apparent selfish purpose while performing the deed and execute his mission with only Heaven's will in mind. In short, a person must conceal his true intentions from the *yetzer hara*.[82]

Other remnants of R. Isaac's teachings will be found in the Appendix.

R. Isaac's Son, the Tzaddik, R. Yehiel Mikhel of Zloczew

R. Isaac's distinguished son, R. Yehiel Mikhel, the maggid of Zloczew, was among the foremost tzaddikim of his time. [When controversy over the new movement of Hasidism flared up in Brody—the center of Torah scholarship in Galicia, as was Vilna in Lithuania—R. Yehiel Mikhel played a central role as a Hasidic advocate. Already in 1772, responding to the letter sent from Vilna signed by the Gaon Elijah, the Galician rabbis assembled at Brody to issue a *herem* (excommunication) against those who followed the Hasidic way. At the thunderbolt of the publication of the powerful, first Hasidic book, *Toldot Ya'akov Yosef*, in 1780, the rabbis of Lithuania issued a new denunciation of the sect in 1781, even to the point of forbidding marriage with its members or burying their dead, and they sent out communications to other communities to this effect. In that very year the *bet din* of Brody decreed that the book be burned publicly, an act rarely committed by Jews against Jews. The location chosen for their demonstration was in front of the house of R. Yehiel Mikhel!][83]

82. R. Isaac Yehiel Safrin of Komarno, *Zohar Hai* [Lwów: Ziss and Nik, 1875–81], Exodus, p. 7d; *Netiv Mitzvotekhah, shevil hatorah*, 4; *Heykhal Haberakhah* [Lwów: Balaban, 1865], *leket 'imrey peninim*, published after the section on Deuteronomy [pp. 206–11].
An allusion to the stratagem of concealment was noted by R. Tzvi Hirsch of Zydaczów in the verse (Gen. 12:4), "So Abram went as the Lord had spoken unto him, and Lot went with him." "Lot," according to its Hebrew root, suggests "enclosure" or "cover," as in the expression, "wrapped [*lutah*] in a cloth" (1 Sam. 21:10). [Abram, went "under wraps," as it were, in the service of God (*Heykhal Haberakhah*).]
83. [Dubnow, *Toldot Hahasidut* (Tel Aviv: Dvir, 1933–32), pp. 165–66; J. Perl, *Megaleh Temirin* (Lwów, 1864), p. 3, n. 4. According to *Shivhey Habesht* (Ben-Amos, #251), R. Yehiel Mikhel argued before the heavenly court against the burning of R. Jacob Joseph's book (see Dresner. pp. 63–71).]
According to *Kinat Soferim*, #1496, *Shem Ushe'erit*, p. 30, R. Mikhel died at the age of fifty-two in 1786, which places his birth in 1734. [See n. 17. R. Yehiel Mikhel would then have been orphaned at the age of ten. Cf. M. H. Kleinman, *Mazkeret Shem Hagedolim* (Piotrkow, 1907), p. 3b; Alfasi, *Hahasidut* (Tel Aviv: Maariv, 1974), p. 57; and Ben Menahem, "Hahasidut Me'et Y. Alfasi," *Sinai* (1974):188. The latter places his birth at 1731.]
The story goes that R. Isaac once paid an unexpected visit to the noted R. Abbali, rabbi of *Sdey Lavan* [Hebrew for "White Field," euphemism for the Polish town of Belaya Tserkov ("White Church"), a name which Jews refrained from uttering]. The two went to the adjoining village and there concluded a match between R. Mikhel and the daughter of a

R. Yehiel Mikhel was a close disciple of the Besht, may his memory be for a blessing. After his marriage, he isolated himself for a period of a thousand days, during which he neither spoke to nor saw anyone, devoting every moment to serving the Lord with marvelous *devekut.*

. . . the holy rabbi of Opatów said "I know that in each generation there is one tzaddik who holds the key to the Torah, but I did not know who that tzaddik was. Then I came to the holy rav, R. Yehiel Mikhel, and heard him expound the Torah. When he opened his holy mouth to speak, all the points in Torah which were unclear to me were settled. The moment he ceased teaching, however, the questions returned. It was then that I realized that the key to Torah lay in his hands.[84]

Legends surround R. Mikhel's birth.
It is related that R. Isaac was accustomed

at the birth of each of his sons to hasten immediately to view the newborn child. After scrutinizing the infant, he would conclude with, "This is not what I had in mind" (*Nisht dos hob ikh gemeint*), and would go up to his room, as was his wont. Whereupon the child would fall into a coma and then die.

This occurred many times—whenever his wife give birth—and many souls thus departed this world. When the holy rav, R. Yehiel Mikhel, was born, R. Isaac's wife became furious with him and absolutely refused to show him the baby until he had given her his most solemn assurance that he would not say what he always said. When he came to gaze upon the infant's holy countenance, he said, "Alas! Many more beautiful souls than this were let go! (*O va asakh sheynere neshomos avek gelost!*)."[85]

In the name of R. Uri, the "Seraph" of Strzeliska, the story is told that R. Isaac redeemed one thousand souls from the agony of metempsychosis before be brought [succeeded in bringing?] the soul of his son, R. Yehiel Mikhel, into the world.[86]

---

certain R. Moses, proprietor of a tavern (*vein hoiz*) (Yehiel Mikhel of Zloczew. *Mayim Rabbim* [Warsaw, 1903; rpt. Jerusalem: n.d., 1964], p. 139.

84. [Twersky,] *The Geneology of Chernobyl and Ruzhin* (Hebrew) [Lublin: Tzveke, 1930; rpt., Jerusalem, n.d.], p. 103. [Cf. *'Emunat Tzaddikim*, p. 26b.]

85. Ibid. ["*Ikh hob shoyn a sakh sheynere kinder fin dir avek geshikt.*" (I have already sent away many lovelier children than you.) *Devarim 'Arevim*, p. 10b. Cf. *Raza De'uvda, sha'ar ha'otiyot* (Kiryat Sighet, 1971), p. 4, where the tale is told in the name of R. Meir of Przemyślany. See above, n. 65.

This bizarre tale may be better understood in reference to the passage Heschel brings below in the name of R. Uri of Strzeliska which states that "R. Isaac had redeemed one thousand souls from the agony of metempsychosis (*gilgul*) before he brought (succeeded in bringing?) the soul of his son, R. Yehiel Mikhel, into the world."]

86. The encomium by R. Shalom Mordekhai Hakohen, rabbi of Brezan, to *Mayim Rabbim*, p. 4.

[How are we to understand the bizarre tale just recounted above regarding the birth of R.

[Even after R. Isaac's death, according to the Hasidic legends, the father kept a special eye on the fate and behavior of his son:]

A certain terrible sinner (may Heaven preserve us!) once came to the holy rabbi, R. Zusya of Hanipol, of blessed memory. Just by his face, the holy rabbi recognized him for what he was and strove to turn him from his evil course. The man accepted upon himself henceforth the responsibility of conducting himself properly, but said that he had not the strength to make amends for the past by means of bodily mortifications and fasts. The holy rav, R. Zusya, of blessed memory, replied that should the former sinner agree to do what it is he told him, R. Zusya himself would assume the bodily penance for the man's transgressions and thereby assure the sinner a place in the world to come. To this the man agreed.

Yehiel Mikhel? It may be that R. Isaac was trying for a near-perfect child and was not satisfied with what he was getting. One is reminded of the statement in the Talmud of Rava: "Whose mother bears a child akin to R. Simon (ben Lakish) should have children. If not, better that she not bear children at all" (*BT* Makot 17b; see *Devarim ʿArevim*, p. 10b). If this is the meaning of the story, then the passage in the name of R. Uri may simply be chronological: namely, before the birth of R. Yehiel Mikhel, R. Isaac redeemed a thousand souls. (In a personal communication M. Shulvass reported a tale which may relate to R. Isaac's behavior from a different point of view. The children of a holy man died at birth one after the other. His wife at last complained to him why he did not intercede with Heaven to allow them to live. He went to the cemetery with her, and when they came to the rows of tiny graves where their children were buried, he proceeded to kick the small gravestones. At this, a cross jumped out of each grave, hinting that had they lived they would have converted. Perhaps R. Isaac saw some sin in the later life of his children severe enough to warrant his action. Cf. *BT* Berakhot 10a on the debate between King Hezekiah and Isaiah.)

On the other hand the statement of R. Uri may not be chronological, but causal: namely, that "R. Isaac had redeemed one thousand souls from the agony of metempsychosis (*gilgul*) *before he succeeded in bringing* the soul of his son, R. Yehiel Mikhel, into the world." In other words, with the birth of R. Yehiel Mikhel there was no longer a need for R. Isaac to redeem those in a state of *gilgul*. We might then understand the death of his children on the basis of the kabbalistic notion of *gilgul*. There are two basic forms of *gilgul*: (1) "to enable a man to complete his spiritual nature by performing those religious acts which he had left undone" (Werblowsky, *Joseph Karo* [London: Oxford Univ. Press, 1962], p. 240), and (2) "to serve as atonement for past sins" (ibid.). This latter *gilgul*, "'to receive punishment . . . is the mystery of sucklings who die' (Alkabetz, *Shorshey Shai*, quoted by Werblowsky), who having atoned for sins committed in a former existence have no further need to live." Alkabetz reviews the matter: "Sometimes the righteous who were perfect in their works and committed no mortal sins nevertheless transmigrate in order to acquire further merit, as in the process of refining silver which is refined over and over again . . . Even so, the righteous transmigrate in order to be purified to the utmost; *they do not die as infants* [in their fourth and subsequent incarnation] after they have been in the world three times without sinning, for there is no danger that they would sin now . . . But those who have sinned in a previous existence and have subsequently improved their ways, yet (still) require *gilgul* to atone for mortal sins committed or to take away the uncleanness of their impurity, [having been reborn for that purpose *they*] *die as infants*. This prevents them from sinning and losing their chance of salvation."

It would thus seem that R. Yitzhak, who was one of the masters at delivering those poor souls lost in the hells of *gilgul*, possessed the gift of recognizing in the visage of his newborn children that their salvation was in their death, lest they live, sin, and be lost forever.]

The holy rav proceeded to mortify his own body for the other's transgressions. No one knew of this, until he was once discovered by members of his household rolling about in the snow, almost unconscious from the terrible cold. His family prevented him from continuing, despite his plea that they let him do it just once more since his soul was in mortal danger.

On the following day, the holy rav, R. Mekhele Zlotchover, of blessed memory, son of the holy rav, R. Itzik [i.e., Isaac] Drobitcher, came to visit. Recognizing the mark of sin on R. Zusya's face, he was terrified and asked for an explanation. R. Zusya told him what had happened, that he had agreed to mortify his body for the transgressions of a fellow Jew. R. Mikhel reproached him strongly for endangering his life, but R. Zusya was so immersed in his own thoughts that he paid no note to his visitor's remarks.

Second thoughts soon came to R. Mekhele about how he had criticized R. Zusya. "Not enough," he said to himself, "that R. Zusya had sacrificed himself for a fellow Jew; he also gets rebuked for this!" R. Mikhel began apologizing, but as he spoke, R. Zusya, realizing for the first time that he had been scolded, grieved. In turn, an accusation was lodged in Heaven against the holy rav, R. Mikhel, for having hurt the feelings of the holy rav, R. Zusya, and it was decreed that R. Mekhele must depart this world. The news reached his father, R. Itzikl Drobitcher, in the Upper World, and he began to intercede on behalf of his son's soul. The verdict was modified: if R. Itzikl could persuade the rav, R. Zusya, to pardon R. Mekhele, he would not be punished.

So the holy rav, R. Itzikl, descended from the Upper World to beseech the rav, R. Zusya, to forgive his son. The request was readily granted. He not only forgave him, but also prayed for R. Mekhele's life and good health.

Now, the rav, R. Zusya, had not seen the face of the holy R. Itzikl, but had only heard his voice. When R. Zusya asked why he could not see him, R. Itzikl replied that he had not as yet completely removed the mark of sin that was upon him. R. Zusya then asked for R. Itzikl's help and was told to go to the *mikveh* and meditate on certain *kavanot*. After doing so, he was able to view R. Itzikl's visage, radiant as the noonday sun.

Later, the holy rav, R. Itzikl, appeared to his son, R. Mekhele, of blessed memory, and cautioned him to beware of upsetting R. Zusya,[87] for great was his station in Heaven.[88]

[R. Isaac is said to have been involved in yet another Heavenly reaction to his son, R. Mikhel—this time one which was more complimentary:]

87. See *Pirkey 'Avot* 2:15.
88. *Sihot Yekarim* [of Elimelekh Zev Stern; Satumare, 1930; rpt. Brooklyn: Y. Z. Veishoiz, 1962], p. 5.

R. Moses Teitelbaum, the rabbi of Sátoraljaújhely (Uhel), told the
following story:

> In Heaven, Rashi, of blessed memory, once encountered the
> holy rav, R. Itzikl of Drohobycz. He inquired of R. Itzikl what
> special merit and *mitzvah* his son, the holy rav R. Mikhel, the
> maggid of Zloczew, possessed which would explain the great stir
> he creates in all the heavens. R. Itzikl suggested that it was his
> son's study of the Torah for its own sake. Rashi, of blessed mem-
> ory, thought the explanation inadequate. R. Itzikl then added
> that his son had taken upon himself a regimen of much fasting
> and other bodily deprivations. Rashi remained dissatisfied with
> the answer. Told that, furthermore, R. Mikhel performs many
> acts of kindness, distributes much charity, and the like, Rashi was
> still unconvinced. Then the father said that his son had turned
> many aside from evil ways and had brought about the repentance
> of many sinners. It was this statement that satisfied Rashi, of
> blessed memory, . . . as to why R. Mikhel was causing a stir
> among the Heavenly Host.[89]

Appendix

Several other remnants of R. Isaac's teachings have been preserved:

> [A] I have heard it said in the style of Musar in the name of
> that venerable and wondrously pious man of God, Our Master,
> R. Isaac, known as "R. Isaac Drobitcher," may the memory of
> the righteous be for an eternal blessing, that people, as a rule,
> nurse their angry feelings toward their fellows until Yom Kippur
> eve. Then they beg each other's forgiveness. But this is not cor-
> rect. Rather, each night before falling asleep one ought to forgive
> one's fellow for any wrong he had committed that day, declaring,
> "May the Master of the World pardon those who have wronged
> me." [See *BT* Megillah 18a.] A person who has been sinned
> against at nightfall must forgive the wrongdoer before the rising
> of the sun, as the *Zohar* informs us [see *Zohar* 1:201b], and not
> keep anger pent up within him for an entire year.
> This lesson can be derived from the verse: ". . . This is the
> offering made by fire which ye shall bring unto the Lord: per-
> fectly whole, year-old he-lambs (*kevasim beney shanah temimim*)
> . . . , two, day by day . . . the one lamb (*keves*) shalt thou offer
> in the morning, and the other lamb (*keves*) shalt thou offer at
> dusk" (Num. 28:3–4).

This is the offering . . . which ye shall bring unto the Lord—
that is, you will please the Lord if you do the following:

"Whole, year-old, he-lambs"—that is, what you are accustomed to retain "pent up in your heart" [*kavush*, a play on *keves*,
the singular of *kevasim*] for a whole year until the eve of the Day
of Atonement, should rather be given "two, day by day"—that
is, twice daily.

The one lamb (*keves*) shalt thou offer in the morning"—that is,
what is pent up (*kavush*) within your heart you must make
amends for in the early morning. "And the other lamb shalt thou
offer at dusk"—that is, make amends for before you go to sleep.

"Gracious are the words of the wise" (Eccles. 10:12).

(*Torey Zahav* by R. Benjamin of Zalozce, *parshat pinḥas*)

R. Isaac's life reflected this teaching. The story is told in the name of R.
Isaac's son, R. Yehiel Mikhel of Zloczew—that he instructed his children
"that they pray for the welfare of their enemies" (see *Mayim Rabbim*,
p. 95).

[B Another homily quoted in R. Isaac's name:]

On the verse, "And he may not come into the holy place at all
times (*bekhol ʿet*)" (Levit. 16:2), I have heard this teaching from
the lips of the noted rav and maggid, our master and teacher, R.
Yehiel Mikhel, of blessed memory, in the name of his father, the
noted Hasid, our master, the rav, R. Isaac, of blessed memory:

In the words of the Psalmist, "he who does righteousness at all
times (*bekhol ʿet*)" (Psalms 106:3), the Talmud (*BT* Ketubot 50a)
comments that this refers to one who supports sons and daughters
in childhood. Mistakenly, people might feel relieved of the need
to give charity to others, claiming that just by maintaining their
own children they have already fulfilled their measure of charitable deeds. To discredit this view, the verse emphasizes, "He
may not come into the holy place (with his allegation of) 'at all
times,' i.e. with the claim that support of his own children is
charity enough [which the Talmud calls "righteousness at all
times"]. That, in fact, is insufficient to permit his entrance into
the holy place: the Lord's inner sanctum. The sanctification of the
soul requires open-handed charity to others. (*Ginzey Yosef, parshat ʾaharey*)

Interestingly, this same homily is attributed to the "Seer" of Lublin by
R. Isaac of Niesuchojeze (Nezkhiz) in his *Toldot Yitzḥak, parshat
ʾaharey*.

[C Another teaching attributed to R. Isaac:]

This is a statute of the Torah (Num. 19:2) [This verse introduced the strange laws on the red heifer. Its ashes were used in
the purification ceremonies conducted for those who had become

ritually unclean (*tamey*) after contact with a corpse.] Focusing on the word "statue," Rashi writes: "Satan and the nations taunt Israel, asking, 'What is this *mitzvah*?' and 'What is the reason behind it?' It is because of this that the Torah [introduces the laws of the red heifer as] a 'statue' (*hok*). That is to say: It is the Lord's decree which you are not permitted to question."

In a book published close to the time of R. Isaac, one finds the following:

This is what I have heard in the name of the late sage, the Hasid who was illustrious in his generation, I refer to our master and teacher, R. Isaac, may the memory of the righteous be a blessing, known to all as R. Itzik Drobitcher. That sage asked why it was particularly in regard to the red heifer that Satan asks Israel to tell him the reason for its performance." [There are also other commandments, e.g. *sha'atnez*, the prohibition against weaving flax and wool together (Levit. 19:19), for which there are no obvious reasons.]

R. Isaac's answer turns on the fact that an exoteric reason for the red heifer is in fact given by R. Moses Narboni, whose remarks are cited *in extenso* by Rashi himself (to Num. 19:22). In brief, the red heifer is said to atone for the sin of the golden calf (Exod. 32)—let the mother cow, as it were, come and clean up the mess made by her child (*Tanhuma* to *parshat hukat*, #5). The esoteric rationale for the red heifer, on the other hand, is so difficult to divine that it is to this problem that King Solomon was referring when he said, "I said I shall become wise, but it is beyond me (Eccles. 7:23)." [See *Numbers Rabbah*, chap. 19.]

We know of several instances where even here associations to the golden calf are deliberately avoided so as not to stir up the eternal wrath of God connected with that event [as the verse (Exod. 32:34) says, "Nevertheless, on the day when I visit, I will visit their sin upon them."] The comments of our Sages, may their memory be a blessing, are well-known on the subject. On the passage in Isaiah (6:2) describing the seraphim—"Each one had six wings; with twain he covered his face and with twain he covered his feet, and with twain he did fly"—the Sages, recalling that the feet of the seraph resembled calves' hooves [see Ezek. 1:7], say that it hid them with its wings so as not to evoke the memory of the golden calf [see, for example, *Pirkey Rabbi Elie'zer*, chap. 4]. It is because of this that the *piyut*, "And the flaming *hayot*," of the Morning Service of *Rosh Hashanah*, says, "They cover their feet so as not to bring to mind (the sin of) the calf produced by fire." Similar reasoning led the Sage (*BT* Rosh Hashanah 26a) to explain why the High Priest did not enter the Holy of Holies on the Day of Atonement dressed in his golden vestments. Gold calls up the association to the golden calf, the catastrophic sin. The High Priest, of course, is performing an atonement service. Gold—the "prosecuting attorney," as it were—cannot become part of the defense.

"It is thus Satan's intention," said R. Isaac, "to ask the reason for the *mitzvah* of the red heifer in particular, hoping that the explanation of its connection with the golden calf would come up and provide him with fuel for his accusations against the Jewish people. To prevent this, . . . it is called 'statue,' [that is to say: it is the Lord's decree which] you are not permitted to question."

"'Gracious are the words of the wise.' May his [R. Isaac's] lips stir in his grave [as we repeat his teaching]." [See *BT* Yevamot, 97a.]

[Heschel does not name the primary source.]

This same explanation is cited in *Kedushat Levi*, end of *parshat ki tisa'* in the name of another *tzaddik*, "the pious rav, our master R. Abraham Hayim, may his light shine, of the holy community of Zloczew." [See also *'Orah Lahayim*, *parshat hukat* (Jerusalem, 1960), which attributes this homily to R. Yehiel Mikhel; and *Sefer Habesht*, ed. Maimon (Jerusalem, 1960), p. 302, where it is reported to have been heard from R. Naftali of Ropczyce (1760–1827).]

It was R. Isaac's practice to review each of the "Four Portions" [added to the regular Sabbath readings during the month of Adar; the third in the series was the "Portion of the (Red) Heifer"] on the Friday before it was read in the synagogue. His preparation involved two recitations of the biblical text and one of the aramic *targum* [the intensive review demanded for the regular weekly portion. See *Shulhan Arukh*, *'orah hayim*, #285. R. Isaac's was a scrupulous act since the "Four Portions" are biblical texts which come up for review throughout the year in the normal course of the cycle of readings. For just that reason, Festival readings, for example, need not be examined beforehand (#285:6)]. Several of R. Isaac's descendants kept up this tradition. See *Mayim Rabbim*, p. 87.

Endnotes

ONE. RABBI PINHAS OF KORZEC

Note 51 (from page 11)

Shivḥey Habesht, p. 18b [Ben-Amos, #124]. By that time, apparently, R. Pinhas was already well known and used to travel with the rabbi of Rowne (Rovno) to collect funds for the redemption of captives.

[The full text of the tale from *Shivḥey Habesht* which recounts how R. Pinhas and his father declared themselves as the Besht's disciples follows:

"I heard from the rabbi of our community that once R. Pinhas of Korzec and the rabbi of the holy community of Rowne (Rovno) traveled about collecting ransom money in order to redeem a relative of theirs who was in prison. Said R. Pinhas to the rabbi of Rowne: 'I heard the Besht observes the Sabbath in the holy community of Kaminka. Let us go to him. Perhaps he will help us, and it will no longer be necessary for us to weary ourselves with travel (to collect money).'

"They decided to go to him, and hurried to reach him before he went to the *mikveh*, since afterward it would be impossible to discuss anything with him. But when they met him, he had already been to the *mikveh* and was dressed in his Sabbath clothes.

"In the *bet midrash* his (the Besht's) followers advised them: 'Let yourselves be seen by him and he will certainly know your needs even without your telling him.'

"And so they did. They came to the door of the *bet midrash*, and when he saw them he motioned to them with his hand to leave.

"After that R. Pinhas heard that his father, our teacher and rabbi, Abraham Abba, had arrived at the holy community of Miropol across the river. He went to visit him, since he was worried lest his father, who thought little of the Besht, would want to keep the Sabbath with him. For R. Abraham always used to say to his son: 'Why are you going to the Besht?' Therefore, R. Pinhas feared that his father might show disrespect to the Besht and bring shame upon him, God forbid. R. Pinhas asked him (his father) where he would observe the Sabbath. "Why should I go to the Besht?" he replied. 'I will observe the Sabbath here and preach here.'

"In the morning (however), when the Besht started the prayer of 'O Give Thanks Unto the Lord,' R. Abraham came to the *bet midrash* of Kaminka and stood near the holy ark before which the Besht was praying. R. Pinhas's father was praying in a loud voice, and R. Pinhas was afraid that his father would disturb the Besht and that the Besht would scold him. But the Besht uttered not a word to him, until after the morning prayer.

"It was the Sabbath and also *Rosh Ḥodesh* (the first of the month), which required that they take out two scrolls of the Torah. The Besht took one of the scrolls. R. Pinhas's father took the other one, following the Besht to the reader's

183

stand. The Besht, seeing him [R. Abraham] holding the Torah scroll, scolded him and told someone: 'Take the Torah scroll from him.'

"R. Abraham did not answer back, which surpised R. Pinhas. After the prayer, R. Abraham went to one of the elders of the town across the river. He ate there and slept a while, and then he went to preach in the synagogue. But he returned to the Besht for the third meal.

"It was the custom of the people of Kaminka that when the Besht visited with them, they placed a table for themselves on the side, while the Besht and the guests sat around the main table. When they saw R. Abraham coming, they called him to sit with them since they knew that he was an outspoken Lithuanian (Lithuania was the center for *Mitnagdim*, the opponents of the Hasidim), and he might interrupt the Besht's talk and disturb him. They called to him: 'R. Abraham, come sit with us,' and they gave him a glass of mead.

"When the Besht began to speak, R. Abraham left his seat. He placed himself squarely in the center of the room just opposite the Besht, staring him in the face! R. Pinhas was afraid to make him stop, for one is bidden to honor one's father. So it was that R. Abraham faced the Besht, to R. Pinhas's embarrassment. When the Besht stopped preaching, he returned to his place. They then lit the candles and ate some meat.

"The Besht began speaking again: 'I have one more remark to make. I did not intend to say it, but I heard it said in paradise in my name.' When the Besht began to speak, R. Abraham once again rose up from his seat, placed himself just across from the Besht until he finished, and then returned to his place. They recited the grace after food and prayed the evening service. After the prayer, R. Abraham said to R. Pinhas: 'It is himself and no one else, he himself and no one else.'

"R. Pinhas said: 'What have you seen in him?'

"He said to him: 'Do you think that I did not mind his scolding me at the reading of the Torah? But I waited until the end. Let me tell you, my son, that (previous) night I had a dream in which I entered paradise and the Prince of the Torah entered and repeated a torah said by the Besht. When I awoke from my sleep I remembered it very well, and it was for that reason that I came here. And what I had already heard, I heard again from his holy mouth!'

"I did not hear from the rabbi anything about the prisoner, and I forgot to ask about him."]

Note 147 (from page 27)

"Upon the death of his son, R. Meir, R. Levi Isaac of Berdichev grieved bitterly. R. Abraham Joseph of Hasivata, and R. Abraham Leib, the rabbinic judge of Teplik, came to console him. R. Abraham Joseph said to the rabbi of Berdichev:

"'When the maggid of Miedzyrzecz learned that R. Mikhele, the friend of R. Zev, had died, he said: "At a time when one is obliged to make his influence felt in the world, it is not good to mourn."

"'And when R. Pinhas learned . . .'

"The moment the rav of Berdichev heard the name of R. Pinhas, he shouted: 'Sha! Sha! Sha!'

"Upset, R. Abraham Leib said to R. Abraham Joseph: 'Why did you have to speak of R. Pinhas? You should have been silent.'

"Later the rabbi of Berdichev said: 'Do you understand [*Farshtays du shertze*], since you first spoke of my master [i.e., the Maggid of Miedzyrzecz], how could I then listen about another tzaddik? Nonetheless, tell me about R. Pinhas, since you have already begun.'

"So R. Abraham continued: 'R. Pinhas related a parable: When a great fighter dies in the midst of battle, the other soldiers dare not leave the battle and busy themselves with the fallen one, even though he is a hero.'"

"The rabbi of Berdichev replied: 'The maggid could say what he did, because news of the death came to him [in that case] after the *shiva*, but I am still in the period of the *shiva* where the law requires one to mourn despite the reasons you have given.'" (MS. Kitvey Kodesh, chap. 8, p. 6b.)

The rabbi Mikhele mentioned in this story was not the maggid of Zloczew, for he had died, according to a tradition, on the 26th of Elul, 1786. Perhaps the above-mentioned R. Mikhele is the one spoken of in the records of R. Solomon of Sadagura (p. 198b):

"R. Zev [of Zhitomir, author of the book, *'Or Hame'ir*] had a friend, a noted tzaddik, who died while quite young. Once they were with the maggid, heard Torah from him, and later returned home. It was after midday in the springtime. They got down from the wagon and ordered the wagon driver to follow them. They walked along, discussing what their master had said and lost themselves in conversation. They did not notice the onset of evening and then morning. Ten o'clock in the morning still found them walking and talking. Until at last the wagon driver interrupted them: 'You haven't prayed the *minhah* (afternoon) service. You haven't prayed *ma'ariv*. Don't you intend to pray *shaharit* either?'"

It is told that R. Zev of Zhitomir brought his book [*'Or Hame'ir*] to the son of R. Pinhas in the hope that he would publish it. After spending all night examining the manuscript, he told R. Zev why he refused his request: "I know that you have learned more from my father than from the maggid, yet the maggid you mention many times while my father's name isn't mentioned at all in the book." (I heard this story from the Monestrishter Rebbe in New York.) *'Or Hame'ir* was first printed in Korzec in 1798. The printing house of R. Moses Shapiro, the son of R. Pinhas of Korzec, had already been opened in 1794 in Slavuta (see H. Lieberman, "*Letoldot Hadefus Ha'ivri Beslavita,*" *Kiryat Sefer* 27 [1951]:117). This story reflects the conflict between R. Zev and the family of R. Pinhas.

Two. Rabbi Gershon Kutover

Note 18 (from page 48)
[The following reports in *Shivhey Habesht* describe R. Gershon's early antipathy to the Baal Shem Tov:

"... the great rabbi, our rabbi and master, Gershon of Kuty ... received all his father's papers (after his death) and among them he found the engagement contract, showing that his father had made a match between his daughter, Rabbi Gershon's sister, and some man whose name was Israel. He was amazed that his father, who was prominent, could make a match with a person of low rank, and, moreover, with someone whose background and family lines were unknown ... [The Baal Shem Tov] disguised himself by putting on clothes like those worn by loafers ... changed his manner of speech, and he went to the holy community of Brody to the house of ... Rabbi Gershon. There were two rabbinical courts supervised by Rabbi Gershon which were holding sessions in his house ... The Baal Shem Tov was standing at the door ... Rabbi Gershon thought that he was a beggar. He took a coin with the intention of giving it to him, and the Baal Shem Tov told him, 'I have a secret to tell you.' They went to a room, and the Baal Shem Tov showed him the engagement contract and said: 'Give me my wife.'

"When the rabbi saw the man, his dress, and heard his language, he was astonished and frightened at what his father, God bless his memory, had done. He called his sister and told her the whole situation. She answered: 'Since our father has arranged this, we should not reverse the decision. It is surely God's will, and perhaps a virtuous child will be born from the marriage.'

" . . . Before the wedding took place the Baal Shem Tov . . . talked with his bride secretly and told her the truth . . . He made her swear that she would not reveal anything, even if she would undergo many periods of great poverty.

"After the wedding, our rabbi and master, Rabbi Gershon, wanted to study with him in the hope that the Baal Shem Tov would learn something, but the Baal Shem Tov concealed his knowledge and pretended to be unable to learn. The rabbi said to his sister: 'Really, I am disgraced by your husband, and if you want to divorce him, it is acceptable to me. If not, I will buy you a horse, and you may go and lodge with him wherever he will lodge. I cannot bear this shame' (Ben-Amos, #8).

" . . . the Baal Shem Tov had a horse, but it was stolen from him . . . Rabbi Gershon ridiculed him, and every time that he came to the town he teased him and said: 'Israel, has the horse been returned to you?' (Ben-Amos, #30).

"Once he went on a journey and took the Baal Shem Tov along as his coachman. In the course of the journey our master and rabbi, Rabbi Gershon, fell asleep, and the Baal Shem Tov drove the horse into a marsh filled with mud and mire from which it was impossible to pull them free. Just then his brother-in-law, Rabbi Gershon, woke up. He realized that they were in serious trouble. He thought that the Baal Shem Tov was a simpleton, and he feared that if he sent him to the village to find some Gentiles to haul out the horses, he would wander wherever he pleased. He preferred to go and find help himself. He was forced to climb from the wagon into the mire, and he walked to a certain village. He was returning with several people to pull the horses from the mud when he looked up and saw the Baal Shem Tov coming toward him. He asked: 'Who pulled you out?'

"He answered: 'I struck the horses just once and they simply walked out.'

"Our rabbi and master, Rabbi Gershon, said: 'It is impossible to obtain even this service from him. He is good-for-nothing' (Ben-Amos, #13).

"Once the Baal Shem Tov borrowed a copy of the *Zohar* from the rabbi of the holy community of Kuty. On his way back home he encountered his brother-in-law, Rabbi Gershon, who asked him: 'What do you have under your arm?'

"He did not want to tell him. Rabbi Gershon climbed down from the wagon, took the *Zohar* from under his arm, and said in wonder: '*You* need the *Zohar*!?'" (Ben-Amos, #30; ##19, 20, 28, 30, 46, 56, 80, 151).]

Note 32 (from page 51)
He taught Kabbalah to R. Ezekiel Landau. I have discussed him elsewhere. [Again, as in the previous note, no published work of Heschel's deals with this figure. Evidently by the time of the publishing of his article on R. Gershon (1950), Heschel was engaged in studies on several other early Hasidic figures, among whom was R. Hayim. Heschel's files reveal part of his material.

An analysis of the attitude of the leaders of the Brody community to the Baal Shem Tov and his followers would contribute significantly to the history of early Hasidism. A *herem* against the Hasidim was issued from Brody, and in 1781, one year after its publication, the book, *Toldot Ya ʿakov Yosef*, by R. Jacob Joseph of Polonnoye (Polnoy), was burned in Brody in front of the house of R. Yehiel Mikhel (later of Zloczew), "a fervent disciple of the Baal Shem Tov" (N. M. Gelber, *History of the Jews of Brody* [Hebrew] [Jerusalem: Mosad Harav Kook, 1956], p. 115) and son of R. Isaac of Drohobycz (Drobitch) (see pp. 152–81).

On the other hand, the Baal Shem Tov must have had his supporters there, for it was in Brody that he chose to disclose his identity. "When the time for him (the Baal Shem Tov) to reveal himself approached, it happened that one of the students of our master and rabbi, Rabbi Gershon, went to visit him (the Baal Shem Tov) . . . He commanded his guest to go to our master and rabbi, R. Gershon, but he was not to reveal anything. Instead, he was to proceed to 'the group of the great Hasidim' in the town (Brody), and also to the rabbi of the community and to say these words: 'There is a great light living near your community, and it will be worthwhile for you to seek him out and bring him to the city'" [Ben-Amos, #15]. Dinur understands this passage as implying a following for the Baal Shem Tov at the *kloiz* ("The Beginning of Hasidism and Its Social and Messianic Element" [Hebrew], *Zion* 9 [1944]:187–97). Gelber disagrees, arguing that "we cannot grant that among the scholars of the *kloiz* there were many who were sympathetic to the school of the Baal Shem Tov. On the contrary, the leaders of the *kloiz*, such as R. Hayim Tzanzer and R. Ezekiel Landau, were opponents of the Hasidim of the BE Baal Shem Tov" (*History of the Jews of Brody*, p. 109). Heschel treats the friendship between R. Ezekiel Landau and R. Gershon Kutover in this essay, and begins to treat the relationship between the latter and R. Hayim in his unpublished notes.

"According to Hasidic tradition," writes Heschel in his notes, "the sages of the *kloiz* were opposed to the Baal Shem Tov. This relationship was important because these sages were eminent in themselves and exerted great influence in their time. At the leadership of these scholars was R. Hayim, the son of Menahem Tzanzer, better known as R. Hayim Tzanzer. He did not serve as the rabbi of a community but was the most celebrated kabbalist of his generation in Galicia. R. Ezekiel Landau, the author of *Noda 'Bihuda*, was his student in Kabbalah."

R. Hayim's eminence as a kabbalist is reflected in the well-known *Seder Tefilah Mikol Shanah* (Lwów, 1787), referred to as the *"Sidur of R. Usher,"* i.e., R. Asher the son of Solomon Zalman Margoliot, one of the "members of the *kloiz* of our community (Brody)." An approbation appears there from ". . . the distinguished rabbis who sit on the thrones of judgment and of Torah in the holy community of Brody." In this approbation, the source of kabbalistic authority for the work is ascribed to "the great light, the noted Hasid, distinguished in halakhic as well as mystical learning, wise in all matters, the inspired man, R. Hayim Tzanzer." In his introduction to his *Sidur*, while R. Asher indicates that he consulted the previously published prayerbook which was then used by some of the early Hasidim, the *"Sidur* of the Gaon, Hasid, and kabbalist, our master, R. Shabetai of Raszków," and that R. Asher's own work had the approval of the sages, he notes with emphasis that "particularly, there was that mighty tree for me to rest upon, our master and teacher, the rav, the distinguished luminary, the divine kabbalist, R. Hayim Tzanzer of Brody, may his memory be for a blessing, whom I have served faithfully, especially as regards the true, awesome wisdom (Kabbalah) . . ."

R. Hayim Tzanzer, one of the two signatories of the *herem* against the amulets of Jonathan Eibeschütz (Piekarz, "Beginnings of Hasidism," p. 79), and, according to one source, "an adversary of the Baal Shem Tov" (Gelber, *History*, p. 63), was, in fact, an in-law of R. Jacob Joseph, who quotes him in his work. Piekarz explores the similarities of R. Hayim's little-known writings to those of the early Hasidim, and concludes: "There is no doubt that he was familiar with the teachings of the first Hasidic teachers" (*Beginnings of Hasidism*, p. 223). The Baal Shem Tov held R. Hayim in high regard, suggesting that he possessed the soul of R. Yohanan ben Zakkai. See *Sipurey Kedoshim* (Lwów [Leipzig?], 1866) for stories about the Baal Shem Tov and R. Hayim.

Scholem, in his "Two Letters from the Land of Israel," p. 436, n. 16, claims that the fact that this distinguished leader of the *kloiz* and supposed "foe" of the Baal Shem Tov was none other than the in-law of the Baal Shem Tov's literary disciple, R. Jacob Joseph, was previously "unknown to students of Hasidism." However, this writer's doctoral dissertation, "The Tzaddik," Jewish Theological Seminary of America, 1954, Appendix 2, "Persons Mentioned in the Works of R. Jacob Joseph," pp. 288–89, alludes to it, while Heschel's notes prior to that time identify him as such.

There is a further fact of note both in regard to the relationship of the Baal Shem Tov to the leaders of the *kloiz*, and more particularly, to the family of R. Gershon Kutover. The latter's son, R. Yakir, was the son-in-law of R. Moses Ostrer, another of the leading figures of the *kloiz* and the cosignatory with R. Hayim Tzanzer on the *herem* against the amulets of Eibeschütz. Gershon Scholem, in his article, "Two Letters from the Land of Israel," indicates how in Amsterdam he found the manuscript containing a letter of R. Yakir to his father-in-law, R. Moses. This editor has seen a communication from Heschel, reflecting his search for this very manuscript in 1950. Both Scholem and Heschel were aware that it had been offered at auction in Amsterdam in 1899. Heschel had written Dr. M. Rapp, the son-in-law of Professor A. Freimann, then deceased, whose catalog of Hebrew manuscripts (since published by the American Academy for Jewish Research, 1973) was in the former's home, to search it for the possible record of the manuscript's location.]

Note 81 (from page 63)

In the epistle of R. Abraham Gershon published in *Birkat Haʾaretz*, p. 63a, it is mentioned that R. Abraham Shver Zalk (according to Cahana, and also according to the *Ginzey Nistarot*, his name was Shverzalshk) was among those who encouraged him to accept the Jerusalem rabbinate. In the manuscript version, his name is given as "R. Abraham Shverdlov." I think that he was R. Abraham Shverdlik of Jerusalem, who married the widow of R. Eleazar Rokeah of Amsterdam. Cf. the story in *Shivhey Habesht*, p. 11c [Ben-Amos, #63]. Rivlin's hypothesis, expressed in Frumkin's *History of the Sages of Jerusalem* (Hebrew), pt. 3, p. 71, n. 6, that he was the Hasid, R. Abraham of Brody, who had come to Palestine in the company of R. Eleazar Rokeah and who settled in Jerusalem and died on 7 Elul 1746, cannot be sustained.

In the *Pinkas* Constantinople [JTS MS. 4008], pp. 157a and 167a, I found two lists of Ashkenazim in Palestine receiving financial support [through the Constantinople authorities. Names of the recipients, amounts received, as well as the total allocation, are cited. Y. Barnai, "Jewish Community in Jerusalem," pp. 218–24, principally following A. Yaari, *Emissaries of the Land of Israel* (Hebrew) (Jerusalem: Mosad Harav Kook, 1951), pp. 523–30; *Travels to the Land of Israel* (Hebrew), (Tel Aviv: Histadrut, 1947), pp. 382–423, 774, presented the two lists of names cited by Heschel in this footnote and attempted to identify the people mentioned. In the parentheses are the names according to Barnai's reading. Heschel may have emended them. Barnai dates the second list 1756]:

1755

25. To the sage, R. Gershon
    Kutover
14. To his son, the sage, Yakir   (To my son, the sage, Yakir)

25. To the leader (*nagid*), Itzik of
    Lachowicze (Lehovitz)
20. To Mr. (?, Heb.: *m*) Leib   (To Mr. Leib from Apt)
15. To Mr. Feibush (Mr., as   (.18)
    above, and in all cases
    below.)
18. To Mr. Dov Ber of Brody   (.15)
12. To R. Hirtz of Posen
 8. To R. Aaron of Brody   (To the . . . Aaron of Brody)
 8. . . . Petahia   (To the sage, R. Petahia)
 6. To R. Yehoshua of Szydlow   (To the R. Yosha of Szydlow)
 7.
 8.
166.

4 Elul 1757

25. To the sage, R. Gershon   (To the sage, R. Abraham
    Kutover   Gershon)
14. To his son, the sage, Yakir
13. To the sage, R. Jacob
    Ashkenazi
 8. To the sage, Joshua of   (To the sage, R. Yosha of
    Szydlow (Shidlov)   Szydlow)
14. To the sage, Petahiah
18. To the sage, Dov Ber of
    Brody
14. To the sage, Leib of Opatów   (To the sage, Leib of Opatów)
    (Apt)
15. To the sage, Itzik of
    Lachowicze (Lehovitz)
15. To the sage, Feibush
15. To the sage, Hirtz of Posen   (To the sage, Hirtz of Posen)
12. To the sage, Nata Block   (To the sage, Nata Blokh)
 8. To the sage, Elia
171.

[It is significant that R. Gershon received support in an amount higher than that allotted others. See p. 87, n. 181. The same document, the *Pinkas* Constantinople, points to the large percentage of Ashkenazi immigrants coming from the districts of Podolia and Volhynia where the influence of the Baal Shem Tov was strongest and to which the early geographical origins of Hasidism can be traced. The communities listed there are: Brody, Bolehov, Posen, Zolkiew, Dubno, Vishnitz, Lwów, Aleski, Lublin, Elmi, Sitria, Przemyśl, Zalozce, Lintz, Beresteczko, Satanów, Miedzybórz, Grodno, Prague, Vienna, and Amsterdam. (Cf. Y. Barnai, "Jewish Community in Jerusalem," pp. 193–237.)]

THREE. RABBI NAHMAN OF KOSÓW

Note 149 (from page 148)
R. Ber of Miedzyrzecz, *'Or Torah: rimzey torah* (Korzec: Abraham Madpis, 1804), *parshat re'eh*; *Maggid Devarav Leya'akov* (Korzec: Tzvi Hirsch b. Aryeh Leib and Samuel b. Isaachar Ber Segal, 1784), p. 38b [ed. Schatz, Jerusalem: Magnes Press, 1976, p. 256, #160].

[Involuntary seminal emission is held to be one of the most serious of transgressions according to kabbalistic teaching, which, for example, suggests that "devils" are born from it. In breaking with this tradition, the Besht proposes that there may be a positive side to such an occurrence, for example, the deliverance from a death decree. He spoke, of course, of a purely involuntary event, which in the case of pious ones (*ḥasidav*), and under these circumstances, may be a "good." In any case, after the fact, one's concern should not be so much over what has already transpired, which may lead to depression, but to the ever-present task of "purifying one's thoughts," even transforming evil thoughts to the service of God.

[In his book *Kotzk* 1:358, n. 5, Heschel adds to this thought. "The Baal Shem's opinion concerning *tumʾat keri*, cited in *Degel Maḥaneh ʾEfrayim, parshat ekev* (in the section beginning with: 'The words, "And it shall come to pass because," also hint . . .'), is explained by R. Isaac of Komarno in the following manner: After Adam's sin, good and evil became confused in all things, so that sometimes even in the wholly righteous a spark of evil is found. His fate should be death, so that this evil be extinguished. The Lord, however, takes pity upon him, as it is written. "Precious in the sight of the Lord is the death of His pious ones," and the episode of *keri* is made to occur instead, after which the filth no longer adheres to him, and the evil spark passes quickly into oblivion. This has happened to many pious, saintly, and wholly righteous men." (*ʾOtzar Hahayim* to Deut. 21:22.) (See Heschel, *Kotzk*, 1:235–48, 356–61; 2:627–33, 681–88. See also R. Binyamin of Zalozycz, *Torey Zahav* (Mogilev: Asher Zelig, 1816), *parshat tetzey* for a further statement in the name of the Besht).

The viewpoint of the Besht was not accepted by the majority of the Hasidic leaders who came after him, for example R. Nahman of Braslav. Compare the words of R. Eliezer Halevi Horovitz, rabbi of Tarnogród, in his *Noʿam Magidim Ukevod Hatorah* (Lwów: P. Balaban, 1873), *parshat metzoraʿ*, p. 76b: "Many people who have an episode of *keri*, heaven forbid, do not consider themselves sinful, but think: 'I have done nothing. It happened involuntarily and by accident.' This is truly the way of the fool. For if a spirit of impurity had not passed over him by day, he would have not come to an impure action at night."

The maggid of Miedzyrzecz spoke of the severity of this failing in his homily on Psalms 17:14. See the end of *Maggid Devarav Leyaʿakov*, [ed. Schatz, pp. 331–33, #207]; *ʾOr Torah, psalms*. And his student, R. Yehiel Mikhel, in his "Patterns of Conduct," suggested that one fast if an involuntary seminal emission occurred at night (*Mayim Ḥayim*, p. 12). See the section on prayer at the end of *Tzemaḥ David* by R. David of Dynów (New York: S. B. Rokach, 1953), regarding an incident which occurred in the days of R. Menahem Mendel of Rymanów: "Souls from the supernal world had come before him, protesting" that R. Yehiel Mikhel Zlotchov "was the senior judge of the heavenly court and exceedingly strict regarding *keri* (may heaven save us!), for he had been holy and pure in his lifetime and was never guilty of this transgression. Because of their requests to the rabbi of Rymanów, another was appointed head of the heavenly tribunal. They returned to thank him for making their lot more bearable. For the sin depends upon the generation." Cf. *ʾOhev Yisraʾel, parshat vayeḥi*; R. Nahman of Brazláw, *Tikkun Hakelali*; the story about R. Hayim ibn Atar, *ʾOt Berit Kodesh*, p. 1; *Yesod Veshoresh Haʿavodah* [of Alexander b. Moses Ziskind of Horodny (Nowy Dwor, 1782)], *shaʿar* 10, chap. 3; *shaʿar* 12, chap. 2, and *shaʿar hakolel*, chap. 5; *Kav Hayashar*, chap. 68.

Cf. *Zohar* 1:54b: "When a man dreams in his sleep, female spirits often come and disport with him, and so conceive from him and subsequently give birth. The creatures thus produced are called 'plagues of mankind'"; and *Likutey Torah* by R. Hayim Vital, *parshat bo*: "The mystery of the sin of *keri* ascends to the upper knowledge which is called 'the firstborn.' "

The sages of the Talmud hold that involuntary seminal emission brings impurity to man, but is not a heinous sin punishable by the court. From the passage, "Then shalt thou keep thee from every evil thing (Deut. 23:10), R. Pinhas ben Yair deduced that "one should not indulge in evil thoughts by day that might lead one to impurity by night" (*BT* Ketuvot 46a). On the other hand, "a Tanna taught before R. Nahman: He who has a nocturnal emission on Yom Kippur, let him be anxious over this for the entire year. And if he survives the year, he is assured of being destined for the future world" (*BT* Yoma 88a). *Keri* is one of the six characteristics which are noted as a good sign for one who is sick (*BT* Berakhot 57b). Regarding the patriarch Jacob's words of blessing to Reuben, his firstborn, "My strength and the beginning of my power" (Gen. 49:3), the sages say that Reuben was born from Jacob's very first seminal emission (i.e., he had never before had *keri*) (*Genesis Rabbah* 98:4). Said Abaye: "Is everybody like our Father Jacob concerning whom it is written: 'My strength and the *beginning* of my power'?" (*BT* Yevamot 76a).

Glossary

ʿ**Amidah**: (lit.: standing) core of the Jewish prayer service, recited standing three times daily

ʾ**Amoraʾim**: sages of the talmudic period (roughly the third through the sixth century C.E.)

ʾ**Anaʾ Bakoaḥ**: mystic prayer based on the kabbalistically derived forty-two letter name of God

ʾ**Asham talui**: sacrifice brought when the commission of sin is not certain

ʾ**Av bet din**: chief judge of a local rabbinic court

Baal Shem Tov: (lit.: Master of the Good Name) the popular name given to R. Israel b. Eliezer, the founder of Hasidism

Besht: acronym formed from the name Baal Shem Tov

Bet midrash: house of study and prayer

Borkhu: (lit.: "Bless the Lord") the prayer leader's call to prayer

Davenen: Yiddish for "to pray"

Dayan: rabbinic judge

Devekut: attachment to God, a goal of Jewish mysticism

Din: divine judgement; a source of the demonic

Gabaiʾ: collector of charitable funds

Gadlut: a state of expanded spiritual consciousness

Galut: Diaspora

Get: writ of divorce

Gevir: nobleman, a man of wealth

Hakham: (lit.: wise person) the title of a Sephardic sage

Hametz: leaven of the kind prohibited during Passover

Hatan torah: (lit.: bridegroom of the Torah) the one called to the Torah to conclude the yearly cycle of readings on the festival of Simhat Torah

Haver: colleague

Herem: writ or the state of excommunication

Hitlahavut: religious ecstasy

Hol hamoʿed: intermediate days of the festivals of Passover and Sukkot

Hutzpah: gall, nerve

Katnut: a state of constricted spiritual consciousness

Kavanah: inner devotion during the performance of a religious act

Kavanot: in Kabbalah, systematic meditations during prayer

Kelipot: (lit.: shells) forces of evil

Keri: nocturnal seminal emission

Kloiz: conventicle for prayer and study
Kolel: body of Jews in Palestine receiving funds from abroad
Ma'ariv: the evening service
Maggid: preacher
Malkhut: the tenth *sefirah* (see below), identified in Kabbalah with the *Shekhinah*
Melamed: teacher of young children
Mikveh: ritual bath
Minḥah: afternoon prayer
Minyan: prayer quorum of ten men
Mishnah: the oldest code of postbiblical Jewish law, comprising the teachings of
the Tanna'im, edited around the beginning of the third century C.E.
Mitnagdim: opponents of the Hasidim
Mitzvah: divine commandment and, by extension, a good deed
Mokhiaḥ: (lit.: chastiser) a preacher
Parashah: section of the Torah
Pinkas: minute book of a community
Rav: rabbi; legal authority
Rosh Hashanah: Jewish New Year
Rosh ḥodesh: first day of a Jewish month
Rosh yeshivah: dean of a talmudic school
Sefirah: hypostasis of a divine attribute emanating from the godhead and consti-
tuting part of the world of emanation, which, according to the Kabbalah, is that
aspect of God which one may know and love, and with which one may commune
during prayer and the performance of the commandments
Seliḥah: penitential prayer
Shaḥarit: morning service
Shaliaḥ tzibur: leader of the prayer service
Shekhinah: indwelling presence of God on earth; in the Kabbalah described in
female terms and identified with the tenth *sefirah*, *Malkhut*
Shema yisrael: the declaration of faith in God derived from Deuteronomy 6:4 and
recited twice daily
Shoḥet: ritual slaughterer
Talit: prayer shawl
Tanna'im: sages of the mishnaic period
Tefillin: phylacteries
Tish: (lit.: table) communal meal at the rebbe's table
Tzaddik: (lit.: righteous one) master of a Hasidic sect; holy man
Yetzer hara': evil inclination
Yiḥud: prayer designed to proclaim (and in Kabbalah, to bring about) the unity of
God and the Shekhinah
Yir'at shamayim: fear or awe for God; piety
Yom Kippur: Day of Atonement
Zohar: kabbalistic classic, first published in Spain in the thirteenth century

Gazetteer

The following list contains the names of Eastern European towns and villages mentioned in this book. The towns are listed by their Slavic names; when the Yiddish name for the town is significantly different from the Slavic it is given in parentheses. Names followed by the abbreviation "Y" are given in their Yiddish forms, since their Slavic forms are unknown or unidentifiable—MSC.

Anipol (Hanipol)
Bar
Barivke
Belaya Tserkov (Sde Lavan)
Belz
Berdichev
Beresteczko (Brestemtika)
Bershad
Bershat (Y.)
Bialozórka
Bilgoraj (Bilgorey)
Bolechów
Brazlaw (Bartzlav)
Brody (Brod)
Brzeziny (Berzan)
Buczacz (Buchach)
Cernăuţi (Tchernovitz)
Chernobyl
Dinowitz (Y.)
Dolina (Dalina)
Drohobycz (Drobitch)
Dubnów
Dynów (Dinov)
Gliniany (Gline, Glona)
Grodno
Hasivata (Y.)
Horochów (Horchov)
Horodenka
Józefów (Yuzefaf)
Kalbiel
Kalinblat (Y.)

Kaminka (Y.)
Karlin
Karsna
Kedainai (Kaidenov)
Khmelnik (Y.)
Kobryn
Kock (Kotzk)
Kolmyja (Kolomea)
Komarno
Konstantynów (Konstantin)
Kopyczyńce (Kopitshinitz)
Kopys (Kapust)
Korzec (Koretz)
Kosów (Kosov)
Kowel (Kavla)
Kozienice (Kozhnitz)
Kuty (Kutov, Kitov)
Lady
Ladzien (Ladishin)
Laszniów (Leshnov)
Lechovice (Lechovitz)
Lezajsk (Lizhensk)
Linitz (Y.)
Liter
Lubartów (Levertov)
Luck (Lutzk)
Lwów (Lvov, Levov, Lemberg)
Mezyrów (Mezirov)
Miedzybórz (Mezbizh)
Miedzyrzecz (Mezeritch)
Mikolajow (Miklayov)

195

Miropol
Mogilev (Mohalev)
Munkacs (Munkatch)
Nadwórna (Nadvorne)
Nemirov
Niesuchojeze (Nezkhiz)
Nikolsburg
Olesko (Alesk)
Opatów (Apta, Apt)
Ostróg (Ostraha)
Piotrkow (Pietrokov)
Pistýn
Podhajce (Podheitz)
Podkamien (Pidkamin)
Polonnoye (Polnoy)
Poryck (Poritzk)
Przemyśl (Premishl)
Przemyślany (Primishlan)
Przysuche (Pshishkhe)
Radvil (Y.)
Raszków (Rashkov)
Ropczyce (Ropshitz)
Rowne (Rovno)
Rymanow
Rzeszow (Risha)
Sadagura (Sadigora)
Sasów
Satanów
Sátoraljaújhely (Uhel)
Satumare (Satmar)
Shepetovka (Shepitevka)
Shklov
Shpola
Siluva (Tshidlov)

Slavuta (Slavita)
Slutsk
Sokal (Skahal)
Stanav
Stepan (Stepin)
Stolin
Stretin
Strzeliska (Strelisk)
Swierze
Sydlow (Shidlov)
Szynowo (Shinov)
Tarnopol
Teplik (Y.)
Tetiev (Titiov)
Titshilnik (Y.)
Tomaspol (Tomashpoly)
Torczyn (Tortzin)
Tshidnov (Y.)
Turka
Uman
Vitebsk
Vladmir-Volynski (Ludmir)
Yampol (Yampoli)
Zalozce (Zalozitz)
Zalrave
Zamość (Zameshtesh)
Zasláw
Zawalow (Zvalov)
Zeiahel (Zevehl)
Zhitomir
Zloczew (Zlotchov)
Zolkiew (Zholkva)
Zydaczów (Zidishov)

Select Bibliography

MANUSCRIPTS

MS. Cincinnati. Hebrew Union College #62.
MS. Hebron Letter of R. Gershon Kutover. R. Barukh Zak, Admor of Kobryn.
MS. Kitvey Kodesh. R. Isaac Joel Rabinowitz, Admor of Monestrisht.
MS. Kopitshinitz. R. Abraham Joshua Heschel, Admor of Kopitshinitz.
MS. Megilat Yuhasim. R. Samuel Zanvil Kahana.
MS. *Pinkas* Constantinople. Jewish Theological Seminary #4008.
MS. Shapiro. R. Solomon Shapiro.
MS. Sipurim Yekarim. Location unknown.
MS. Uman. R. Isaac Joel Rabinowitz, Admor of Monestrisht.

ARTICLES AND BOOKS

Aaron of Zhitomir. *Toldot 'Aharon*. Berdichev: Israel Beck, 1817.
Aaron b. Tzvi Hakohen of Opatów. *Keter Shem Tov*. Zolkiew, 1794–95; rpt. Tel Aviv: Zarsky and Rosenberg, 1960.
Abraham of Slonim. *Yesod Ha'avodah*. Warsaw: Meir ir Y. Halter, 1892.
Abraham b. Tzvi. *Mishneh Avraham*. Zhitomir, 1868.
Abraham David Wahrman of Buczacz. *'Eshel 'Avraham*. Buczacz: Dratler, 1906.
Abraham Hamalakh b. Dov Ber of Miedzyrzecz. *Hesed Le'avraham*. Cernăuti: Meshulam Heller, 1851.
Abraham Hayim b. Gedaliah. *'Orah Lahayim*. Berdichev, 1817; rpt. Jerusalem: Wolf and Stutsberg, 1961.
Abraham Isaac of Zinkevitz. *Sipurey Tzaddikim*. Vienna, 1922.
Adler, E. N. *Jews in Many Lands*. Philadelphia: Jewish Publication Society, 1905.
Alfasi, Y. *Hahasidut*. Tel Aviv: Zion 1969; rpt. Maariv, 1974.
———. "A New Source for the *Nusah Ha'ari* of the Hasidim" (Hebrew). In *Temirin*, vol. 1. Edited by I. Weinstock. Jerusalem: Mosad Harav Kook, 1972, pp. 287–304.
Alkalai, Joseph. *'Amar Yosef*. Salonica: Betzalel Halevi Ashkenazi, 1831.
'Asefat 'Amarim to Psalms. Edited by Isaiah Borokovitz. Warsaw, 1883.
Ashkenazi, Benjamin Zev b. David. *Sha'are Binyamin*. Zolkiew: Mann and Segal, 1752.
Assaf, S. "Toward the History of the Rabbinate in Germany, Poland, and Lithuania" (Hebrew). *Reshumot* 2 (1922):259–300.
Avigri, Isaac. "Linguistic Contributions from the Field of Hasidism" (Hebrew). *Metzudah* 3–4 (1945):229–48.
Azulai, H.Y.D. *Ma'agal Tov Hashalem*. Edited by A. Freimann. Jerusalem: Mekitzey Nirdamim, 1934.

————. *Simḥat Haregel ʿal Rut*. Livorno: Castillo and Saadun, 1782.

Babad, Joshua Heschel b. Isaac. *Sefer Yehoshuʿa*. Zolkiew: Meyerhoffer, 1829.

Bachrach, Jacob. *Vikuḥa Raba*. 5th ed. Munkács, 1894; rpt. Warsaw: M. Kleinman, 1913.

Bachrach, Yair Hayim. *Havat Yaʾir*. Frankfurt a.M.: Johannes Wust, 1699.

Balaban, M. *Dzieje Żydów w Galiczji*. Lwów: Nakl. Ksieyarni Polskiej B. Poloniec Kiego, 1916.

————. "Hasidism: On Recent Hasidic Literature" (Hebrew). *Hatekufah* 18 (1923):487–502.

————. *Letoldot Hatenuʿah Hafrankit*. Tel Aviv: Dvir, 1934.

————. Review of *Reb Yisrael Baal Shem Tov* by S. Setzer. In *Bicher Velt* 1, nos. 4–5 (1922):406–7.

Barnai, Y. "The Jewish Community in Jerusalem in the Middle of the Eighteenth Century" (Hebrew). *Shalem* 2 (1976):193–240.

————. "Notes on the Immigration of R. Abraham Gershon Kutover to Eretz Yisrael" (Hebrew). *Zion* 42 (1977):110–19.

————. "Pekidei Ereẓ Israel Bekushta." *Encyclopaedia Judaica*. 1974 Yearbook, pp. 249–50.

Barukh b. Abraham of Kosów. *ʿAmud Haʿavodah*. Cernăuti: Johann Eckardt und Sohn, 1863; rpt. Józefów: Setzer, 1883.

————. *Yesod Haʾemunah*. Cernăuti, 1863; rpt. as *Neḥmad Venaʿim*. Józefów: Setzer, 1883.

Barukh of Miedzybórz. *Butzina Dinnehora*. Lwów: Karl Bodvisser, 1880.

Bauminger, M. S. "More About the Letter of the Baal Shem Tov to His Brother-In-Law, R. Gershon of Kutov" (Hebrew). In *Sefer Margaliot*. Edited by Y. Raphael. Jerusalem: Mosad Harav Kook, 1973.

Beillis, Shlomo. "The Beginnings of 'Yung Vilna'" (Yiddish). *Die Goldene Keit* 101 (1980):18–20.

Ben Hamelekh Vehanazir. Edited by A. M. Haberman. Tel Aviv: Mosad Harav Kook, 1950.

Benjamin b. Aaron. *Torey Zahav*. Mogilev: Asher Zelig, 1816.

Benjamin Wolf b. Matityahu. *Toharot Hakodesh*. Amsterdam 1733; rpt. Bialozórka: Mordecai b. Samuel, 1806.

Ben Menahem, N. Review of *Haḥasidut* by Y. Alfasi. *Sinai* 74 (1974):187–91.

Benveniste, Hayim. *Dina Deḥayey*. Constantinople: Reuben and Nissim Ashkenazi, 1742.

Ben Zion, Ariel. *Sar Shalom Sharʿabi*. Jerusalem: Zutot, 1930.

Berger, Israel. *ʿEser ʾOrot*. Piotrkow: Palman, 1910.

Bernfeld, Simon. *Sefer Hadimaʿot*. Berlin: Eshkol, 1923–26.

Bet Pinḥas. Bilgoraj, 1926.

Betzalel b. Solomon. *Nofet Tzufim*. Lwów: Abraham Joshua Heschel, 1865.

Biber, M. M. *Mazkeret Lagedoley ʾOstraha*. Berdichev: H. Y. Sheftel, Mefitzey Haskalah, 1907.

Birkat Haʾaretz. Edited by Barukh Hakohen. Jerusalem: Frumkin, 1904.

Bodek, M. M. *Seder Hadorot Haḥadash*. N.p., n.d.

[Bodek, M. M.] *Mifʿalot Hatzaddikim*. Lwów, 1857; rpt. Warsaw: Joshua Gershon Munk. n.d.

Braver, Abraham. "Joseph the Second and the Jews of Galicia: A Historical Inquiry" (Hebrew). *Hashiloah* 23 (1910):29–39, 147–54, 331–43, 427–34.

————. "On the Quarrel Between R. Shneur Zalman of Ladi and R. Abraham of Kalisk." *Kiryat Sefer* 1 (1924):142–49, 226–37.

Brilling, D. "On Emissaries from the Land of Israel to Germany." *Sura* 4 (1964):250–75.

———. "The Activity of the Jerusalem Emissary Petahya b. Jehudah Wahl Katzenellenbogen in Western Europe (1735–1750)" (German). In *Festschrift I. E. Lichtigfeld*. Edited by E. Roth and F. Bloch. Frankfurt a.M., 1964.

Brisk, A. *Helkat Mehokek*. Jerusalem: S. Halevi Zuckerman, 1901–10.

Bromberg, A. *Hasidic Leaders* (Hebrew). Jerusalem: Hamakhon Lahasidut, 1963.

Buber, Martin. "Replies to My Critics: On Hasidism." In *The Philosophy of Martin Buber*. Edited by P. A. Schilpp and M. Friedman. La Salle, Ill.: Open Court, 1967.

Buber, S. *Anshey Shem*. Cracow: Y. Fischer, 1895.

Cazes, Benjamin. *Megillat Sefer*. Constantinople: Reuben and Nissim Ashkenazi, 1750.

Cohen, Moses. *Kehunat ʿOlam*. Constantinople: Jonah B. Jacob, 1740.

Cohen-Tzedek, Joseph. *Shem Ushʾerit*. Cracow: Y. Fischer, 1895.

David b. Tzvi Elimelekh. *Tzemah David*. New York: S. B. Rokach, 1953.

David ibn Zimra. *Magen David*. Amsterdam: Asher Anshel b. Eliezer, 1713.

Davidson, Israel. *Thesaurus of Medieval Hebrew Poetry*. New York: Jewish Theological Seminary, 1925.

Degel Mahaney Yehudah. Edited by Brandwein. Jerusalem: Bros. Brandwein, 1957.

Deinard, E. *Shibalim Bodedot*. Jerusalem: Lunz, 1915.

Deutsch, Hananya Yom-Tov Lipa. *Toharat Yom-Tov*. 9 vols. New York: Shulsinger, 1951.

Dimitrovsky, H. Z. "On the Nature of Pilpul" (Hebrew). In *Salo Wittmayer Baron* Jubilee Volume. New York: American Academy for Jewish Research, 1974.

Dinaborg (Dinur), B. "The Beginning of Hasidism and Its Social and Messianic Element" (Hebrew). *Zion* 9 (1944):186–97.

Dov of Bolechov. *Zikhronot*. Edited by M. Vishnitzer. Berlin: Klal Verlag, 1922.

Dov Ber of Miedzyrzecz. *Maggid Devarav Leyaʿakov: Likutey ʾAmarim*. Korzec, 1781, 1784; rpt., edited by R. Schatz-Uffenheimer. Jerusalem: Hebrew University Press, 1976.

——— and Levi Isaac of Berdichev. *ʾOr Haʾemet*. Zhitomir, 1901; rpt. Jerusalem: Yahadut, 1967.

———. *ʾOr Torah*. Korzec: Abraham Madpis, 1804.

Dresner, S. "Hasidic Truth." *Shefa* 2, no. 4 (1981):23–25.

———. *Levi Yitzhak of Berdichev*. New York: Hartmore House, 1975.

———. *The Zaddik*. New York-London: Abelard-Schuman, 1960; rpt. New York: Schocken, 1974.

Dubnow, S. *Divrey Yemey ʿAm ʿOlam*. Tel Aviv: Dvir, 1933–40.

———. "The First Hasidim in the Land of Israel" (Hebrew). *Pardes* 2 (1894):201–14.

———. *The History of the Jews in Russia and Poland*. Philadelphia: Jewish Publication Society, 1916, 1920.

———. *Toldot Hahasidut*. Tel Aviv: Dvir, 1930–32.

Duckesz, Edward [Ezekiel]. *Hokhmey AHW*. Hamburg: Goldschmidt, 1908.

———. *ʾIva Lemoshav*. Cracow: E. Gräber, 1903.

Duran, Simon b. Tzemah. *Sefer Tashbatz*. Amsterdam: Naftali Hirz Levi Emden, 1738.

Ehrman, D. *Devarim ʿArevim*. Munkacs: Ehrman, 1903.
Eibeschütz, Jonathan. *Luhot Haʿedut*. Altona: Aaron Katz, 1755.
Eisenstadt, Israel Tuviah. *Daʿat Kedoshim*. St. Petersburg: Behrman, 1897–98.
Eisenstadt, Meir. *Panim Meʾirot*. Amsterdam: Solomon b. Joseph Proops, 1715.
Eisenstein, J. D. *ʾOtzar Yisraʾel*. New York: Jewish Encyclopaedia Publishing Co., 1906–13.
Elbogen, Ismar. *Der jüdische Gottesdienst in seiner geschichtlichen Entwicklung*. Leipzig: Fock, 1913. Hebrew version: *Hatefilah Beyisraʾel*. Tel Aviv: Dvir, 1972.
Emden, Jacob. *Sefer Hitʾavkut*. Altona, 1762–69.
———. *Shevirat Luhot Haʾaven*. Zolkiew (Altona), 1756 (1759).
ʾEmunat Tzaddikim. Warsaw, 1900; rpt. Brooklyn: N. L. Levin, n.d.
Epstein, Aryeh Leib. *Sefer Pardes*. Konigsberg: Johann Friedrich Drist, 1759.
Frank, Azriel Nathan. *Meshumadim in Poilen*. Warsaw: M. Y. Fried, 1923.
Friedberg, Ch. B. *The Families Landau* (Hebrew). Padgorza, 1905.
———. *History of the Family Horovitz* (Hebrew). Antwerp, 1928.
Friedman, Israel. *ʿIrin Kadishin Teninaʾ*. Bartfeld: 1887.
Frumkin, A. *History of the Sages of Jerusalem* (Hebrew). Jerusalem: Solomon Press, 1928–30.
Funn, S. Y. *Keneset Yisraʾel*. Warsaw: Boimritter and Ganskar, 1886.
Ganar (Malakhi), A. "The History of the Jewish Settlement in Hebron" (Hebrew), *Hator*. Jerusalem, 1929.
Gaon, M. D. *Oriental Jews in the Land of Israel* (Hebrew). Jerusalem: Azriel, 1938–48.
Gedaliah of Linitz. *Teshuʿot Hen*. Berdichev: G. Segal, 1816; rpt. Jerusalem: S. Reifen, 1964.
Gelber, N. M. *Aus Zwei Jahrhunderten*. Vienna and Leipzig: Löwit, 1924.
———. "The Baptismal Movement among the Polish Jews in the 18th Century" (German). *Monatsschrift für Geschichte und Wissenschaft des Judentums* 67 (1924):225–40.
———. "From the Pinkas of the Old Jewish Cemetery in Brody" (German). *Jahrbuch der Judisch Literarischen Gesellschaft* 13 (1920):119–41.
———. *History of the Jews of Brody* (Hebrew). Jerusalem: Mosad Harav Kook, 1956.
Gelernter, Hayim. *ʿOneg Hayim Lashabat*. Munkács, 1908; rpt. New York, 1973.
Gepner, Jacob. *ʾOr Ki Tov*. Jerusalem: Mifal Helkat Mehokek, 1968.
Gottlieb, Samuel Noah. *ʾOhaley Shem*. Pinsk: Glauberman, 1912.
Graf, Moses. *Zera Kodesh*. Furth, 1696; rpt. Brooklyn, 1973.
Granatsztajn, Y. *The Disciples of the Baal Shem Tov in the Land of Israel* (Hebrew). Tel Aviv, 1982.
Grossman, Levi Halevi. *Shem Usheʾerit*. Tel Aviv: Betzalel, 1943.
Gurland, Jonas. *Lekorot Hagezerot ʿal Yisraʾel*. Przemyśl, Cracow, and Odessa, 1887–92.
Gutman, M. *Mitorat Hahasidut: Torat Rabenu Pinhas Mikoretz*. Bilgoraj, 1941; rpt. as *Torat Rabenu . . .* Tel Aviv: Mosad Harav Kook, 1950, 1953.
Hager, Y., and Berger, Y. *ʿAteret Yaʿakov Veyisraʾel*. Lwów, 1881.
Halberstam, Hayim. *Sheʾelot Uteshuvot Divrey Hayim*. Warsaw: Abraham Kahana, 1930.
Halperin, Israel. *Eastern European Jewry* (Hebrew). Jerusalem: Magnes Press, 1968.
———. *The First Immigration of Hasidim to the Land of Israel* (Hebrew). Jerusalem and Tel Aviv: Schocken, 1947.

————. *Pinkas of the Council of the Four Lands* (Hebrew). Jerusalem: Mosad Bialik, 1945.

————. "On the Relationship between the Jewish Councils and Communities of Poland and Palestinian Jewry" (Hebrew). *Zion* 1 (1936):82–88.

Halperin, M. M. *Kevod Ḥakhamim*. Jerusalem, 1896.

Hasidic Letters from Eretz-Israel (Hebrew). Edited by Y. Barnai. Jerusalem: Yad Ben-Zvi, 1980.

Hass, Simha. *'Ahavat Tziyon*. [Horodna, 1790.]

————. *Neti'ah shel Simḥah*. Zolkiew, 1763.

Hayim Jacob b. Jacob David of Safed. *Sama' Deḥayey*. Amsterdam: Joseph Dayan, 1739.

Hayim Meir b. Abraham Samuel Heilman. *Bet Rabi*. Berdichev: H. Y. Sheftel, 1900.

Hazan, S. *Hama'alot Leshlomo*. Alexandria: F. H. Mizrahi, 1894.

Herford, R. T. *Christianity in Talmud and Midrash*. London: Williams, 1903.

Herz, Nathan B. Naftali. *'Alim Laterufah*. Warsaw: Bratzlav Publishing, 1930.

[Heschel, Abraham Joshua.] *Between God and Man: From the Writings of Abraham J. Heschel*. Edited by Fritz A. Rothschild. 1959; rpt. New York: Free Press, 1965.

————. "Hasidism as a New Approach to Torah." *Jewish Heritage* 14, no. 3 (1972):14–21.

————. *Kotzk: In Gerangel far Emesdikeit*. Tel Aviv: Hamenorah, 1973.

————. *Man's Quest for God*. New York: Scribner's, 1954; rpt. as *Quest for God*, New York: Crossroad, 1982.

————. *A Passion for Truth*. New York: Farrar, Strauss and Giroux, 1973.

————. "R. Gershon Kutover: His life and Immigration to the Land of Israel" (Hebrew). *Hebrew Union College Annual* 23 (1950–51):17–71.

————. "Rabbi Isaac of Drohobycz" (Hebrew). *Hado'ar Jubilee Volume*. New York: Hado'ar, 1957, pp. 86–94.

————. "Rabbi Nahman of Kosów, Companion of the Baal Shem Tov" (Hebrew). In *The Harry A. Wolfson Jubilee Volume*. Edited by Saul Lieberman et al. New York: American Academy for Jewish Research, 1965. Hebrew section, pp. 113–41.

————. "Rabbi Pinhas of Koretz" (Hebrew). In *Alei Ayin: The Salman Schocken Jubilee Volume*. Jerusalem: Schocken, 1948–52, pp. 213–44.

————. "Reb Pinhas Koritzer" (Yiddish). *Yivo Bleter* 33 (1949):9–40.

————. "In Search of Exaltation." *Jewish Heritage* 13, no. 3 (1971):29–30, 35.

————. *The Theology of Ancient Judaism* (Hebrew). London and New York: Soncino, 1962–65.

————. "Toward An Understanding of Halakhah." *Yearbook of the Central Conference of American Rabbis* 63 (1953):386–91.

————. "The Two Great Traditions." *Commentary* 5 (1948):416–22.

————. "Unknown Documents in the History of Hasidism" (Yiddish). *Yivo Bleter* 36 (1952):113–35.

Hillman, David Tzvi. *'Igrot Ba'al Hatanya Uveney Doro*. Jerusalem: Hamesorah, 1953.

Horodezky, S. A. *Hahasidut Vehahasidim*. Berlin: Dvir, 1922.

————. *'Oley Tziyon*. Tel Aviv: Gazut, 1947.

————. *Torat Hamagid Mimezritch Vesiḥotav*. Berlin: Eynot, 1923.

Horowitz, Eliezer. *No'am Magidim Ukhevod Hatorah*. Lwów: Pessel Balaban, 1873.

Horowitz, Isaac. *Mat'amey Yitzhak*. Piotrkow: Moses Elias and Eleazar Schonfeld, 1904.

Horowitz, Jacob Isaac. *Divrey 'Emet*. Zolkiew, 1828; rpt. [Israel]: A. N. Bernata, 1965.

Horowitz, M. *Frankfürter Rabbinen*. Frankfurt: Commissionsverlag der Jaegerśchen Buchhandlung, 1885.

Horowitz, Naftali. *'Ohel Naftali*. Lwow: Zeidman and Oisshnit, 1910.

Horowitz, Shmelke of Nikolsburg. *Divrey Shmu'el*. Lwów: Moses Hakohen, 1862.

Horowitz, Tzvi. *On the History of the Polish Jewish Communities* (Hebrew). Jerusalem: Mosad Harav Kook, 1978.

Imrey Tzaddikim. Edited by D. Frankel. Husiatyn: Philip Kabalha, 1899.

Isaac Bekhor David. *Divrey 'Emet*. Constantinople: Reuben and Nissim Ashkenazi, 1760.

Isaac Shapira of Niesuchojeze. *Toldot Yitzhak*. Warsaw: G. Schriftgiesser, 1868.

Israel of Satanów. *'Ateret Tif'eret Yisra'el*. Lwów, 1865; rpt. Warsaw: Samuel Orgelbrand, 1871.

Israel b. Aaron [Jaffe] of Shklov. *'Or Yisra'el*. Frankfurt a.O.: M. Gottschalk, 1712.

Israel b. Shabbetai of Kozienice. *'Avodat Yisra'el*. Jozefów, 1842; rpt. New York: Friedman, 1972.

Issachar Dov Baer of Zloczew. *Mevaser Tzedek*. Dubnów: Judah Leibush and Gershon Ben Zion Margaliot, 1798.

Jacob Joseph of Polonnoye. *Ben Porat Yosef*. Korzec: Abraham Samson Katz of Raszkow and Abraham Dov of Khmelnik, 1781.

―――. *Ketonet Pasim*. Lwów: Abraham Joshua Heschel b. Judah Gershon, 1866.

―――. *Toldot Ya'akov Yosef*. Korzec: Abraham Samson Katz of Raszków and Abraham Dov of Khmelnik, 1780.

―――. *Tzafnat Pa'neyah*. Korzec: Abraham Samson Katz of Raszków and Abraham Dov of Khmelnik, 1782.

Jacob Joseph b. Judah Leib Hakohen. *Rav Yevi*. Slavuta: Eliakim Getz et al., 1792.

Jacobs, Louis. *Hasidic Prayer*. New York: Schocken, 1973.

―――. *Hasidic Thought*. New York: Behrman, 1976.

―――. *Jewish Mystical Testimonies*. New York: Schocken, 1977.

Joseph b. Solomon Darshan of Posen. *Yesod Yosef*. Frankfurt a.O., 1679; rpt. Jerusalem, 1967.

Joseph Moses Elkanah of Zabarov. *Brit 'Avram*. Brody, 1875.

Joshua Abraham b. Israel of Zhitomir. *Ge'ulat Yisra'el*. Pt. 2. Ostróg: Aaron and Son, 1821.

Kahana, S. *'Anaf 'Etz 'Avot*. Cracow: Kahan, 1903.

Kahana, A. *Hahasidut*. Warsaw: Lewin-Epstein, 1922.

Kamelhar, I. *Dor De'ah*. Bilgoraj: Kamelhar, 1933.

―――. *Mofet Hador*. Munkács: Kahn and Fried, 1934; rpt. Jerusalem: Yam Hatalmud, 1968.

Kaminker, Samuel. *Sheney Hame'orot*. Kishinev: Joshua b. Joseph and Reuben b. Asher Fikman, 1896.

Kanafi, Joseph. *The Sign of the Holy Covenant* (Hebrew). Livorno, 1884.

Katz-Shteiman, H. "Concerning Y. Barnai's Notes on the Immigration of R. Abraham Gershon of Kutov to the Land of Israel" (Hebrew). *Zion* 42 (1977):302–5.

Kitover, Israel Halevi. *Shevil Ha'emunah.* In Saadia Gaon, *Sefer Ha'emunot Vehade'ot.* Józefów: Setzer, 1885.

Kleinman, M. H. *Mazkeret Shem Hagedolim.* Piotrkow, 1907; rpt. Beney Brak: Binah, 1967.

———. *Zikaron Larishonim.* Piotrkow, 1882; rpt. Brooklyn: Moriah, 1976.

Kovetz Teshuvot Harambam Ve'igrotav. Edited by Lichtenberg. Leipzig: H. L. Schnaus, 1859.

Landau, Ezekiel. *Doresh Letziyon.* Prague, 1827; rpt. Warsaw: Goldman, 1880.

———. *Noda' Bihudah.* Prague: M. Katz, 1776.

———. *Derushey Hatzlah.* Warsaw: 1899.

Lernowitz, Samuel. *Kevod Hatorah.* Lwów, 1873.

Letters of the Baal Shem Tov and His Disciples (Hebrew). Edited by D. Frankel. Lwów: Frankel, 1923.

Levi b. Solomon of Brody. *Bet Levi.* Zolkiew: Aaron and Gershon Siegel, 1732.

Lieberman, H. "How Jewish 'Researchers' Explore Hasidism" (Hebrew). *'Ohel Rahel.* Vol. 1. Brooklyn: Empire Press, 1980, pp. 1–49.

———. "Note on the History of Hebrew Printing at Slavuta" (Hebrew). *Kiryat Sefer* 27 (1951):117–19. *'Ohel Rahel*, pp. 199–202.

Likkutey Rav Hai Ga'on (Ner Yisra'el). *Likkutim Meharav Pinhas Mikoretz,* Lwów, 1800; rpt. [Israel], 1968.

Likkutey Yekarim. Edited by Meshulam Pheibush Heller. Lwów: Judah Solomon Rappaport, 1792; rpt. Mezyrów, 1794, as *Likkutim Yekarim.*

Loewenstamm, Saul. *Binyan 'Uri'el.* Amsterdam: Y. and A. Proops, 1778.

Lunz, A. *"The Book Ahavat Tziyon: The Nature and Author of its Forgery"* (Hebrew). *Yerushalayim* 4 (1892):137–52.

———. "Dovev Siftey Yesheynim." *Yerushalayim* 2 (1887):141–59.

———. "Kivrey 'Eretz Hatzvi." *Yerushalayim* 1 (1882):125.

[Luria, Isaac.] *Mahberet Hakodesh.* Korzec: Kruger, 1783.

Lutzker, Solomon. *Divrat Shlomo.* Zolkiew, 1848; rpt. Jerusalem: Maayan Hokhmah, 1955.

Mahler, R. *Yidn in Amoliken Poilen.* Warsaw: Farlag Yiddish Bukh, 1958.

Malki, Ezra b. Raphael. *Malki Bakodesh.* Salonica: Betzalel Halevi, 1749.

Mann, Menahem. *She'erit Yisra'el.* Amsterdam, 1771.

Margaliot, Jacob. *Kevutzot Ya'akov.* Przemyśl, 1897.

Margaliot, Judah Leib. *Korban Reyshit.* Frankfurt a.O.: Judah Leib b. Asher Zelig, 1778.

Margaliot, R. "To Remove Slander" (Hebrew). *Modia* (1938).

Mastboim, Joel. *Galicia.* Warsaw: Farlag Jacobson-Goldberg, 1929.

Meir b. Yavitz. *Mayim Hayim.* Zhitomir: Hanina Lipa and Joshua Heschel Shapiro, 1857.

Meisels, Uziel. *Tif'eret 'Uzi'el.* Warsaw: N. Schriftgiesser, 1863.

———. *Tif'eret Tzvi.* Zolkiew: Gershon Litteris, 1803.

Menahem Mendel b. Joseph of Rymanow. *'Ateret Menahem.* Bilgoraj: Lifschitz, 1910.

Menahem Mendel of Vitebsk. *Likutey 'Amarim.* Lwów: Shalom Zwerling, 1911.

Meyuhas b. Samuel. *Sefer Peri Ha'adamah.* Salonica, 1752.

Michelson, Abraham Hayim Simhah Bunim (ed.). *Dover Shalom.* Premyśl: Amkroit and Freund, 1910.

Miropol, Samuel. *Tif'eret Shemu'el.* New York: Orios Press, 1926.

Modena, David. *Ruah David Venishmat David.* Salonica: Betzalel Ashkenazi, 1747.

Mordecai of Niesuchojeze. *Rishpey ʾEsh Hashalem.* Brody: M. L. Harmelin, 1874.

Moses of Dolina. *Divrey Mosheh.* Zolkiew: S. P. Stiller, 1865.

Moses of Kozienice. *Beʾer Mosheh.* Lwów, 1805.

Moses of Satanow. *Mishmeret Hakodesh.* Zolkiew, 1745.

Moses Israel. *Sheʾelot Uteshuvot Masʾat Moshe.* Constantinople: Jonah b. Jacob, 1734–42.

Nash, Stanley. *In Search of Hebraism: Shai Hurwitz and His Polemics in the Hebrew Press.* Leiden: Brill, 1980.

Navon, Judah. *Kiryat Melekh Rav.* Constantinople: Reuben and Nissim Ashkenazi, 1751.

Perl, J. *Megaleh Temirin.* Vienna: A. Strauss, 1819; rpt. Lwów, 1864.

Piekarz, M. *Bimey Tzemihat Hahasidut.* Jerusalem: Mosad Bialik, 1978.

Pinhas of Korzec. *Midrash Pinhas.* Edited by Y. Weiss. Jerusalem: 1943.

———. *Nofet Tzufim.* Piotrkow: H. Palman, 1911.

———. *Tosefta Lamidrash Pinhas.* Edited by Betzalel Joshua of Galina. Lwów: 1896.

———. *Likkutim Meharav Pinhas Mikoretz.* In Likkutey Rav Hai Gaon (Ner Yisrael). Lwow, 1800; rpt. [Israel], 1968.

Pinhas [Lerner] of Dinowitz. *Siftey Tzaddikim.* Warsaw: Isaac M. Alter, 1928.

Porush, S. *Encyclopaedia of Hasidism: Books* (Hebrew). Jerusalem: Mosad Harav Kook, 1980.

Rabinowitz, Joshua Heschel. *Masekhet ʾAvot ʿIm Beʾur Torat ʾAvot.* New York: Rechtman, 1926.

Rapoport-Albert, A. "Confession in the Circle of R. Nahman of Braslav." *Bulletin of the Institute of Jewish Studies* (London) 1 (1973):65–97.

Rappaport, Hayim Hakohen. *Mayim Hayim.* Zhitomir: Shapiro, 1857.

Rappaport, Isaac b. Judah Hakohen. *Batey Kehunah.* Smyrna: Jonah Ashkenazi and David Hazan, 1736–41.

Riecher, Jacob. *Shevut Yaʿakov.* Prague, 1689; rpt. Brooklyn: M. J. Finkelstein, n.d.

Rodkinson, Michael Levi. *Toldot Baʿaley Shem Tov.* Königsberg: Petzall, 1886.

Rorio, Mordecai. *Shemen Hamor.* Livorno: A. Rorio, 1793.

Rosanes, M. *History of the Jews of Turkey* (Hebrew). Sofia: Amichpat, 1937–38.

Rosenbaum, Tzvi Hirsch. *Raza Deʿuvda.* Kiryat Syget: Mifitzey Hasefarim, 1971.

Rosenstein, Isaac David. *Peʾer Layesharim.* Jerusalem: Zuckerman, 1921.

Rubenstein, A. "A Letter of the Baal Shem Tov to R. Gershon of Kutov" (Hebrew). *Sinai* 67 (1970):120–39.

———. "On a Manuscript of the Letter of the Baal Shem Tov to R. Gershon of Kutov" (Hebrew). In *Sefer Margaliot.* Edited by Y. Raphael. Jerusalem: Mosad Harav Kook, 1973:175–88.

———. "A Possible New Fragment of the *Shivhey Habesht?*" (Hebrew). *Tarbiz* 35 (1965):174–91.

———. "Stories of Self-Disclosure in *Shivhey Habesht*" (Hebrew). *Aley Sefer* 6–7 (1979):157–86.

Rubin, A. "The Concept of Repentence Among the Hasidey Ashkenaz." *Journal of Jewish Studies* 16 (1965):161–76.

Sabelman, Abraham Isaac. *Sipurey Tzaddikim Hehadash.* Vienna, 1922; rpt. Jerusalem: Hotzaat Sefarim, n.d.

Safrin, Isaac Judah Yehiel. *Heykhal Haberakhah* [Pentateuch]. Lwów: Pessel Balaban, 1865.

———. *Netiv Mitzvotekhah.* Jerusalem, 1947; rpt. New York: Sefarim Kedoshim, 1970.

———. *Notzer Hesed*. Lwów: Eliezer Tzvi Safrin, 1856.

———. *Zohar Ḥai*. Lwów: Ziss and Nik, 1875–81.

Samuel of Szynowo. *Ramatayim Tzofim*. In *Tana Devey ʾEliyahu*. Warsaw, 1881; rpt. Jerusalem: Levin-Epstein, 1961.

Schatz-Uffenheimer, R. "Man's Relations to God and World in Buber's Rendering of the Hasidic Teaching." In *The Philosophy of Martin Buber*. Edited by P. A. Schilpp and M. Friedman. LaSalle, Ill.: Open Court, 1967.

Schechter, Solomon. *The Chassidim*. London: Jewish Chronicle, 1887.

Scholem, Gershom. *Devarim Bago*. Tel Aviv: Am Oved, 1975.

———. "The Historical Figure of R. Israel Baal Shem Tov" (Hebrew). *Molad* 18 (1960):335–56, pp. 287–325.

———. *Major Trends in Jewish Mysticism*. 3d ed. New York: Schocken, 1961.

———. "Two Letters from the Land of Israel" (Hebrew). *Tarbiz* 25 (1956): 429–40.

Sefer Habesht. Edited by Maimon. Jerusalem: Mosad Harav Kook, 1960.

Shapiro, Elimelekh b. Hayim. *Divrey ʾElimelekh*. Warsaw: Halter and Schuildberg, 1890–91.

Shapiro, Moses Judah Leib of Sasow. *Likutey Ramal*. Cernăuti, 1866.

Shapiro, Pinhas. *Midrash Pinḥas*. Bilgoraj, 1930. See Pinhas of Korzec.

Shapiro, Tzvi Elimelekh of Dynów. *ʾIgra Depirka*. Lwów, 1858; rpt. [Israel] H. Z. Schwartz, 1981.

Shivḥey Habesht. Kopys: Israel b. Isaac Jaffe, 1815.

———. Edited by Mondschein, Joshua. Jerusalem: Hanabal, 1928.

———. Translated by Dan Ben-Amos and Jerome R. Mintz. Bloomington: University of Indiana Press, 1970.

Shneur Zalman of Ladi. *Likutey ʾAmarim (Sefer Hatanya)*. Brooklyn: Kehot, 1973.

Shneurson, M. M. *Derekh Mitzvotekhah*. Poltava: Elijah Akiba Rabinowitz, 1911.

Shohet, A. "The Jews of Jerusalem in the Eighteenth Century" (Hebrew). *Zion* 1 (1936):377–410.

Shulman, E. *Yung Vilno*. New York, 1946.

Simon Menahem Mendel of Gowarczow. *Sefer Baʿal Shem Tov*. Lodz, 1938.

Sipurey Kedoshim. M. M. Bodek (?), Leipzig (?), Lwów (?), 1866.

Stern, Elimelekh Zev. *Siḥot Yekarim*. Satumare, 1930; rpt. Brooklyn: Y. Z. Veishoiz, 1962.

Strashun, Mathias. *Likutey Shoshanim*. Munkacs, 1889.

Tama, Mordecai. *Peʾer Hador*. Amsterdam: Janson, 1765.

Teitelbaum, Mordecai. *Harav Miladi Umifleget Ḥabad*. Warsaw: Toshiah, 1910–13.

Teitelbaum, Moses. *Yismaḥ Mosheh*. Lwów: Franz Galinski, 1851.

Teomim, Hayim. *Zikaron Larishonim*. Kolomyja, 1914; rpt. Jerusalem, 1969.

Teomim, Meir. *Birkat Yosef Veʾeliyahu Rabbah*. Zolciew, 1747.

———. *Nofet Tzufim*. In *Rav Peninim*, by Joseph Teomim. Frankfurt a.O, 1782.

Tishby, Isaiah. *Mishnat Hazohar*. 3d ed. Jerusalem: Mosad Bialik, 1971.

Todros b. Tzvi of Rowne. *Halakhah Pesukah*. Turka, 1765.

Toledano, Y. M. "From Manuscripts" (Hebrew). *Hebrew Union College Annual* 5 (1928):403.

Twerski, A. D. *The Geneology of the Families Twerski and Friedman* (Hebrew). Lublin, 1932; rpt. 1938.

———. *The Geneology of Chernobyl and Ruzhin* (Hebrew). Lublin: Tzveke 1930; rpt. Jerusalem, n.d.

Twersky, Menahem Nahum. *Yismaḥ Lev.* Slavuta, 1798.

Tzavaʾat Harivash. New York: Kehot, 1975.

Tzvi Elimelekh Shapira of Dynów. *ʾIgra Depirka.* Lwów, 1858; rpt. [Israel]. H. Z. Schwartz, 1981.

Vital, Hayim. *Likutey Torah Neviʾim Uketuvim.* Zolkiew, 1775; rpt. Tel Aviv: Hotzaʾat Kitvey Rabbenu Haʾari, 1963.

Weinryb, B. *The Jews of Poland.* Philadelphia: Jewish Publication Society, 1972.

Werfel [Raphael], Yitzhak. *Hasidism and the Land of Israel* (Hebrew). Jerusalem: Hotzaat Hasefarim Haeretz Yisraelit, 1940.

Wertheim, A. *Halakhot Vehalikhot Baḥasidut.* Jerusalem: Mosad Harav Kook, 1961.

Wurm, A. *Z Dziejòw Zydostwa Brodskiego.* Brody: Nakladem Gminy Wyzananiowej Zydowskiej, 1935.

Yaari, A. "Biographical Miscellany" (Hebrew). *Kiryat Sefer* 13 (1936):121–30.

———. "Bibliographical Miscellany" (Hebrew). *Kiryat Sefer* 20 (1943):passim.

———. *Emissaries of the Land of Israel* (Hebrew). Jerusalem: Mosad Harav Kook, 1951.

———. Notes to G. Scholem's "Two Letters from the Land of Israel" (Hebrew). *Tarbiz* 26 (1956):109–12.

———. *Taʿalumat Sefer.* Jerusalem: Mosad Harav Kook, 1954.

———. Two Basic Recensions of *Shivhey Habesht* (Hebrew). *Kiryat Sefer* 39 (1964):249–72, 394–407, 559–61.

———. "Two Kuntresim from the Land of Israel" (Hebrew). *Kiryat Sefer* 23 (1946–47):140–59.

Yehiel Mikhel b. Isaac of Zloczew. *Mayim Rabbim.* Warsaw: A. Schriftgiessen, 1899; rpt. Jerusalem, 1964.

Yerahmiel Moses of Kozienice. *Shemaʿ Shelomo.* Piotrokow, 1928.

Yitzhak-Isaac b. Joel Hakohen. *Brit Kehunat ʿOlam.* Lwów: Judith bat Tzvi Hirsch, 1796.

———. *Sheʾelot Uteshuvot Zikhron Kehunah.* Lwów: Kugel, Lewin, and Co., 1863.

Yitzhak Isaac of Korzec. *Hakaneh ʿal Hamitzvot.* Poryck, 1786.

Yizraeli, M. *The Letter of 5508.* Jerusalem, 1978.

Zimmels, H. J. *Ashkenazim and Sephardim.* London: Jews College Publications, 1958.

Ziskind [Susskind], Alexander b. Moses. *Yesod Veshoresh Haʿavodah.* Nowy Dwor, 1782; rpt. Warsaw: Tzvi Hirsch, 1814.

Index